*Software Performance
and Scalability*

Software Performance and Scalability

A Quantitative Approach

Henry H. Liu

A JOHN WILEY & SONS, INC., PUBLICATION

Published by John Wiley & Sons, Inc., Hoboken, New Jersey
Published simultaneously in Canada

For general information on our other products and services or for technical support, please contact our Customer Care Department within the United States at (800) 762-2974, outside the United States at (317) 572-3993 or fax (317) 572-4002.

Wiley also publishes its books in a variety of electronic formats. Some content that appears in print may not be available in electronic formats. For more information about Wiley products, visit our web site at www.wiley.com.

Library of Congress Cataloging-in-Publication Data:

Liu, Henry H.
   Software performance and scalability : a quantitative approach/Henry H. Liu
         p. cm.
   Includes bibliographical references and index.
   ISBN 978-0-470-46253-9 (cloth)
   1. Computer software—Development.   2. System design.   I. Title.
   QA76.76.D47L577 2009
   005.1—dc22   2009005654

10   9   8   7   6   5   4   3   2   1

To my family

Contents

PREFACE   **xv**

ACKNOWLEDGMENTS   **xxi**

Introduction   **1**
Performance versus Scalability / 1

PART 1 THE BASICS   **3**

1. Hardware Platform   **5**

1.1   Turing Machine / 6
1.2   von Neumann Machine / 7
1.3   Zuse Machine / 8
1.4   Intel Machine / 9
    1.4.1   History of Intel's Chips / 9
    1.4.2   Hyperthreading / 9
    1.4.3   Intel's Multicore Microarchitecture / 13
    1.4.4   Challenges for System Monitoring Tools / 17
1.5   Sun Machine / 17
1.6   System Under Test / 18
    1.6.1   Processors / 18
    1.6.2   Motherboard / 19
    1.6.3   Chipset / 20

1.6.4   Storage / 22

1.6.5   RAID / 24

1.6.6   Networking / 27

1.6.7   Operating System / 29

1.7   Odds Against Turing / 30

1.7.1   Memory Leaks / 30

1.7.2   SLAs / 35

1.8   Sizing Hardware / 35

1.9   Summary / 37

Recommended Reading / 37

Exercises / 38

2. **Software Platform**   **41**

2.1   Software Stack / 42

2.2   APIs / 44

2.2.1   Windows APIs / 45

2.2.2   Java APIs / 45

2.2.3   Google APIs / 46

2.3   Multithreading / 47

2.4   Categorizing Software / 53

2.4.1   Systems Software / 53

2.4.2   Application Software / 54

2.4.3   Middleware Software / 55

2.5   Enterprise Computing / 55

2.5.1   What Is Enterprise Software? / 55

2.5.2   Enterprise Software Architecture / 57

2.5.3   Monolithic Architecture / 57

2.5.4   Client/Server Architecture / 58

2.5.5   Three-Tier Architecture / 59

2.5.6   N-Tier Architecture / 60

2.5.7   Software Componentry / 61

2.5.8   Service-Oriented Architecture / 61

2.6   Summary / 63

Recommended Reading / 64

Exercises / 64

3. **Testing Software Performance and Scalability**   **65**

3.1   Scope of Software Performance and
        Scalability Testing / 67

3.1.1   Performance Regression Testing / 68

3.1.2   Performance Optimization and
           Tuning Testing / 70

3.1.3   Performance Benchmarking Testing / 75

3.1.4 Scalability Testing / 75

3.1.5 QA Testing Versus Performance Testing / 82

3.1.6 Additional Merits of Performance Testing / 82

3.2 Software Development Process / 83

3.2.1 Agile Software Development / 83

3.2.2 Extreme Programming / 84

3.3 Defining Software Performance / 86

3.3.1 Performance Metrics for OLTP Workloads / 87

3.3.2 Performance Metrics for Batch Jobs / 92

3.4 Stochastic Nature of Software Performance Measurements / 95

3.5 Amdahl's Law / 97

3.6 Software Performance and Scalability Factors / 99

3.6.1 Hardware / 100

3.6.2 Operating System / 103

3.6.3 Database Statistics / 107

3.6.4 SQL Server Parameterization / 108

3.6.5 Database Deadlocks / 110

3.6.6 Licensing / 110

3.7 System Performance Counters / 111

3.7.1 Windows Performance Console / 112

3.7.2 Using *perfmon* to Diagnose Memory Leaks / 118

3.7.3 Using *perfmon* to Diagnose CPU Bottlenecks / 119

3.7.4 Using *perfmon* to Diagnose Disk I/O Bottlenecks / 121

3.7.5 Using Task Manager to Diagnose System Bottlenecks / 125

3.7.6 UNIX Platforms / 128

3.8 Software Performance Data Principles / 129

3.9 Summary / 131

Recommended Reading / 132

Exercises / 133

PART 2 APPLYING QUEUING THEORY   **135**

4. Introduction to Queuing Theory   **137**

4.1 Queuing Concepts and Metrics / 139

4.1.1 Basic Concepts of Queuing Theory / 140

4.1.2 Queuing Theory: From Textual Description
to Mathematical Symbols / 141

4.2 Introduction to Probability Theory / 143

4.2.1 Random Variables and Distribution Functions / 143

4.2.2 Discrete Distribution and Probability
Distribution Series / 144

4.2.3 Continuous Distribution and Distribution
Density Function / 145

4.3 Applying Probability Theory to Queuing Systems / 145

4.3.1 Markov Process / 146
4.3.2 Poisson Distribution / 148
4.3.3 Exponential Distribution Function / 150
4.3.4 Kendall Notation / 152
4.3.5 Queuing Node versus Queuing System / 152

4.4 Queuing Models for Networked Queuing Systems / 153

4.4.1 Queuing Theory Triad I: Response Time, Throughput, and Queue Length (Little's Law) / 154
4.4.2 $M/M/1$ Model (Open) / 155
4.4.3 Queuing System: With Feedback versus Without Feedback / 159
4.4.4 Queuing Theory Triad II: Utilization, Service Time, and Response Time / 159
4.4.5 Multiple Parallel Queues versus Single-Queue Multiple Servers / 160
4.4.6 $M/M/m/N/N$ Model (Closed) / 162
4.4.7 Finite Response Time in Reality / 166
4.4.8 Validity of Open Models / 169
4.4.9 Performance and Scalability Bottlenecks in a Software System / 170
4.4.10 Genealogy of Queuing Models / 171

4.5 Summary / 172
Recommended Reading / 174
Exercises / 175

5. Case Study I: Queuing Theory Applied to SOA   **177**

5.1 Introduction to SOA / 178
5.2 XML Web Services / 179
5.3 The Analytical Model / 181
5.4 Service Demand / 183

5.4.1 Web Services Handle Creation / 184
5.4.2 XML SOAP Serialization/Deserialization / 184
5.4.3 Network Latency / 185
5.4.4 XML Web Service Provider / 186
5.4.5 Database Server / 186
5.4.6 Data Storage / 187

5.5 MedRec Application / 188

5.5.1 Exposing a Stateless Session EJB as an XML Web Service / 188
5.5.2 Consuming an XML Web Service Using SOAP / 189

5.6 MedRec Deployment and Test Scenario / 189

5.7   Test Results / 191

    5.7.1   Overhead of the XML Web Services Handle / 192

    5.7.2   Effects of Caching Web Services Handle / 193

    5.7.3   Throughput Dynamics / 194

    5.7.4   Bottleneck Analysis / 195

5.8   Comparing the Model with the Measurements / 198

5.9   Validity of the SOA Performance Model / 200

5.10 Summary / 200

Recommended Reading / 201

Exercises / 202

6. Case Study II: Queuing Theory Applied to Optimizing and Tuning Software Performance and Scalability   **205**

6.1   Analyzing Software Performance and Scalability / 207

    6.1.1   Characterizing Performance and Scalability Problems / 207

    6.1.2   Isolating Performance and Scalability Factors / 208

    6.1.3   Applying Optimization and Tuning / 215

6.2   Effective Optimization and Tuning Techniques / 220

    6.2.1   Wait Events and Service Demands / 221

    6.2.2   Array Processing—Reducing V_i / 223

    6.2.3   Caching—Reducing Wait Time (W_i) / 226

    6.2.4   Covering Index—Reducing Service Demand (D_i) / 228

    6.2.5   Cursor-Sharing—Reducing Service Demand (D_i) / 229

    6.2.6   Eliminating Extraneous Logic—Reducing Service Demand (D_i) / 231

    6.2.7   Faster Storage—Reducing Data Latency (W_i) / 232

    6.2.8   MPLS—Reducing Network Latency (W_i) / 233

    6.2.9   Database Double Buffering—An Anti Performance and Scalability Pattern / 235

6.3   Balanced Queuing System / 240

6.4   Summary / 244

Recommended Reading / 245

Exercises / 246

PART 3   APPLYING API PROFILING   **249**

7. Defining API Profiling Framework   **251**

7.1   Defense Lines Against Software Performance and Scalability Defects / 252

7.2   Software Program Execution Stack / 253

7.3   The *PerfBasic* API Profiling Framework / 254

7.3.1   API Profile Logging Format / 255

7.3.2   Performance Log Parser / 256

7.3.3   Performance Maps / 258

7.3.4   Performance Summarization File / 260

7.4   Summary / 260

Exercises / 261

8. Enabling API Profiling Framework   263

8.1   Overall Structure / 264

8.2   Global Parameters / 265

8.3   Main Logic / 266

8.4   Processing Files / 266

8.5   Enabling Profiling / 267

8.6   Processing Inner Classes / 270

8.7   Processing Comments / 271

8.8   Processing Method Begin / 272

8.9   Processing Return Statements / 274

8.10 Processing Method End / 275

8.11 Processing Main Method / 276

8.12 Test Program / 277

8.13 Summary / 279

Recommended Reading / 279

Exercises / 280

9. Implementing API Profiling Framework   281

9.1   Graphics Tool—*dot* / 281

9.2   Graphics Tool—ILOG / 284

9.3   Graphics Resolution / 286

9.4   Implementation / 287

9.4.1   driver / 287

9.4.2   Global Parameters / 289

9.4.3   logReader / 291

9.4.4   logWriter / 292

9.4.5   Node / 293

9.4.6   Link / 293

9.4.7   CallRecord / 294

9.4.8   utility / 294

9.4.9   parser / 295

9.4.10 xmlProcessor / 298

9.4.11 analyzer / 299

9.4.12 adapter / 300

9.5   Summary / 300

Exercises / 301

**10. Case Study: Applying API Profiling to Solving Software
Performance and Scalability Challenges** **303**

10.1   Enabling API Profiling / 304

    10.1.1   Mechanism of Populating Log Entry / 305

    10.1.2   Source and Target Projects / 306

    10.1.3   Setting *apf.properties* File / 306

    10.1.4   Parsing Workflow / 308

    10.1.5   Verifying the Profiling-Enabled
Source Code / 310

    10.1.6   Recommended Best Coding Practices / 311

    10.1.7   Enabling Non-Java Programs / 312

10.2   API Profiling with Standard Logs / 313

    10.2.1   Generating API Profiling Log Data / 313

    10.2.2   Parsing API Profiling Log Data / 314

    10.2.3   Generating Performance Maps / 316

    10.2.4   Making Sense Out of Performance Maps / 319

10.3   API Profiling with Custom Logs / 320

    10.3.1   Using Adapter to Transform
Custom Logs / 320

    10.3.2   Generating Performance Maps with
Custom Logs / 321

10.4   API Profiling with Combo Logs / 325

    10.4.1   Client Side Performance Map / 325

    10.4.2   Server Side Performance Map / 327

10.5   Applying API Profiling to Solving Performance and
Scalability Problems / 333

    10.5.1   Baseline / 333

    10.5.2   Optimization / 335

    10.5.3   Analysis / 336

10.6   Summary / 337

Exercises / 338

**APPENDIX A   STOCHASTIC EQUILIBRIUM
AND ERGODICITY** **339**

A.1   Basic Concepts / 339

    A.1.1   Random Variables / 339

    A.1.2   Random Variable Vector / 340

    A.1.3   Independent and Identical Distributions (IID) / 341

    A.1.4   Stationary Processes / 342

    A.1.5   Processes with Stationary
Independent Increments / 342

A.2   Classification of Random Processes / 343
    A.2.1   General Renewal Processes / 343
    A.2.2   Markov Renewal Processes / 343
    A.2.3   Markov Processes / 343
A.3   Discrete-Time Markov Chains / 345
    A.3.1   Transition Probability Matrix and C-K Equations / 345
    A.3.2   State Probability Matrix / 347
    A.3.3   Classification of States and Chains / 348
A.4   Continuous-Time Markov Chains / 349
    A.4.1   C–K Equations / 349
    A.4.2   Transition Rate Matrix / 349
    A.4.3   Imbedded Markov Chains / 350
A.5   Stochastic Equilibrium and Ergodicity / 351
    A.5.1   Definition / 351
    A.5.2   Limiting State Probabilities / 353
    A.5.3   Stationary Equations / 354
    A.5.4   Ergodic Theorems for Discrete-Time Markov Chains / 354
    A.5.5   Ergodic Theorems for Continuous-Time Markov Chains / 356
A.6   Birth–Death Chains / 357
    A.6.1   Transition Rate Matrix / 357
    A.6.2   C–K Equations / 358
    A.6.3   Limiting State Probabilities / 359
    A.6.4   Ergodicity / 359

**APPENDIX B   MEMORYLESS PROPERTY OF THE
EXPONENTIAL DISTRIBUTION**   **361**

APPENDIX C   M/M/1 QUEUES AT STEADY STATE   **363**

C.1   Review of Birth–Death Chains / 363
C.2   Utilization and Throughput / 364
C.3   Average Queue Length in the System / 365
C.4   Average System Time / 365
C.5   Average Wait Time / 366

INDEX   **367**

Preface

Software platforms are a written product of the mind.
—D. S. Evans, A. Hagiu, and R. Schmalensee

WHY THIS BOOK

Few people would disagree with the fact that building a large-scale, high-performance, and scalable software system is a complex task. This is evidenced by the magnitude of required up-front and ongoing financial costs and personnel commonly seen at every large software development organization. Seeking effective, efficient, and economical approaches to developing large-scale software is of interest to the entire software community.

Regardless of its complexity and scope, every software development project is driven by a few common factors:

- It is required to be *on schedule* because of urgency to be first to market in order to gain a competitive edge.
- It is required to be *within budget* under the pressure of showing profit and return on investment (ROI) as soon as possible.
- It is required to provide customers with all major *functionalities* at a minimum.
- And it is required to meet customer's expectations on *performance* and *scalability* to be *usable*.

While management is responsible for providing sufficient budget to cover personnel, development, test infrastructure, and so on, we, the technical staff (developers, quality assurance engineers, and performance engineers), are accountable for delivering the software product under development on schedule and within budget while meeting high standards on performance and scalability.

However, it's not uncommon to see that performance and scalability are pushed aside by the following higher priority activities:

- Analyzing system functionality requirements
- Deciding on the right architecture and design patterns
- Choosing appropriate programming paradigms and efficient development tools
- Starting coding and delivering early builds that meet major functionality requirements as soon as possible
- Implementing automated functionality test frameworks

Performance and scalability are often an afterthought during the last minute of product release. And even worse, performance and scalability issues might actually be raised by unsatisfied customers as soon as the product is rushed to the market. Under such circumstances, intense pressure builds up internally, and panic and fire-fighting-like chaos ensues.

On the other hand, software performance and scalability are indeed very challenging technical issues. Precautions must be taken with every major effort to improve the performance and scalability of a software product. A few industrial pioneers have issued warnings:

- "More computing sins are committed in the name of efficiency (without necessarily achieving it) than for any other single reason—including blind stupidity." —W. A. Wulf
- "Premature optimization is the root of all evil." —Tony Hoare and Donald Knuth
- "Bottlenecks occur in surprising places, so don't try to second guess and put in a speed hack until you have proven that's where the bottleneck is." —Rob Pike

So, how can we implement an effective, efficient, and economical approach to building performance and scalability into software? Establishing a very capable performance and scalability test team would certainly help. However, it is my observation that this approach is insufficient for guaranteeing that performance and scalability issues are dealt with properly, as it may easily exclude software developers from taking performance and scalability concerns into account in the first place. It's a reactive and less efficient approach to let the performance and scalability test engineers find the performance and scalability defects and then fix them with the developers. It's a lot more costly to fix software performance and scalability defects without having the developers take care of them in the first place.

That's the motivation behind this book, which promotes a proactive approach of letting the software developers build the performance and scalability *into* the product and letting the performance and scalability test engineers concentrate on the performance and scalability verification tests with a larger volume of data, more representative workloads, and more powerful hardware. This approach requires a mindset shift for the software developers that their job is just to make the software work and the performance and scalability problems can be fixed outside their job scope. Software developers should think consciously from performance and scalability perspectives whenever they make a design or an implementation decision.

Software developers already possess strong, valuable, and hard-to-obtain software design and implementation skills. Regardless of their experience, they can complement their existing coding skills by acquiring from this book knowledge about designing and implementing performance and scalability into their products in the first place during the various life cycles of development.

Of course, it's impractical to have only the software developers take care of all the performance and scalability challenges. Building a software system that performs and scales is a cross-team effort. This book provides a common knowledge platform for all stakeholders to work together to tame the challenging performance and scalability issues so that the product they are all responsible for is *built to perform and scale.*

WHO THIS BOOK IS FOR

If you are reading this book, probably you are interested in learning how you can help design and build performance and scalability into your software for which you are one of the stakeholders, either from the technical or management perspective. No matter what your roles are, I am very confident that you will learn something from this book that can help you become more knowledgeable, more productive, and more efficient in solving your performance and scalability issues.

I wrote this book with some specific groups of readers in my mind. In deciding what material to include in this book and how to write it, I tried my best to make this book pertinent and useful for the following groups of readers:

- Software developers who have the most influence on how well the software product they develop will actually perform and scale. If software developers are equipped with adequate knowledge and experience in software performance and scalability, fewer defects will slip out of their hands into the builds they deliver.
- Software engineers who conduct the performance and scalability tests to make sure that the product will not be released to the market without catching and resolving major performance and scalability defects. Nowadays, it's very hard to find experienced software performance engineers. Most of the engineers who conduct the performance and scalability tests are from other job responsibilities, such as quality assurance, system administration, database administration, or programming. This book can help them get up to speed quickly in helping resolve software performance and scalability issues they discover through their tests.
- Software performance managers and development managers who are interested in understanding software performance and scalability problems at a high level so that they can lead more effectively in getting various performance and scalability defects resolved in time.

- The book can also be used as a textbook in various ways. First of all, it can be used as a textbook for university courses related to computer performance evaluation and software non-functional testing at the upper-division undergraduate and graduate levels. It can be used as a required supplement to the computer organization texts now in use that every CS and CpE student must take. It is an ideal text as well to supplement a course in queuing theory that is available in many universities for the students majoring in mathematics, probability and statistics.

Many books available today on the subject of software performance and scalability do not provide the same level of *quantitativeness*, which is one of the most distinctive merits of this book. In my opinion, *quantitativeness* is a requirement for dealing with software performance and scalability issues, as performance and scalability are quantitatively measurable attributes of a software system.

I hope that the quantitative approach and the real-world quantitative case studies presented throughout this book can help you learn about software performance and scalability faster and more effectively. And more importantly, I am confident that by applying everything you learn from this book to your product, you can make a huge difference in improving the performance and scalability of your product to the satisfaction of your company and customers.

HOW THIS BOOK IS ORGANIZED

Software Performance and Scalability: A Quantitative Approach is the first book to focus on software performance and scalability in a quantitative approach. It introduces the basic concepts and principles behind the physics of software performance and scalability from a practical point of view. It demonstrates how the performance and scalability of your products can be optimized and tuned using both proven theories and quantitative, real-world examples presented as case studies in each chapter. These case studies can easily be applied to your software projects so that you can realize immediate, measurable improvements on the performance and scalability of your products.

As illustrated in Figure A, this book elaborates on three levels of skill sets for coping with software performance and scalability problems.

Level 3: API Profiling

Level 2: Queuing Theory

Level 1: The Basics

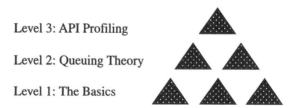

Figure A *Three levels of skill sets for solving software performance and scalability challenges.*

Specifically, this book consists of the following three parts:

- *Part 1: The Basics*. This part lays the foundation for understanding the factors that affect the performance and scalability of a software product in general. It introduces the various hardware components of a modern computer system as well as software platforms that predetermine the performance and scalability of a software product. It concludes with how to test *quantitatively* the performance and scalability of a software product. Through quantitative measurements, you can determine not only which hardware and software platforms can deliver the required performance and scalability for your products, but also how to optimize and tune the performance and scalability of your products over time.

- *Part 2: Applying Queuing Theory*. Queuing theory is the mathematical study of waiting lines or queues for a system that depends on limited resources to complete certain tasks. It is particularly useful as a *quantitative* framework to help identify the performance and scalability bottlenecks of a computer software system. The efficacy of queuing theory in solving software performance and scalability problems is demonstrated in two subsequent chapters using quantitative case studies.

- *Part 3: Applying API Profiling*. API profiling provides *quantitative* information about how a software program is executed internally at the API level. Such information is useful in identifying the most expensive execution paths from performance and scalability perspectives. Based on such information, developers can design more efficient algorithms and implementations to achieve the best possible performance and scalability for products. This part introduces a generic API profiling framework (*perfBasic*), which can be implemented easily in any high-level programming languages. It concludes with a case study chapter showing quantitatively how one can use the *performance maps* generated with the API profiling data out of this API profiling framework to help solve software performance and scalability issues.

In order to make this book more suitable as a textbook for an upper division undergraduate or graduate level course for computer and software engineering students, exercises have been provided at the end of each chapter. In most cases, the exercises have been designed to encourage the reader to conduct his/her own research and come up with the *quantitative* solutions to the exercises. In addition, the reader is encouraged to think and practice, rather than simply writing a program or filling in a formula with numbers. Dealing with software performance and scalability problems is more challenging than simply coding, and oftentimes, it's really passion and discipline that can make a difference.

I have made every effort to make this book concise, practical, interesting, and useful for helping you solve your software performance and scalability problems. I hope you'll enjoy reading this book, apply what you learn from this book to your work, and see immediate positive results. In addition, be conscious that by developing high-performance and scalable software that consumes less electric power to run, you are not only contributing to the success of your company and your customers, but also helping reduce global warming effects, for which we are all responsible.

HOW TO REACH THE AUTHOR

All mistakes and errors, if any, in the text are my responsibility. You are more than welcome to email me your comments about the contents of this book, or errors found therein, at *henry@perfmath.com* For any downloads and updated information about the book, visit the book's website at *http://www.perfmath.com*.

Henry H. Liu, PhD

Folsom, California
September 2008

Acknowledgments

First, I would like to thank all of the colleagues I had worked with in the field of physics research. Some of the greatest physicists that I was so lucky to have had a chance to work for and with include: Professor S. Liu, Professor J. Xie, Dr. J. Le Duff, Professor Dr. A. Richter, Dr. J. Bisognano, Dr. G. Neil, and Dr. F. Dylla. Because of them, my previous physics research career had been so enjoyable and fruitful. I'd like to mention that my current career as a software performance engineer has benefited tremendously from my previous career as a physicist. Although I left physics research and jumped to computers and software about a decade ago, the spirit of pursuing a subject in a rigorous, quantitative, and objective manner cultivated through my earlier physics research career has never left me. I have had this hopelessly immutable habitude of trying to deal with every software performance issue as quantitatively as possible as if it were a physics research subject. I have been totally soaked with that spirit, which gives me the power and energy for pursuing every challenging software performance and scalability problem quantitatively, and thus this book—*Software Performance and Scalability: A Quantitative Approach*.

With my career as a software performance professional, I'd like to especially thank Pat Crain, who introduced me to applying queuing theory to solving software performance challenges. Pat also encouraged me to write my first research paper on software performance, which was presented and awarded the best paper award in the category of software performance at the 2004 CMG Conference held in Las Vegas. I owe a debt of gratitude to Keith Gordon, who was the VP of the software company I worked for. Keith had enthusiastically read draft versions of my papers prior to publication and had always encouraged me to publish and share my software performance experience with the greater software community. I also feel excited to mention one of my fellow software performance engineers, Mary Shun, who encouraged me to write a book on software performance someday. Many thanks and this is it, Mary!

Special thanks are also due to Engel Martin, one of the greatest software performance group managers I have ever worked for. While taking on a tremendous amount of managerial responsibilities, Engel has demonstrated an extremely sharp and accurate sense of software performance and scalability issues at high levels. The atmosphere Engel created within the group he manages has always made me feel comfortable to express my opinions freely and to make my own judgments objectively on technical issues, as I used to as a scientist, for which I am truly grateful.

I would like to take this opportunity to thank the nonanonymous yet never-met authors of some hundreds of books I bought in mathematics, physics, computers, and software. The books they wrote fed my knowledge-hungry mind at various stages of my careers.

I sincerely thank those anonymous referees who offered very useful opinions on how to make this book more valuable to the readers and more suitable as a textbook for an upper division undergraduate or graduate level course for students majoring in computers and software. Their very helpful suggestions have been incorporated in the various parts of this book.

I also owe thanks to Dr. Larry Bernstein, who kindly recommended my book proposal to Wiley. The structure of this book has been deeply influenced by his seminal works published by Wiley in the series of *Quantitative Software Engineering*.

Paul Petralia at Wiley-Interscience mentored me as a first-time book writer through each step of the entire process. It would have not been such a smooth process without Paul's guidance and high professionalism. Michael Christian helped me achieve the next milestone for the book—to get it into production at Wiley—with his hard work and high efficiency. My production manager, Shirley Thomas, production editor, Christine Punzo, compositor (Techset Composition Ltd.), and illustration manager, Dean Gonzalez, at Wiley were the hard-working, efficient engines behind completing the last stage of publishing this book. Needless to say, without such a highly efficient and professional team at Wiley, my software performance experience accumulated over a decade would have still been scattered in various publications and work notes. So many thanks to everyone involved at Wiley.

I'd like to thank my wife, Sarah Chen, who sacrificed so much to take care of our newborn son, William, most of the time, in order to let me sit down and focus on writing this book using my weekends, nightly hours, and even vacation times.

You as a reader are greatly appreciated as well. Your interest in this book has shown your strong motivation to further the success of your company and also your willingness to help contain global warming by developing high-performance and highly scalable software that burns less electric power.

HENRY H. LIU

Introduction

All good things start with smart choices.
— Anonymous

PERFORMANCE VERSUS SCALABILITY

Before we start, I think I owe you an explanation about what the difference is between *performance* and *scalability* for a software system. In a word, performance and scalability are about the *scalable performance* for a software system.

You might find different explanations about performance versus scalability from other sources. In my opinion, performance and scalability for a software system differ from and correlate to each other as follows:

- *Performance* measures how fast and efficiently a software system can complete certain computing tasks, while *scalability* measures the trend of performance with increasing load. There are two major types of computing tasks that are measured using different performance metrics. For OLTP (online transaction processing) type of computing tasks consisting of interactive user activities, the metric of *response time* is used to measure how fast a system can respond to the requests of the interactive users, whereas for noninteractive batch jobs, the metric of *throughput* is used to measure the number of transactions a system can complete over a time period. Performance and scalability are inseparable from each other. It doesn't make sense to talk about scalability if a software system doesn't perform. However, a software system may perform but not scale.

- For a given environment that consists of properly sized hardware, properly configured operating system, and dependent middleware, if the performance of a software system *deteriorates rapidly* with increasing load (number of users or volume of transactions) prior to reaching the intended load level, then it is not scalable and will eventually underperform. In other words, we hope that the performance of a software system would sustain as a flat curve with increasing load prior to reaching the intended load level, which is the ideal scalability one can expect. This kind of scalability issue, which is classified as *type I* scalability issue, can be overcome with proper optimizations and tunings, as will be discussed in this book.

- If the performance of a software system becomes unacceptable when reaching a certain load level with a given environment, but it cannot be improved even with upgraded and/or additional hardware, then it is said that the software is not scalable. This kind of scalability issue, which is classified as *type II* scalability issue, cannot be overcome without going through some major architectural operations, which should be avoided from the beginning at any cost.

Unfortunately, there is no panacea for solving all software performance and scalability challenges. The best strategy is to start with the basics, being guided by queuing theory as well as by application programming interface (API) profiling when coping with software performance and scalability problems. This book teaches how one can make the most out of this strategy in a quantitative approach.

Let's begin with the first part—the basics.

Part 1

The Basics

I went behind the scenes to look at the mechanism.
—Charles Babbage, 1791–1871, the father of computing

The factors that can critically impact the performance and scalability of a software system are abundant. The three factors that have the most impact on the performance and scalability of a software system are the raw capabilities of the underlying hardware platform, the maturity of the underlying software platform (mainly the operating system, various device interface drivers, the supporting virtual machine stack, the run-time environment, etc.), and its own design and implementation. If the software system is an application system built on some middleware systems such as various database servers, application servers, Web servers, and any other types of third-party components, then the performance and scalability of such middleware systems can directly affect the performance and scalability of the application system.

Understanding the performance and scalability of a software system *qualitatively* should begin with a solid understanding of all the performance bits built into the modern computer systems as well as all the performance and scalability implications associated with the various modern software platforms and architectures. Understanding the performance and scalability of a software system *quantitatively* calls for a test framework that can be depended upon to provide reliable information about the true performance and scalability of the software system in question. These ideas motivated me to select the following three chapters for this part:

- Chapter 1—Hardware Platform
- Chapter 2—Software Platform
- Chapter 3—Testing Software Performance and Scalability

Software Performance and Scalability. By Henry H. Liu
Copyright © 2009 IEEE Computer Society

The material presented in these three chapters is by no means the cliché you have heard again and again. I have filled in each chapter with real-world case studies so that you can actually feel the performance and scalability pitches associated with each case quantitatively.

1

Hardware Platform

What mathematical problems should a computing machine solve?
—Konrad Zuse, 1934

To build new specifications from given specifications by a prescription.
—His answer in 1936

Computing is the deviation of result specifications to any specifications by a prescription.
—His extended definition in 1946

What performance a software system exhibits often solely depends on the raw speed of the underlying hardware platform, which is largely determined by the central processing unit (CPU) horsepower of a computer. What scalability a software system exhibits depends on the scalability of the architecture of the underlying hardware platform as well. I have had many experiences with customers who reported that slow performance of the software system was simply caused by the use of undersized hardware. It's fair to say that hardware platform is the number one most critical factor in determining the performance and scalability of a software system. We'll see in this chapter the two supporting case studies associated with the Intel® hyperthreading technology and new Intel multicore processor architecture.

As is well known, the astonishing advances of computers can be characterized *quantitatively* by Moore's law. Intel co-founder Gordon E. Moore stated in his 1965 seminal paper that the density of transistors on a computer chip is increasing exponentially, doubling approximately every two years. The trend has continued for more than half a century and is not expected to stop for another decade at least.

The quantitative approach pioneered by Moore has been very effective in quantifying the advances of computers. It has been extended into other areas of computer and software engineering as well, to help refine the methodologies of developing better software and computer architectures [Bernstein and Yuhas, 2005; Laird and

Brennan, 2006; Gabarro, 2006; Hennessy and Patterson, 2007]. This book is an attempt to introduce *quantitativeness* into dealing with the challenges of software performance and scalability facing the software industry today.

To see how modern computers have become so powerful, let's begin with the Turing machine.

1.1 TURING MACHINE

Although Charles Babbage (1791–1871) is known as the father of computing, the most original idea of a computing machine was described by Alan Turing more than seven decades ago in 1936. Turing was a mathematician and is often considered the father of modern computer science.

As shown in Figure 1.1, a Turing machine consists of the following four basic elements:

- A *tape*, which is divided into cells, one next to the other. Each cell contains a symbol from some finite alphabet. This tape is assumed to be infinitely long on both ends. It can be read or written.
- A *head* that can read and write symbols on the tape.
- A *table* of instructions that tell the machine what to do next, based on the current state of the machine and the symbols it is reading on the tape.
- A *state register* that stores the states of the machine.

A Turing machine has two assumptions: one is the unlimited storage space and the other is completing a task regardless of the amount of time it takes. As a theoretical model, it exhibits the great power of abstraction to the highest degree. To some extent, modern computers are as close to Turing machines as modern men are close to cavemen. It's so amazing that today's computers still operate on the same principles

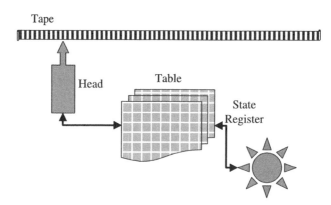

Figure 1.1 *Concept of a Turing machine.*

as Turing proposed seven decades ago. To convince you that this is true, here is a comparison between a Turing machine's basic elements and a modern computer's constituent parts:

- Tape—memory and disks
- Head—I/O controllers (memory bus, disk controllers, and network port)
- Table + state register—CPUs

In the next section, I'll briefly introduce the next milestone in computing history, the von Neumann architecture.

1.2 VON NEUMANN MACHINE

John von Neumann was another mathematician who pioneered in making computers a reality in computing history. He proposed and participated in building a machine named EDVAC (Electronic Discrete Variable Automatic Computer) in 1946. His model is very close to the computers we use today. As shown in Figure 1.2, the von Neumann model consists of four parts: memory, control unit, arithmetic logic unit, and input/output.

Similar to the modern computer architecture, in the von Neumann architecture, memory is where instructions and data are stored, the control unit interprets instructions while coordinating other units, the arithmetic logic unit performs arithmetic and logical operations, and the input/output provides the interface with users.

A most prominent feature of the von Neumann architecture is the concept of stored program. Prior to the von Neumann architecture, all computers were built with fixed programs, much like today's desktop calculators that cannot run Microsoft Office or play video games except for simple calculations. Stored program was a giant jump in making machine hardware be independent of software programs that can run on it. This separation of hardware from software had profound effects on evolving computers.

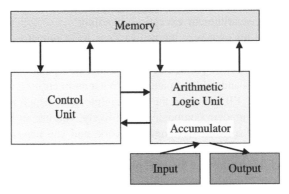

Figure 1.2 *von Neumann architecture.*

The latency associated with data transfer between CPU and memory was noticed as early as the von Neumann architecture. It was known as the *von Neumann bottleneck*, coined by John Backus in his 1977 ACM Turing Award lecture. In order to overcome the von Neumann bottleneck and improve computing efficiency, today's computers add more and more cache between CPU and main memory. Caching at the chip level is one of the many very crucial performance optimization strategies at the chip hardware level and is indispensable for modern computers.

In the next section, I'll give a brief overview about the Zuse machine, which was the earliest generation of commercialized computers. Zuse built his machines independent of the Turing machine and von Neumann machine.

1.3 ZUSE MACHINE

When talking about computing machines, we must mention Konrad Zuse, who was another great pioneer in the history of computing.

In 1934, driven by his dislike of the time-consuming calculations he had to perform as a civil engineer, Konrad Zuse began to formulate his first ideas on computing. He defined the logical architecture of his Z1, Z2, Z3, and Z4 computers. He was completely unaware of any computer-related developments in Germany or in other countries until a very late stage, so he independently conceived and implemented the principles of modern digital computers in isolation.

From the beginning it was clear to Zuse that his computers should be freely programmable, which means that they should be able to read an arbitrary meaningful sequence of instructions from a punch tape. It was also clear to him that the machines should work in the binary number system, because he wanted to construct his computers using binary switching elements. Not only should the numbers be represented in a binary form, but the whole logic of the machine should work using a binary switching mechanism (0–1 principle).

Zuse took performance into account in his designs even from the beginning. He designed a high-performance binary floating point unit in the semilogarithmic representation, which allowed him to calculate very small and very big numbers with sufficient precision. He also implemented a high-performance adder with a one-step carry-ahead and precise arithmetic exceptions handling.

Zuse even funded his own very innovative Zuse KG Company, which produced more than 250 computers with a value of 100 million DM between 1949 and 1969. During his life, Konrad Zuse painted several hundred oil paintings. He held about three dozen exhibitions and sold the paintings. What an interesting life he had!

In the next section, I'll introduce the Intel architecture, which prevails over the other architectures for modern computers. Most likely, you use an Intel architecture based system for your software development work, and you may also deploy your software on Intel architecture based systems for performance and scalability tests. As a matter of fact, I'll mainly use the Intel platform throughout this book for demonstrating software performance optimization and tuning techniques that apply to other platforms as well.

1.4   INTEL MACHINE

Intel architecture based systems are most popular not only for development but also for production. Let's dedicate this section to understanding the Intel architecture based machines.

1.4.1   History of Intel's Chips

Intel started its chip business with a 108 kHz processor in 1971. Since then, its processor family has evolved from year to year through the chain of 4004–8008–8080–8086–80286–80386–80486–Pentium–Pentium Pro–Pentium II–Pentium III/Xeon–Itanium–Pentium 4/Xeon to today's multicore processors. Table 1.1 shows the history of the Intel processor evolution up to 2005 when the multicore microarchitecture was introduced to increase energy efficiency while delivering higher performance.

1.4.2   Hyperthreading

Intel started introducing its hyperthreading (HT) technology with Pentium 4 in 2002. People outside Intel are often confused about what HT exactly is. This is a very relevant subject when you conduct performance and scalability testing, because you need to know if HT is enabled or not on the systems under test. Let's clarify what HT is here.

First, let's see how a two physical processor system works. With a dual-processor system, the two processors are separated from each other physically with two independent sockets. Each of the two processors has its own hardware resources such as arithmetic logical unit (ALU) and cache. The two processors share the main memory only through the system bus, as shown in Figure 1.3.

TABLE 1.1   Evolution of the Intel Processor Family Prior to the Multicore Microarchitecture Introduced in 2005

Year	Processor	CPU Speed	Addressable Memory
1971	4004	108 kHz	640 bytes
1972	8008	200 kHz	16 kilobytes (kB)
1974	8080	2 MHz	64 kB
1978	8086	10 MHz	1 MB
1985	80386	16 MHz	4 GB
1989	80486	50 MHz	4 GB
1993	Pentium	66 MHz	4 GB
1995	Pentium Pro	200 MHz	4 GB
1997/98	Pentium II/Xeon	300/400 MHz	4/64 GB
1999	Pentium III/Xeon	500/555 MHz	4/64 GB
2001	Xeon/Itanium	1.7/0.8 GHz	64 GB/1 TB
2001	Pentium 4/Xeon	2 GHz	4 GB
2003	Pentium 4 HT/Xeon	3/3 GHz	4/64 GB
2004	Itanium 2	1.6 GHz	1 TB
2005	Pentium 4/Xeon MP	3.7/3.6 GHz	4/64 GB

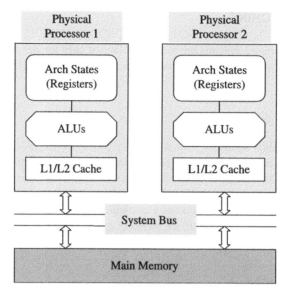

Figure 1.3   *Two physical processors in an Intel system.*

As shown in Figure 1.4, with hyperthreading, only a small set of microarchitecture states is duplicated, while the arithmetic logic units and cache(s) are shared. Compared with a single processor without HT support, the die size of a single processor with HT is increased by less than 5%. As you can imagine, HT may slow down single-threaded applications because of the overhead for synchronizations between

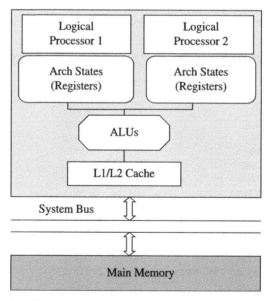

Figure 1.4   *Hyperthreading: two logical processors in an Intel system.*

the two logical processors. However, it is beneficial for multithreaded applications. Of course, a single processor with HT will not be the same as two physical processors without HT from the performance and scalability perspectives for very obvious reasons.

■ Case Study 1.1: Intel Hyperthreading Technology

How effective is hyperthreading? I had a chance to test it with a real-world OLTP (online transaction processing) application. The setup consisted of three servers: a Web server, an application server, and a database server. All servers were configured with two single-core Intel® Xeon™ processors at 3.4-GHz with hyperthreading support. The test client machine was on a similar system as well. The details of the application and the workload used for testing are not important here. The intention here is to illustrate how effective hyperthreading is with this specific setup and application.

Figure 1.5 shows the average response times of the workload with and without hyperthreading for different numbers of virtual users. The workload used for the tests consisted of a series of activities conducted by different types of users. The response time measured was from end to end without including the user's own *think times.* It was averaged over all types of activities.

With this specific test case, the effectiveness of HT depended on the number of users, ranging from 7%, to 23%, and to 33%, for 200, 300, and 400 users, respectively. The maximum improvement of 33% for 400 users is very significant.

As a matter of fact, the effectiveness of HT depends on how busy the systems are without HT when an intended load is applied to the systems under test. If CPUs of a system are relatively idle without HT, then enabling HT would not

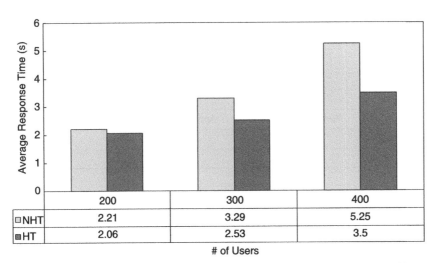

Figure 1.5 *Performance enhancements from hyperthreading (TH) in comparison with non-hyperthreading (NTH) based on a real-world OLTP application.*

help improve the system performance much. However, if the CPUs of a system are relatively busy without HT, enabling HT would provide additional computing power, which helps improve the system performance significantly. So the effectiveness of HT depends on whether a system can be driven to its fullest possible utilization.

In order to help prove the above observation on the circumstances under which HT would be effective, Figure 1.6 shows the CPU usages associated with the Web server, application server, and database server for different numbers of users with hyperthreading turned off and on, respectively. I have to explain that those CPU usage numbers were CPU utilizations averaged over the total number of processors perceived by the Microsoft Windows® 2003 Enterprise Edition operating system. With hyperthreading not turned on, the two single-core processors were perceived as two CPUs. However, when hyperthreading was turned on, the two single-core processors were perceived by the operating system as four processors, so the total CPU utilization would be the average CPU utilization multiplied by four and the maximum total CPU utilization would be 400%.

As is seen, the average CPU utilizations with HT turned on were lower than those with HT off. Take the Web server for 200 users as an example. With HT off, the average system CPU utilization was 27%. However, with HT on, the average system CPU utilization turned to 15%. This doesn't mean that the physical CPUs were about twice busier with HT off than with HT on. If we take into account the fact that those CPU utilization numbers were averaged over the total number

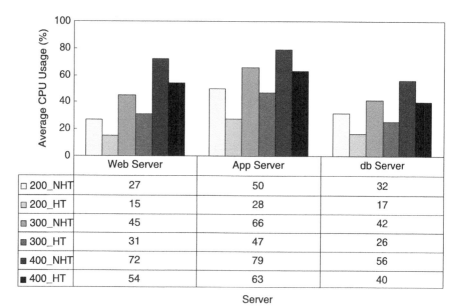

Figure 1.6 Comparisons of server system CPU utilizations between nonhyperthreading (NHT) and hyperthreading (HT).

of CPUs, it means that with HT off, each of the two CPUs of the Web server was 27% busy, whereas with HT on, each of the four CPUs of the same Web server was 15% busy; so overall the four CPUs in the case of HT-enabled did more work than the two CPUs in the case of HT-disabled; thus the overall system performance has been improved.

In the next section, I'll help you understand what Intel's multicore microarchitecture is about. Of course, multicore is a lot more powerful than hyperthreading, since a dual-core processor is closer to two physical processors than a single-core hyperthreaded processor is.

1.4.3 Intel's Multicore Microarchitecture

In contrast to hyperthreading, the Intel multicore microarchitecture shares nothing above L2 cache, as shown in Figure 1.7 for a dual-core configuration. Therefore both single-threaded and multithreaded applications can benefit from the multiple execution cores. Of course, hyperthreading and multicore do not contradict each other, as one can have each core hyperthreading enabled.

The Intel multicore microarchitecture resulted from the marriage of the other two Intel microarchitectures: NetBurst and Mobile, as shown in Figure 1.8. Note that Intel started to enter the most lucrative market of high-end server systems as early as Pentium Pro. That's how the NetBurst microarchitecture was born with the Xeon family of processors. The Mobile microarchitecture was introduced to respond to

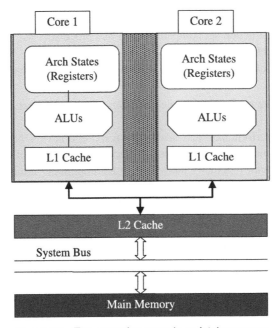

Figure 1.7 *Two execution cores in an Intel processor.*

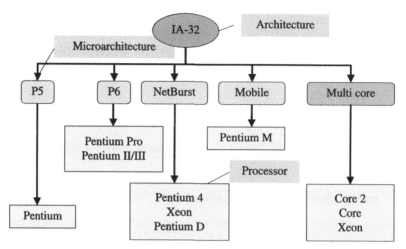

Figure 1.8   History of the Intel 32 bit microarchitecture.

the overheated mobile computing demands, for which low-power consumption was one of the most critical requirements. Combining the advantages of high performance from NetBurst and low power consumption from Mobile resulted in the new Intel multicore microarchitecture.

It's very necessary to differentiate among those three terms of *architecture, microarchitecture*, and *processor*:

- Processor architecture refers to the instruction set, registers, and memory data-resident data structure that is public to the programmer. Processor architecture maintains instruction set compatibility so that processors will run the programs written for generations of processors.
- Microarchitecture refers to the implementation of processor architecture in silicon.
- Processors are productized implementation of microarchitecture.

For software performance and scalability tests, one always needs to know the detailed specs of the systems being tested, especially the details of the processors as the brain of a system. It actually takes time to learn all about Intel processors. Here is a more systematic approach to pursuing the details of the Intel processors used in an Intel architecture based system. One should start with the processor number, which uniquely identifies each release of the Intel processors. It's not enough just to know the marketing names of the Intel processors. If you are using Intel architecture based systems for your performance and scalability tests, it's very likely that you are using Intel Xeon processor based systems.

Table 1.2 shows the specs of the latest Intel server processors. The specs include CPU type, CPU clock rate, front-side-bus (FSB) speed, L2/L3 cache, and hyper-threading support. It's interesting to see that Intel architecture is moving toward more and more cores while keeping increasing front-side-bus speed and L2/L3 cache. Hyper-threading support becomes less important as more and more cores can

TABLE 1.2 Intel 32-Bit Server Processors Classified by CPU Model, CPU Clock Rate, FSB (Front Side Bus) Speed, L2 and L3 Cache, and HT (Hyper-Threading) Support

CPU	Clock Rate (GHz)	FSB (NHz)	L2/L3 (MB)	HT
Xeon	3.00–3.80	800	2/–	Yes
Xeon MP	2.83–3.66	667	1/0–8	Yes
Dual-Core	1.66–3.50	667–1600	2/0–16	Some
Quad-Core	1.60–3.20	1066–1333	4–12/–	No
Six-Core	2.13–2.66	1066	9/12	No

be packaged in a single processor. Also the clock rate is not necessarily going higher with more cores. Most of the architectural design decisions were based on the goal of increasing performance by maximizing the parallelism that a multi-core processor can support.

On the desktop side, Intel has recently released a product family of Intel Core™ i7 processors. The Core™ i7 processors adopted a combination of multi-core with hyper-threading to maximize the multi-tasking capability for CPU processing power demanding applications. To maximize the I/O performance, Core™ i7 incorporated many advanced Intel technologies such as Intel® Smart Cache, Intel® QuickPath Interconnect, Intel® HD Boost, and integrated memory controller, etc., into the design. See Figure 1.9 for the image of an Intel Core™ i7 processor.

Now let's say you are using a Dell® PowerEdge® 6800 server. From looking up Dell's website, you would know that this system is using Intel's *3.0 GHz/800 MHz/ 2 × 2 MB Cache, Dual-Core Intel® Xeon 7041 Processor*. Then from Intel's website about *viewing processor number details* page for Xeon processors, you will find further details about the Dual-Core Xeon 7041 processor: for example, its system type is MP, which means that it can be configured with at least four or more processors. Some processors are labeled UP or DP, which stands for uniprocessor (UP) or dual-processor (DP). Also, it's capable of hyperthreading (HT).

Figure 1.9 *Intel Core™ i7 processor.*

It's very important that you are not confused about the terms of processor, UP/DP/ MP, multicore, and hyperthreading when you communicate about exactly what systems you are using. Here is a summary about what these terms imply hierarchically:

- *Processor* implies the separate chip package or socket. A system with one, two, or N processors with N > 2 are called one-way (UP), two-way (DP), or N-way systems (MP).
- A processor could be a dual-core or quad-core processor with two or four cores in that processor. *Cores* are called *execution engines* in Intel's term.
- You can have hyperthreading turned on within each core. Then you would have two computing threads within each core.

Next, I'll provide a case study to demonstrate how important it is to keep up with the latest hardware advances in order to tap the highest possible performance and scalability potentials with a software application. A newer, faster computer system may even cost less than the older, slower one purchased just a couple of years ago.

■ **Case Study 1.2: Performance and Scalability Comparison Between Intel's Single-Core and Multicore Processors**

Figure 1.10 shows how effective the Intel multicore architecture could be compared with its single-core architecture, demonstrated with a real-world enterprise application that inserts objects into a database. The same tests were conducted with two different setups. In each setup, two identical systems were used, one for the application server, and the other for the database server.

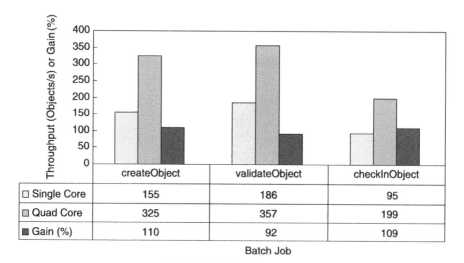

	createObject	validateObject	checkInObject
□ Single Core	155	186	95
▨ Quad Core	325	357	199
■ Gain (%)	110	92	109

Batch Job

□ Single Core   ▨ Quad Core   ■ Gain (%)

Figure 1.10   *Performance and scalability advantages of the Intel quad core over its single-core architecture.*

With the above test setups, the single-core setup was configured with two identical systems, each of which was equipped with four single-core Xeon processors at 3.67 GHz, whereas the quad-core setup was configured with two identical systems as well, each of which was equipped with two quad-core Xeon processors at 1.86 GHz. The total CPU power was the same between the single-core and quad-core systems. However, the quad-core setup outperformed the single-core setup consistently across all three different types of batch jobs by about a factor of 2, while the cost of each quad-core system was about only half of a single-core system. This shows how important it is to upgrade your hardware in time in order to get the maximum performance and scalability for your application while spending less.

New microarchitecture poses challenges for traditional system monitoring tools in terms of how CPU utilizations should be interpreted when logical or virtual processors are exposed to operating systems as if they were physical processors. This issue will be briefly discussed in the next section.

1.4.4 Challenges for System Monitoring Tools

It is confusing with hyperthreading and multicore with regard to how many physical CPUs a system actually has. For example, when you open up your Windows Task Manager on your system, you might see four CPUs displayed. Then you would wonder whether it's a four-way system, or two-way system dual-core per processor, or actually a single-processor dual-core system with hyperthreading enabled. If you are not sure, ask your system administrator to find out what's actually inside the box regarding the number of CPUs, cores, and hyperthreading.

Keep in mind that with your performance and scalability testing, you need to know exactly what systems you are using, because what systems you use will determine what performance and scalability you will observe for the software you test. Keep also in mind that the traditional operating system utilities fall behind the multicore and hyperthreading technologies. Whether it's a physical processor, a hyperthreaded logical processor, or a core, they all appear as a CPU to the operating system, which imposes challenges for interpreting the log data you collect with the processor performance counter.

Next, I'll introduce Sun machines, which are popular for IT production systems.

1.5 SUN MACHINE

Sun Microsystems® processor lines started with MicroSPARC I at 40–50 MHz introduced in 1992. Table 1.3 shows all Sun processors since 1998. The earlier Sun processors may have been retired in every IT organization. Note that UltraSPARC IV and IV+ are dual-core processors, whereas T1 and T2 are multicore, multithreading processors based on Sun's *CoolThread* technology. T1 and T2 were code-named *Niagara* and *Niagara II* processors. T1 has six pipeline stages, whereas T2 has eight pipeline stages, as shown in Figure 1.11.

TABLE 1.3 **Sun UltraSPARC Processors Since 1998**

Model	Speed (MHz)	Year	Threads/Core × Cores = Total Number of CPUs
UltraSPARC IIi	333–480	1998	1 × 1 = 1
UltraSPARC III	750–900	2001	1 × 1 = 1
UltraSPARC IIIi	1064–1593	2003	1 × 1 = 1
UltraSPARC IV	1050–1350	2004	1 × 2 = 2
UltraSPARC IV +	1500–1800	2005	1 × 2 = 2
UltraSPARC T1	1000–1400	2005	4 × 8 = 32
UltraSPARC T2	1400	2007	8 × 8 = 64

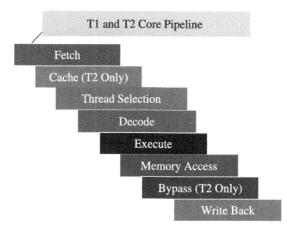

Figure 1.11 *Core pipelines for Sun T1 and T2 multicore, multithreading processors.*

It is helpful to understand how the new generation of Sun processors work. Essentially, one physically packaged processor can contain multiple cores, and one core can contain multiple threads. *Cores* don't share anything above L2 cache, whereas *threads* share everything below the register level. Those threads are termed *computing threads* in Sun's *throughput computing* marketing programs.

One can use the command "*psrinfo –vp*" to check out the processor type and the number of CPUs on a Sun system. However, it's necessary to make sure how many physical processors and logical CPUs or how many *cores* or *threads* are actually installed on the system.

In the next section, I'll show you how you can get to know quickly about your performance and scalability testing systems based on the latest Intel processors.

1.6 SYSTEM UNDER TEST

1.6.1 Processors

Your machine, whether it's a server class machine or a development desktop, is no doubt much more powerful than the machines built more than half a century ago. That's because modern processors have become millions of times faster.

TABLE 1.4 Comparison of Performance Between the IAS Machine and a Typical Modern Machine with Intel Xeon Processors

Spec	IAS	Modern Machine	Improvement (Times)
Memory	5 kB	12 GB	>2 million
Addition time	62 (μs)	1.3 (ns)	50 thousand
Multiplication time	713 (μs)	1.7 (ns)	400 thousand

In order to see the astronomical disparity, Table 1.4 compares the performance of one of the von Neumann machines with one of the typical Intel servers. This von Neumann machine was named the IAS machine, which was the first electronic digital computer built by the Institute for Advanced Study (IAS) at Princeton, New Jersey, USA, in 1952. A 3-GHz, dual-core, Intel Xeon 7041 processor is chosen arbitrarily for comparison. This processor is based on the Intel Core microarchitecture. In order to explain how we arrived at its performance for comparison, we need to explain the concepts of latency and throughput in the context of the Intel Core microarchitecture.

In the context of the Intel Core microarchitecture, latency is the number of processor clocks it takes for an instruction to have its data available for use by another instruction. Throughput is the number of processor clocks it takes for an instruction to execute or perform its calculations. A floating-point addition operation takes a latency of 3 processor clocks and a throughput of 1 processor clock. A single-precision floating-point multiplication operation takes a latency of 4 processor clocks and a throughput of 1 processor clock. Thus we can derive that the addition time and multiplication time of a modern Intel Xeon processor would be about 1.3 nanoseconds and 1.7 nanoseconds, respectively. Given its multicore and multithreading capability, a modern processor could be a million times faster than one manufactured half a century ago.

Even different models of the modern processors manufactured within a few years apart could exhibit drastically different performance and scalability with your software, as we have demonstrated with the preceding case study of the Intel multicore versus single-core comparison.

In the next few sections, let's expand more into the other parts of a computer system that have significant impact on the performance and scalability of a software system in general.

1.6.2 Motherboard

A powerful processor would starve to death without commensurate peripheral components to keep feeding it with instructions and data. In other words, a powerful processor needs a highly efficient environment to support it. That environment is provided by a motherboard, as shown in Figure 1.12.

The server motherboard shown in Figure 1.12 contains two dual-core processors, sixteen memory slots for installing up to 16 GB of RAM, two network ports, internal redundant arrays of inexpensive disks (RAIDs) controllers, peripheral component interconnect (PCI) slots, and a chipset. If you have a system of your own, you can

Figure 1.12 Intel server board SE7520BB2 (courtesy of Intel).

actually open the box yourself and get familiar with all the components on the motherboard.

Keep in mind that all the components on a motherboard are crucial for achieving super high performance out of today's Intel architecture based systems. When you evaluate your performance and scalability test results, you definitely need to know all the specs of your systems under test. This is also very necessary when you document your test results. I'd like to emphasize again that what performance and scalability you get with your software has a lot to do with what you have *inside* your systems.

You may often hear the other two terms of *chip* and *chipset*. A chip is basically a piece of integrated circuit that may contain millions of transistors. There are different types of chips. For example, processor chips contain an entire processing unit, whereas memory chips contain blank memory. Figure 1.13 shows the Intel Xeon uniprocessor (left) and multiprocessor (right) chips.

In the next section, I'll clarify what chipsets are.

1.6.3 Chipset

A chipset is a group of integrated circuits ("chips") that are designed to work together and are usually marketed as a single product. It is also commonly used to refer to the specialized chips on a motherboard. For example, the Intel E7520 chipset consists of three chips for facilitating data exchange between processors and memory through the front-side bus, and also between processors and secondary storage through the PCI bus.

Figure 1.14 shows that a chipset is partitioned into a memory bridge and an I/O bridge. These two bridges are normally called *north* and *south* bridges. The chipset

Figure 1.13 Intel Xeon processor chips (courtesy of Intel).

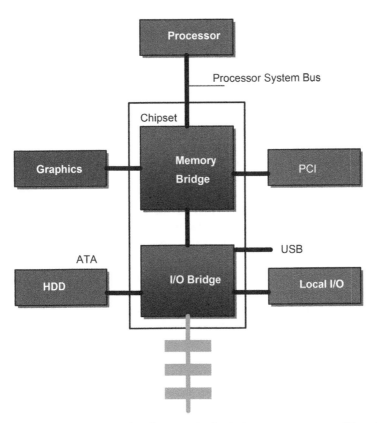

Figure 1.14 Chipset acting as hubs of communication between a processor and its peripheral components.

determines the type of processor, memory, and I/O components that a particular system can support. The chipset's efficiency directly affects the overall system performance.

Unfortunately, the components within a chipset are built-in and not very tunable from system performance perspectives. However, you can choose high-end components when you make a purchase to guarantee that you would get the highest possible performance while your budget permits.

Next, let's concentrate on the storage, which is as important as CPUs, since it determines how fast data can be moved among various data storage levels. Some examples will be presented in Chapter 6 to show how important I/O could be for enterprise applications from the system performance perspective.

1.6.4 Storage

Storage hierarchy is another important factor in determining the performance of a system. Figure 1.15 shows the various levels of storage based on the proximity of the storage layer to the processor, in the sequence of registers, caches, main memory, internal disks, and external disks.

In order to understand the impact of storage on the performance of a system, let's take a look at what each level of storage does for the system following the hierarchical sequence as shown in Figure 1.15:

- Registers are internal to a processor. They hold both instructions and data for carrying out arithmetic and logical calculations. They are the fastest of all forms of computer storage, since they are integrated on a CPU's chip, functioning as switches representing various combinations of 0's and 1's, which is how computers work as we all know.

- Cache memory consists of L1, L2, and L3 caches. L1 cache stores both instructions and data for reuse in order to increase the performance or "throughput" of a computer. L2 and L3 caches store the segments of programs that have just been executed, as well as the data already fetched from main memory for reuse in order to reduce the chances of refetching from the main memory. From L1 to L3, the access speed gets slower while the capacity gets larger.

- Main memory stores programs and data needed by the programs to be executed. Typically, modern computer systems are either 32-bit or 64-bit systems. The addressable memories for 32-bit and 64-bit systems are 4 GB and 1 TB, respectively, although the actual memory installed may be smaller or larger. Main memory is volatile in the sense that if the system is turned off, everything stored on it will be lost. Main memory communicates with the processor through the FSB (front-side bus).

- Hard disks are used for nonvolatile, mass storage of persistent data. There are a few different types of hard disks, for example, IDE (integrated drive electronics), SATA (serial advanced technology attachment), and SCSI (small computer system interface). IDE disks are traditionally used for home PCs. SATA disks

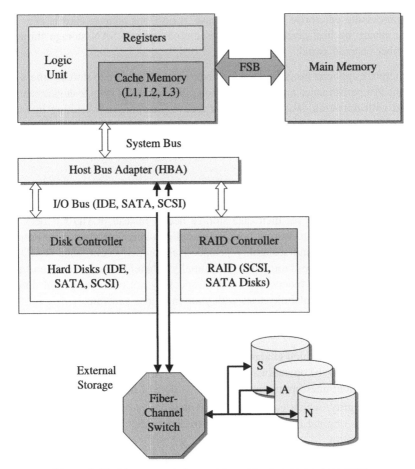

Figure 1.15 Memory and storage hierarchies in a computer system.

are used for video/audio production because of their affordability and large capacity (e.g., >700 GB). SCSI drives are used for more demanding work-stations and enterprise server systems.

• Note that disks can be used as separate ones or configured as RAID (redundant array of inexpensive disks). I'll discuss more about RAID later, but for the time being, just take it as a logical approach to reorganizing disks for built-in redundancy for failure protection and parallel access to multiple disks for better performance.

• Hard disk drives are accessed over one of a number of bus types, including IDE, SATA, SCSI, and fiber channel. Host adapter or host bus adapter bridges the computer's internal system bus to its I/O bus to enable communications between a processor and its peripheral disk storage devices. Note that most enterprise storage adopts external SAN (storage area network) storage for storing and processing enterprise data. In this case, a host bus adapter card is needed to connect the host computer with the remote external SAN storage through a fiber-channel switch.

Enterprise applications typically adopt external SAN storage to store business critical data. For performance and data protection purposes, SAN storage devices are configured with mirroring, striping, and error recovery techniques, resulting in various levels of RAID. Let's get to the details of RAID in the next section.

1.6.5 RAID

RAID stands for redundant arrays of inexpensive disks. We mentioned RAID in the previous section, but did not elaborate on it. Most of the IT organizations rarely use local independent disks for their data storage needs. Instead, RAID has been used as a standard approach to storing both static and dynamic enterprise data. From the software performance and scalability perspectives, properly configured RAID may improve data read/write throughput substantially. Therefore, we recommend using RAID rather than local independent disks, especially not one single local disk, for the performance and scalability tests with your enterprise software.

No matter how it is configured, the purposes with a RAID configuration are one, or more, or all of the following:

- Fault tolerance, which guarantees that if some disks of a RAID fail, the system can continue to be operational for sufficiently long so that the failed disks can be fixed without interrupting normal business uses of the system.
- Data integrity, which guarantees that if the data is partially lost or corrupted, the entire original data set can be recovered based on the remaining healthy and valid data.
- Higher data transfer throughput relative to a single or more separate disks, as data can be read from or written to multiple disks in parallel.

With a RAID configuration, multiple physical disks appear as one logical unit to the operating system. There are software RAID configurations and hardware RAID configurations. With a software RAID configuration, an abstraction software layer sits above the disk device drivers, which manage data transfer between physical disks and the operating system. Since this software layer consumes the CPU time of a local system, a software RAID configuration in general is much slower than a hardware RAID configuration. Therefore, if performance is a concern, a hardware RAID configuration is preferred over a software RAID configuration.

With a hardware RAID, a RAID controller is used to perform all calculations for managing the disks and maintaining the properties specified for a RAID configuration. This offloads RAID-related computing tasks from the main CPUs of the host system to RAID controller hardware, which improves the overall system performance. Another advantage of using a hardware RAID is that the built-in cache from a hardware RAID can help improve the overall system performance further.

A RAID could be internal or external to a system. An internal RAID uses the internal local disks and built-in on-board RAID controller of a system to realize a RAID configuration. An external RAID uses a fiber-channel switch to connect a RAID provided by an SAN (storage area network) to the host system.

How to configure and administrate a RAID is beyond the scope of this book. Here we will only provide enough information about the most commonly used RAID configurations so that you know how to choose a RAID configuration for conducting your performance and scalability tests for which I/Os are important.

RAID configurations are also termed *RAID levels*. The following RAID levels are most commonly seen in today's IT environment:

- RAID 0 (stripping). This RAID configuration spreads data across multiple disks. As shown in Figure 1.16a, multiple disks are connected to a RAID controller, which in turn is connected either internally or externally through a fiber channel

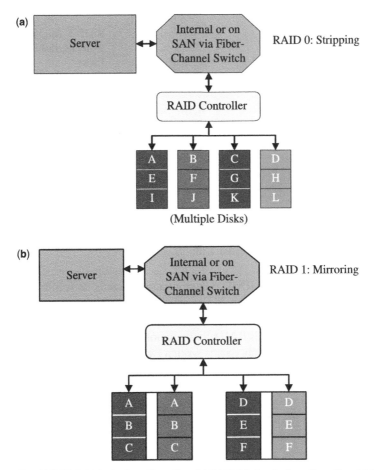

Figure 1.16 *(a) RAID 0 (stripping) configuration; (b) RAID 1 (mirroring) configuration; (c) RAID 10 (mirroring + stripping) configuration; and (d) RAID 5 (stripping + parity) configuration.*

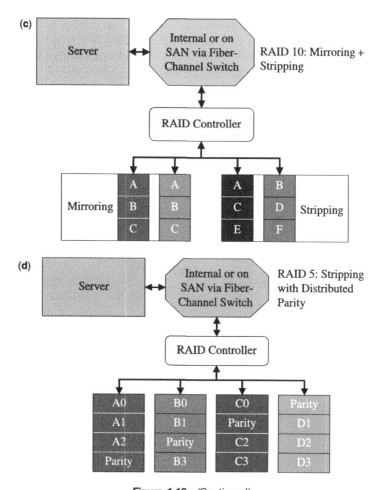

Figure 1.16 (Continued).

to the system. With the RAID 0 configuration, there is no redundancy or error recovery as data blocks are just written to multiple disks sequentially in a round-robin fashion.

- RAID 1 (mirroring). This RAID configuration duplicates data on multiple disks. As shown in Figure 1.16b, data is written twice on mirroring disks, which provides data redundancy but not error recovery. Also note that with RAID 1, twice the data storage capacity is required. This RAID configuration might be used in production, but not in performance and scalability testing environment.
- RAID 10. This RAID configuration is a combination of mirroring and stripping with mirroring first and then stripping, as shown in Figure 1.16c.
- RAID 5 (stripping with distributed parity). This RAID configuration spreads both user data and error correction data across multiple disks, as shown in

TABLE 1.5 Comparison Among Various RAID Levels

RAID Level	Advantages	Disadvantages
0	High read and write performance	No fault tolerance
1	Fault tolerance and twice the read throughput of single disks	Same write performance of single disks
10	Fault tolerance and high read and write performance	More disk space used than RAID 5
5	Fault tolerance and high read and write performance with less disk space used than RAID 1	Might be slower than RAID 0 because of parity calculations

Figure 1.16d. With this RAID configuration, error recovery is provided through distributed parity. Further details about various parity distribution algorithms are beyond the scope of this book, and interested readers should consult more specific texts about this subject.

There are other RAID levels such as RAID 2, 3, 4, 6, 7, 0 + 1, and 50, which represent different combinations of stripping, mirroring, and parity algorithms. Since these RAID levels are not used as commonly as the four RAID levels of 0, 1, 10, and 5, they are not explained here. From the performance and scalability testing perspectives, it's sufficient just to know those four most typical RAID configurations.

In a production environment, typically it's either RAID 10 or RAID 5 that is adopted. There is a tendency to recommend RAID 10 over RAID 5 in the published literature for database-intensive enterprise applications. See Table 1.5 for a summary of the advantages and disadvantages of those four typical RAID levels of 0, 1, 10, and 5.

For performance and scalability tests, I typically use RAID 0, which is not only easy to set up but also a good compromise between storage capacity and performance. If you don't have the option of using a RAID configuration other than the local disks, you should use at least three separate local disks for your enterprise data so that you do not always hit one disk hard with your I/O-intensive applications.

In addition to processors, main memory, and secondary storage, networking is another important factor that affects the performance and scalability of a software system under test. In the next section, I'll briefly introduce the concepts that are crucial for understanding the impact of networking on the performance and scalability of a software system.

1.6.6 Networking

Networking is essential for computers to communicate with each other, as computers rarely stand alone. Computers may sit on a LAN (local area network) to communicate with each other, for which the network latency is negligible. If computers communicate with each other across the continents, then the network latency would be a great concern.

Figure 1.17   Intel Pro/1000 MT Dual Port Server Adapter.

In understanding how computer networking works, it's important to understand the following physical and logic entities:

- *Network Adapter.* A network adapter is the physical hardware that enables networking connectivity from a computer to a computer network. Figure 1.17 shows a typical Intel® Pro/1000 MT Dual Port Server Adapter which enables two Gigbit copper server connections in a single PCI slot. This adapter is designed to automatically scale with growing networks by auto-negotiating 10/100/1000 Mbps performance. It can enhance server performance further by teaming the two connections or teaming with other Intel® Pro Server Adapters to achieve multi-Gigbit scalability and redundant failover capability.

- *Network Bandwidth.* Network speed is typically measured by the amount of data that can be transferred in unit time. It is quantified by megabits/second (Mbps) or gigabits/second (Gbps). For example, your home network might be able to run at a maximum theoretical speed of 36 Mbps with your wireless port or at a maximum theoretical speed of 100 Mbps with your regular wired port. When you have two computers at home, you can actually connect your two computers through a crossover cable, which would be much faster than going through the wireless port if you have large amounts of data to transfer from one computer to the other. This is the simplest example of how network bandwidth could determine the networking performance of computers.

- *Network Types.* A network might be as simple as two computers connected through a crossover cable or as complicated as the entire Internet. Between these two extremes, there are many different types of networks whose names end with "AN," such as LAN, (local area network) and WAN (wide area network).

- *Network Latency.* Network latency is a different concept from network bandwidth. It measures how long it takes for a network packet to travel from point A to point B. Typically, network latency is less than 1 ms on a LAN, about 40 ms on a WAN, and 400 ms across continents. You can use the command of *ping <IP> -l size* to check out the latency for the systems that you are concerned with.

- *Network Protocol.* A network protocol governs how data is exchanged between various end points, which are typically the network ports of the computers which send and receive network data packets. The most popular network protocols are the TCP/IP protocols, which stand for transmission control protocol and Internet protocol. A network protocol essentially is the language that all computers and network routers use when they are configured to communicate with each other with that protocol.

From the software performance and scalability testing perspectives, you should have well-isolated networks for the computer servers under test, otherwise the results would be unpredictable. If you have to run your tests with your servers sitting on your corporate business network, you should verify your performance testing results at different times, for example, during busy morning hours and idle night hours, to isolate the effects of the shared network.

If your enterprise applications support global deployment architecture, you may want to use the servers spread across the continents to mimic the effects of network latency from a customer's usage perspectives.

As a software performance engineer, sometimes you may need to troubleshoot some network problems yourself. For example, one of the simplest tasks is to check if a remote server is up using the command *"ping [serverName | serverIPAddress]"* which works both on Windows and UNIX platforms. You can add the *"-l byteSize"* option to the *ping* command to obtain the network latency between two systems for a given packet size.

Another a little bit more advanced command is *"netstat"* which is helpful for checking the availability of the network ports on a system. Network ports cannot be shared among different applications on a system, and each application requires its own port number. For example, to check if a port number, say port 3269, is available, use the command *"netstat −a | find "3269""* on Windows or *"netstat −a | grep 3269"* on UNIX.

Usually, these two commands (*ping* and *netstat*) are sufficient for trouble-shooting some very basic network problems. For more complicated network issues, you need to contact your network administrator who has the authority to check the network routers and switches, etc.

1.6.7 Operating System

In addition to hardware, operating systems play a critical role in determining not only the performance and scalability but also the reliability of a software product. It's beyond the scope of this text to discuss in detail how to configure an operating system for the maximum performance, scalability, and reliability for a software product. However, one should be aware of some of the major features of an operating system, for example, the version and the latest service pack, and whether it's a 32-bit or 64-bit system.

It is especially important to know whether the operating system in use is 32-bit or 64-bit, as the performance, scalability, and reliability of a software product may be eventually limited by the amount of addressable memory space and the amount of total physical RAM. You can check whether an operating system is 32-bit or 64-bit by running some OS-specific script, for example, the *sysdm.cpl* script from the Run dialog box on Windows, or *isainfo −v* on Solaris.

In the next section, we'll discuss what would happen if those Turing assumptions were not satisfied in reality.

1.7   ODDS AGAINST TURING

The Turing model has been very useful as an abstract model for studying the concepts of computing. However, there is a gap between academic research and practical engineering. In this section, I'll show you what it implies when the assumptions made behind the Turing model could not be satisfied in reality.

Of those two assumptions associated with the Turing model, one is related to the unlimited memory or storage, and the other is related to the unlimited time for completing a computing task. Essentially, with these two assumptions, the Turing model doesn't care about how much memory a computer has and how fast the CPUs are. In reality, violation of the first assumption would result in system crashing and violation of the second assumption would result in slow performance, which would result in loss of revenues for customers and possibly penalties on the software vendor as well.

Although today's systems can be built with more and more RAM and faster and faster CPUs, various resource-intensive applications have been pushing the hardware resource limits as well. Issues such as memory leaks and slow CPUs still hinder adequate performance for more and more demanding software systems. Software developers and performance professionals must be committed to making sure that these two typical issues have been addressed properly with their products.

The effect of slow CPUs on the performance and scalability of a software system is obvious, and the impact of memory leaks is obvious as well. If a software product has severe memory leaks, sooner or later, it will crash with out-of-memory errors. In the next section, I'll help you understand what memory leaks are and how to monitor memory leaks. However, be aware that fixing memory leaks might be an unattainable task due to the difficulties of determining where memory leaks occur in the source code.

1.7.1   Memory Leaks

What is memory leak? Memory leak is a term describing the phenomenon of continuous memory consumption growth as a software application keeps running. We cannot expect zero memory growth. In the meanwhile, we cannot tolerate unlimited memory consumption growth without seeing software malfunctioning.

Software applications run as *processes* on computer systems. It's necessary to monitor the processes of a software application to see whether they have memory leaks or not over time.

Let's first take a look at a few memory-related performance counters from the *perf-mon* utility on the Windows platform. I typically use the following *process*-related performance counters to monitor memory consumption of the processes I care about:

- *Private bytes*. This counter represents the current size, in bytes, of memory that a process has allocated that cannot be shared with other processes.
- *Working set*. This counter represents the current size, in bytes, of the working set of a process. The working set is the set of memory pages touched recently by the threads in a process. If free memory in a computer is above a threshold, pages are left in the working set of a process even if they are not in use. When free memory falls below a threshold, pages are trimmed from working sets. If they are needed, they will then be soft-faulted back into the working set before leaving main memory.
- *Virtual bytes*. This counter represents the current size, in bytes, of the virtual address space a process is using. Use of virtual address space does not necess-arily imply the corresponding use of either disk or main memory pages. Virtual space is finite, and a process can limit its ability to load libraries.

These explanations of each counter are from *perfmon* help. I found that *private bytes* and *working set* are essentially the same, since they are not distinguishable from each other when they are drawn on the same chart, as you will see soon. *Virtual bytes* is more like a chunk of memory allocated for a process at a certain point of time. When *private bytes* or *working set* gets close to *virtual bytes*, more vir-tual memory will be allocated, which leads to a staircase-like pattern for virtual bytes when more and more memory spaces are needed by a running process.

■ **Case Study 1.3: Memory Leaks**

Figure 1.18 shows memory leaks from an application server process. The virtual bytes went beyond 2 GB three times. The working set and private bytes curves overlapped and spiked whenever the virtual bytes went beyond 2 GB.

This memory leak test was conducted on a Windows 2003 server. The 32-bit Windows operating system has a 4-GB total addressable address space, which is divided into two 2-GB for the operating system itself and applications, respectively.

One can also monitor memory leaks using the *perfmon* counter of *Available Memory in MBytes*, as shown in Figure 1.19. It's interesting to note that *Available Memory in Mbytes* shown in Figure 1.19 is almost a reverse reflection of the *virtual bytes* shown in Figure 1.18.

Figure 1.20 shows the application server process CPU usage associated with the memory leaks shown in Figure 1.18. It's interesting to note that whenever the virtual bytes reached that 2-GB limit, the application server restarted itself, resulting in all memory releases in the application server process. Similar measures in pro-duction environment can be taken in combating memory leaks by manually restart-ing the applications during the maintenance windows, either weekly or biweekly.

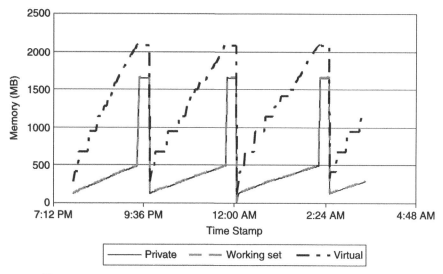

Figure 1.18 *An example of memory growth of an application server process.*

Of course, memory leaks are not remedyless. One can use certain tools such as IBM/Rational Purify™ to detect and fix memory leaks effectively. Figure 1.21 shows the memory consumption of the same application server with the same test after the memory leaks were fixed. It's seen that all memory consumption curves were flat. The virtual memory started with 278.5567 MB and ended with 278.5567 MB.

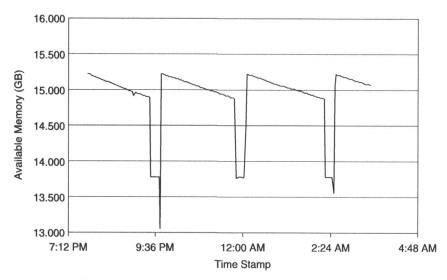

Figure 1.19 *Total available memory on the application server.*

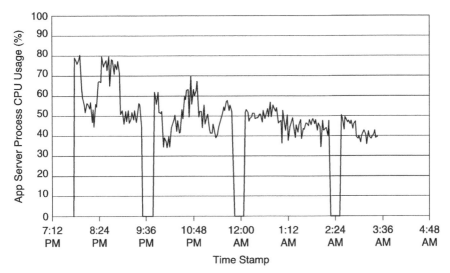

Figure 1.20 *Application server restarted itself whenever its memory leaked beyond the 2-GB limit.*

Although a 32-bit system has a 4-GB addressable virtual address space only, more than 4-GB physical memory can be installed on 32-bit editions of Windows systems with the help of the Intel's Physical Address Extension (PAE) technology. In addition, the 2 GB/2 GB default partition can be adjusted to 3 GB for an application and 1 GB for the kernel with a combination of the 4-GB tuning (4GT) feature and the IMAGE_FILE_LARGE_ADDRESS_AWARE value of the LOADED_IMAGE

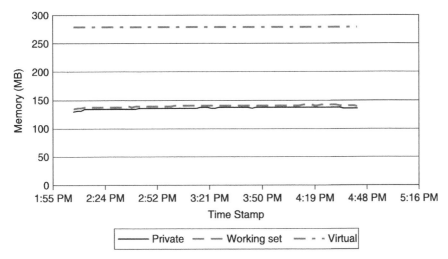

Figure 1.21 *Flat memory growth after memory leaks were fixed.*

structure. On 64-bit editions of Windows, one can increase the 2-GB limit up to 4 GB by setting the parameter IMAGE_FILE_LARGE_ADDRESS_AWARE for a 32-bit application.

One might think that moving to a 64-bit version of an operating system might help combat the memory barrier to some extent. Keep in mind that for the same application with the same workload it might take more memory in a 64-bit environment than in a 32-bit environment. This needs to be taken into account when sizing the physical memory requirements for your applications.

Although the maximum addressable space in a 64-bit environment can be as large as 1 TB, the actual addressable space will still be limited by the amount of physical memory installed on the system. Of course, one can adjust the virtual memory (swap space on UNIX or paging file size on Windows) to allow an application to use a largest possible addressable space. Both the swap space on UNIX and paging file size on Windows are configured very conservatively by default. On Windows, the paging file size is typically 2 GB or less by default, while on UNIX, the swap space is configured to be the same as the amount of total physical memory available by default. However, you should check the virtual memory configured on your system if you know that memory is one of the most limiting resources for your application.

On Windows, you can reconfigure paging file size by accessing *Performance Options* from *System Properties* → *Performance* → *Settings* → *Advanced* → *Virtual Memory* [*Change*]. On Solaris, follow the below procedure:

- Run command "*mkfile −v 10000 m /export/data/mySwapFile*" to create your swap file. This command creates a 10GB swap file named *mySwapFile* in the directory */export/data*. Of course, you can be flexible with the amount of space, file name and the directory name to suit your needs.
- Add an entry of "*/export/data/mySwapFile - - swap − no −*" in the file */etc/vfstab*.
- Issue the command "*swap −a /export/data/mySwapFile*".
- Check the swap file added with the command "*swap −l*".

The actual amount of virtual memory (swap or paging file size) to configure is application-dependent. The general rule of thumb is not to exceed 2−3 times the total amount of physical memory installed on the system.

Some of the latest Intel Xeon-based systems support both 32-bit and 64-bit operating systems. Xeon processors are intrinsically 32-bit, but can be extended to 40 bits with Intel's EM64T technology. Therefore, when you have a 64-bit operating system running on a Xeon-based system, the maximum amount of physical memory that can be installed might be limited to 64 GB. Check with the vendor of your system to make sure the exact configurations you have on your system.

In the next section, I'll discuss the service level agreements (SLAs) that have something to do with the other assumption made for the Turing model.

1.7.2 SLAs

Today's business corporations strongly depend on software to manage their daily operations and generate revenue. Apparently, the software they buy should not only do what it is supposed to do, but it should also perform adequately. This means that we do not have unlimited time for the software program to do what it is supposed to do. For some critical business services, there are certain performance requirements that must be met in order to achieve the projected business objectives. When such software performance requirements are written into a service contract, they effectively constitute a service level agreement (SLA) as part of a service contract between service providers and their customers. So the purpose of an SLA is to help make sure that a service provider lives up to its commitments by providing the level of services that both parties agreed upon.

The customers want to get what they paid for, and they cannot tolerate unbounded performance of the software they purchase without having their critical businesses impacted. For example, a stock exchange software program must guarantee the completion of a buy or sell order transaction within a certain amount of time; otherwise the customer may lose money. For Web-based online retailers, their transaction systems must be able to process purchases within a reasonable time frame so that users would not lose patience and go away, causing loss of revenue.

However, just as life insurance doesn't guarantee life, SLAs don't guarantee levels of service. When SLAs are broken in production, the customers would lose revenue and the service providers may get monetary penalties, which would cause hardships to both parties. That's why it's important to have performance designed and built into a product before deploying at a customer's site so that SLAs, if any, will not be broken. This book provides many performance optimization and tuning techniques that can be applied in general to help make sure that the SLAs bound to a software product will be satisfied.

1.8 SIZING HARDWARE

Sizing hardware for a software system is about establishing a quantitative, empirical formula describing the performance that a specific hardware platform is capable of delivering, or for a given performance requirement, what hardware platform would be required to achieve it. Such a sizing guideline would be extremely handy for the customers to decide on what hardware to acquire, or for a software provider to troubleshoot the customer performance escalations caused by undersized hardware.

In order to arrive at an effective sizing guideline, one should try to optimize and tune the software under test for the best possible performance and leave the hardware as the only factor that determines the performance of the software. This section provides an example of the throughput of the software being predominated by the CPU power of both the database server and the application server. The sizing formula has worked very well for many real customer occasions.

App Server
(4 CPUs @ 3.68 GHz)

Database Server
(4 CPUs @ 3.68 GHz)

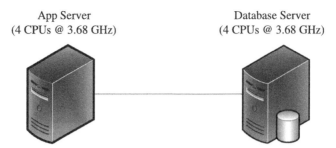

Figure 1.22 *A test configuration for sizing hardware.*

■ Case Study 1.4: Sizing Hardware

Figure 1.22 shows the test configuration, which consists of two servers, a database server, and an application server, for an enterprise software application. The two server systems were identical, with four single-core Intel Xeon processors at 3.68 GHz on each system. Both the application server and the database server were optimally configured with the best performance optimization and tuning practices obtained through extensive internal lab tests. In addition, the two server systems were located on the same subnet, which was another important test condition.

With a specific enterprise application batch job and a rigorous, repeatable test procedure, the following sizing formula, at which level this configuration was capable of processing, was found:

2 Transactions per second per CPU GHz of the application server

with the assumption that the database server is equal to or more powerful than the application server. The CPU power or CPU GHz of the application server was defined as follows:

Total CPU GHz of the application server = 4 × 3.68 GHz = 14.72 GHz

Based on the above specs, this setup was able to deliver a throughput of 29 transactions/second.

This sizing formula has been consistently verified with several internal and external customer tests. It has been used successfully for resolving a few customer performance escalations, which fell into the following categories:

- Undersized hardware attributed to the low throughput, which was improved to what the sizing formula predicted after upgrading the hardware.
- Inappropriately configured database and application caused low throughput, which was improved to what the sizing formula predicted after configuring the systems to the recommended optimal settings.

This case study is provided as a reference for you to size your application when applicable. Keep in mind that a sizing formula needs to be adjusted with time as the performance of the application gets improved or degraded due to the changes that have to be introduced in the worst case.

1.9 SUMMARY

Understanding software performance and scalability begins with understanding computers, because it's the hardware that will eventually determine the performance and scalability of a software program after all optimizations and tunings have been exhausted on the software side. In order to help enhance the consciousness of the dependency of software performance and scalability on the underlying hardware platform, we have spent this entire chapter going over all major aspects of computers such as CPUs, memory, disks, and networking. Hopefully, this helps establish a baseline for necessary hardware knowledge required for doing performance and scalability test work, whether it's for benchmarking, sizing, optimization, or tuning.

This chapter is about hardware in general. The next chapter will be about software in general. Chapter 3 will be focusing on all concepts associated with testing software performance and scalability in general. These three chapters constitute the foundations for performing actual software performance and scalability test work. I hope that after studying these three chapters, you will be able to start asking the right questions about software performance and scalability and carry out your tests efficiently to help resolve any performance and scalability challenges associated with your products.

RECOMMENDED READING

For Moore's law, see his publication:

Gordon E. Moore, Cramming more components onto integrated circuits, *Electronics*, Vol. 38, No. 8, April 19, 1965.

To understand computers in general, the following two textbooks are excellent sources:

W. Stallings, *Computer Organization and Architecture—Designing for Performance*, 4th edition, Prentice Hall, 1996.

D. Patterson and J. Hennessy, *Computer Organization & Design—The Hardware/Software Interface*, Morgan Kaufmann, 1994.

See the following texts for quantitative approaches applied to refining software engineering and development:

L. Bernstein and C. M. Yuhas, *Trustworthy Systems Through Quantitative Software Engineering*, John Wiley & Sons, 2005.

S. Gabarro, *Web Application Design and Implementation: Apache 2, PHP5, MySQL, JavaScript and Linux/UNIX*, John Wiley & Sons, 2006.

L. Laird and M. Brennan, *Software Measurement and Estimation: A Practical Approach*, John Wiley & Sons, 2006.

The following text is an excellent source for applying the quantitative approach to understanding computer hardware architecture:

J. Hennessy and D. Patterson, *Computer Architecture: A Quantitative Approach*, 4th edition, Morgan Kaufmann, 2007.

EXERCISES

1.1. Get to know your computers. If you have access to a system (Windows or UNIX or Linux), find out the following specs on the system:
- System model
- Operating system
  The exact version
  32 bit or 64 bit
- Processors
  Processor model
  Number of sockets or processors
  Number of cores per processor
  CPU clock rate
  Hyperthread support if applicable
  Front-side bus speed if applicable
  L1/L2/L3 caches
  Any other differentiating features
- Memory
  Total amount of physical memory
- Network ports
  Number of network ports and the speed that is supported
- Storage
  File system
  Internal or external
  RAID level if applicable

1.2. This applies to the 32-bit Windows 2-GB limit. Develop a memory-intensive 32-bit sample application and run it on 32-bit Windows. Observe how the application would crash when the 2-GB limit is reached. Apply the Microsoft/Intel memory tuning techniques on the 32-bit Windows to increase the memory to 3 GB for the application and rerun. Observe the application behavior as the memory usage goes up with the application.

1.3. There is a popular perception that UNIX is faster than Windows. Envision the potential pitfalls and consequences of a recommendation based on such a perception if not verified with actual performance and scalability tests.

1.4. This concerns sizing hardware. The tests show that a setup similar to Figure 1.22, except that each server was equipped with two quad-core CPUs at 1 GHz, was able to deliver a throughput of 19 transactions/second. Apply the sizing formula introduced in Section 1.8 to this test configuration and calculate the expected throughput. Compare the measured throughput with the calculated throughput and what conclusion could you draw from it?

1.5. This concerns sizing hardware. A customer reported a low throughput of 0.8 transactions/second with a setup similar to Figure 1.22, except that both the application server and the database server were installed on a same system with 3 RISC processors at 1.6 GHz each. Based on the regression test, it was known that the application performance had been degraded by about 25%. Using the sizing formula in Section 1.8 with a 25% degradation taken into account, it was calculated that this test configuration should be able to process 3.6 transactions/second. The customer was advised to apply all recommended database and application configuration settings, rerun the test, and look for an expected throughput of 3.6 transactions/second. The customer reported back that processing 15,900 transactions took about 71 minutes after the database server and application server were optimally configured as advised. Compare the newly measured throughput from the customer with the calculated throughput and what conclusion could you draw from it?

1.6. This concerns sizing hardware. A customer reported a low throughput of 2.8 transactions/second with a setup similar to Figure 1.22, except that the application server was equipped with four CPUs with the clock rate either at 2.2 GHz or 3 GHz and the database server had a total CPU power of 16 GHz. The exact CPU frequency of the application server was not provided and the 2.2 GHz or 3 GHz was looked up from the vendor's website based on the server model. In this case, it was estimated using the sizing formula in Section 1.8 that this setup should be able to deliver a throughput of 18–24 transactions/second based on the uncertainty of the application server CPU frequency. After further communications with the customer, it was found that the reported low throughput was due to turning the logging on. The customer was advised to rerun the test with logging off and expect a throughput in the range of 18–24 transactions/second. The customer reported back that a throughput of 22 transactions/second was achieved after logging was turned off and they were happy with that throughput. Calculate the impact of logging on the performance of the system in this case and what conclusion could you draw from it?

1.7. How can you effectively prevent customers from starting with undersized hardware for your software applications? What are the benefits of doing so?

2

Software Platform

Well, it's a very, very exciting time ... and that's where vision is ...
—Bill Gates

In the simplest sense, software controls what computers do. Since there are an unlimited number of things that computers can do, there are an unlimited number of software programs developed for various kinds of computing tasks. Regardless of the computing tasks, all software programs share some commonalities in how they are created and how they run on computers.

Understanding the performance and scalability of a software system quantitatively requires a good understanding of how a software program is developed inside out. Poorly designed and implemented software will not run fast on fast hardware. Even well-designed software may not perform and scale optimally on fast hardware without going through a full cycle of optimization and tuning for the best possible performance and scalability.

In this chapter, we'll begin with the concept of the software stack, which consists of multiple layers. How each layer performs and scales is critical to the overall performance and scalability of a system as a whole. Then I'll elaborate on the concept of application programming interfaces (APIs), which are the building blocks for constructing various software programs. Because of its absolute importance for performance and scalability, multithreading is discussed with the help of a quantitative case study. I'll also categorize different types of software so that we would know our battlefields for combating software performance and scalability issues. The last section is dedicated to introducing enterprise computing, which probably is one of the largest fields of computing where software performance and scalability are most critical.

I am sure that the topics covered in this chapter are not new to you. However, when reading each section, try to think consciously from software performance and scalability perspectives, which is how each section was prepared. Let's start with the software stack first.

Software Performance and Scalability. By Henry H. Liu
Copyright © 2009 IEEE Computer Society

2.1   SOFTWARE STACK

Computers do not have their own intelligence and they do not speak our languages. They can only understand electronic signals that have two states: *on* and *off*. These electronic signals are represented in *binary numbers* of 0 and 1. A mixed string of 0's and 1's can constitute instructions or commands that instruct computers what to do.

Without showing computer instructions in assembly language, you may still remember what assembly languages are from your college computer classes. Assembly language is the symbolic version of the computer instructions that is a step closer to our language. An assembly statement is translated into a mixed string of 0's and 1's by an assembler whose job is to translate instructions from symbolic version to binary version. For example, an assembly statement of *add x, y* would be translated into a string of 0's and 1's by an assembler as shown below:

```
add x, y (assembly)
=>10001101100011100011011100110110 (binary)
```

Although much closer to the way we humans think, assembly language is still not flexible enough for constructing complicated programs, as it requires programmers to write one line for every instruction that a computer can understand, forcing programmers to think like machines.

Note that an assembler is a software program as well. Following a similar line of thinking that we could write a program (the assembler) to translate a program (written in assembly language) into machine code, why couldn't we write another program to translate programs written in some high-level programming languages into a program in the format of assembly language? This wonderful idea resulted in the birth of compilers, which can compile $x + y$ into *add x, y* as shown below:

$$x + y => add\ x, y$$

This concept of high-level programming language was a huge leap in advancing the use of computers. It liberated programmers from thinking like a machine to thinking in a more natural language expressed in English words and algebraic notation. It also opened the door to the ideas of creating programs for dedicated purposes such as *I/O* (input/output) *libraries* and common system management software, which is called *operating system*.

Some of the most popular high-level programming languages in the 1970s and 1980s include FORTRAN, COBOL, C, and C++. The first three are procedure-oriented programming languages, whereas C++ is an object-oriented programming language. Programs written in these languages are enabled to call libraries for common functions such as I/O. They are made executable by being compiled and then assembled into machine code. Their executable form is called *binaries*, which are run with the coordination of operating systems. So the procedure of developing such software consists of the following:

- Coding the logic of a program in a high-level programming language
- Compiling the developed program with linking to libraries to be called

- Assembling the developed program into machine code
- Running the developed program on specific computer hardware with the assistance of a specific operating system

The dependency of one program on another forms the software stack as shown in Figure 2.1. Apparently, the performance of a software program developed in high-level programming languages depends not only on how the application logic was designed and implemented, but also on the workings of the compiler, the assembler, the operating system, and the hardware.

With given computer hardware and operating system, one can often achieve better performance with the programs written in high-level programming languages by applying various compiler optimization options during the compile stage. Compilers were designed and implemented for yielding the optimal performance for the programs they compile by targeting specific underlying computer hardware.

With the advent of Java in the 1990s, another revolutionary idea was introduced, that is, the Java virtual machine (JVM). JVM was designed to bridge the gaps among different operating systems by abstracting various program run-time environments. Java has become more and more popular, partially because of the new waves of Internet-based computing. The programs written in Java can be run on different platforms without being modified or recompiled, be it Windows or UNIX. This reflects something very deep: all programs written in Java are a universal abstraction in the format of *byte code*. We come back to what Alan Turing depicted seven decades ago!

The idea of JVM was extended to virtual systems that can be configured with virtualization software such as VMWare™. This level of virtualization allows you to run multiple applications on multiple operating systems on a single physical system. This introduces another layer of virtualization software in the software stack, as shown in Figure 2.2. It is interesting that one can install a VMWare server directly on the bare metal hardware or on a host operating system such as Windows or Linux.

Apparently, as stated previously, every layer of the software stack shown in Figure 2.2 is a performance and scalability factor for the programs built to run on

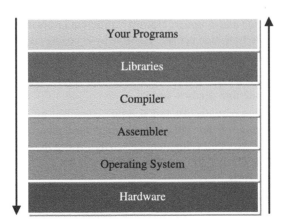

Figure 2.1 *Software stack.*

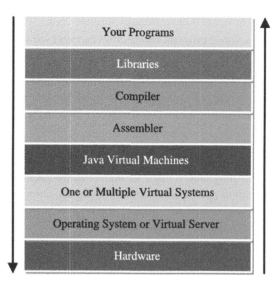

Figure 2.2   Virtual machines and virtual systems in the software stack.

that stack. Some layers are more tunable than others from the software performance and scalability perspectives. It's important to make sure that all optimization opportunities at every layer have been tapped properly.

In the next section, I'll discuss application programming interfaces (APIs), which are as pivotal to software as nerves are to the human body. The performance of a software system eventually drills down to its API performance.

2.2   APIs

Software programs are built in a layered approach. Different layers constitute various components, which consist further of subcomponents. Layered approaches have the advantage of *divide and conquer*. However, different layers need to communicate with each other properly, which is made possible by exposing collections of common functions as APIs. It's important to understand the following:

- An API is an abstract specification about the basic functions provided for building software that needs to use it.
- The software that provides the functionality described by an API is said to be an *implementation* of the API. An API implementation is presented to users as a part of a software development kit (SDK). An SDK contains not only the implementation of an API, but also the documents and code samples about how to use the APIs.
- Access paths to APIs must be specified when calling programs are compiled and built.

- An API is different from an ABI (application binary interface). An API defines the interface between source code and libraries so that the same source code will compile on any system supporting that API, whereas an ABI allows compiled object code to function without changes on any system using a compatible ABI.

In the next few subsections, we'll look at some of the most well-known examples of APIs to get an idea about what APIs exactly are and why they are important from the performance and scalability perspectives. Let's start with the Windows APIs first.

2.2.1 Windows APIs

A Microsoft Windows system is built with many different classes of APIs, which include the following:

- *Base Services API.* This provides access to the fundamental resources available to a Windows system.
- *Graphics Device Interface API.* This provides the functionality to output graphic content to monitors, printers, and other output devices.
- *User Interface API.* This provides the functionality to create and manage screen windows and most basic controls such as buttons and scrollbars, the functionality to receive mouse and keyboard input, and other functionality associated with the GUI part of Windows.
- *Common Dialog Box Library API.* This provides applications with standard boxes for opening and saving files, choosing color and font, and so on.
- *Common Control Library API.* This gives applications access to some advanced controls provided by the operating system.
- *Windows Shell API.* This allows applications to access, change, and enhance the functionality provided by the operating system shell.
- *Network Services API.* This gives access to the various networking capabilities of the operating system. Winsock is one of its most well-known subcomponents.

I am sure that Windows is part of your daily work, so you are already familiar with what Windows APIs do to fulfill whatever tasks you need to accomplish using various application programs installed on your system.

Next, let's take a look at Java APIs, which are another huge category in developing software applications.

2.2.2 Java APIs

Java APIs include the essential APIs for the following common functionalities:

- *Character and String API.* This performs character and string operations.
- *Collection API.* This groups multiple elements into a single unit (collection). Collections let you store, retrieve, manipulate, and transmit data from one method to another.
- *Error Handling API.* This enables handling errors using exceptions.

- *JavaBean Technology API*. This can be used to create reusable, platform-independent software components that you can combine into applets, applications, or composite components.
- *Language Basics API*. This enables supporting basic data types and operations using variables, arrays, operators, flow of control, and scope.
- *Number and Math Operation API*. This enables supporting fundamental and complex mathematical operations.
- *Input and Output API*. This enables exchanging data between a program and external storage, including serialization and custom protocol handling.

Even if you have never programmed in Java, it should still be easy to picture why those Java APIs are needed for constructing high-level applications.

Another interesting example of APIs is Google APIs. I have included more Google APIs than Windows APIs and Java APIs just in case you want to know upon what APIs this most popular search engine has been built.

2.2.3 Google APIs

Google API is the newest API kid on the block. Google APIs are helping Google make a lot of money everyday as Windows APIs do for Microsoft. It's interesting to see what APIs have been working behind the scenes for a multibillion dollar business. The following is a list of Google APIs that are available in public from Google's website at `http://code.google.com/apis/`:

- *AdSense API*. This enables you to integrate AdSense signup, ad unit management, and reporting into your Web or blog hosting platform.
- *AdWords API*. This lets developers engineer computer programs that interact directly with the AdWords server.
- *Google Base Data API*. This allows client applications to view and update stored data in the form of Google data API ("GData") feeds.
- *Google Data API*. This provides a simple standard protocol for reading and writing data on the Web.
- *Google Earth KML*. This keyhole markup language is a grammar and file format for modeling and storing geographic features such as points, lines, images, and polygons for display in the Google Earth Client. KML gives you the ability to do amazing things with Google Earth.
- *Google Apps API*. This provides domain administration APIs for customers.
- *Google Maps API*. This integrates Google's interactive maps with your data on your site.
- *Google Search Appliance API*. This allows search administrators to have complete control over how search results are requested and presented to end users.
- *Google Toolbar API*. This lets you create custom buttons for the Google Toolbar using XML.

- *Google SOAP Search API.* This enables software developers to query billions of Web pages directly from their own computer programs. The Google Web search API uses the SOAP and WSDL standards.

I hope you have been convinced that APIs are the basic building blocks for software as atoms and molecules are for matter in the physical world. It's important to recognize that high-performance software stems from the high-performance APIs on which it is built.

In the next section, I'll discuss multithreading, which is one of the most important implementation choices for achieving high performance and scalability for a software system.

2.3 MULTITHREADING

First of all, a *thread* is different from a *process* in computer science. A *process* is a stand-alone program, while *threads* typically are spawned within a process without crossing the boundary of that process.

Multithreading is one of the most important software technologies for boosting the performance and scalability of all types of software. It allows multitasks to be executed simultaneously or in parallel to make the most of the computer hardware with multiple CPUs. Even on a single-user system such as a PC, multithreading can help create the illusion of simultaneity to an end user by switching among different tasks sufficiently fast. For example, you can enjoy streaming video while surfing the Internet on your single-processor laptop.

Multithreading is a *must* for enterprise software. Enterprise software typically runs on multiprocessor computers, which are designed for running multithreaded programs or multiple programs in parallel. I had an experience in helping solve an application performance escalation for a high-profile customer. It turned out that the performance issue that the customer was experiencing was largely due to a single-threaded application running on a 12-CPU 400-MHz outdated system. There couldn't be a worse combination of massive CPUs, low CPU clock rate, and single-threaded application for creating performance issues.

This book is not about programming, so we do not delve into the details of how to write a multithreaded program in C/C++ or Java. However, I'd like to share the multithreaded performance of a real-world, multithreaded enterprise application to help you gain insights into the common performance and scalability characteristics of multithreaded enterprise applications in general.

■ **Case Study 2.1: Multithreading**

This application creates objects in a database by calling the APIs of an application server directly. As you can imagine, this would involve heavy disk activities and it's really important to interlace disk I/Os incurred through the database server with the validation logic on the application server. The test environment was simple. It consisted of the following test configuration:

- A 4-CPU Intel Xeon 3.6-GHz Windows 2003 system used as the database server with Oracle 10g installed. It had an internal RAID 0 stripped across four physical disks with a single channel RAID controller.
- An identical Intel Xeon 3.6-GHz Windows 2003 system used as the application server. Both the database server and the application server had 12 GB of RAM and gigabits per second network connections.
- The object creation program was a multithreaded Java program that could be configured to run with multiple threads.

So what kind of throughput in terms of objects/second would you expect out of such a configuration? It depends on how many threads you would run with such an application. Figure 2.3 shows the throughput of this application with different numbers of threads from 1 to 15 configured with the object creation client program.

With this test, the application server was configured with a thread pool of 46 threads, which was an empirical thread number for the best possible performance and scalability for this enterprise application. From the test results shown in Figure 2.3, we can see the following:

- The measured throughput doesn't scale up linearly with the number of threads configured for creating objects in the client program. Does this mean that the application is not scalable or the underlying platform of Windows 2003 or Intel architecture is not scalable? We will leave this question to be answered later.
- No substantial gain in throughput was observed beyond 8 threads, which was also equal to the total number of CPUs out of both the database server and the application server. In general, the maximum throughput is achieved when every processor is fully busy.
- Although it's far from linearly scalable, the three-digit multithreaded throughput that can be achieved with this application is quite impressive. That's about a factor of 4 improvement compared with the single-threaded throughput. This clearly shows how important it is for the software to take advantage of the underlying hardware in order to achieve the best possible performance and scalability.

Now let's try to answer the question of why it wasn't linearly scalable and what was the bottleneck.

Remember that whenever we analyze a performance or scalability issue, we always start with CPU utilizations of each system being tested. On Windows, we use a Microsoft performance monitoring tool called *perfmon*. With this tool, you can capture almost every performance metric you can imagine on a Windows system. But most of the time, we only need to monitor a few that will be most likely responsible for the performance problem that an application is experiencing.

Perfmon works by monitoring certain system resources called the *performance object* in *perfmon*'s term with certain performance metrics called *performance*

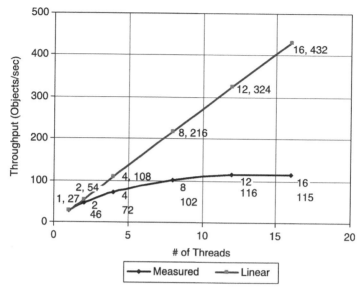

Figure 2.3 *Performance of a real-world, three-tier, multithreaded enterprise application. Each data point is labeled with its x (horizontal) and y (vertical) values and the Linear line represents the ideal linear scalability for comparison purposes.*

counters. For monitoring system CPU utilizations, we use the *Processor* performance object with the *%Processor Time* performance counter. The following excerpt is Microsoft's definition of what this counter is about:

% Processor Time [counter] is the percentage of elapsed time that the processor spends to execute a non-idle thread. It is calculated by measuring the duration that the idle thread is active in the sample interval, and subtracting that time from interval duration. (Each processor has an idle thread that consumes cycles when no other threads are ready to run.) This counter is the primary indicator of processor activity, and displays the average percentage of busy time observed during the sample interval. It is calculated by monitoring the time that the service is inactive and subtracting that value from 100%.

As explained in the above excerpt, this counter essentially measures how busy a system is. With our multithreaded application being discussed here, we'd like to know how CPU utilizations of the application server and database server evolve as we increase the number of threads for the object creation program.

The CPU utilizations recorded for both the application server and database server during each test run are displayed in Figure 2.4. It is seen that both application server and database server CPUs leveled off at 12 threads. The maximum CPU utilization was 35% for the application server and 46% for the database server. Apparently, both servers were less than half busy, which indicates that the bottleneck was somewhere else.

As this is an enterprise application that involves a lot of disk I/O activities, we certainly need to check out the disk activities incurred during each test run. Before

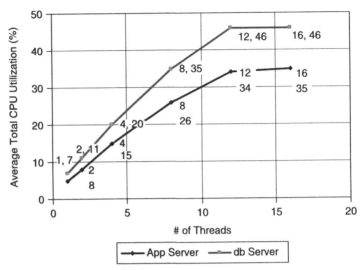

Figure 2.4 *CPU utilizations of the application server and database server with increasing number of threads for the object creation program.*

showing the disk activity data, let's become familiar with the following disk counters first:

- *% Idle Time*. This counter reports the percentage of time during the sample interval that the disk was idle.
- *Disk Reads [Writes]/sec*. This counter is the rate of read [write] operations on the disk.
- *Avg. Disk Read [Write] Queue Length*. This counter is the average number of read [write] requests that were queued for the selected disk during the sample interval.
- *Avg. Disk sec/Read [Write]*. This counter is the average time, in seconds, of a read [write] operation associated with the disk.

It's important to keep in mind that *perfmon* doesn't seem to record *%Disk Time* for actual disk busy time correctly, so we used $100 - \%Idle\ Time$ for the *%Disk Busy Time* as a workaround. Figure 2.5 shows the disk utilizations of the RAID 0 logical disk for this application with increasing number of threads. As seen, the disks were quite busy during each test, ranging from an average utilization of 23% for 1 thread to 60% for 16 threads.

Next, we want to see whether these disk activities were read or write operations. This can easily be determined by looking at the disk reads and writes/second counters. The result is shown in Figure 2.6. It's so clear from the data shown in Figure 2.6 that the disk activities were overwhelmingly dominated by write operations, ranging from 87 writes/second for 1 thread to 456 writes/second for 16 threads. The read operations were a few per second only with all numbers of threads.

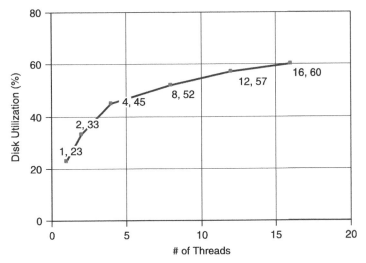

Figure 2.5 *Disk utilizations of the RAID 0 logical disk with increasing number of threads for the enterprise application that incurred a lot of disk read and write activities.*

When disks are flooded with I/O requests, the read and write queues that hold those I/O requests for processing will accumulate. This can easily be verified with the average disk read and write queue lengths. The associated queue length data is shown in Figure 2.7, in which only average write queue length is shown, since average read queue length is close to zero for each test run across all numbers of threads.

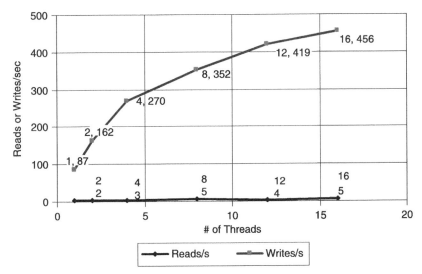

Figure 2.6 *Read and write operations incurred during each test run with increasing number of threads.*

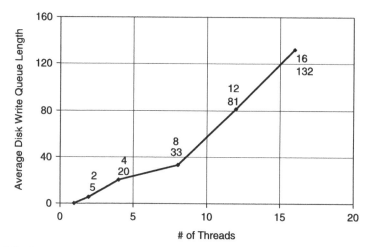

Figure 2.7 *Average disk write queue length incurred during each test run with increasing number of threads (average disk read queue length was omitted as it was less than one for every test run from 1 through 16 threads).*

A rule of thumb is that a resource is a bottleneck when the queue length associated with it is over 2 per unit. Since the RAID 0 configuration used for this test had four disks, the threshold would be 8. This threshold of 8 had been exceeded with a write average queue length of 20 with 4 threads. With 16 threads, the associated average write queue length even went up to 132, which was over 16 times the threshold value of 8. It is clear that the system was disk write bottlenecked. It's necessary to point out that whenever you test the performance and scalability of an enterprise application that incurs excessive I/O activities, always look out for potential I/O bottlenecks. Most likely, disk I/O would become the bottleneck prior to CPUs. Diagnosing bottlenecks properly helps you to come up with the right solutions that can help further improve system performance. I'll provide many such examples in the later chapters of this book.

The consequence of excessive I/O request accumulation in write queue is increasing disk write time for each write operation. This is further confirmed by Figure 2.8, which shows that the average disk write time had increased from 4 milliseconds with 1 thread to 233 milliseconds with 16 threads. This explains why throughput was not going up much beyond 8 threads, as with more than 8 threads, disk write time began to go up drastically. Faster disk storage with more I/O channels will help alleviate this bottleneck to some extent.

I hope this section has convinced you that multithreading is critical for any application where performance and scalability matter. I also hope you have gotten a preview about how performance and scalability bottlenecks can be nailed down quickly and decisively by following a disciplined and quantitative methodology, as has been demonstrated with this real-world multithreaded enterprise application.

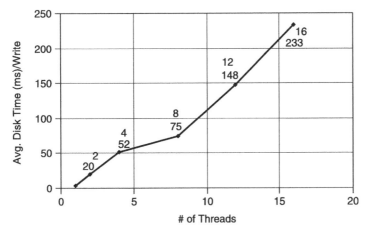

Figure 2.8 *Average disk write time in milliseconds with increasing number of threads for the object creation program.*

In the next section, I'll try to categorize software so that we know what our battlefields are when we come to fight software performance and scalability problems, whether it's during the development stage or after being deployed at a customer's site.

2.4 CATEGORIZING SOFTWARE

Software is built in a layered approach. The layer that is closest to the hardware is categorized as systems software, the layer that is closest to the user is categorized as application software, and the layer between the two is classified as middleware software.

In order to illustrate the above categorization methodology, let's look at some of the examples at each layer. Let's start with the systems software first.

2.4.1 Systems Software

Systems software is anything that has to be part of hardware in order for the entire system to function as a complete computing platform. There are three types of systems software:

- *BIOS (Basic Input/Output System)*. BIOS is sometimes called firmware. It is run when a PC computer is powered on. The primary function of the BIOS is to set up the stage for other software programs stored on hard drives, floppies, and CDs to load, execute, and assume control of the PC. This process is commonly known as booting up. With Intel architecture based systems, one can enable or disable hyperthreading (HT) at the BIOS level during the start-up process. This is the most reliable way of knowing whether your system has HT turned on or not.

- *Device Drivers*. Device drivers are interfaces in the form of software that control how various hardware components interact with the operating system. A device driver is a layer between a hardware device and an operating system. It translates commands written in high-level programming languages into the machine language that the hardware devices can understand. For example, when you buy a printer, you need to install the printer driver on your PC to enable printing, if it's not already included with your operating system.

- *Operating System* (*OS*). An operating system is software that can translate user commands into machine instructions for the computer hardware to execute. It also coordinates the use of hardware resources by performing basic tasks such as controlling and allocating memory, scheduling system requests, controlling input and output devices, facilitating networking, and managing disk storage usage through a file system. Popular operating systems available today on the market include Windows from Microsoft, Mac from Apple, various flavors of UNIX operating systems such as IBM's AIX, HP's HP-UX, and Sun's Solaris, and also the free operating system, Linux.

Systems software provides a platform or run-time environment for application software to run on computers. Computers are useful because there are so many applications that can be run to do useful things. In the next section, we'll look at what types of applications are typically run on computers.

2.4.2 Application Software

Application software refers to the class of software that can help individuals or business organizations do something more efficiently by employing the capabilities of a computer or networked computers. There are many types of application software based on their purposes:

- *Business Software*. This class of application software addresses the needs of business organizations for more efficient business processes and management. ERP (Enterprise Resource Planning) is one of the typical types of business software, which has modules such as CRM (Customer Relation Management), HR (Human Resources), SC (Supply Chain), Financials, Manufacturing, and so on. ITSM (IT Service Management) is another typical type of business software, which includes components such as HD (Help Desk), CM (Change Management), PM (Problem Management), and IM (Incident Management). More broadly, any type of software used in an enterprise that helps facilitate accessing and managing enterprise data belongs to the category of business software.

- *Media and Entertainment Software*. This class of application software addresses the needs of individuals or organizations for consuming digital media such as video gaming, video conferencing, and streaming media.

- *Product Engineering Software*. This class of application software addresses the needs of professional individuals for enhancing their productivity and efficiency. It includes CAD (Computer Aided Design), CAE (Computer Aided Engineering), and IDE (Integrated Development Environment).

Based on other classification schemes, you may also encounter:

- *Internal Applications*. This class of applications is developed for internal use only. They are also called in-house applications.
- *Single-User Applications*. This class of applications is intended for individual users such as Microsoft Office Suite, Turbo Tax for filing tax returns, and any other applications you can run on a PC.
- *Web Applications*. This class of applications is made available through the Internet. Users employ a Web browser to access such applications. All online search portals such as Google, Yahoo, and MSN belong to this category. Pure play online retailers such as Amazon.com and eBay, as well as the Web shopping sites from traditional retailers, belong to this category as well.
- *Database-Centric Applications*. This class of applications is characterized by its strong dependencies on databases. Most of the business software applications are typical database-centric applications.

Application software tops the software stack. There is another layer in the middle between an operating system and an application that provides specialized functionalities. This is the so-called middleware software that will be introduced in the next section.

2.4.3   Middleware Software

The middleware software business began with those messaging software products such as IBM's MQ, Microsoft's MSMQ, and those pure players such as Tibco and webMethods. During the past decade, it has expanded substantially to include application servers such as IBM's WebSphere, BEA's WebLogic, and Microsoft's .NET platform. Specialized infrastructure server software such as email servers and network and security management servers belong to this category as well.

Middleware software is designed to support enterprise computing which is the topic for the next section.

2.5   ENTERPRISE COMPUTING

Enterprise computing is a broad concept that refers to all the necessary building blocks needed for establishing an enterprise application ecosystem that can support business operations more efficiently. The entire platform for enterprise computing includes computer hardware, networks, all supporting middleware software systems, and enterprise applications.

However, we'll focus on the software aspect of enterprise computing only. Let's start with understanding what enterprise software is first.

2.5.1   What Is Enterprise Software?

The word *enterprise* refers to a business organization in general. Enterprise software refers to a special class of software that enables running businesses on computers.

At the highest level, one can divide enterprise software into two categories: infrastructure enterprise software and application enterprise software.

Infrastructure enterprise software provides a platform on which application enterprise software is run. All application server software and database server software belong to this category. Here are some examples of the infrastructure enterprise software systems:

- J2EE application server software such as BEA's WebLogic, IBM's WebSphere, and Microsoft's .NET platform that includes many server components for different purposes.
- Database server software such as Oracle, DB2 (IBM), and SQL Server (Microsoft).

Application enterprise software is characterized by the business functions it supports and automates, such as:

- Intranet portal application
- Internal inventory management application
- Sales order entry application
- Accounting system
- Production scheduling system
- Customer relationship management system
- Customer billing system
- IT service management system

Application enterprise software typically depends on backend databases to support enterprise data management and information retrieval. Figure 2.9 shows the architecture of a generic enterprise Web application. It consists of a database server,

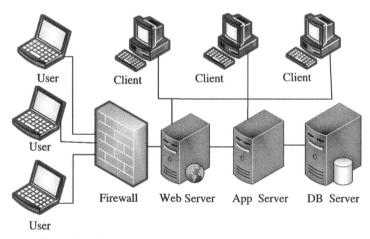

Figure 2.9 Architecture of a typical enterprise Web application.

an application server, and a Web server. Enterprise data such as customer profiles, purchase orders, internal HR data, and so on is stored on the dedicated databases. An application server implements the business logic that may involve retrieving data based on authorized permissions, applying certain business rules such as data validation when inserting new data and modifying existing data, and so on. A Web server receives users' requests, processes the requests, and renders the responses back to the user. External clients need to go through the firewall to access the application. Internal clients can either access the application server directly or access the Web server without going through the firewall.

How an enterprise application is accessed by its users adds another layer of complexity to the performance and scalability of the application. In the next few sections, we'll explore various common enterprise software architectures. A good understanding of the architecture that a software system is built upon is necessary for understanding the performance and scalability characteristics of the system and coming up with better design, implementation, and testing strategies.

2.5.2 Enterprise Software Architecture

Software architecture conveys two major pieces of information about software:

1. The software components that constitute a whole system to provide certain functions at the system level.
2. How the components communicate with each other to fulfill the system functions.

With application enterprise software, the system functions are divided into various tasks such as:

1. Storing, retrieving, and managing data.
2. Applying business logic, which is also known as application logic.
3. Optionally displaying data to users through user interfaces.

Based on how these tasks are implemented in software, application enterprise software architecture has gone through a series of evolutions since the inception of software in the 1960s with the advent of computers. The following sections describe how each generation of application enterprise software architecture evolved chronologically. A minimum understanding of various enterprise software architectures is required for being able to help solve efficiently the performance and scalability challenges facing large-scale enterprise software applications.

2.5.3 Monolithic Architecture

Monolithic architecture was the product of mainframe times. In a mainframe system, all computing resources are assembled into a single stand-alone system. All software functions such as data and application logic reside on the same mainframe system. User access to the system is provided with terminals, as shown in Figure 2.10.

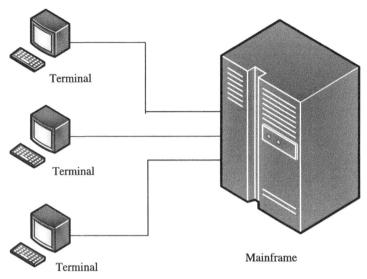

Figure 2.10 A mainframe computer for monolithic applications.

Terminals don't have much computing power other than being used as display devices for entering commands to the system and displaying data from the system.

2.5.4 Client/Server Architecture

Mainframe systems were powerful, yet expensive and hard to maintain. As time went by, especially with the advent of the PC (personal computer) era with its economy of

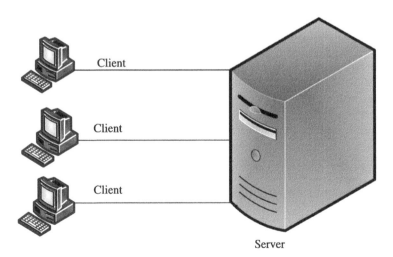

Figure 2.11 Client/server or two-tier architecture.

scale achieved through massive production, a new generation of software architecture, the client/server architecture, emerged, as shown in Figure 2.11.

With client/server architecture, system functions are cut in the middle of the application logic function; namely, some of the application logic is deployed with data on a more powerful server system, and some of the application logic is deployed on less powerful and much cheaper client systems together with the user interface.

Client/server architecture is also known as two-tier architecture, as there is a clear boundary between the client and the server. Email servers and file servers are some of the typical examples of client/server architecture. Although it's relatively old, client/server architecture is still widely in use today.

2.5.5 Three-Tier Architecture

The next natural step seems to be separating data, application logic, and user interface onto three separate, independently deployable tiers, and that's the three-tier architecture, as shown in Figure 2.12.

A three-tier architecture typically consists of a datatier with database servers, an application logic tier with application servers, and user interface tier that consists of internal clients who can access the application server either directly through the client applications without going through a Web server or through a Web server.

Note that tiered architecture is defined from the deployment and operational point of view in order to meet performance and scalability requirements. One can install all three tiers on one physical server machine for development purposes, but it still is called three-tier architecture because of the separable deployment options of all three tiers.

Internet applications such as Web applications and electronic commerce websites are typical examples of the three-tier architecture. For example, almost

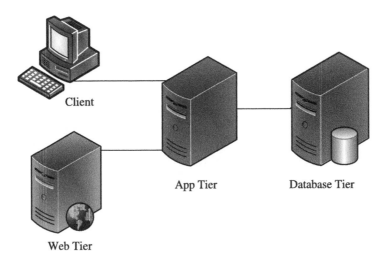

Figure 2.12 Three-tier architecture.

every company has a website that users can browse to ascertain the services and products it provides and also register for more service privileges and restricted accesses. The behind-the-scenes supporting infrastructure of an Internet application consists of the following:

- A front tier running on one or more Web servers that redirect user requests and provide static content
- A middle tier running on one or more application servers, such as J2EE servers, that handle dynamic content and user-specific requests such as retrieving user profile
- A back end tier running on one or more database servers that manages and provides access to the data

We are not done with tier segregation yet. As business logic becomes more and more complicated, application tier might be split further into multiple tiers, which leads to the concept of N-tier architecture. Let's elaborate on N-tier architecture in the next section.

2.5.6 N-Tier Architecture

In some literature, the term N-tier implies any number of tiers, from 2 to more than 3 tiers. In some context, the term N-tier implies blurred boundaries and resultant complexities among various application tier components from the functionality point of view. The latter seems to be a more logical extension to the reality that one application component can rarely fulfill all business logic.

Let's take a mobile phone company billing application system as an example of N-tier architecture. Such an application may need to be able to support tens of millions

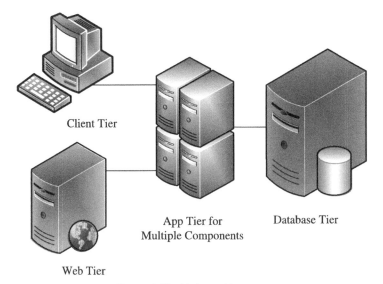

Client Tier

App Tier for
Multiple Components

Database Tier

Web Tier

Figure 2.13 N-tier architecture.

of customers. As shown in Figure 2.13, the application architecture may need to have at least the following application components working collaboratively to fulfill various functions:

- Accounting component that manages user account
- Product catalog component that provides service plans for users to choose from
- Sales order component that can process online purchases from users
- Billing component that bills customers for their purchases and uses of the services according to the available service contracts

In this architecture, each application component is reusable and might be a mature stand-alone application by itself. It's also possible that different application components might come from different vendors, and some integration work is required to make all of them work together. This extension naturally leads to the new generations of software architecture, for example, software componentry and service-oriented architecture (SOA), which are our subjects for the next two sections.

2.5.7 Software Componentry

Software componentry is based on the idea that software components, like the equivalent of hardware components, can be made swappable so that composite software can be built using commercial off-the-shelf (COTS) components. The motivation for using COTS components is that they will reduce the overall system development cost and time because the components can be bought instead of being developed from scratch. However, it comes with a significant side effect that the software component integration work and dependency on a third-party component vendor may incur significant additional cost.

The concept of COTS is further extended to the concept of modifiable off-the-shelf (MOTS). A MOTS product is typically a COTS product with its source code modifiable. A MOTS product can be customized by the purchaser, by the vendor, or by another party to meet the customer requirements. Because a MOTS product is adapted for a specific purpose, it can be purchased and used immediately. However, since MOTS software components are developed by external sources, a purchaser has less control over the course of change down the road. This may create some dependency on the MOTS component vendor and impose upgrade challenges as well.

During the past few years, software architecture evolved from COTS and MOTS to SOA. SOA is the newest generation of software architecture. It is promising in saving software development cost and providing flexibility for composing new services, as will be introduced in the next section.

2.5.8 Service-Oriented Architecture

Service-oriented architecture (SOA) provides a new perspective for simplifying the process of building large-scale, increasingly complex, and interwoven application enterprise software systems. It has been gaining massive momentum as it promises

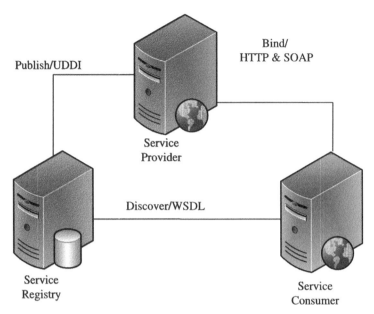

Publish/UDDI

Bind/
HTTP & SOAP

Service
Provider

Discover/WSDL

Service
Registry

Service
Consumer

Figure 2.14 XML Web services architecture.

to solve enterprise application integration challenges more cost effectively than using the traditional proprietary messaging protocol based approaches.

In achieving the goals of simplifying application integration, SOA emphasizes the use of loosely coupled software services. In an SOA environment, resources are distributed over networks and are made available as independent services, which can be accessed without the knowledge of their underlying platform implementation.

At the highest level, an SOA-based enterprise application consists of *service providers* and *service consumers*. A service consumer sends service requests to its service provider, which renders the service requests and sends service responses back to the service consumer. How the service requests and responses are represented or formatted and how the service consumer and service provider communicate with each other constitute the watershed for different styles of SOAs.

XML Web services are the most popular implementation of SOA today. XML Web services infrastructure enables service publishing, discovery, and message exchange between a service provider and its consumer. As shown in Figure 2.14, there are three entities involved in XML Web services infrastructure: service provider, service registry, and service consumer. The infrastructure follows three open standards in the format of specifications: UDDI (Universal Description, Discovery, and Integration) for service publishing, WSDL (Web Services Description Language) for service discovery, and HTTP (HyperText Transport Protocol) and SOAP (Simple Object Access Protocol) for message exchange between a service provider and its consumer.

The term *bind* in Figure 2.14 describes the built-in infrastructure function of enabling a service provider and its service consumer to communicate with each other through exchanging messages that they both understand. Here is how it works step by step:

- The request and response messages are encoded in text format by following a special XML dialect called Simple Object Access Protocol (SOAP).
- The SOAP messages are sent back and forth between a service consumer and its provider using the HTTP through a URL, although it may use other protocols such as FTP or SMTP.
- Behind the scenes, the components developed in languages such as Java or C# fulfill the service requests. The interfaces from those components are coded in language-specific binary format. Therefore, SOAP serialization and deserialization must happen when the SOAP messages arrive at and leave the component interfaces.

You can learn more about the performance and scalability characteristics of the XML Web services based applications presented quantitatively in Chapter 5.

2.6 SUMMARY

In this chapter, we started with understanding the software stack in general by using a layered approach, which is also the approach that should be taken when investigating and solving software performance and scalability issues. Although there are many factors that can affect and determine the performance and scalability of a software system, it's really important to make sure that the APIs as basic building blocks are intrinsically highly performing and scalable by design.

Modern computer architecture is moving toward implementing multithreading at the chip level. Therefore, implementing multithreading at the software level is a must for achieving the best possible performance and scalability. We illustrated this notion with a real-world, multithreaded enterprise application. We also offered a simple analysis of what was preventing that application from being more scalable. The underlying bottleneck with that application was from the disk I/Os, which is typical with many large-scale enterprise applications that require the fastest possible storage for retrieving data from and writing data to disks.

We then categorized different types of software in order to help define the battlefields for software performance and scalability work. We further elaborated various architectures of enterprise software, which is where performance and scalability work is needed most.

In the next chapter, I will cover what you need to know about measuring the performance and scalability of a software system quantitatively. It is interesting that everybody has opinions, and sometimes even strong opinions, about software performance and scalability, but only those who are educated and bound by disciplines can succeed.

RECOMMENDED READING

The following texts are recommended in general for understanding software, computers, and software architecture:

F. Buschmann, R. Meunier, H. Rohnert, P. Sommerlad, and M. Stal, *Pattern-Oriented Software Architecture—A System of Patterns*, John Wiley & Sons, 1996.

T. Erl, *Service-Oriented Architecture—A Field Guide to Integrating XML and Web Services*, Prentice Hall, 2004.

D. Patterson and J. Hennessy, *Computer Organization & Design—The Hardware/Software Interface*, Morgan Kaufmann, 1994.

D. Schmidt, *Pattern-Oriented Software Architecture—Patterns for Concurrent and Networked Objects*, Volume 2, John Wiley & Sons, 2000.

W. Stallings, *Computer Organization and Architecture—Designing for Performance*, 4th edition, Prentice Hall, 1996.

For characterization of XML Web services infrastructure overhead, refer to the following publication:

H. H. Liu and P. V. Crain, An analytic model for predicting the performance of SOA-based enterprise software applications, in *CMG 2004 Proceedings*, Las Vegas.

EXERCISES

2.1. Explain conceptually the differences between Java virtual machine and computer server virtualization technologies such as VMWare^{TM}.

2.2. Write a simple, multithreaded program in any programming language with which you are familiar. Measure the performance of your program on a computer that has at least two CPUs by varying the number of threads. Plot a curve showing when the performance of your program starts to level off as you increase the number of threads. Explain and justify the underlying bottleneck by using the quantitative system resource consumptions collected during the executions of your program.

2.3. What's the most reliable way of determining whether your Intel architecture based system is hyperthreading enabled or not?

2.4. Give your vision of the next generation of software architecture after SOA.

3

Testing Software Performance and Scalability

Don't guesstimate. Measure it!
—The author

For the software product you develop, it's necessary to incorporate performance and scalability testing into your development life cycles. Thorough performance and scalability tests can provide a quantitative basis for further optimization and tuning opportunities so that the maximum possible performance and scalability can be achieved for your product. High performance and scalability could be one of the advantageous selling points for your product against any competitors. High performance and scalability will also make your customers happy after the deals are closed and your customers start to deploy and use your product. Your customers would be frustrated if they cannot easily get your product up and running after paying a premium for the product.

Let's assume you agree that testing the performance and scalability of your software product must be part of your product development life cycle. Then, how can you maximize the productivity, efficiency, and effectiveness of your software performance and scalability testing work? This book helps you achieve such goals. In order to be successful, you'll need to have the right mindset, right hardware, and right skill set.

Your mindset needs to be adapted for designing and executing software performance and scalability tests. We all know that mindset is the drive behind how we make decisions, what we do, and what we can accomplish. In this sense, mindset

Software Performance and Scalability. By Henry H. Liu

transition is the most important thing to accomplish in order to turn your software performance and scalability testing work into values for your organization. Your previous background as a software developer, a database administrator, a system administrator, or a quality test engineer is very helpful for doing software performance and scalability testing work. However, your previous experience doesn't guarantee you immediate success. You need to try your best to think very carefully about how you should design and conduct your performance and scalability tests, how you should evaluate your quantitative test results, and how you can help turn your performance and scalability test work into values for your organization. With such a strong performance and scalability oriented mindset, you have advantages for delivering solid test results even if you may need to sharpen your technical skills with time.

However, mindset transition doesn't happen in days, weeks, or even months. It is generally agreed in the software community that it takes at least five years for a software engineer to become proficient in testing, optimizing, and tuning the performance and scalability of a software system. But don't be discouraged by that notion. The performance and scalability issues of a software system can be treated quantitatively and precisely more like a science than a black art. If you are willing to learn and willing to follow those proven best practices as presented in this book, you can become effective and successful immediately with your software performance and scalability work.

With the right mindset, the next important thing is to have the right computer hardware for testing the performance and scalability of your software product. Don't be tempted into using low-end, development, or QA systems for conducting performance and scalability tests. A general rule of thumb is that the systems you use for performance and scalability tests should be at least two to four times more powerful than your development or QA systems in terms of the total CPU gigahertz power as the product of the number of CPUs and CPU frequency. Low-end computer hardware tends to mask the real performance and scalability issues.

With the right mindset and the right hardware, the final thing you need is the right technical skill set. The right technical skill set includes not only the ability to design and conduct the tests, but also the ability to determine whether the test results are valid. Avoid rushing to conclusions prematurely based on invalid test results. Software performance and scalability testing is not just about taking measurements. Try to think whether the measured numbers make sense. It's obvious that some subsequent action items need to be derived and carried out following your performance and scalability tests. What action items you come up with should be driven by your dependable, quantitative measurements about the performance and scalability of your product. Making conclusions based on invalid test results will not yield anything that can be materialized into performance and scalability benefits for your product.

To help you acquire the right technical skill set, this chapter introduces all the basic concepts, terminologies, and methodologies associated with software performance and scalability testing.

I'll start in Section 3.1 with the scope of software performance and scalability testing. This will help put your software performance and scalability testing into proper perspective.

In Section 3.2, I'll introduce the software development process adopted nowadays in many software development organizations. A software development process defines the environment into which you must fit yourself so that you will be recognized as a vital member of the team. It also defines the protocols with which you and your co-workers can exchange ideas and work collaboratively to build performance and scalability into your product. Feeling comfortable with the environment and protocols can help you enhance your productivity and efficiency significantly.

In Section 3.3, I'll concentrate on defining the performance metrics for both OLTP (online transaction processing) type and batch job type of software systems. I'll use concrete case studies to help you understand those metrics.

In Section 3.4, I'll discuss the stochastic nature of software performance and scalability test results. It's very important to understand that software performance and scalability test results contain errors, just like any other measurements in other disciplines.

In Section 3.5, I'll introduce Amdahl's law. This law essentially is the compass for determining what you should do to improve the performance and scalability of your product in a larger scope.

In Section 3.6, I'll enumerate those common factors that are critical in determining the performance and scalability of a software system. Your ability to effectively diagnose and solve performance and scalability problems strongly depends on your understanding of those performance and scalability factors.

In Section 3.7, I'll show you how to use system performance counters to analyze various performance and scalability factors so that you can quickly learn how to focus on the most important factors for a specific performance or scalability issue.

In Section 3.8, some software performance data principles will be introduced and elaborated.

Finally, in Section 3.9, I'll summarize all the topics covered in this chapter. A list of texts will be recommended for further study if you feel that you want to learn more about some subjects.

This chapter only teaches you the basics about testing software performance and scalability. To become proficient in coping with software performance and scalability issues, you need to grasp queuing theory and API profiling, which will be presented in Parts II and III of this book.

Let's begin with the scope of software performance and scalability testing in the next section.

3.1 SCOPE OF SOFTWARE PERFORMANCE AND SCALABILITY TESTING

We begin with the scope of software performance and scalability testing to help you put your tests in perspective. Knowing exactly what you are testing for can help ensure success for your testing.

Common nonfunctional software performance and scalability tests can be classified into the following four categories:

- *Performance regression testing* for tracking performance changes due to code changes from release to release. This will help ensure that no surprises will be encountered by your customers after they apply upgrades to their production environment.

- *Performance optimization and tuning testing* for supporting ongoing optimization and tuning efforts for making your software perform better and better.

- *Performance benchmarking testing* for knowing what performance the customers should expect with your software if they use similar, realistic workloads with similar hardware that is a good approximation of what will actually be used in production.

- *Scalability testing* for checking out whether your software can meet customers' growing business needs. This is similar to *stress testing* in that it puts more loads on your software to see not only whether it will perform but also whether it will break.

These four different types of tests are not stand-alone islands. In fact, they complement each other:

- You can start with performance regression testing for identifying common use scenarios that are important for your customers. These scenarios can be used for defining other types of tests later. Performance regression testing can also serve as a baseline for further performance testing.

- Additionally, without a rigorous performance regression testing process in place, the performance of your software may degrade significantly without being noticed and you may end up with no *testable* versions of your software available for your larger scale benchmarking and scalability tests, which are intended for publishing good numbers, not bad numbers.

- The best practices out of your ongoing performance optimization and tuning tests can be applied to benchmarking testing and scalability testing.

- Benchmarking testing and scalability testing can help expose the performance problems that you may not have found out using small data volumes with your performance regression or optimization and tuning testing.

Let's elaborate more on each type of software performance and scalability testing in the following sections.

3.1.1 Performance Regression Testing

Software developers and QA engineers are familiar with the concept of *regression testing*. It's a measure to verify whether newly introduced code changes have broken anything that worked previously.

However, we should not assume that this concept applies to functional testing only. Regression testing applies to performance testing as well. The purpose of performance regression testing is to check whether the performance of the software has been degraded by the changes introduced to the source code.

It is very necessary to conduct performance regression testing when changes are made to the software that has already been deployed at the customer's site. And it should be conducted before pushing changes to the customer's production environment. I had an opportunity to explore a case where the customer's online shopping website became too slow for online shoppers to place purchase orders, after a new change to the software in use was introduced. Intense investigation on the software vendor's side found out that it was caused by inadvertently missing caching the data when new changes were introduced to the software, which used to be cached at the application level. You can image what turmoil it had brought up when the customer's website was no longer capable of taking customer orders and the executives of the two companies started their dialogs about the issue.

Software performance regression testing is important not only for minimizing the risks to a customer's business but also for internally tracking performance degradations and improvements due to changes at the source code level, which are inevitable with ongoing development. Whether intentional or inadvertent, changes to the source code can cause severe performance degradations to the software under development. The adverse effects of changes on the performance of software can only be caught with standard performance regression testing. For example, developers might keep changing SQL queries as needed for changed business logic without actually realizing that it may invalidate existing database table indexes for those SQL queries. Regular performance regression testing can help prevent things like this from happening.

Performance regression testing doesn't have to be conducted as frequently as for functionality regression testing. Functionality regression testing needs to be conducted for every nightly build, whereas performance regression testing only needs to be conducted on a per-iteration basis, which typically is every 2–4 weeks per iteration.

Performance regression testing doesn't have to cover as many scenarios as functionality regression testing does. It should concentrate on a few scenarios with which performance matters most for the customers. Functionality regression testing tends to be fine-grained down to the API level with variations of API signatures, whereas performance regression testing is more coarse-grained, focusing on the solution scenarios, which mimic how the software is actually used by customers.

Performance regression testing should be automated as much as possible. Managing all regression test data could become a daunting task with time.

■ Case Study 3.1: Performance Regression Testing

Before moving on to the next section, I'd like to share with you a performance regression testing experience for a real product that I worked on as a performance engineer.

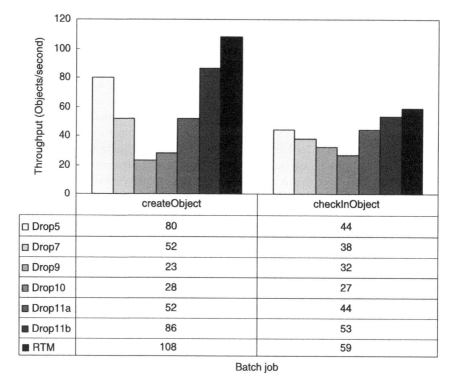

Batch job	createObject	checkInObject
□ Drop5	80	44
□ Drop7	52	38
▨ Drop9	23	32
▨ Drop10	28	27
▨ Drop11a	52	44
■ Drop11b	86	53
■ RTM	108	59

Figure 3.1   *Performance regression tests for the two batch jobs of a real software product from initial drops to the final RTM.*

Without the necessity of going into the details of the application, Figure 3.1 shows how the throughput of the two batch jobs of an application had evolved over time from drop to drop and to the final release to market (RTM). Behind those up–down–up bars were enormous performance optimization and tuning efforts engineered into the product through effective collaborations between the performance team and the development team.

It is clear from this case study that the performance of a software product can indeed be degraded as new changes are introduced. An effective performance regression testing process can effectively help prevent performance defects from slipping into the release without being noticed.

3.1.2   Performance Optimization and Tuning Testing

In this section, I'll share some of my software performance testing experiences and observations with you. Specifically, I'll concentrate on the following aspects of software performance testing:

- What software performance testing is all about
- Why productivity and efficiency are especially important for software perform-ance testing

- A common software performance testing procedure that should be followed for your software performance testing work
- What deliverables should result from your software performance testing

Throughout this section, I'll use *software performance testing* to imply *software performance optimization and tuning testing*. *Performance testing* seems to be a generic term and a broad concept, but to clarify, by *performance testing* I mean the following two different types:

1. Performance testing for optimizing software at the code implementation level. This requires some level of API profiling and database query analysis, identifying hot APIs and SQL queries, arriving at proper optimization recommendations, and then evaluating the recommendations with your developers for possible changes at the source code level for performance improvements.

2. Performance testing for tuning the performance of your software by varying the configuration parameters of the hardware platform, software platform, and the application without incurring changes at the source code level. Establishing the out-of-the-box (OOTB) baseline performance for your software is the first step for this type of performance testing. Then, you can tune the hardware and software configurations as well as your application configurations for the maximum possible performance.

It's very important that you write up your performance tuning guide and communicate your sizing guidelines and best performance tuning practices to both your internal customer support group and external customers. Your guidelines for sizing the hardware and tuning the performance of your software can help your customers have a smooth start-up and long-term satisfaction with your software.

Performance testing should be part of the entire life cycle of your software development. You should keep refining your test methodologies and testing tools to achieve the highest possible productivity and efficiency. Productivity and efficiency are everything for software performance testing. It's not unusual to find out that people have been spending months of time without actually getting anything down. I typically attribute this kind of unfortunate phenomenon to the following three factors:

1. Software performance testing has its own unique challenges compared with functionality testing and writing code. Most often, you may need to spend a lot of time just to get everything up and running. For functionality testing and writing code, you find something broken and you fix it—that's your achievement. However, that is not the case at all with software performance testing. With software performance testing, you can't claim full credit by saying "I found that it doesn't work." Your job as a performance engineer is to help establish baseline performance for your product and help make it perform better by applying optimizations and tunings. If you don't end up with some reliable baseline numbers and optimization and tuning recommendations that

can lead to better performance for your product, your time is essentially wasted or your company is not benefiting from your work.

2. Software performance testing requires you to think carefully about every detail of your performance testing. You might think that you got some numbers, but it only turned out that the numbers you got are not reliable or are meaningless in the worst case. For example, you did not realize that your testing is benefiting from cached data, which would not be cached in a real production environment. Another common mistake is to take data in an unstabile environment. For example, you repeat the same test 10 times and get results that are drastically different. How can you evaluate such results meaningfully? The errors in test results must be controlled to less than a few percent for your data to be truly useful unless the underlying performance factors such as the network traffic across a WAN are the study objects.

3. In a more general sense, a software performance job requires sharp, independent, and creative thinking abilities. Technical skills are easy to obtain, but thinking abilities are hard to obtain within a short period of time. You need to think constantly how you can improve your productivity and efficiency by doing things in more efficient ways. As you keep thinking and practicing, you'll gradually become a fully fledged software performance engineer who can solve software performance problems in a matter of hours while others might spend weeks or even months without success.

In addition, a rigorous procedure is necessary for your software performance testing. You should always follow the same procedure for your software performance testing unless you are establishing a new baseline. Software performance testing typically consists of the following steps:

- Designing your workloads based on customer's use requirements on performance. This is especially important when your company has SLAs (service level agreements) with customers, by which violating performance requirements may incur monetary penalties. When you do not have SLAs with customers, you need to extract performance requirements based on common use scenarios of the customers so that you can know what your goals are.

- Designing and developing test scripts or in-house tools to drive your workloads. For OLTP (online transaction processing) workloads, most likely you'll need to develop your test scripts to be used with one of those commercial performance load test tools such as LoadRunner®, SilkPerformer®, Empirix®, or Quantify®. For batch jobs typically running in the background, you'll need to develop your own specific scripts or tools to drive the test.

- Deciding on appropriate hardware. I have emphasized a few times that software performance testing is not just about getting performance numbers. Starting with outdated or very low-end hardware is a major mistake that you cannot afford to make. For some large-scale applications, you may not be able to get the production-level hardware, but the hardware you choose for your performance testing should be much more powerful than those development and functionality testing systems. If your application software is database intensive, use adequate storage for your data or, at least, do not put all your database data and transaction log files on a single local hard drive. You should not raise false performance alarms based on significantly undersized hardware.

- Setting up your testing environment. This may include installing your software with all middleware software installed. Then you need to populate data, which is one of the foundation pieces of the initial work for your testing. Next, execute your tests a few times to ensure that your environment is not only working but also stable. Your test bed is like the soil for your plants and flowers—you can't expect good outcomes with an environment that is not well prepared.

- At this point, you need a detailed procedure about how you conduct your tests. You may not want to raise false performance alarms using the test results out of different test procedures. For example, when you change the number of threads or any other configuration parameters for your software, you may need to restart your server for that change to take effect. Then with every drop you test, you need to follow the same procedure of restarting the server after making configuration changes for your software; otherwise, you might be surprised that somehow your software is a lot slower than it used to be and may even raise a false alarm.

- When everything including a test procedure is in place, you are ready to take your performance baseline. Baseline is where you get started with a set of configuration parameters that are known to be optimal with the given hardware. As you learn more about your software, you may establish new baselines by taking your best known methods into account. For example, initially you might have taken your baseline with an OOTB number of threads configured for your software. You might then have learnt that the performance of your software could be a factor of 5 better or more if the number of threads was set to a much higher value. Then the performance data taken with this new number of threads would be your new baseline. The baseline may change with time. It's a series of newly improved performance levels that challenge you to push the performance of your software to the next level after you implement your newly established optimizations and tunings.

- After establishing baseline, your next step is to analyze those factors that affect the performance of your software most—the performance bottlenecks. Later, I'll show you in detail how to analyze performance bottlenecks based on queuing theory and performance counters.

- After identifying affecting performance factors or bottlenecks, you need to think how those bottlenecks can be removed by implementing optimizations at the application level or tunings external to your software. You should not immediately request faster hardware, as faster hardware is only for lean software that has gone through full cycles of performance optimization and tuning. I'll elaborate more on software performance optimization and tuning throughout the rest of this book.

- It's very important that you get *reliable*, quantitative performance data, use your data to arrive at your recommendations for further optimization and tuning, and use your data to drive your recommendations to the successful end of being accepted, implemented, and verified. Only at this point can you be assured of your value to your company's business.

Deliverables out of your software performance testing should include at a minimum the following:

- Performance numbers such as response times or throughputs that matter most for your customers. It's better to put your test results in a more presentable manner so that it can easily be communicated with others, including your management.
- An exact list of test conditions used for obtaining your test results. This should include:
    - The hardware specs such as the number of CPUs, CPU clock rate, memory, disk space, and network as well as operating system and service packs.
    - The exact software stack that was tested. Some installation options that matter to your performance testing should be documented as well.
    - Hardware and software configurations changed relative to their default settings. This may include database configurations and any configurations that are specific to your software, such as the number of threads or the amount of memory configured.
- Database activity reports such as Oracle statspack or automatic workload repository (AWR) reports.
- Performance counter log data such as obtained with Windows *perfmon* utility or any UNIX scripts.
- Performance test log files that were created during the test.
- And, most importantly, a bottleneck analysis that gives directions on how you can further optimize and tune the performance of your software.

Software performance defects typically are managed through a bug tracking system for your software development. You should submit your defects in time and then follow through with the developers to make sure that they are resolved and checked into the next build or release of your software. Until then, your organization has benefited from your software performance testing work.

Performance testing can be done at the level of each software component. A complete application system may include many software components that work together to fulfill their promises to users. Performance testing at the system level belongs to benchmarking testing, which is one step closer to customer deployment. Let's discuss more about benchmarking testing in the next section.

3.1.3 Performance Benchmarking Testing

Benchmarking testing typically is market driven or has targeted customers in mind. It's a way to show how well your software can perform and how well your software can meet your customers' needs against your competitors by using more realistic workloads and closer-to-production hardware. Outcomes from benchmarking tests would be regarded as milestones for your software that you and your company would be proud of if the numbers look good.

Benchmarking testing is more of a team effort than an individual's effort. However, it can't be successful without thorough performance work by each performance engineer on each software component.

For benchmarking testing, planning and execution are more emphasized than seeking new optimization and tuning opportunities. For this reason, we won't spend more time on this topic.

3.1.4 Scalability Testing

Scalability testing is similar to stress testing in that it takes your performance testing to the extreme to find out where the limits are. You may hear people say this software can support up to that many users or it can process up to that much volume of transactions, and that's about scalability testing. This kind of testing is interesting, because every business is expected to grow with time as is the processing capability of the software they purchase to support their business operations.

Scalability testing resembles optimization and tuning oriented performance testing except that it's measured more by quantitative metrics, such as the maximum number of users and the volume of transactions the software under test can support. It typically is an extension to your regular performance testing with more users and larger data sets.

As you increase the load, whether it's measured by the number of users or by the size of the data sets, you may see completely different behaviors with your software than you have seen with previous tests using lighter workloads. For this reason, it's very necessary to conduct some level of scalability testing, especially when you have gotten all of the low-hanging fruits during the early stages of your performance testing.

Some specific issues that you may want to focus on with your scalability testing include the following:

- Making sure that the hardware you use for your scalability testing is adequate. The performance limit with your software might be lifted by either scaling up or scaling out the hardware under test. Scaling up means using faster hardware, and scaling out means using more identical systems. Software scaling and hardware scaling are typically coupled with each other. Nonscalable software won't scale on scalable hardware, and scalable software won't run on nonscalable hardware. The worst combination is a single-threaded application running on a massive number of low clock rate CPUs, which won't scale no matter what you do.

- Memory leak is one of the special issues that should be checked out with your scalability tests. The 32-bit operating systems have a maximum addressable memory space of 4 GB, which is split into 2 GB for the kernel and 2 GB for an application process on the Windows platform. This allocation might be repartitioned into 1 GB for the kernel and 3 GB for the application with the help of some switches at the hardware level, but that may still not be enough for memory-hog applications.

- If a database is involved, prepare to add new indexes when the load increases, as database system performance is most sensitive to the size of the data stored in your database. This is illustrated with the next case study.

■ **Case Study 3.2: Scalability of a Batch Job Type of Database-Intensive Application**

One cannot assume that if a software system is scalable on one platform that has been thoroughly tested then it will be scalable on other platforms as well without being verified. This experience is shown quantitatively in Figure 3.2.

With this case study, even with the same volume of data of 44 k objects created with an enterprise application, on platform II (a specific flavor of UNIX), I needed to add a couple of new indexes for some database tables in order to stop rapid throughput deterioration. Those indexes were not needed on platform I

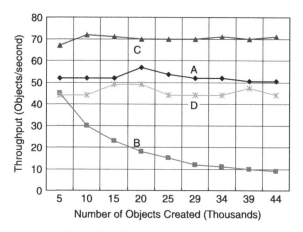

—◆— A: platform I (baseline)
—■— B: platform II (baseline: poor scalability)
—▲— C: platform II (scalability improved after adding 3 indexes)
—✳— D: platform I (after adding 3 indexes)

Figure 3.2 *Dependence of software scalability on platforms illustrated using a batch job of creating 44 k objects from a real product (Note: Curve A shows the baseline established on Windows platform; curve B shows poor scalability on UNIX when the same test was repeated; curve C shows improved scalability after adding three new indexes to two heavily accessed database tables; and curve D shows the same test on Windows with those three indexes added.)*

(Windows 2003) on which I used to conduct all my performance testing for that application.

The performance test setup associated with Figure 3.2 consisted of an application server and a database server. That batch job was designed to create objects through a client program that calls the application server APIs. The evolution of the throughput of this application with time is a measure of how scalable this application is. As shown by curve A, the throughput stays flat on Windows platform. However, when the same test was run on a UNIX platform, it was found that the throughput was going down rapidly, which indicated a poor scalability, as shown by curve B.

The detailed database query analysis revealed that three indexes should be added to two heavily accessed tables. After adding those three indexes, the same test was run on both the UNIX platform and Windows platform. As is shown by curve C, adding those three new indexes had indeed drastically cured the poor scalability on the UNIX platform, along with a significant performance improvement up to a factor of 7. However, the overhead of adding those three indexes caused about 10% performance degradation on the Windows platform, as shown by curve D.

This example has demonstrated that software may exhibit different scalability characteristics on different platforms. So do not take it for granted that if your software is scalable on one platform it will be scalable on all other platforms. Different platforms may have different combinations of CPU and I/O capabilities. The scalability of software depends on the balance of the resource utilizations among various system resources, such as CPU, disk I/O, and so on. So the resource utilization balance established on one platform may become broken on another platform and a new balance needs to be established therein to achieve the desired scalability on the new platform.

Next, let's examine a scalability test study case with an OLTP type application.

■ Case Study 3.3: Scalability of an OLTP Type Application

The workload of an OLTP type application is characterized by the following two input parameters:

- Number of active virtual users for simulating the real users of the application
- Average transaction rate for each user type that simulates the activities from each type of user

The scalability testing for an OLTP type application can thus be conducted by varying the number of active virtual users and the average transaction rate with the scripts defined. Without the necessity of going into the details of this application, Figures 3.3 and 3.4 show the average response times for the designated actions versus the increasing number of active virtual users and average transaction rates, respectively. Note that the response times displayed in these two figures are server response times, which do not include the browser time. Browser time is the time spent on the user's machine for rendering the responses from the server to the user.

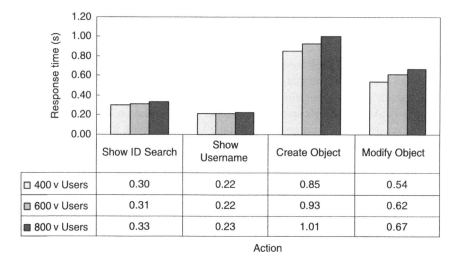

	Show ID Search	Show Username	Create Object	Modify Object
☐ 400 v Users	0.30	0.22	0.85	0.54
▨ 600 v Users	0.31	0.22	0.93	0.62
■ 800 v Users	0.33	0.23	1.01	0.67

Action

Figure 3.3   *Scalability of an OLTP application versus the number of users.*

With the tests conducted by varying the number of active virtual users, the transaction rates were fixed at five times the average transaction rate while increasing the number of users from 400 to 600 and to 800. Note that the response times did not increase linearly with the number of users and that scalable performance has been observed across all user actions.

With the tests conducted by increasing the transaction rate for each user type proportionally, the number of users was fixed at 800 while increasing the transaction rate from average to 2.5 times the average and 5 times the average. Once again, scalable performance has been observed across all user actions. Note that

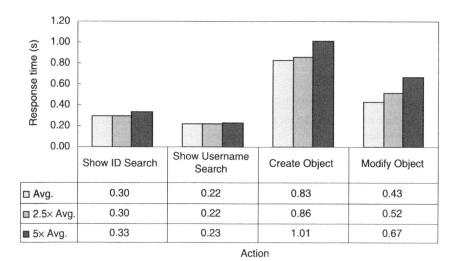

	Show ID Search	Show Username Search	Create Object	Modify Object
☐ Avg.	0.30	0.22	0.83	0.43
▨ 2.5× Avg.	0.30	0.22	0.86	0.52
■ 5× Avg.	0.33	0.23	1.01	0.67

Action

Figure 3.4   *Scalability of an OLTP application versus the transaction rate.*

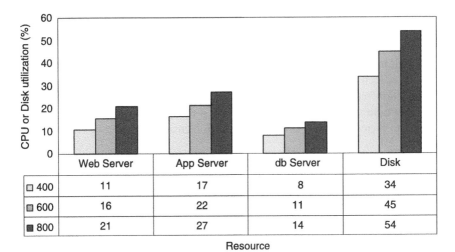

Resource	Web Server	App Server	db Server	Disk
□ 400	11	17	8	34
▨ 600	16	22	11	45
■ 800	21	27	14	54

Figure 3.5 *Resource utilizations associated with scalability tests with an increasing number of users.*

the response times did not increase linearly with the increasing transaction rate either. Both types of scalability tests demonstrated the scalable performance of this application with increasing load.

The scalable performance demonstrated with the scalability tests associated with Figures 3.3 and 3.4 resulted from the fact that none of the resources were driven to the saturated state. This can be verified with the resource consumptions shown in Figures 3.5 and 3.6 for the two scalability test cases, respectively. In these two

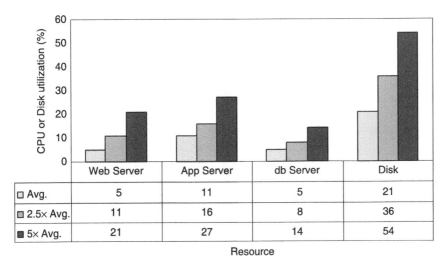

Resource	Web Server	App Server	db Server	Disk
□ Avg.	5	11	5	21
▨ 2.5× Avg.	11	16	8	36
■ 5× Avg.	21	27	14	54

Figure 3.6 *Resource utilizations associated with scalability tests with an increasing transaction rate.*

figures, not only the CPU utilizations but also the database disk utilizations are shown. It is seen that none of the servers had CPU utilizations exceeding 30%, which is very desirable for OLTP type applications.

With this case study, the largest CPU utilization was 27% with the application server, which implied that the system could accommodate more users or higher transaction rates while maintaining acceptable response times. Next, we'll see another case study that will demonstrate that the response times of all user types begin to increase beyond linear scaling with increasing number of virtual users.

■ Case Study 3.4: Scalability of Another OLTP Type Application

It is necessary to point out that we may not always see the ideal scalability as demonstrated in the previous case study. The response times of an OLTP application may increase faster, depending on the power of the hardware system used for each tier of the application.

Figure 3.7 shows the increasing response times of each user type (UT) with the number of virtual users increased from 200 to 300, 400, and 500, respectively. Note that here the response time was defined as the total transaction time for each user type instead of a specific action, in contrast with the preceding case study. The conventional 2-second requirement is imposed on a user action such as clicking on a link or button, not on the entire transaction, which consists of a series of actions.

As seen from Figure 3.8, when the number of users was increased by 150% from 200 to 500, the response time had increased 159%, 170%, and 189% for the user types of 1, 2, and 4, respectively, which is more than 150%, although for user type 3, it's 125%, which is less than 150%.

Thus we can conclude that this OLTP application could scale up to about 500 users with the hardware chosen for each tier of the application. As shown in Figure 3.9, both the Web server CPU utilization and the database disk utilization

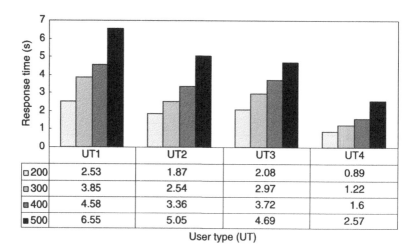

	UT1	UT2	UT3	UT4
□ 200	2.53	1.87	2.08	0.89
▨ 300	3.85	2.54	2.97	1.22
▨ 400	4.58	3.36	3.72	1.6
■ 500	6.55	5.05	4.69	2.57

User type (UT)

Figure 3.7 *Response time vs. the number of virtual users.*

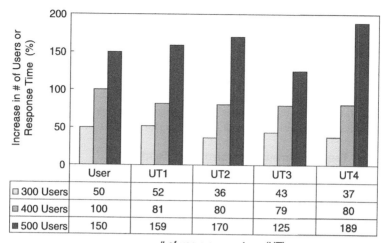

	User	UT1	UT2	UT3	UT4
▫ 300 Users	50	52	36	43	37
▨ 400 Users	100	81	80	79	80
■ 500 Users	150	159	170	125	189

# of users or user type (UT)

Figure 3.8   Scalability of an OLTP application.

approached near or above 70% with 500 virtual users, which is an indicator that the system was running around the saturation point with that many users where the response time of the system began to increase nonlinearly upward. This kind of behavior can be well explained in queuing theory, which will be introduced in the next chapter.

Since scalability testing is a magnified version of performance testing, from testing procedure to optimization and tuning techniques, whatever applies to performance

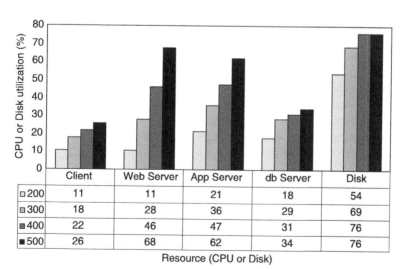

	Client	Web Server	App Server	db Server	Disk
▫ 200	11	11	21	18	54
▨ 300	18	28	36	29	69
▨ 400	22	46	47	31	76
■ 500	26	68	62	34	76

Resource (CPU or Disk)

Figure 3.9   Average system resource utilizations associated with the scalability tests shown in Figure 3.7.

testing applies to scalability testing as well. You can certainly leverage your performance testing skill set for your scalability testing, as performance testing and scalability testing are next to each other on the same scale, one on the left-hand side with lighter loads and the other on the right-hand side with heavier loads.

In your organization, you may have both a QA team and a performance team for the software under development. In the next section, I'll shed some lights on how the QA team and performance team can work together to deliver a high-quality software product that will not only work but also perform and scale.

3.1.5   QA Testing Versus Performance Testing

QA testing is about making sure that a software product works as has been designed from the functionality point of view. It's more about the correctness of a software program with its coded logic, rather than how fast it can complete a specific task. Performance testing works on the basic assumption that the software works, but that it might perform slow, which may make it unusable for its users. These are different sides of the same coin and typically inseparable.

In dealing with QA testing versus performance testing, I'd like to share some observations and experiences I had in my software performance engineer career so that you will not fall into the same traps:

- QA testing should precede performance testing. Using a non-QAed version of software for performance testing may only end up with rediscovering the functionality bugs that the developers and QA engineers are already aware of. Typically, you should use the last known good version of software that has passed QA testing for your performance testing.

- Performance testing is different from QA testing. QA testing doesn't care about what tool to use as long as it can be used to help prove the correctness of the software under test. However, performance testing is a lot pickier on what tools to use. I have seen people trying to adapt QA testing tools for performance testing. They can surely get some performance numbers this way. However, QA testing tools typically carry heavy overhead on the client side, which does not necessarily represent the true performance of the software under test. Also, QA testing tools typically do not measure up with the requirement of volume testing that is a requirement for performance testing. So either use commercial quality performance testing tools or develop your own performance testing oriented tools for doing your performance testing.

Sometimes performance testing may help discover functionality bugs that QA testing did not uncover. These are some additional merits of performance testing that will be briefly touched upon in the next section.

3.1.6   Additional Merits of Performance Testing

Software performance testing is a kind of performance assurance that the software you sell to your customers has adequate performance. Software performance testing is typically conducted prior to deploying your software in your customer's production environment.

It's necessary to realize that adequate software performance testing prior to production deployment has additional merits for other software performance activities, such as performance modeling, capacity planning, performance monitoring, and performance management. A well-optimized, well-tuned, and lean software application consumes less hardware resources, thus helping to arrive at the proper capacity planning without purchasing more expensive hardware.

To reinforce the above notion, I'd like to further elaborate that software design, implementation, SQL queries, and system-level tunings can strongly influence system resource utilizations. Spending money on optimizing and tuning your software may help avoid expensive hardware purchases for your customers, which helps reduce IT costs overall for your customers. This may not happen unless you can integrate software performance engineering effectively into your software development process, which is the topic for the next section.

3.2 SOFTWARE DEVELOPMENT PROCESS

Following an effective software development process can help boost the productivity and efficiency of a software development team. Productivity and efficiency are two key factors for the success of a software project. Getting familiar with the software development process can help assess when performance and scalability concerns should be injected into the life cycle of a software product.

In this section, I'll introduce the most popular software development process that adopts *agile software development*, which is a conceptual framework for undertaking software engineering projects, and *extreme programming*, which is a software engineering methodology. As stated earlier, a software development process defines the environment and protocols under which performance engineers must work in order to be more productive and efficient in solving software performance and scalability problems. Knowing the environment and the protocols is as important as the mindset transition we discussed at the beginning of this chapter. Being able to set oneself into a workplace ecosystem harmoniously is a requirement for all professions.

3.2.1 Agile Software Development

In this section, we introduce agile software development methods. Agile methods emerged in the mid-1990s as "lightweight" software development methods as part of a reaction against traditional "heavyweight" methods such as the heavily regulated, micromanaged waterfall development model. Agile methods are sometimes characterized as being at the opposite end of the spectrum from "plan-driven" or "disciplined" methodologies.

Agile methods are a family of development processes, not a single approach to software development. All agile methods share the following common characteristics:

- Attempting to minimize risk by developing software in short time boxes, called iterations, which typically last one to four weeks. Each iteration has its full life cycle from planning, requirement analysis, design, coding, and testing, to documentation. After several iterations, a release is accomplished, which includes all combined, fully tested changes made during previous iterations.

- Emphasizing real-time, face-to-face communication over the written document among a team of a few or more members. Because of the small amount of written documentation relative to other methods, agile methods are criticized as being undisciplined.

- Emphasizing working software as the primary measure of progress. In this regard, quality assurance tests are conducted for all iterations, while performance and scalability tests might be conducted only prior to the release.

Although this is a brief introduction to agile software development, it should be clear what "agile" elements it is advocating. Usually, you don't want to performance test every nightly build of the software under development. Testing every build is what the QA team would do. Performance testing a non-QAed build will only end up with duplicating the QA engineer's work. As a performance engineer, you should focus on performance issues instead of functionality issues.

In the next section, I'll briefly touch upon extreme programming (XP), which is one of the most popular agile software development methodologies.

3.2.2 Extreme Programming

Extreme programming (XP) prescribes a set of day-to-day practices for managers and developers. The exercise of these practices—which are traditional software engineering practices taken to "extreme" levels—leads to a development process that is more responsive to customer needs than traditional methods.

Extreme programming was created by Kent Beck, Ward Cunningham, and Ron Jeffries during their work on the Chrysler Comprehensive Compensation System (C3) payroll project. The C3 project was started in order to determine the best way to use object technologies, using the payroll systems at Chrysler as the object of research, with SmallTalk as the language and Gemstone as the persistence layer. Kent Beck, a prominent SmallTalk practitioner, was brought in to do performance tuning on the system, but his role was expanded as he noted issues with the development process. He began to refine the development methodology used on the project by implementing some changes, together with Ward Cunningham and Ron Jeffries. The C3 project was unsuccessful and was eventually cancelled, but Kent Beck published his book, *Extreme Programming Explained*, in 1999, which has since influenced the software development process heavily.

The main aim of XP is to reduce the cost of change. In traditional system development methods, the requirements are determined at the beginning of the development project and often are fixed from that point on. This means that the cost of changing the requirements at a later stage will be high. XP sets out to reduce the cost of change by introducing basic values, principles, and practices to make system development more flexible with respect to changes.

Three major XP values are:

- Communication
- Simplicity
- Feedback

Building software requires communicating requirements to developers. In formal software development methodologies, requirements are communicated to developers through documentation. XP favors frequent verbal communication instead of written documentation.

XP encourages starting with the simplest possible solution and evolving to better ones. The difference between this approach and traditional development methods is the focus on designing and coding for the needs of today instead of those of tomorrow or the future. Designing and coding for uncertain future requirements implies the risk of spending resources on something that might not be needed.

Feedback is another essential element of XP. Feedback can be multidimensional, namely, from unit tests about the correctness of an implementation, from the customer about the functionality and features, and from the team about implementation planning.

XP does not contradict software performance testing at all. Whenever possible, apply XP values to your software performance work to maximize the values of your performance testing work to improve the chances of your product's success. For example, you should:

- Count on frequent verbal communications with your developers instead of waiting for formal documents about the design of your software. Don't be discouraged if you find out that there are not many formal documents around. By talking to your developers frequently, you can always get the most up-to-date education on how your software is designed and implemented.
- Be aware that simple designs often bode well with high performance. By doing your performance testing, you might be able to help drive the complexity out of your product. For example, there could be some business logic computations that simply burn CPU cycles for operations that don't need to be performed. In some cases, some database triggers that are fired under certain conditions may not have to be fired at all.
- Frequently check with your customers to get feedback on how they use your software and how your software meets their performance requirements for their businesses. This can help you to build more realistic workloads even if you may not be able to get customer data to drive your workloads in your performance test environment.

In summary, mindset transition and fitting yourself into the working environment and protocols defined by your software development process are some of the *soft* skill sets that you should possess in order to achieve the maximum productivity and efficiency with your software performance work. Next, we'll focus on the hard-core, technical skill sets that you should have for testing the performance and scalability of your software.

3.3 DEFINING SOFTWARE PERFORMANCE

Everybody is familiar with the concept of *performance* regardless of the context. It's essentially the speed at which some activity or work is completed from start to finish. It can be perceived as fast, normal, or slow. However, when it comes to software, we are most concerned with the performance associated with two types of computing tasks or workloads:

- OLTP (online transaction processing)
- Batch jobs

OLTP refers to the computing tasks of processing the requests from the interactive users who use a software system real-time, while batch jobs refer to the regularly scheduled computer programs that run in the background in order to finish some amount of work within a specified time window.

An OLTP workload is simply a representation of the interactive user activities. It is often characterized by the types of user activities and the number of users associated with each type of user activity. A batch job workload specifies the amount of work to be processed without the necessity of user intervention.

A workload can be a real workload or a synthetic workload. A real workload is arrived at by analyzing the real-world production site operations. A synthetic workload is composed based on the hypothetical use cases constructed from customer requirements analysis.

In testing the performance and scalability of a software system, it's more desirable to use customer data and real workloads. However, very often, one has to use synthetic data and synthetic workloads for the following reasons:

- No real-world data or customer data are available because of legal issues and other sensitivities associated with customer data, or the software is a new product and there is no customer yet.
- Synthetic workload is more flexible as it can easily be modified to answer various kinds of *what–if* questions.
- A synthetic workload is still valuable if it is sufficiently representative.

The performance metrics for OLTP and batch jobs are intuitive and easy to understand quantitatively. However, it can be difficult in reality for people to get used to using a quantitative metric, such as response time in seconds for OLTP activities or throughput in objects or transactions/second for batch jobs, to describe a performance problem. You may often hear users complaining that the system is *slow*, but they won't tell you quantitatively how slow it is. You have to characterize the performance of the system quantitatively in the user's environment so that you can compare it with the expected performance based on your own benchmarking tests. Then you can decide what needs to be done to bring the reportedly poor performance back to the level you would expect.

Next, I will describe the performance metrics for both OLTP and batch jobs.

3.3.1 Performance Metrics for OLTP Workloads

Since OLTP workloads tend to simulate real user activities, the performance of an OLTP type software system is measured by *response time* experienced by the users. The response time is the time duration measured from a user's perspective from initiating an action to receiving the response from the system. For example, the user login response time is the time duration from a user clicking on the login button to actually seeing the next screen indicating that the user has successfully logged in.

It's important not to confuse *response time* with *think time*. *Think time* measures the time duration spent by a user on preparing input and digesting the content of the response until initiating the next action to the system, whereas *response time* measures the time spent by the system actually processing the user request. A system would be idle when a user is *thinking* or entering input.

Every load test tool provides the option for specifying think times. It must be clarified that the differentiation between response time and think time leads to the differentiation between *active* users and *concurrent* users to a system. The following formula summarizes clearly the subtlety of active users (N_{active}) versus concurrent users ($N_{\text{concurrent}}$):

$$N_{\text{concurrent}} = N_{\text{active}} \left(\frac{Response\ time}{Response\ time + Think\ time} \right) \tag{3.1}$$

From Equation (3.1) it is clear that there are always more active users than concurrent users with nonzero think times. Concurrent users are those who are actually stressing the system. In reality, people may just say "users" without qualifying whether they mean concurrent or active users. Or when they say concurrent users, they actually mean active users.

Calling active users concurrent users is a misnomer. To see why this is so, the following case study is provided to show the enormous difference between the number of active users and the number of concurrent users when the think time gets large compared to the response time.

■ **Case Study 3.5: Active Users Versus Concurrent Users**

Let's say that an OLTP lab test indicates that an average response time of 2 seconds can be achieved with an average think time of 90 seconds for 460 active users. Then how many concurrent users can this OLTP system support, and how many active users can this OLTP system support with different average think times? The answers are summarized in Figure 3.10. The number of concurrent users this application can support is 10. However, the number of active users this application can support depends on think times. It is seen that the think times have large impacts on how many active users this OLTP system can actually support.

Unless specifically requested by the customer, an OLTP benchmarking effort should always use the number of active users to quantify the actual number of users a system under test can support. Of course, think times specified in the load test scripts must be as realistic as possible. In addition, think times should be static and as

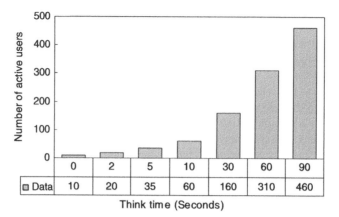

Figure 3.10   *Number of active users that an OLTP system can support with think times varying from 0 to 90 seconds.*

consistent as possible over time, as dynamic think times can introduce artificial effects into the tests, which may result in a false statement about how many active users a system can actually support.

Most of the time, you need a commercial quality load test tool to measure the performance of an OLTP system with simulated OLTP workloads. You should consult the original documents about how to use such tools. You may want to take a formal course to help make sure that the tools will be used properly. Any test can generate some numbers about the performance of a software system. However, numbers make sense only when each step of the test is carried out properly.

An OLTP workload simulating a real-world use scenario typically yields the following artifacts after a load test is complete:

- Evolution of the active number of virtual users simulated
- Evolution of the overall response time for the entire test duration
- Evolution of the response time for each individual user activity
- HTTP throughput in terms of hits per second on the Web server
- Evolution of transaction rate over time
- Distribution of response times in terms of percentiles

To help understand the artifacts of an OLTP test better, Case Study 3.6 is provided.

■ Case Study 3.6: Performance Test on an OLTP System

Figure 3.11 shows some artifacts from a typical OLTP performance test using a real product. The test started at 9:13 PM and lasted about one hour. The entire setup consisted of a Web server, an application server, and a database server, which is a typical N-tier architecture. Four different user groups were specified, with some users creating objects and some users searching and modifying objects.

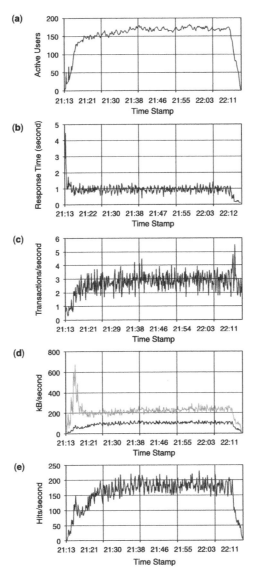

Figure 3.11 (a) Number of active users recorded; (b) overall average response time; (c) transaction rate; (d) data transfer rate (upper curve: HTTP response data in kB/s; lower curve: HTTP request data in kB/s); and (e) HTTP hits (request + response) per second recorded at each instant during an OLTP performance test run.

The charts show the number of active users, overall response time for all user groups, transaction rate, Web server HTTP data exchange rate, and hits per second recorded at each sampling interval during the test, respectively.

Note that in Figure 3.11d, which shows data transferred to and from the Web server, the lower curve shows the request data and the upper curve shows the

TABLE 3.1 Summaries on the Artifacts of a Typical OLTP Workload Test

Artifact	Measured Data for Each Attribute
Number of active users	182
Overall response time	Minimum: 0 s
	Average: 0.94 s
	Maximum: 28 s
	Standard deviation: 2.9 s
Transactions	Total: 10,344
	Average rate: 2.7/second
Data transfer	Total: 1,175 MB
(request + response)	Transfer rate: 307 kB/s
Web server hits	Total: 600,064
	Average rate: 157/second

response data. The transfer rate of hundreds of kilobytes per second shown on the chart is far below the typical network bandwidth of gigabits per second. This low network utilization indicates that the network is not the bottleneck. How to conduct performance bottleneck analysis will be covered in more detail in later chapters.

Charts like Figure 3.11 are interesting for showing how the test evolved from start to finish. Eventually, we have to use statistical averaging to help communicate the performance test results quantitatively, such as Table 3.1 for the OLTP test illustrated above.

When each test is completed, it's necessary to check the number of errors that occurred. If the error percentage is below a few percent, the test is valid and acceptable. However, if you get a lot of errors, the test is not valid and you need to resolve those errors. Occurrence of errors is traceable with an OLTP load test tool, as shown in Figure 3.12, which shows zero errors occurred.

Response times can be further drilled down to per user group activity. For example, with the OLTP load test example shown earlier, there were four user groups specified together with their assigned weights or percentages:

- repCreateOrder user group (30%)
- viewModifyOrder user group (15%)

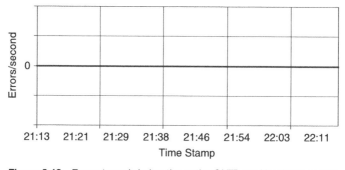

Figure 3.12 Errors traced during the entire OLTP workload test period.

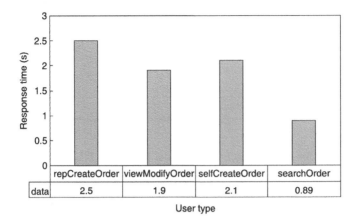

Figure 3.13 *Average response times for each user group.*

- selfCreateOrder user group (15%)
- searchOrder user group (40%)

The above distribution implies that the user scenario assumed that 30% of the users were customer representatives who were creating orders, 15% of the users were viewing and modifying orders, 15% of the self-service users were creating orders, and 40% of the users were searching orders. The ratios can be adjusted to answer various types of what–if questions.

Figure 3.13 shows the average response times for each user group from the OLTP load test example shown earlier, which were 2.5 s, 1.9 s, 2.1 s, and 0.9 s for those four user groups, respectively. Note that those response time numbers do not include think times. Think time is the user's own time and is not controllable by computer systems.

While average response time is one of the widely used metrics for measuring the performance of OLTP systems, some people prefer using *percentiles* to more realistically quantify actual response times perceived by actual users. Figure 3.14 shows the

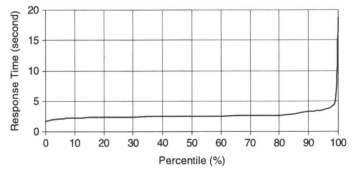

Figure 3.14 *Percentile response times for repCreateOrder user group (50th percentile—2.5 s; 90th percentile—3.3 s; 95th percentile—3.5 s; 99th percentile—4.8 s).*

TABLE 3.2 Comparison Between Average and 90% Percentile Response Times for Different User Groups Associated with the OLTP Example

User Group	Average (s)	90th Percentile (s)
repCreateOrder	2.5	3.3
viewModifyOrder	1.9	2.4
selfCreateOrder	2.1	2.7
searchOrder	0.9	1.1

percentile chart for the first user group of the earlier OLTP example, from which various percentile response time numbers can be extracted.

The general consensus is that the 90% percentile response time is closer to what a user would perceive in reality. In Figure 3.14, the 90th percentile response time for the first group of users associated with the OLTP workload example discussed earlier is 3.3 s, in comparison with the average response time of 2.5 s. This is shown in Table 3.2 together with the comparisons between 90th percentile response time and average response time for all other user groups as well.

Before concluding this section, it's necessary to clarify that the total elapsed time or transaction time defined for an interactive user action has three parts:

$$OLTP\ Transaction\ time = User\ time + System\ time + Browser\ time \qquad (3.2)$$

where *User time* represents the time from the user, for example, think time and the time for clicking a button or entering a command, *System time* measures the elapsed time or the round-trip time on a server system from when a user request leaves a user's machine to when the response arrives at the user's machine, and *Browser time* measures the time spent locally on a user's machine for rendering the server response. The response times obtained with an OLTP load test tool typically represent the system time only without including *User time* and *Browser time*.

In the next section, we'll discuss the performance metrics for batch jobs.

3.3.2 Performance Metrics for Batch Jobs

The performance of a batch job is measured in *throughput*, in contrast with *response time* for OLTP workloads. Throughput measures the number of tasks completed or the number of objects created within a given period of time. For example, a billing application may need to reconcile customer accounts on a regular basis, say, monthly. The monthly customer account reconciliation job might be scheduled to run within a 2-hour window at night at the beginning of each month. The performance of this batch job can be measured in terms of the number of accounts reconciled within the 2-hour window, which can be translated into throughput, the number of accounts reconciled per hour.

Other examples of batch job throughput may include *objects created per second, documents created per second, purchase orders created per second, tickets created per second*, and so on. For longer batch jobs, it might make more sense to use *per minute* or *per hour* so that you don't end up with fractional entities created per second.

Next, let's examine a specific case study.

■ Case Study 3.7: Performance Test with a Batch Job

Figure 3.15 shows an example of batch job throughput using a real-world enterprise application. The horizontal axis represents the number of objects created in *thousands* with time, and the vertical axis represents the throughput in terms of objects created per second at the instant when a specified number of objects were created. At the end of the run, over one million objects were created. The overall average throughput was 228 objects/second, with one million objects created over a period of 1 hour and 13 minutes. This high throughput was obtained with 20 threads running on a high-end application server system and a high-end database server system. However, the concrete details with this application and the systems used for the test are less important here.

Figure 3.15 shows a well-balanced, healthy, and steady throughput evolution as more and more objects were created. This benefited from a combination of good design, efficient implementation, and heavy performance optimization and tuning efforts put into the product development. This is the ideal case you want to have with your batch jobs, or in other words, you don't want to see throughput going down with time as more and more objects are created. I'll provide an example of throughput deteriorating with time in a later section and show you how to analyze the problem and come up with a solution to fix it.

Although, in general, we always look at the statistic averages of software performance metrics such as response time and throughput, you can also have a microscopic view of the performance metrics at each instant of time. Such microscopic views are especially useful for performance engineers to analyze the performance

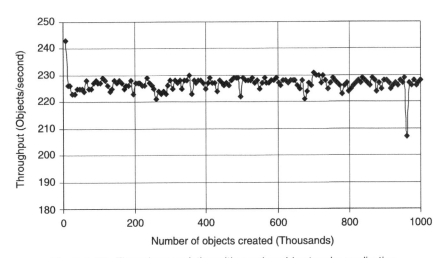

Figure 3.15 *Throughput evolution with a real-world enterprise application.*

test runs to look for ways to understand and improve the performance of the software under development.

Figure 3.16 shows the microscopic views of the throughput evolution associated with the one million object creation test shown in Figure 3.15. Figure 3.16a shows the instantaneous throughput for the creation of the object instances, whereas Figure 3.16b shows the instantaneous throughput for the creation of the object relation instances.

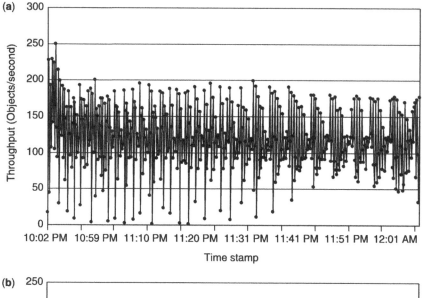

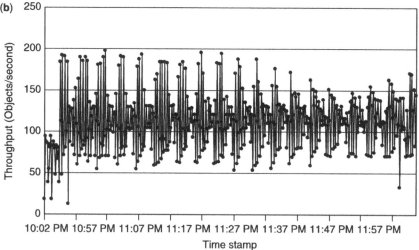

Figure 3.16 (a) Throughput of a batch job that created half a million objects. (b) Throughput of a batch job that created half a million relations.

Figure 3.16 was generated with the data extracted according to the creation time stamps of the object instances from the database with a simple SQL script. The extracted data was then imported into an Excel spreadsheet. Actually, the object instances and object relation instances were created concurrently. Showing the instantaneous throughput of both object types may help one understand which type of object creation is more expensive and how it can be improved.

Apparently, according to Figures 3.11b and 3.15, both response time and through-put fluctuate within a certain range with time. This kind of microscopic, stochastic behavior is intrinsic with software performance measurements, as with any measurements in other fields. It underscores the fact that even under exactly the same test conditions, repeating the same tests may not yield exactly the same test results. This leads to the question of what degree of fluctuation or reproducibility in software perform-ance test results is acceptable—which is the topic of the next section.

3.4 STOCHASTIC NATURE OF SOFTWARE PERFORMANCE MEASUREMENTS

For a software system, its performance can be measured more quantitatively than any other aspect. However, it's a fact that both response time numbers and throughput numbers are stochastic in nature, as illustrated in the previous sections. Let's say we keep the hardware, software, and system configurations the same, and we repeat the same test several times; whether it's an OLTP workload, a batch job, or a simple API level unit performance test, the measured performance numbers, either response time or throughput, may differ from run to run under exactly the same test conditions. In general, one should be cautious in interpreting any performance number changes of less than 10% as improvements or degradations associated with any code changes or system configuration changes. Keep in mind that performance results are statistical numbers and statistics do contain errors.

Fluctuation in software performance test results is an important issue. That's because all software performance tests, whether it's for benchmarking, regression test-ing, optimization, or tuning, strongly depend on the accuracy and reproducibility of the test results. To some extent, we can say that software performance is stochastic in nature. This is a very delicate issue that must be dealt with cautiously. It's necessary to have a good estimate of the fluctuation of the test results so that such fluctuations will not be interpreted as performance gains or losses associated with whatever changes were made to any test conditions. Whenever I hear people say they made a 5% improvement or they lost 5% performance, I always wonder if that's actually real or purely from the test result fluctuation that is something intrinsic with any software performance tests.

In reality, it might be very difficult to control the test conditions no matter how hard you try. For example, if all systems under test are part of a LAN that is shared with other daily business operations in your organization, the performance test numbers taken with the same workload and test procedure during morning hours might differ significantly from those taken at midnight—by "significantly" I mean anywhere from 20% to a factor of 2 or more. However, this should not be the case if your test is not network bottlenecked.

Even if your test is not network bottlenecked, you may still not see the ideal reproducibility or precision that you might expect with all the same test conditions. My recommendation is that, as long as the fluctuation is less than 5%, you should let it go. However, if you are seeing that your test results differ from run to run by more than 10% even with exactly the same test conditions used for repeating the same test, you need to stop doing further tests and think about what is responsible for the noticeable fluctuations in your test results. Continuing to generate invalid performance numbers is no better than generating no numbers.

In general, with a fresh setup in a new environment, I do not recommend taking the first few tests seriously. The first few tests are just warm-up exercises for you. Take this opportunity to check out the hardware and the system configurations. Then evaluate how reproducible your tests are with the same test conditions. This is a prerequisite for establishing confidence in the tests you will conduct.

If you do observe large fluctuations in your test results, here is a list of things that you can check out to help narrow down what is causing the problem:

- Design and configure your test so that it will run for at least 10 minutes. A longer test duration tends to smooth out fluctuations.
- Make sure that data caching at various levels, such as at storage level, file system level, database level, and application level, is taken into account. This is especially true for database-intensive applications.
- Make sure that you use exactly the same procedure. This is very important for regression tests. For example, if you miss updating database statistics, you might see very different test results at the end of your test. The regression test typically is used for checking whether changes made to software are causing performance slow-downs. You certainly don't want to correlate performance slow-downs due to stale statistics or any non-software-related changes to the changes made to your software. This kind of mismatch may cause panic in your organization and compromise your credibility if it happens too often.
- To some extent, only you know what you are doing. You must minimize the fluctuations in your test results to a satisfactory level so that you do not raise false alarms too often.

However, we do want to see positive changes in the performance and scalability of a software system when intentional changes are made either to the software itself, to the hardware on which it is run, or to the configurations with which it is set to run. In this book, all the variables that can affect the performance and scalability of a software system are classified as software performance and scalability factors. Prior to presenting many performance and scalability factors, I'd like to introduce you to Amdahl's law, which is the law for understanding the impact of the performance improvement made with a subsystem on the overall performance of the system.

3.5 AMDAHL'S LAW

Amdahl's law originated from explorations four decades ago on how one could enhance the performance of a computer system by using multiple parallel processors. Here it is adapted for evaluating the performance of a software system that consists of a series of subsystems such as a typical three-tier system composed of a Web server, an application server, and a database server.

Since we prefer to explore multiple factors one at a time, let's assume that we are dealing with a software system that consists of two subsystems. We'll use the *elapsed time* as the performance measure of the system so that it would apply to both OLTP and batch jobs. Amdahl's law helps estimate how much speedup one can have for the entire system if a subsystem is made faster. We often come up with such questions when we try to figure out how we can make a system run faster by improving some parts of it. So Amdahl's law is very applicable for us to evaluate the potential improvement on the performance and scalability of a software system quantitatively by improving the performance of the subsystems.

Let's say that we have a system that consists of subsystem 1 and subsystem 2. The time for the system to process a request is T_1 on subsystem 1 and T_2 on subsystem 2, so the total elapsed time on the overall system is $T_1 + T_2$. Let's further assume that we can potentially improve the elapsed time on the second subsystem by n times, which is termed the *enhancement* for convenience in this book. So the performance gain (G) by making the second subsystem n times faster can be derived as follows:

$$G = \frac{T_1 + T_2}{T_1 + T_2/n}$$

$$\text{or} \quad G = \frac{T_1 + T_2}{T_1 + T_2 - T_2\left(1 - \dfrac{1}{n}\right)}$$

$$\text{or} \quad G = \frac{1}{1 - \dfrac{T_2}{T_1 + T_2}\left(1 - \dfrac{1}{n}\right)}$$

$$\text{or} \quad G = \frac{1}{1 - f\left(1 - \dfrac{1}{n}\right)}$$

$$\text{or} \quad G = \frac{1}{1 - f + \dfrac{f}{n}} \tag{3.3}$$

where $f = T_2/(T_1 + T_2)$ is the *original* fraction of the elapsed time spent on subsystem 2 relative to the *original* total elapsed time of the entire system. For convenience, we call f the *impact factor* in this book. The lower the impact factor associated with a subsystem, the less the gain would be for the overall system when that subsystem is made faster.

When applying Amdahl's law, it's important to keep in mind that the impact factor f is calculated based on the *original* elapsed times on the subsystem and the overall system, respectively. We'll present a case study to show how much gain can be expected for the overall system by making a subsystem 10 times faster ($n = 10$) by varying the impact factor f according to Equation (3.3).

■ Case Study 3.8: Amdahl's Law

Instead of showing a single data point with a specific enhancement (n) and a specific impact factor (f), Figure 3.17 shows how much gain (G) can be expected for the overall system if a subsystem can be made 10 times faster ($n = 10$) with different values for the impact factor (f).

It is not surprising that the larger the impact factor for the subsystem being enhanced, the larger the gain for the overall system. It is seen that with the fixed enhancement of 10 times for the subsystem, on the lower end of $f = 10\%$, the gain for the overall system is 10% as well, while on the higher end of $f = 90\%$, the gain for the overall system is about a factor of 5. Of course, for $f = 1$, namely, the subsystem is the overall system itself, the gain for the overall system is equal to the enhancement for the subsystem.

Although the implication from Amdahl's law is so obvious, in reality, many people simply make bold statements that if they can make some subsystem twice as fast, then they can make the overall system twice as fast as well. Some design decisions are actually based on such obvious fantasies.

In the next section, I'll show you some real-world performance and scalability enhancement examples, which might be hard to quantify with Amdahl's law, but

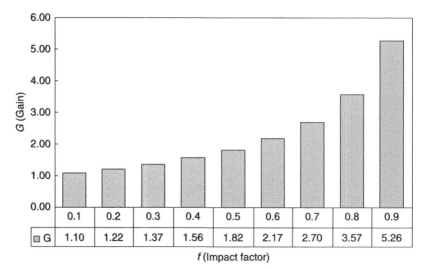

Figure 3.17 *Performance gain (G) for the overall system versus the impact factor (f) for a subsystem with a potential enhancement of 10 times (n = 10), calculated with Equation (3.3).*

they are really effective. Hopefully, you can apply some of the examples here to your product and see immediate improvements on the performance and scalability of your product.

3.6 SOFTWARE PERFORMANCE AND SCALABILITY FACTORS

To some extent, the performance and scalability of a software system might be one of the most mysterious aspects of software. That's because there are so many factors that can affect the performance and scalability of a software system. Some of these factors include:

- Raw performance and scalability of the underlying hardware platform. Since software runs on hardware, hardware certainly is one of the most important factors that determine how fast software can run when some workloads are put on it. There are four categories of hardware factors: CPU, memory, storage, and network. Each category is characterized with different specs:
  a. For CPU, those specs include the CPU architecture, CPU clock speed, number of CPUs, amount of cache on the processor, and the memory bus speed.
  b. For memory, it's not that complicated: most of the time, it's as simple as how much memory is installed on the system.
  c. For storage, one needs to know whether it's internal or external. In addition to the total amount of storage space available, one also needs to know the number of I/O controllers and the number of ports on each controller as well as the number of physical disks. If a certain level of RAID is used, one needs to know how many disks were used to configure that RAID level. The amount of cache at the storage level is critical for helping boost I/O performance as well.
  d. For networks, one needs to know the number of network cards and ports installed on the computer systems under test as well as the maximum bandwidth such as 100 Mbps or 1 Gbps. It's also necessary to know if all servers are on the same subnet of a LAN or if they have to communicate with each other across a firewall or WAN.
- How hardware is configured. All hardware systems are designed for potentially maximizing the performance and scalability of the software applications that run on it. Some examples may include:
  a. With Intel-based servers, you may want to check whether hyperthreading is enabled if applicable, because it may help boost the performance of your application by as much as 30%, as was shown in Case Study 1.1 in Chapter 1.
  b. With local disks on your Microsoft Windows OS based servers, you may want to check whether *Enable disk caching on the disk* is checked, as it may speed up your I/O significantly. You can check this out by following Computer Management | Device Manager | Disk drives | Disk device |

Properties | Policy. You can also enable disk caching on UNIX systems using the disk *format* command. But be careful not to erase all your data on the disks.

c. If you are using Microsoft Windows OS based servers and your application is network intensive, you may want to make sure that the network adapter media type is set to full duplex. You can check this out by following Computer Management | Device Manager | Network Adapters | Ethernet | Properties | Advanced | Speed & Duplex | . . . Full.

- Operating system platform. Given the same hardware, application software installed on different operating system platforms may exhibit different performance and scalability characteristics.

- Database system platform. Given the same hardware and operating system, database-dependent enterprise applications may exhibit different performance and scalability characteristics with different database systems.

- How your database is configured, which is a whole category on its own and I will give some specific examples later in detail.

- Configuration settings of your software itself, for example, whether it's single-threaded or multithreading capable, the number of threads configured if multithreading capable, caching implementation and enabling, and database connection pool settings.

- How your software product is designed and implemented. With given hardware and the available knobs for configuring and tuning hardware systems, this is the most critical factor for determining the performance of your software. One of the objectives of this book is to help you design and implement performance and scalability into your software product by adopting all well-known performance practices and following an effective performance and scalability testing methodology.

This seems to be a long list for software performance and scalability factors, but we only scratched the surface of it. We are not trying to address all software performance and scalability factors in this section. Instead, we simply attempt to raise the awareness that software performance and scalability are determined by numerous factors instead of just one or two. It's not uncommon to see orders of magnitude better performance from the start time to when everything gets settled down.

In the following sections, I'll present a few case studies to help reinforce the notion of *software performance and scalability factors*. These case studies came from my experience with real products and are representative of many software products developed in many organizations. Let's begin with the hardware as one of the most important software performance and scalability factors in the next section.

3.6.1 Hardware

Although it's so obvious that the raw performance and scalability of hardware is very critical for the performance and scalability of a software system, it's not uncommon to find out that a lot of preproduction testing efforts tend to use undersized hardware.

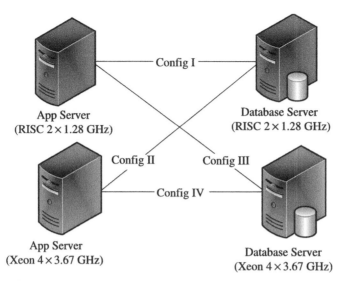

Figure 3.18 *Four different test configurations for showing the dependence of software performance on hardware.*

To demonstrate how important the hardware is for the performance and scalability of a software system, I'd like to share with you one of my real experiences with a customer in resolving critical performance escalations.

To help determine the cause of the customer's performance problem, I installed the identical software stack on two different hardware setups, one consisting of two identical computer servers both using RISC processors, and the other consisting of two identical computer servers both using Intel Xeon processors. Each RISC box had two 1.28-GHz processors, and each Xeon box had four 3.67-GHz processors. One box was used for the application server, and the other was used for the database server.

As shown in Figure 3.18, I had four test configurations based on all possible pairings of the application server to the database server: RISC-to-RISC, Xeon-to-RISC, RISC-to-Xeon, and Xeon-to-Xeon.

Without going into any more details than necessary, the performance of the same software application tested with each configuration is shown in Figure 3.19. It is seen that:

- With both the application server and the database server installed on the two identical RISC-based systems, the application exhibited an average throughput of 6.5 objects/second.
- With the application server installed on a Xeon-based system and the database server on a RISC-based system, the application exhibited an average throughput of 7 objects/second.
- With the application server installed on a RISC-based system and the database server on a Xeon-based system, the application exhibited an average throughput of 12 objects/second.

- With both the application server and the database server installed on the two identical Xeon-based systems, the application exhibited an average throughput of 35 objects/second.

Apparently, in this test case, the faster CPUs delivered better performance. Let's use the total CPU power of a computer system to quantify this interesting performance enhancement from the slower CPUs to the faster CPUs. The total CPU power of a computer system is defined as the product of the number of CPUs and the CPU clock rate. It is interesting to note from Figure 3.20 that the throughput scaled

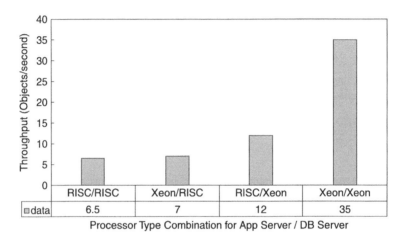

Figure 3.19 *Performance of the same application with different hardware pairings for application server and database server. RISC/RISC, Xeon/RISC, RISC/Xeon, and Xeon/Xeon correspond to the four different configurations labeled in Figure 3.18.*

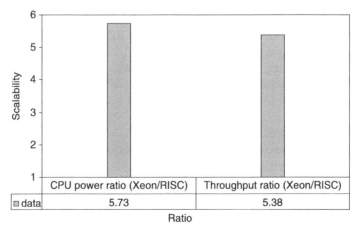

Figure 3.20 *The performance of an enterprise application scales linearly with the hardware CPU processing power.*

almost linearly from RISC to Xeon: a CPU power ratio of 5.73 from RISC-to-RISC configuration to Xeon-to-Xeon configuration yielded a 5.38 times performance improvement, which could potentially cut a one-day job into a few hours.

Convinced by my carefully designed tests and quantitative test results, the customer happily upgraded his hardware and achieved the performance expectation based on his business requirements.

In the next section, I'll demonstrate how the operating system can be a potential performance and scalability factor.

3.6.2 Operating System

Given the same hardware, the performance of the same application may vary, depending on what operating system is installed to host the application. In this section, an example on Windows versus Linux in terms of application performance is presented. Note that the purpose here is not to stir up a war about which platform performs better. Instead, my purpose is to show how the performance of an enterprise application may depend on the operating system on which it is installed to run. Also, to make it a fair comparison, no OS-specific tunings applied to either platform: namely, the performance numbers were taken out-of-the-box for each OS platform.

Because there were four identical Intel Xeon based servers with database involved, there were actually four different test configurations, as shown in Figure 3.21. The Windows 2003 Enterprise Server was installed on two systems and a specific flavor of Linux Enterprise Server was installed on the other two systems so that we had two Windows systems and two Linux systems.

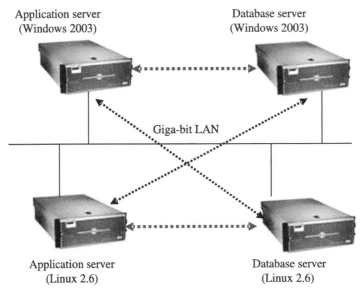

Figure 3.21 *Windows and Linux test configurations.*

These four test configurations were:

1. Win/Win configuration with both the application server and the database server on the two separate Windows systems.
2. Linux/Win configuration with the application server on a Windows system and the database server on a Linux system.
3. Linux/Linux configuration with both the application server and the database server on the two separate Linux systems.
4. Win/Linux configuration with the application server on a Windows system and the database server on a Linux system.

The common factors for this comparison of Windows versus Linux include the following:

- *Hardware.* Four identical server systems with the following specs for each system: 4 Intel Xeon quad-core processors at 2.4 GHz and 16 GB RAM.
- *Enterprise Application.* Two different versions of the same application—one compiled for Windows, and the other for Linux.
- *Database.* Same Oracle 10g except that one was the Windows version and the other was the Linux version.
- *Workload.* Same workload driven from a same-batch job diver inserting objects into the database.

As we stated, the test tool inserts objects into the database through the application server APIs. The same test procedure was repeated on each test configuration with 12 threads concurrently inserting objects into the database. The results are summarized and shown in Figure 3.22.

Based on the test results shown in Figure 3.22, it is seen that:

- With both the application server and the database server on Windows, a throughput of 290 objects/second was achieved, while with both the application server and the database server on Linux, a throughput of 152 objects/second was achieved. This seems to indicate that Linux was about 50% slower than Windows with this specific example.
- With the application server on Linux and the database server on Windows and Linux, respectively, a same throughput of 152 objects/second was achieved, which seems to indicate that it's the application server on Linux that caused the slow-down.

In order to understand why the application seemed to be slower on Linux than on Windows with this specific example, the system resource utilizations were examined for the test configurations of Win/Win and Linux/Linux. As shown in Figure 3.23, it seems that an unusually high kernel CPU utilization of 31% was observed on the

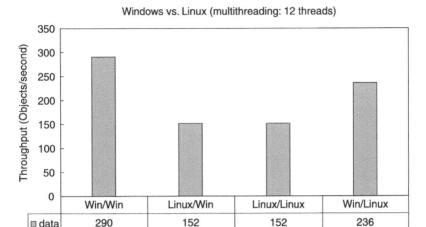

Figure 3.22 *Multi-threading performance comparisons between Windows and Linux.*

application server installed on Linux. This might indicate that multithreading of this application was implemented more efficiently on Windows than on Linux.

In order to verify whether it's an issue of multithreading implementation with the application on Linux, the same test was repeated with only a single thread inserting objects into the databases on the two configurations of Win/Win and Linux/Linux, respectively. Interestingly, as shown in Figure 3.24, the same throughput of 97 objects/second was achieved on both the Windows and the Linux setups. Although it's not 100% conclusive, it does indicate that multithreading implementation with this application might be less efficient on Linux with this specific example.

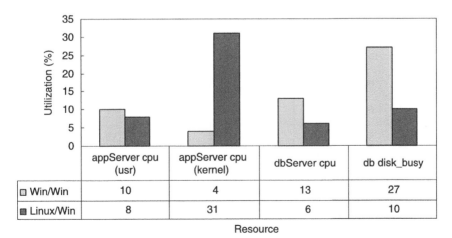

Figure 3.23 *High portion of the kernel CPU utilization on the application server installed on Linux.*

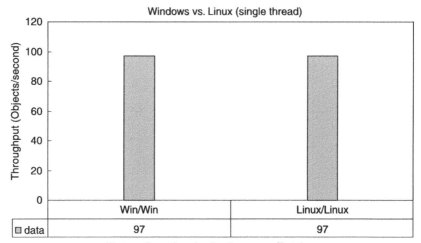

Figure 3.24 *Same performance between Windows and Linux with the same application running in* single thread mode.

Using a similar application but with more complex application logic, a series of tests were run on both Windows and Linux platforms to insert about 190,000 objects into the database by varying the number of threads, respectively. The test results are shown in Figure 3.25. This time, comparable performance of the same application was obtained on Windows and Linux platforms.

As stated earlier in this section, the purpose of this example is not to show which operating system is more superior to the other. Instead, I'd like to caution that the

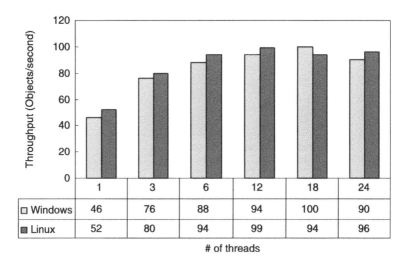

Figure 3.25 *Performance comparison of the same application between Windows and Linux platforms.*

operating system is indeed an important performance and scalability factor even given the same hardware and the same application.

In the next section, I'll show you another important performance and scalability factor for database-intensive enterprise applications.

3.6.3 Database Statistics

It's well known that database performance strongly depends on the most up-to-date statistics for the database server query optimizer to decide on the optimal execution plans. This is especially true with Oracle® 10g, which is extremely flexible for intervening externally on how the optimizer chooses optimal execution plans for frequently executed SQL queries.

Let's first explain what optimizer statistics are. Database optimizer statistics basically are computed profiles for database objects such as tables and indexes. If such statistics are up-to-date and known to the query optimizer, the query optimizer is able to compute all possible execution plans for a query and select the least costly one for the execution of that query.

Very often, when a database-intensive application is found to be significantly slower than it used to be, simply updating the optimizer statistics for a Schema might immediately solve all the performance problems. Figure 3.26 shows the magic effect of database optimizer statistics on the performance of an application. For the same test, it is seen that the throughput was doubled after the Oracle 10g optimizer statistics were updated during the time interval between 22:06:17 and 22:14:28.

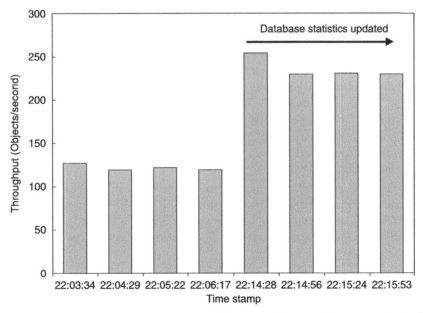

Figure 3.26 *Throughput of the same test doubled after optimizer statistics were updated with Oracle 10g.*

The next example is another powerful demonstration about how critical it is to be able to deal with the peculiarities of the query optimizer of a database product.

3.6.4 SQL Server Parameterization

A database server is essentially an SQL query processing engine. Database servers from different vendors have different designs and implementations on how SQL queries are processed, which differentiates one database server product from another.

The performance and scalability of the database-intensive enterprise applications depend strongly on how the underlying database server is configured and tuned. The performance and scalability factors associated with specific database servers are abundant. This section provides one example showing how the performance of a real-world application can be affected by the database query optimizer of the Microsoft SQL Server 2005.

This example involves a feature in the Microsoft SQL Server 2005 that can be configured to instruct the database query optimizer about how to process the SQL queries with literal values in the *where* clause. The two SQL queries are considered similar if they differ only in the literal values in the *where* clause. For example, the following SQL query contains a literal value for the *city* column in the *where* clause:

```
SELECT customer_account_id, customer_name,
customer_phone_number from customer_table where city=
'ANY_CITY';
```

If the above query is to be executed many times with different literal values for the *city* column, the SQL Server 2005 query optimizer can keep reusing the execution plan for the above query without going through the parsing process every time.

The parameter that controls how the similar SQLs should be processed by the SQL Server 2005 query optimizer is named PARAMETERIZATION. It has two settings: SIMPLE and FORCED. Each setting has a different implication for similar SQLs:

- SIMPLE. This setting is the default setting for the PARAMETERIZATION option. It instructs the SQL Server query optimizer to try to use the same execution plan for all obviously similar SQL queries, but does not enforce parameterization.
- FORCED. FORCED is a more aggressive setting than SIMPLE in terms of parameterization. When the PARAMETERIZATION option is set to FORCED, any literal value that appears in a SELECT, INSERT, UPDATE, or DELETE statement is converted to a parameter during query compilation with certain exceptions.

Figure 3.27 shows how much the performance of a real product had benefited from using a proper setting for PARAMETERIZATION. The same test of inserting 88 k objects with four threads was conducted with the two different settings of SIMPLE

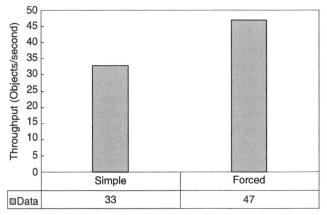

Setting of Parameterization (SQL Server 2005)

Figure 3.27 *SQL server parameterization SIMPLE versus FORCED with a batch job of a real enterprise application.*

and FORCED for the PARAMETERIZATION parameter. As is seen, the throughput was 42% better with FORCED than with SIMPLE.

You can set the PARAMETERIZATION parameter for the SQL Server 2005 by using the following T-SQL statement to enable FORCED parameterization:

```
ALTER DATABASE YOURDATABASE
      SET PARAMETERIZATION FORCED
GO
```

or using the following T-SQL statement to set it back to SIMPLE:

```
ALTER DATABASE YOURDATABASE
      SET PARAMETERIZATION SIMPLE
GO
```

You can also change this parameter through the SQL Server 2005 Management Studio by following the steps of Database | Property | Option | Parameterization. With the Management Studio you can easily verify the current setting of this parameter as well.

Whether your application should use SIMPLE or FORCED should be verified with your tests. Software performance and scalability testing is always specific to the test case that is being tested and one should never take anything for granted without actually testing it. There is no guarantee that whatever applies to one test case would apply to all other cases regardless. The example provided in the next section shows that FORCED parameterization sometimes may work against you if you have deadlock issues and you want to turn on the option of READ_COMMITTED_SNAPSHOT on SQL Server 2005 to help overcome deadlock issues when running your application in multithreaded mode.

3.6.5 Database Deadlocks

Multithreading is a norm for today's enterprise applications. However, an application might work in multithreaded mode on one database platform, but not on another database platform. If an application couldn't run in multithreaded mode on a specific database platform, then the only way to run it on that database platform is to turn to single-threaded mode, in which case, performance and scalability suffer severely.

This case study provides an example of how one could fight the database deadlock issue if the application suffers deadlocks on the SQL Server 2005. As one of the options, one can turn on the READ_COMMITTED_SNAPSHOT on the SQL Server 2005 to effectively avoid deadlocks. Without having this option turned on, the application batch job I tested running with eight threads terminated immediately about 5 minutes after the job was launched. With a single change of turning this option on, the same test of inserting the entire two million objects into the database took 9 hours and 34 minutes, which yielded a high throughput of 58 objects/ second. Running this application in a single-threaded mode would have taken about 2 days and 8 hours to complete!

However, somehow this option of READ_COMMITTED_SNAPSHOT conflicts with the option of FORCED parameterization discussed in the previous section. In my test case, READ_COMMITTED_SNAPSHOT worked only with the SIMPLE parameterization. In addition, if it is used with too many threads on lower-end systems with only one or two CPUs, it may not help prevent deadlock issues. One may see different behaviors with this option in a high-end performance test environment than in a low-end QA environment.

In the next section, I'll share with you another interesting experience with software licensing.

3.6.6 Licensing

Do not ignore the fact that even licensing is a factor that may affect the performance and scalability of your software that requires a license to run. Licensing may specify how many client connections can run concurrently between the client and the application server, which would certainly limit the performance and scalability of the licensed software.

One day I found out that suddenly my test was a lot slower than it used to be and I wasn't able to reproduce my previous test results. Because usually there are so many suspicious factors that can affect the outcome of a test, it took me a while to trouble-shoot what was causing the problem. Eventually, I found that it was because somehow all licenses for the software I was testing were gone. After adding all required licenses without changing anything else, the test results got back to normal. This experience is shown in Figure 3.28, which might be a good reminder that when you find nothing else is responsible, check out the licenses!

According to my experience, much of the software performance and scalability work with a software product is to identify and understand all software performance and scalability factors for that product so that we can come up with better designs, implementations, and more effective tunings to make it perform and scale better.

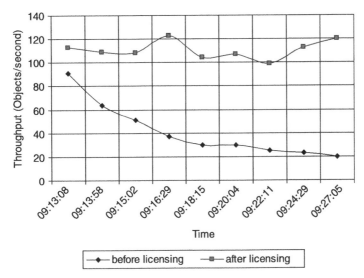

Figure 3.28 *Effects of licensing on the performance and scalability of a software application.*

Keep in mind that experience is important, and software performance and scalability work is not a guessing game. There are effective approaches to nailing down software performance and scalability issues, and all approaches start with *performance counters*, which actually correspond to all performance factors. This is where we transit from discussion of software performance and scalability factors to performance counters in the next section.

3.7 SYSTEM PERFORMANCE COUNTERS

The performance and scalability of a software system are determined by the various performance and scalability factors. Those factors that are affecting the performance and scalability of a software system most are classified as the bottlenecks. System performance counters help capture those bottlenecks.

All operating systems, whether it's Windows, UNIX, or Linux, have built-in system performance counters that can be used to monitor how a system is utilizing its resources. Based on the resource utilizations of a system, one can infer immediately what the system is doing and where the problem areas are. Capturing the system resource utilizations is one of the most fundamental tasks to be conducted for diagnosing software performance and scalability problems.

A performance counter enabled through a system monitoring tool is simply a logical entity that represents one of the aspects of a resource quantitatively. For example, one often needs to know:

- How busy the CPUs of a system are
- How much memory is being used by the application under test

- How busy the disks of a data storage system are
- How busy the networks are

System resource utilizations can be monitored in real time or collected into log files for later analysis. In this section, I describe how this can be done on Windows and UNIX platforms.

3.7.1 Windows Performance Console

On Windows-based computers, the performance monitoring utility program *perfmon* can be used to log performance counters. Since most developers and QA engineers

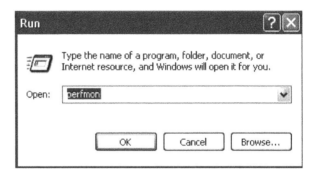

Figure 3.29 *Dialog box for starting up* perfmon.

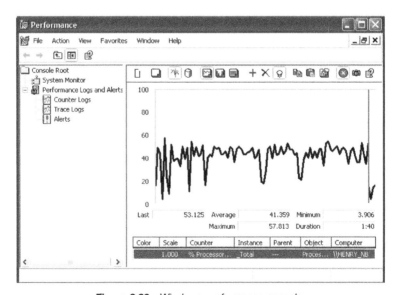

Figure 3.30 *Windows performance console.*

might have not gotten a chance to get familiar with using *perfmon*, we spend a few minutes to show how to use it here.

To start up *perfmon*, click on Start | All Programs | Run, and enter *perfmon* as shown in Figure 3.29.

Then click OK and you should see the Performance Console as shown in Figure 3.30.

The left-hand side of the Console shows two items, System Monitor and Performance Logs and Alerts. When the System Monitor is selected, the right-hand side frame displays the current readings of the added counters. At the bottom of the frame, added counters are shown. For example, Figure 3.30 shows that on the computer \\HENRY-NB, the counter *%Processor_Time* of the Performance Object *Processor* was added to display CPU utilizations. The readings associated with this counter are: Last CPU utilization reading 53.125%, Average CPU utilization 41.359%, Minimum CPU utilization 3.906%, and Maximum CPU utilization 57.813%. This is how to tell how busy the CPUs of a system are.

It might be helpful at this point to get familiar with the above performance console. Placing the mouse pointer on an icon at the top of the right-hand side frame shows what that icon is for. Some of the examples include:

- Clicking on the second icon would clear the display.
- Clicking on the third icon would enable viewing current activities.
- Clicking on the "+" icon would bring up the Add Counters dialog box for adding new counters to the monitoring list.
- Clicking on the "x" icon would remove a counter from the current monitoring list.
- Clicking on the light bulb icon would highlight the display for the counter selected currently.
- Clicking/unclicking on the red-cross icon would freeze/unfreeze displaying the current activities.

Next, let's see how to add various performance counters. Figure 3.31 shows what *Performance object* to select, what *Counters* to select, and whether to select for *All instances* or only some specific instances.

After selecting *Performance object*, *instances*, and *counters* based on your needs, click *Add* to add the desired counters. Click *Close* to exit the Add Counters dialog box. If you want to know what a specific counter is for, select the counter you are interested in, then click *Explain* and you will get a fairly detailed description about that counter.

You can adjust the sampling interval by clicking on the Properties icon and then specify *Sample automatically every n seconds*, where n is the number of seconds you desire as the sampling interval. The default 1 second shown in Figure 3.32 is too fast and you can increase it based on how long your test would last.

Real-time display is meant for short test duration only, and also, you would lose the data after closing it. You can log the counters into a *perfmon* log file and analyze the logs afterwards.

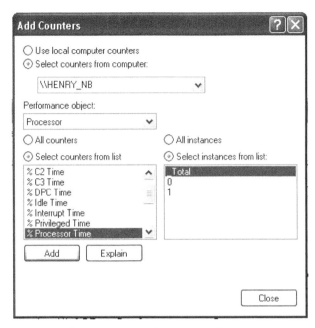

Figure 3.31 *Dialog box for adding* perfmon *counters.*

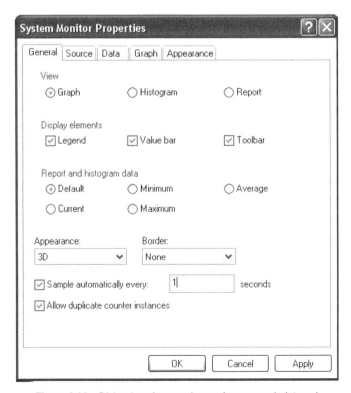

Figure 3.32 *Dialog box for entering* perfmon *sample interval.*

To set up a *perfmon* logging task, follow this procedure:

- Select *Counter Logs* under *Performance Logs and Alerts*, and right-click on *Counter Logs* to select the *New Log Settings* dialog box as shown in Figure 3.33.

- Enter a name and click on OK, which would bring up the dialog box as shown in Figure 3.34.

- From here you can add any counters you are interested in and specify a sampling interval. At the top, it shows the log file name, which will contain the performance log data for later offline analysis.

- You can specify the log format under the Log Files tab, either Binary File or Text File (Comma delimited) for working with Excel to plot charts. Even if you select binary format now, you can re-save logged data in text format later. To change the log format from binary to text with a log file, first import the logged data in binary format, and then specify the time range, add the counters you are interested in, and then display the data. Right click anywhere on the display area and re-save data in text format.

- You specify the schedules under the Schedule tab. You can select to manually start and stop or specify a logging duration to avoid logging too much unnecessary data even after a test is complete.

To analyze the *perfmon* log data, follow this procedure:

- Select the System Monitor entry, and then click on the fourth icon of View Log Data, which should bring up the dialog box as shown in Figure 3.35.

- Click on *Add* and then add the *perfmon* log file you want to analyze, which should bring up a dialog box similar to Figure 3.36.

- Click on the Time Range button to display the time range for which the counters were logged. You can move the sliding bars to adjust the exact range you want. Keep in mind that the average value of a counter is based on the exact range you select, so you may want to adjust to the exact start and stop times of your test. You should keep a daily activity log that records the exact details of your test such as test start/stop time, all test conditions, and test results so that you can easily look back at exactly what you did with your previous test. This is a good habit to have as a software performance engineer.

- Then click on the Data tab to get to the Add Counters dialog box. From there, first delete all counters and then select the counters you are interested in for analyzing your *perfmon* log data.

Figure 3.33 *Dialog box for naming a new* perfmon *log setting.*

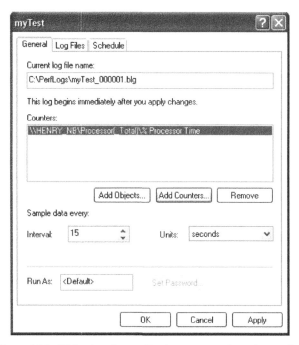

Figure 3.34   *Dialog box for configuring a new* perfmon *log setting.*

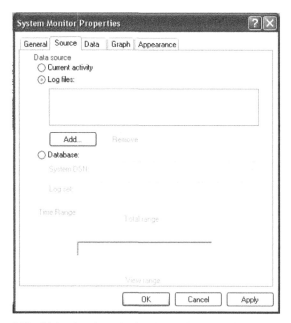

Figure 3.35   *Dialog box for selecting the* perfmon *log file to be analyzed.*

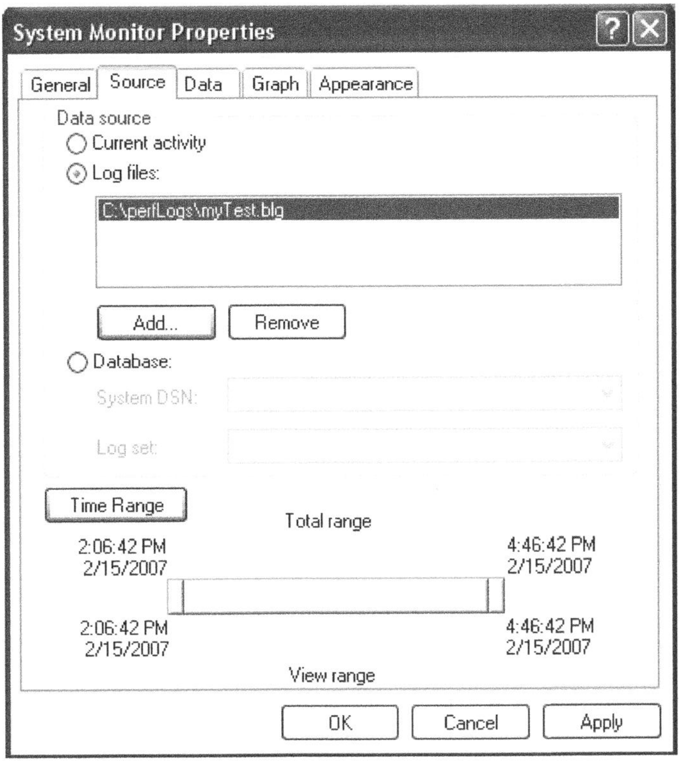

Figure 3.36 *Dialog box with a* perfmon *log file added.*

This seems to be a little bit tedious but it helps you learn *perfmon* quickly without experimenting with it yourself. Initially, it might be difficult for you to decide what counters you should select out of the hundreds of built-in counters. To help you get started, Table 3.3 shows all common *perfmon* counters I typically use for diagnosing my performance issues. You can add more based on your special needs, but this list of counters should be sufficient in general.

Before moving on to the UNIX system performance counters, I'd like to share with you some techniques of using *perfmon* to diagnose common performance and scalability issues such as memory leaks, CPU bottlenecks, and disk I/O bottlenecks. Using *perfmon* to diagnose performance and scalability issues is a very important skill to acquire for testing the performance and scalability of a software system on the Windows platform. *perfmon* is intuitive, easy to learn, and very powerful for diagnosing performance and scalability issues on Windows. This is true not only for troubleshooting the performance and scalability problems you encounter with a complex, large-scale software system, but also for figuring out what's wrong when your desktop or laptop Windows system is too slow for you to bear with.

Let's start with using *perfmon* to diagnose memory leaks.

TABLE 3.3 A Minimum Set of Perfmon Counters to be Logged for Performance Tests in Windows Environment [a]

Performance Object	Performance Counters
Processor	%Processor Time
System	Processor Queue Length
Process	%Processor Time
	Private Bytes
	Thread Count
	Virtual Bytes
	Working Set
Memory	Available MBytes
	Page Reads/sec
	Page Writes/sec
Physical disk or logical disk	%Idle Time (Note: Use 1 − %Idle for %Busy Time)
	Avg. Disk Read Queue Length
	Avg. Disk Write Queue Length
	Avg. Disk Bytes/Read
	Avg. Disk Bytes/Write
	Avg. Disk sec/Read
	Avg. Disk sec/Write
	Disk Read Bytes/sec
	Disk Write Bytes/sec
	Disk Bytes/sec
	Disk Reads/sec
	Disk Writes/sec
Network interface	Bytes Received/sec
	Bytes Sent/sec
	Bytes Total/sec

[a]Select instances that are pertinent to your tests.

3.7.2 Using perfmon to Diagnose Memory Leaks

The first chart I'd like to show is the memory growth chart, which might help you evaluate the memory leak issues associated with your application. Memory leak is a very common factor affecting the performance and scalability of a software system on Windows, especially with 32-bit Windows operating systems. It's one of the toughest issues in developing software, as most of the time, you know your software leaks memory, but it's hard to know where leaks come from. perfmon can only help diagnose whether you have memory leaks in your software; it doesn't tell you where the leaks come from. You have to use some other tools like Purify® to find and fix the memory leaks that your product suffers.

In a 32-bit environment, the maximum addressable memory space is 4 GB. On the Windows platform, this 4 GB is split between the kernel and a process. Although you can extend that 2-GB limit to 3 GB using a 3-GB switch parameter, that 3 GB may still not be enough for some applications with severe memory leak problems. So the best defense is to contain memory growth in your application. Otherwise, when that 2-GB limit is hit, your application will start to malfunction, which makes it totally unusable.

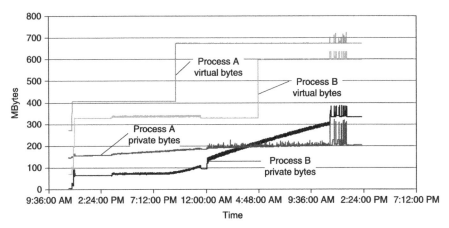

Figure 3.37 *Memory growth associated with two processes of an application written in C/C++ in a Windows environment.*

As a performance engineer, you are obligated to check memory growth with your software product by using a large volume of data. When you observe significant memory growth, you need to communicate it back to your development team so that they can fix it in time. Keep in mind that you need to make sure whether memory growth would come down after your test is complete. If it doesn't, it probably can be classified as *memory leaks*, which sounds more horrible than memory growth. There is also a likelihood that the memory growth you observe is actually memory fragmentation, which is related to how the operating system manages memory. Whether it is memory leak or memory fragmentation, they are equally bad as far as the consequences to the application are concerned.

Figure 3.37 shows memory growth with two processes of an application written in C/C++. The total test duration was about 24 hours. Note that private bytes curves are smoother than virtual bytes curves, which appear stair-cased. One should use private memory to evaluate actual physical memory consumption. It is seen that Process A is much more benign than Process B in terms of memory growth, as its private bytes curve is much flatter. Process B reached 320 MB at the end of the test, which means it might reach the 2-GB memory limit if the test lasts 5 days. From this test, it's clear that it's necessary to take some action against the memory growth for Process B.

In the next section, I'll discuss how to use *perfmon* to diagnose CPU bottlenecks.

3.7.3 Using *perfmon* to Diagnose CPU Bottlenecks

You can monitor the CPU utilizations of a Windows system using the performance object of Processor with the %Processor Time counter if you know you have only one major process such as a database server running on your system. If you have multiple processes running on your system, then use the Process performance object with the %Processor Time counter for the process instances you are concerned with.

The %Processor Time counter for the Processor performance object measures the total average CPU utilization across multiple CPUs, whereas the %Processor Time counter for the Process performance object measures the accumulative CPU utilizations across multiple CPUs. So the maximum value is 100% for the former and $N \times 100\%$ for the latter, where N is the number of total CPUs of an *N-way* Windows system. This is a subtle difference that must be accounted for when interpreting CPU utilizations.

Typically, an application might be deployed on multiple systems, for example, the application server on one physical box and the database server on another physical box. When the application is properly sized, and the application is well optimized and tuned, CPU utilizations across multiple systems should be well balanced to yield sustainable, maximum possible performance and scalability. Figure 3.38 shows such a balanced flow where the application server and database server were about equally utilized, yielding a high throughput of creating 127 objects/second. Over one million objects were created during a period of 2 hours and 11 minutes with the associated test run.

If you see the CPU utilization of the database server is going up while the CPU utilization of the application server is going down, then some tuning is required to bring both of them to a steady state. This phenomenon was called "bifurcating," which might

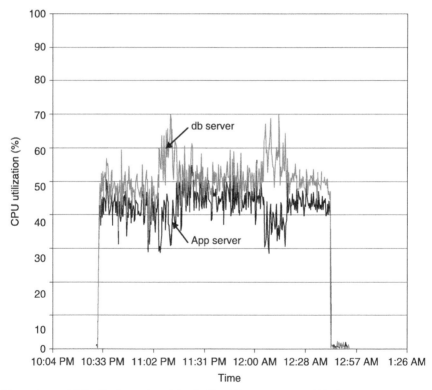

Figure 3.38   *CPU utilizations of two identical Intel Xeon systems on Windows 2003, one as the application server and the other as the database server.*

be very common for applications that are not well tuned [Liu, 2006]. This is a good example that you should not just keep generating performance test numbers. You should examine utilizations of various resources to see if there are opportunities for improving the performance and scalability of your application as well.

The general criteria for defining CPU as the bottleneck on a computer system is that the average CPU utilizations are above 70% or the average processor queue length per CPU is above two. However, there might be a case where other resources, such as disks, may become the bottleneck before the CPU does. This is especially true with database-intensive software applications. Let's look at such a scenario next.

3.7.4 Using *perfmon* to Diagnose Disk I/O Bottlenecks

In this section, I'd like to share with you a chart that shows disk activities. It is very important to make sure that your disk I/O is not the bottleneck if your application is database intensive.

perfmon provides a sufficient number of counters associated with disk activities. However, very often, you may find that the %Disk Time counter may give you some bogus numbers exceeding 100%. As a workaround, use 100 − %Idle Time to calculate the disk %Busy Time, which is equivalent to the average utilization for CPUs. Figure 3.39 shows the average disk utilizations calculated using 100 − %Idle Time for that one million object creation batch job discussed in the preceding section. The database storage used for this test was an internal RAID 0 configuration stripped across three physical disks.

Unlike CPUs, a disk utilization level of above 20% starts to indicate that I/O is the bottleneck, whereas for CPUs the threshold is about 70%. This disparity between

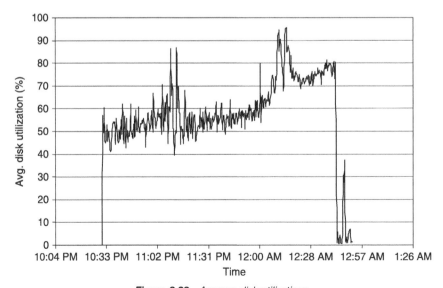

Figure 3.39 *Average disk utilizations.*

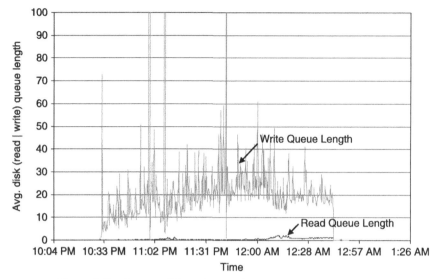

Figure 3.40 *Average disk read queue length and write queue length.*

disks and CPUs is due to the fact that CPUs in general can crank much faster than disks can spin.

Exploring disk activities is a lot more interesting than exploring CPU activities, as we can dig deeper into more metrics such as average (read | write) queue length, average (reads | writes) / sec, average disk sec / (read | write), and disk (read | write) / sec. Let's explore each of these disk activity metrics.

Figure 3.40 shows the average disk read queue length and average disk write queue length recorded during that one million object creation batch job. It is seen that the write queue length is much larger than the read queue length, which implies that a lot more disk write activities occurred than read activities. This is not surprising at all, as during this batch job test, one million objects were created and persisted to the disks, which inevitably incurred a lot more disk writes than reads.

Queue length is a measure of the number of items waiting in a queue to be processed. According to queuing theory, which will be introduced in a later chapter of this book, a resource is considered a bottleneck if its queue length is larger than 2. As we introduced earlier, the database storage used for this test was an internal RAID 0 configuration stripped across three physical disks, which would push the queue length threshold to 6. It's clear from Figure 3.40 that the write queue length was around 20, which had far exceeded the threshold value of 6. This implies that a more capable storage system would help improve the performance and scalability of this batch job further.

Figure 3.41 shows the average number of reads and writes per second that occurred during this test. There were about 300 writes/second and 50 reads/second, which once more confirmed that more writes than reads occurred during the test period for the one million object creation batch job. Remember that the throughput for this

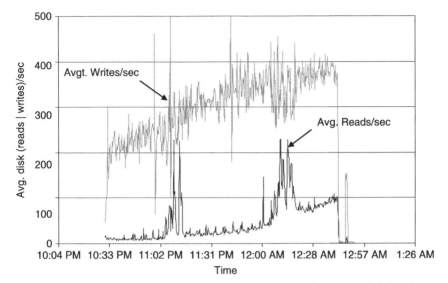

Figure 3.41 *Average number of reads and writes per second that occurred during the one million object creation batch job.*

batch job was 127 CIs/s, which implies that about 2 to 3 writes occurred per object creation on average. This seems to be normal for most database write-intensive applications.

In addition to knowing the disk queue lengths and I/O rates associated with a test, it's also insightful to know how long it takes on average per read and per write. Normally, disk times should range from 5 milliseconds to 20 milliseconds with normal I/O loads. You may get submillisecond disk times if the database storage has a huge cache, for example, from a few gigabytes to tens of gigabytes.

For this test, each disk has only a 256-MB cache, so we would expect disk read and write times to be well above 1 millisecond. Actual disk read and write times associated with this test are shown in Figure 3.42. As is seen, the average disk write time is much longer than the average disk read time, as we already know from the previous analysis that there were a lot more requests accumulated up in the write queue than in the read queue. You have confidence when all metrics are consistent with each other.

Charts are very useful for qualitatively characterizing each performance factor. However, they are less precise for *quantifying* each performance factor. To get more quantitative, you can use the View Report functionality of *perfmon* to obtain the average value of each performance counter, such as shown in Figure 3.43 with the following quantitative values for some of the indicative disk performance counters:

- Average disk utilization: 60%
- Average disk time per read: 11 milliseconds
- Average disk time per write: 73 milliseconds
- Average disk write queue length: 22

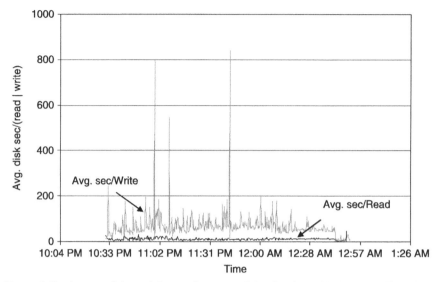

Figure 3.42   Average disk read time and average disk write time with the one million object creation batch job. Note that avg. disk sec / (read | write) are perfmon counter names and the actual units are in milliseconds.

- Disk reads/sec: 46
- Disk writes/sec: 297

Keep in mind that you need to narrow the time range of your *perfmon* log data down to the exact range corresponding to the start and end times of your test; otherwise, the averaged values won't be accurate.

Performance Console allows you to monitor system resource utilizations over an extended period of time when the test is running. It's convenient for post-testing performance and scalability analysis. However, sometimes, you may want to use another Windows utility tool—Task Manager—for checking the resource consumption on the current Windows system. This is the topic for the next section.

PhysicalDisk	1D:
%Idle Time	40.126
Avg. Disk Read Queue Length	0.502
Avg. Disk sec/Read	0.011
Avg. Disk sec/Write	0.073
Avg. Disk Write Queue Length	21.783
Disk Reads/sec	46.197
Disk Writes/sec	297.044

Figure 3.43   Perfmon report.

3.7.5   Using Task Manager to Diagnose System Bottlenecks

We'll see in this section that Task Manager is more convenient than *perfmon* for some tasks. For example:

- You may want to have a quick look at how busy the CPUs of a system are overall right now.
- You may want to check how well balanced the CPU utilizations are across multiple CPUs of the system. This actually is an easy way to tell whether the software is running in multithreaded mode by examining whether all CPUs are about equally busy simultaneously.
- You may want to check which processes are consuming most of the CPU power on this system right now.
- You may want to check how much memory is used right now. And you can drill down to which processes are consuming most of the memory.
- You may want to check the network utilization right now.
- You can even see in real time if memory is leaking or not. If you see the memory consumption of a process is only going up, then there are probably memory leaks with that process.

First, to start up Task Manager, press CTRL + ALT + DELETE and you should get a dialog box similar to Figure 3.44.

As shown in Figure 3.44 under *Performance* tab, this system has two CPUs and both of them were busy, which means that the application is a multithreaded application. It also shows that a total memory of 374 MB was used up to that moment.

You can check the network utilizations by clicking on the *Network* tab, and check the users currently logged in by clicking the *Users* tab. But the most important tab for troubleshooting a performance issue with a system is the *Process* tab.

Computer programs run on a computer system as *processes*. Each process has an ID and a name to identify itself on the system it is running. By clicking on the *Process* tab on the Windows Task Manager dialog box, you can bring up a list of processes that are running currently on the system, as shown in Figure 3.45.

A few notes about this *Process* tab:

- You may want to check the box of *Show processes from all users* at the left bottom corner of the screenshot in Figure 3.45 in order to see the processes that you are looking for.
- You can't see your processes unless they are running right now.
- You can sort by CPU Usage or Memory Usage to look for the most CPU-intensive or memory-intensive processes running on this system right now.
- You can decide on what metrics you want to be displayed by clicking on the View | Select Columns ... which would bring up the list of metrics you can select, such as shown in Figure 3.46.

As you can see from the screenshot in Figure 3.46, you can select the Memory Usage, Memory Usage Delta, and Peak Memory Usage from the view options

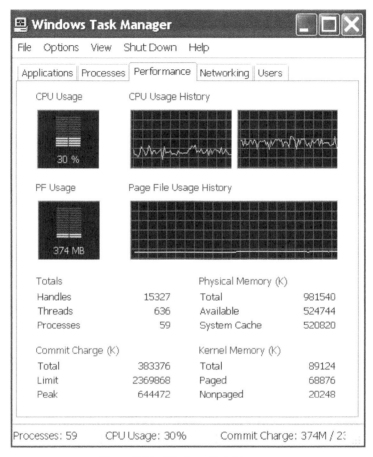

Figure 3.44 *Windows Task Manager.*

made available. These counters give a complete view of the process memory consumption. When a memory-intensive application is running, you will see the memory usage for that process keeps growing with more positive memory usage deltas than negative ones. If the memory usage doesn't come down after the process completed its task and is waiting for more new tasks, that's an indication that there is a memory leak issue with that process.

This concludes our discussion on performance counters on Windows systems. Most software development work is done on Windows, which is why we covered more topics on Windows.

However, for enterprise software applications, UNIX or Linux platforms are the most likely choice for some customers, so you might need to test out your software on these platforms as well. Instead of repeating what is already available in many UNIX/Linux texts, in the next section, I'll show you a simple script that can be used to capture the CPU and memory consumptions for the processes that you are

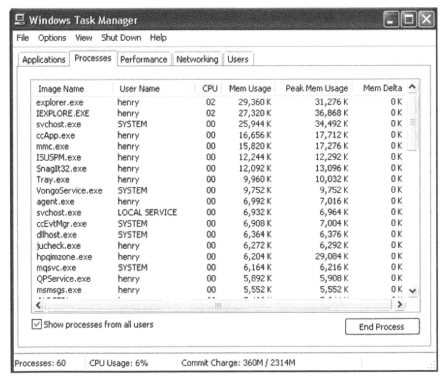

Figure 3.45 *Process view from Windows Task Manager.*

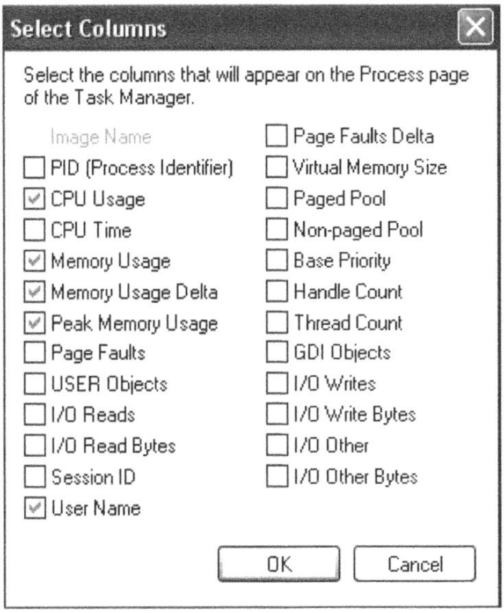

Figure 3.46 *Select columns for process view.*

concerned with. This probably is sufficient for most of your performance test needs. In a production environment, UNIX/Linux systems are typically managed by professional administrators who have developed special ways of capturing various system performance counters or simply use tools provided by vendors. That is beyond the scope of this book.

3.7.6 UNIX Platforms

On UNIX and Linux systems, vendors provide their own system performance monitoring tools, although some common utilities such as *sar* might be available on all specially flavored platforms.

Performance troubleshooting often requires monitoring resource utilizations on a per-process basis. This might be a little bit more challenging on UNIX systems than on Windows systems. On Windows, you use *perfmon* to configure which processes and what counters you want to monitor. On UNIX systems, you need a script to do the same job. Here, I'd like to share one script that I often use on a specially flavored, popular UNIX platform for capturing CPU and memory utilizations when my tests were running. Since it's written in *bash* shell, it could be run on other UNIX and Linux systems as well.

Here is the script that you can adapt to your needs for monitoring systems resource usages on a per-process basis in your UNIX or Linux environment:

```
#!/bin/bash
sleepTime=60
pattern="yourPattern"
x=0
procId=$(ps -eo pid,pcpu,time,args | grep $pattern |\
    grep -v grep | awk '{print $1}')
echo "procId="$procId
while [$x -ge 0]
do
 date=$(date)
 ps0=$(ps -o vsz,rss,pcpu -p $procId)
 x=$((x+1))
 echo $x $date $ps0 | awk '{print $1, $3, $4, $5, $8,\
    $11/1000.0, $9, $12/1000.0, $10, $13, $14}'
 sleep $sleepTime
done
```

As you see, this is a *bash* script. You need to specify how often you want to sample (*sleepTime*) and enter a string (*pattern*) that represents your process. Then you extract the process ID of that process. Using that process ID, you keep polling in an infinite loop for the counters you want to record. In this script, I was most interested in three counters, *vsz*, *rss*, and *pcpu*, which represents the virtual memory size, resident memory size, and CPU usage associated with that process. The counters *vsz* and *rss* are equivalent to the virtual bytes and private bytes counters of *perfmon* on Windows, respectively. These counters are very useful for monitoring memory growth associated with a process.

To execute this script, change to the *bash* shell environment and issue the following command:

```
prompt> ./scriptFileName > filename.txt &
```

The output is directed to a text file that you can analyze later. The text file is formatted with comma, so you can import it into an Excel spreadsheet to draw the charts you are interested in. Remember that this is an infinite loop, so you need to bring it to the foreground using the command *fg* and stop it after you are done.

If you cannot run this script, you might need to execute the command *chmod 700 scriptFileName* to set proper permissions.

Also, this simple script can be modified to monitor multiple processes in a single script.

In the next section, I'll propose several software performance data principles to help enforce the notion that software performance and scalability testing is not just about gathering data. It's about getting data that has value for your company and your customers.

3.8 SOFTWARE PERFORMANCE DATA PRINCIPLES

Before concluding this chapter, let's discuss a few software performance data principles that can help ensure that decisions made for improving performance and scalability of a software system are based on properly collected performance data. Actions based on improperly collected performance data will not yield the intended results.

When collecting software performance and scalability test data, the following principles should be observed:

Principle 1: *Hardware Principle.* Software performance and scalability tests are different from QA tests. Development and QA tests are typically conducted on very low-end systems, while performance and scalability tests should be conducted on high-end systems. There are two main reasons for the requirement of using high-end systems for performance and scalability tests:

- Low-end systems exhibit very different performance and scalability behaviors than high-end systems do. The performance and scalability problems observed on the low-end systems may simply be caused by undersized hardware, which might be absent if high-end systems are used.
- Testing the performance and scalability of a software system requires using sufficient load, which may not be doable with low-end systems.

The general principle for choosing proper hardware for software performance and scalability tests is that it should be close to what the customer will use in production, or at least much more powerful than the systems used for development and QA tests. Remember that the performance and scalability of a software system strongly depend on the hardware used for testing, and therefore do not pick undersized hardware just because it's available. If your software is enterprise class software, it doesn't make sense to run your performance and scalability tests on a single desktop with the entire software stack including the database installed on it.

Principle 2: *Platform Principle.* Here the word *platform* refers to a collection of software systems above the hardware layer on which a software application depends, for example, the operating system, database system, and any other type of middleware systems. If the software supports both Windows and UNIX, then commensurate tests should be conducted on both operating systems. Likewise, if the software supports both Oracle and Microsoft SQL Server, then commensurate tests should be conducted on both database systems. Too many permutations should not be used as an excuse for limiting the performance and scalability tests to one combination of platforms only. You might be surprised that your software performs and scales well on one platform, but not on others, as some database queries might be quite okay on one platform, but not on other platforms. In that case, you might need to add additional indexes. Do not take it for granted that your software performs and scales well on the platform you tested and therefore it will perform and scale well on other platforms as well.

Principle 3: *Reality Principle.* The test scenarios and workloads should closely mimic how your customers would use your product. Sometimes, it might be difficult to know exactly how a software system will be used by real users. It's acceptable to start with some hypothetical scenarios, but it should be taken as an iterative process; namely, the scenarios should be refined over time.

Principle 4: *Volume Principle.* Although it's acceptable to use lighter workloads for performance regression tests, one should make sure that tests using large volumes of users and data are conducted as well to reveal the true performance and scalability of a software system in real usage scenarios. Such tests are especially interesting to customers, as they want to know if the software they plan to purchase will meet their requirements with the number of users and volume of data they run. In addition, the foundation data that your test depends on should be realistic. Synthetic data might be too perfect and sometimes may not reveal the functionality and performance problems that only real users can discover. For example, when you create customer account data yourself, you may not have the correct relationships among the various entities created. This is often a difficult issue to deal with: you use your own manufactured data for your functionality and performance testing, but customers may see different functionality and performance behaviors when they use your software with their real data in a real-life environment.

Principle 5: *Reliability Principle.* Your performance and scalability test results should be reproducible with acceptable fluctuations when exactly the same test conditions are followed. This is the reliability principle for evaluating your software performance and scalability test data. The reproducibility requirement is not absolute in the sense that it allows a reasonable level of fluctuations, which ideally should be only a few percent or less. This will help avoid interpreting nondeterministic factors into performance issues and raising false performance alarms or following to wrong avenues toward solving a software performance problem.

Principle 6: *Quality Principle.* This principle measures the overall quality of the test results. In some cases, test results may satisfy all the preceding principles but may not be of high quality. For example, if the tests keep using cached data that will not be cached in the production environment due to too many users or too large a volume of data, then the test results would be invalid no matter how good they look and how reproducible they are. It's hard to define a measure of quality in general for performance and scalability test data, since it is software dependent. Only you can define the quality of your test data as you are most familiar with how your software will be used in production. Do not jump to conclusions immediately with your test results. Think hard and make sure that your test results are valid and then derive your actions based on your test data.

This is by no means a complete list of all software performance data principles. Based on your own situations, you can derive more to make sure that your test results make sense and deliver values for your organization.

Hopefully, at this point, you have gotten the concept of software performance and scalability factors. I hope you have also learned how to use Windows *perfmon* and the UNIX utilities to log various performance counters to help you identify the various factors that are critical for the performance and scalability of your software. If you have achieved these goals, you are now equipped with the necessary technical skill set to conduct software performance and scalability testing. However, that may not be enough. In the next few chapters, I'll help you learn how to analyze, optimize, and tune the performance and scalability of your software based on queuing theory and API profiling so that you will become proficient in coping with software performance and scalability challenges in general.

3.9 SUMMARY

In this chapter, we started with defining the scope of software performance and scalability testing in general, which includes four different categories: regression testing, performance testing, benchmarking testing, and scalability testing. We then elaborated with concrete case studies for the categories of regression testing and scalability testing.

We then drew a boundary between QA testing and performance testing. We emphasized that performance testing should use well-QAed versions of software so that performance work will not overlap with QA work.

We briefly introduced agile software development and extreme programming. The motivation for learning about the software development process is to help understand how software performance and scalability work can be incorporated into the software development process most effectively and efficiently.

We defined software performance metrics for both OLTP and batch jobs. OLTP workloads are measured in response times, whereas batch jobs are measured in throughput. We used concrete examples to demonstrate what artifacts one should expect from both OLTP and batch job performance tests.

We emphasized the stochastic nature of software performance measurements so that one would not interpret intrinsic fluctuations in measurements as performance gains or degradations when testing the changes introduced either to source code or to system and application configurations.

We then introduced Amdahl's law, which is very helpful for evaluating the performance gain to the overall system based on the enhancements on the subsystems.

The central part of this chapter is about understanding software performance and scalability factors such as hardware, operating system, database configurations, and application configurations. We presented plenty of real-world case studies showing various common performance and scalability factors that can be expected with a software system.

We presented step-by-step procedures about how to use *perfmon* and Task Manager to monitor the potential performance and scalability factors and how to further identify bottlenecks that limit the performance and scalability of a software system.

At this point, you should be very knowledgeable about software performance and scalability in general. You should have no difficulties in actually designing and conducting software performance and scalability tests. However, I encourage you to study through the rest of this book so that you will become much more effective and efficient in helping solve challenging software performance and scalability problems.

RECOMMENDED READING

There are quite a few very good classic texts on software performance and scalability in general that every software stakeholder should have on his/her bookshelves. I especially recommend the following:

N. Gunther, *The Practical Performance Analyst*, McGraw-Hill, 1998.

D. A. Menasce, V. A. F. Almeida, and L. W. Dowdy, *Scaling for E-Business*, Prentice Hall PTR, 2000.

D. A. Menasce, V. A. F. Almeida, and L. W. Dowdy, *Performance by Design*, Prentice Hall, 2004.

C. U. Smith and L. G. Williams, *Performance Solutions—A Practical Guide to Creating Responsive, Scalable Software*, Addison-Wesley, 2002.

Some older but still very helpful texts include:

E. D. Lazowska, J. Zahorjan, G. S. Graham, and K. C. Sevcik, *Quantitative System Performance: Computer System Analysis Using Queuing Network Models*, Prentice Hall, 1984.

R. Jain, *The Art of Computer Systems Performance Analysis*, John Wiley & Sons, 1991.

The following text is most authoritative on agile and extreme programming:

K. Beck, *Extreme Programming Explained: Embrace Change*, Addison-Wesley, 1999.

For Amdahl's law, consult the following texts:

G. M. Amdahl, Validity of the single-processor approach to achieving large scale computing capabilities, in AFIPS Conference Proceedings, Volume 30, AFIPS Press, 1967, pp. 483–485.

J. Hennessy and D. Patterson, *Computer Architecture: A Quantitative Approach*, 4th edition, Morgan Kaufmann, 2007, pp. 29–32.

The following publication is quoted in Section 3.7.3 for associating sustainable performance of software with the balance of system resource utilizations in an N-tier deployment architecture:

H. H. Liu, Applying queuing theory to optimizing enterprise software applications, in CMG 2006 Proceedings, Reno.

EXERCISES

3.1. List the top two reasons why performance regression testing is critical for each release (major or patch level) of a software product.

3.2. While figuring out how the performance of an large-scale enterprise application can be improved, a developer decides that he wants to create *one* object in the database with API logging turned on and find out where most of the execution time is spent. What can you make of it?

3.3. With a database-intensive enterprise application, a developer states that she could reduce the number of executions for an SQL query by half, and therefore she expects the application will perform twice better. What can you make of it?

3.4. A Web application is deployed on a setup consisting of a Web server, an application server, and a database server. The performance test analysis shows that 70% of the total elapsed time with a specific type of user activity was on the database server. Let's say that the amount of elapsed time spent on the database server for this type of user activity can be reduced by five times by applying some database configuration tunings. What would be the expected performance gain for the overall system?

3.5. Design and develop a simple Windows 32-bit program in any high-level programming language with which you are familiar. Make sure that your program will be CPU and memory intensive to some extent. Run your program and log all the common performance counters with *perfmon*. Based on the *perfmon* data collected when running your program, write a test report showing the CPU and memory consumptions associated with your program.

3.6. Table 3.4 shows the load test results of an OLTP application with the given user types and the number of users for each user type. In the table, R represents the

TABLE 3.4   An OLTP Load Test Profile

User Type	# of Users	R (s)/($R + Z$) (s)	# of Concurrent Users
UT01	60	2.53/62.38	( )
UT02	40	1.87/78.44	( )
UT03	40	2.08/74.22	( )
UT04	60	0.89/42.06	( )

average response time and Z represents the average think time. Calculate the number of concurrent users for each user type. What's the percentage of the users who were stressing the system concurrently?

Part 2

Applying Queuing Theory

Mathematics is the language with which God has written the universe.
—Galileo Galilei, 1564–1642

No human investigation can be called real science if it cannot be demonstrated
mathematically.
—Leonardo da Vinci

Coping with the performance and scalability of a software system effectively depends not only on the quantitative measurements as described in Part I but also on the quantitative analysis based on proven theories such as queuing theory. It's more reliable to count on queuing theory than on gut instincts in identifying bottlenecks that limit the performance and scalability of a software system, since queuing theory can provide more quantitative and objective guidance. Queuing theory is helpful not only for arriving at the conclusions about where the bottlenecks are but also for giving the prescriptions about how the bottlenecks can actually be removed.

This part is dedicated to queuing theory augmented with case studies as follows:

- Chapter 4—Introduction to Queuing Theory
- Chapter 5—Case Study I: Queuing Theory Applied to SOA
- Chapter 6—Case Study II: Queuing Theory Applied to Optimizing and Tuning Software Performance and Scalability

Please note that the material presented in this part is not an introduction to queuing theory in general and in depth. I'd like to help you learn the part of queuing theory that is most relevant in the context of the performance and scalability of a software system. In other words, queuing theory is introduced in this book from a practical point of view, rather than from an academic point of view.

Software Performance and Scalability. By Henry H. Liu
Copyright © 2009 IEEE Computer Society

4

Introduction to Queuing Theory

Numbers are the highest degree of knowledge. It is knowledge itself.
—Plato

Queuing theory is not developed specifically for improving the performance and scalability of a software system. It's generic and applicable in many fields. It's developed for computing and optimizing the efficiency of any system that achieves its objectives by consuming multiple resources optimally. Queuing theory can be applied to computing and optimizing the efficiency of the following:

- Industrial production processes such as automobile manufacturing process, semiconductor manufacturing process, or any manufacturing process that requires optimally utilizing various resources to achieve maximum possible efficiency
- Customer call centers that handle large volumes of customer service requests everyday
- Telecommunication systems consisting of networks, switches, and routers that process large volumes of network packets everyday
- Computer systems that execute large volumes of requests from active users or transactions regularly scheduled as batch jobs

What are the benefits of learning queuing theory for solving your software performance and scalability challenges?

Queuing theory can help you understand all software performance and scalability concepts more formally. You might have heard that software performance is more of an art than a science. This is a misconception. As you will see, in the framework of queuing theory, all software performance concepts such as response time, throughput, and number of requests can be described with corresponding mathematical symbols; and the interrelations among those concepts can be described quantitatively with a number of mathematical equations as performance laws. A good understanding of all software performance concepts more formally in the framework of queuing theory is beneficial for being able to cope with software performance and scalability challenges more effectively.

Queuing theory can help you understand software performance and scalability more scientifically. The performance and scalability of a software system depend on the use scenarios and the raw performance and scalability of the underlying hardware and software platforms. A use scenario can be an online user activity or a batch job. The underlying hardware platform consists of various components such as the computer CPUs, memory, networks, and storage. The supporting software platform consists mainly of the operating system and all middleware systems. The performance metrics for online user activities and batch jobs are response time and throughput, respectively. Queuing theory unifies all those aspects and metrics with quantitative performance laws mathematically. After grasping queuing theory, you will get accustomed to coping with software performance and scalability challenges with a more scientific approach, similar to the way adopted by scientists in many traditional disciplines. This is another requirement for being able to cope with software performance and scalability challenges more effectively.

Queuing theory can help you identify software performance and scalability bottlenecks more efficiently from a practical point of view. As we stated earlier, queuing theory provides the laws that govern the performance and scalability of a software system that operates using multiple hardware resources. By applying queuing theory, you can easily identify the bottlenecks that limit the performance and scalability of your software system. Based on the bottlenecks identified, you can apply various optimization and tuning techniques or upgrade your hardware to help push the performance and scalability of your software to the next level.

Queuing theory can help you analyze the root causes of your software performance and scalability problems more objectively. Software performance and scalability factors are abundant, and it's impractical to test out every possible permutation or use trial-and-error tactics until the real root causes are found. Being guided by queuing theory can help you narrow down the root causes of your software performance and scalability issues more efficiently than relying on gut instinct.

Queuing theory can help you come up with more dependable sizing guidelines for your software products. For many software development organizations, it's often necessary to publish dependable sizing guidelines to help customers plan appropriate hardware capacities ahead of production deployment. Based on your quantitative performance and scalability test results obtained with a certain test architecture, which is a combination of your use scenarios, test methodologies, hardware platforms, operating system platforms, database backend platforms, and middleware platforms, you can apply queuing theory to analyze your test results and come up with meaningful sizing guidelines for your customers.

Overall, a minimum understanding of queuing theory from the software performance and scalability perspectives is necessary to cope with software performance and scalability challenges effectively. It's also a necessary training for establishing an appropriate performance-oriented mindset and mentality. This chapter and the next two queuing theory case study chapters will help you achieve such objectives.

This chapter is organized as follows. In Section 4.1, I'll begin with an introduction to the basic queuing concepts and the mathematical symbols used to formulate queuing theory. Whenever you learn a new theory, you should always start with its basic concepts and the mathematical symbols used to express the theory. Familiarity with all basic concepts and consciously memorizing all the mathematical formulas as well as all the mathematical symbols will help you grasp the theory faster. Of course, learning any theory is not just about memorizing the symbols and mathematical equations mechanically. The importance is that you understand all the implications behind the theory and know how to use the theory to solve real problems.

In Section 4.2, I'll give a brief introduction to probability theory, which is very necessary as probability and statistics are the foundations on which queuing theory was developed. Also, a review of the basic concepts of probability theory such as random variables and distribution functions is a necessary preparation for understanding how queuing theory is established mathematically.

In Section 4.3, I'll introduce Markov random processes, Poisson and exponential distributions, and Kendall notation. Kendall notation is the framework with which a queuing system is characterized. I'll briefly touch upon the difference between a queuing node and a queuing system, which is a preparation for understanding more complicated queuing systems.

Section 4.4 presents what I hope you would eventually learn about all important queuing models for networked queuing systems. I'll concentrate on Little's law and some variations of the open models and closed models that are very useful in solving real software performance and scalability problems.

I'll take a practical approach to introducing queuing theory without involving complicated mathematics. I'll try to be as concise and precise as possible so that after you read this chapter, you will be able to apply the concepts and useful formulas of queuing theory to your software performance and scalability work.

Appendices A through C introduce more advanced concepts such as stochastic equilibrium and ergodicity about random processes. This provides the flexibility for those who wish to learn things in a bottom-up approach (like myself). It is also strongly recommended for the college and graduate students who wish to get a more formal training on queuing theory in general.

Let's begin with the basic concepts and metrics of queuing theory.

4.1 QUEUING CONCEPTS AND METRICS

Basic concepts are the building blocks for any theory. By getting familiar with the basic concepts of a theory, you know immediately what problems that theory is trying to solve. This is the first step to begin with when learning any new theory. Let's begin with the basic concepts of queuing theory before moving to the abstract probability theory that describes queuing theory more rigorously.

4.1.1 Basic Concepts of Queuing Theory

In fact, it's not that hard to grasp the basic concepts of queuing theory. Everybody has the experience of visiting a banking center. When we deposit or withdraw at a banking center, most of the time, we have to wait in line in order to be serviced by a teller. We don't want to wait too long in line and we care about how long it takes for a teller to complete servicing us so that we can leave for the next thing on our busy daily agenda.

With this simple banking example, we already touched upon most of the concepts of queuing theory. Using the banking center example, some important basic concepts that queuing theory is based upon can be illustrated as follows:

- *Server*. This is banking center fulfilling the customer's service requests.
- *Customer*. This is the initiator of service requests.
- *Wait Time*. This is the time duration a customer has to spend waiting in line.
- *Service Time*. This is the time duration from when a teller starts to service a customer to when the customer is leaving the teller and the next customer is called in for service.
- *Arrival Rate*. This is the rate at which customers arrive for service.
- *Service Rate*. This is the rate at which customers are serviced.
- *Utilization*. This is the portion of a teller's time actually servicing customers rather than idling.
- *Queue Length*. This is the total number of customers waiting or being serviced or both.
- *Response Time*. This is the sum of wait time and service time for one visit to a teller.
- *Residence Time*. This is the total response time if the teller is visited multiple times for one transaction.
- *Throughput*. This is the rate at which customers are serviced. A banking center certainly is interested in knowing how fast it can service customers without losing them because of long wait times.

So from banking efficiency and customer satisfaction perspectives, we already know that both a banking center and customers are interested in:

- Minimizing wait time so that the banking business would be more efficient and customers would be happier
- Minimizing service time by training tellers to become more and more proficient so that the banking center can run its business more efficiently
- Knowing the average customer arrival rate so that the banking center will neither over- nor understaff.
- Minimizing both response time and residence time by refining the transaction processes
- Striving for the highest possible throughput to stay profitable while making customers happy

As you may have seen, by thinking in the framework of queuing theory, it's a lot easier to brainstorm various ways of improving the productivity and efficiency of the processes we are concerned with.

Let's further construct a case to see what typical problems queuing theory can help resolve in the context of software performance and scalability. The question can be formulated as follows:

For a given average arrival rate λ and a given service rate μ, how many parallel servers (m) are required in order for the system to operate under steady-state conditions?

This problem can be answered by requiring that the system load intensity (ρ) defined as $\rho = \lambda / m\mu$ must be smaller than one or $\lambda/m\mu < 1$ or $m > \lambda/\mu$, where m is the minimum number of parallel servers required to maintain the steady-state operating condition for the system. If a system is not designed properly to guarantee that the steady-state condition of $\rho = \lambda/m\mu < 1$ is satisfied, then it will begin to mal-function or even crash sooner or later because of the load exceeding the system's processing capacity.

Using this banking example as an easy entrance to understanding queuing theory, we can now formally transit to queuing theory in a more rigorous format in the context of software performance and scalability.

4.1.2 Queuing Theory: From Textual Description to Mathematical Symbols

An analytical theory identifies important phenomena in reality and represents them in mathematical symbols, and further formulates them in succinct equations to become quantitative. This transition from being qualitative in textual description to being quantitative in mathematical format is inevitable and we all need to embrace it when it comes down to grasping a theory.

With the help of a graphic representation of a queue as shown in Figure 4.1, we can now begin to correlate the basic concepts of queuing theory we introduced earlier with their corresponding mathematical symbols. In Figure 4.1 we have replaced *customer* in the banking example with *request*, which is more pertinent to the context of software performance and scalability. However, throughout this chapter, *customer*, *software service request*, and *user* will be interchangeable whenever it's more pertinent to the concrete context.

To elaborate further, each bean in Figure 4.1 represents a request, which could be a system or user call from a caller to a callee. There is a queue in front of the server, which stores all arriving requests for the server to process. In the context of software

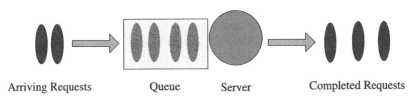

Arriving Requests   Queue   Server   Completed Requests

Figure 4.1 *Graphic representation of a queuing system.*

TABLE 4.1 Mathematical Symbols Used in Queuing Theory

Symbol	Semantics
S	Service time
V	Number of visits to the server
D	Service demand
R	Response time
R'	Residence time
X	Throughput
λ	Arrival rate
U	Utilization
W	Wait time
N	Total queue length (waiting and/or being serviced)

application running on one or more computer systems, the server could be any type of resource, for example, a software server or any hardware components such as processors, disks, and networks. The power of a theory is that it can be developed based on an abstract model that represents a bunch of entities in reality and can then be applied to each of the entities from which the generic abstract model was built. This is one of the most fascinating aspects of theories that have attracted a lot of bright minds to work on them diligently.

In the preceding section, we introduced all the basic concepts of queuing theory. Without further delay, let's see how some of the basic concepts of queuing theory and their corresponding symbols correlate with each other. This correlation is shown in Table 4.1.

Each symbol in this table represents one metric of a queuing system. This set of symbols represents the complete set of metrics for a queuing system. Queuing theory weaves these concepts and symbols into formulas in a meaningful way so that the behavior of a queuing system can be studied analytically. Analytical formulas are powerful because they provide insight into how one metric can affect others if it changes. In addition, analytical formulas are arrived at based on abstract models, and therefore they are widely applicable.

Keep in mind that to help facilitate communications with others, it's necessary to stick to the same symbols commonly used in the literature; for example, S always represents service time, V the number of visits to the same server, D service demand, R response time, R' residence time, X throughput, λ arrival rate, U utilization, W wait time, and N queue length. As another benefit, sticking to a fixed set of symbols can help you remember those analytical formulas that we will introduce later. It's easier to think in *symbols* than in text descriptions when learning a theory.

Queuing is a dynamic process. The number of arriving requests to a queue is stochastic or random in nature, and the service time is not a constant either. This puts us in a position of relying on certain probability distributions to study queuing processes. Probability distributions are not only a prerequisite for discussing queuing theory, but also a powerful testimony for the errors that are inherent in software performance measurements. Certain errors will exist in our measurements no matter how well we control the test environment. I emphasized this in Chapter 3 to avoid interpreting small errors in measurements as performance gains or losses.

How the entities represented by those symbols in Table 4.1 are correlated with each other mathematically is the gist of queuing theory. We'll get there after a brief introduction to probability theory in the next section. Keep in mind that queuing theory is built on probability theory and statistic laws.

4.2 INTRODUCTION TO PROBABILITY THEORY

Probability theory is the branch of mathematics concerned with analysis of random phenomena. The central objects of probability theory are events, random variables, and stochastic processes. These objects are mathematical abstractions of nondeterministic events or measured quantities that may either be single occurrences or evolve over time in an apparently random fashion.

Probability theory is the mathematical foundation for statistics. It is essential to understanding a lot of natural phenomena, human activities, and behaviors of various complex systems. A great discovery of the 20th century in physics was the probabilistic nature of physical phenomena at the atomic scale, described in quantum mechanics. Another amazing example is the pre-presidential election polling in the United States: it's said that none of the actual presidential election outcomes have deviated from what was predicted from the pre-presidential polling that samples only thousands of potential voters out of millions. Of course, probability theory has contributed a lot to understanding the performance of both computer hardware and software.

There are two branches of probability theory: discrete probability theory, which deals with events that occur in countable sample spaces, and continuous probability theory, which deals with events that occur in a continuous sample space. They both share the same theoretical framework and complement each other. And they both begin with random variables and probability distribution functions, as you'll see from the following sections.

4.2.1 Random Variables and Distribution Functions

In probability theory, a random variable is a variable whose values are random and to which a probability distribution is assigned. For example, when tossing a coin, there can be only two outcomes: heads or tails. When rolling a die, the possible outcome space is extended to $\{1, 2, 3, 4, 5, 6\}$, as a die has six sides. In these cases, the outcome of tossing a coin or rolling a die is a value assigned to a discrete random variable; the probability for each occurrence of the outcome of each experiment is either $1/2$ or $1/6$.

Tossing a coin or rolling a die is like doing an experiment. As we have seen from the above description, the outcome of each experiment can be expressed using the value of a variable X. If you don't like gambling, another example might be that every time you measure the number of customers arriving at a banking center over a period of time, you would get a number that represents the number of arriving customers you counted over that period of time. A series of counting over multiple observation intervals would constitute an experiment, which would yield a value set assigned to a *variable* that represents the number of customers arriving at a banking center.

Although varying with certain random factors, for example, you can never predict exactly how many customers you are going to see coming to the bank over the next period of time, the values of this variable X follow a certain probability distribution law. This kind of variable is called a *random variable* and can be represented using uppercase letters such as X or T. Representing a random variable with concrete values embodies the quantification of a random phenomenon, which is a great step toward describing random phenomena quantitatively and mathematically.

Given a random variable X, the probability that its values do not exceed a real number x is a function of x, or in other words, it depends on the concrete value of x which represents the state of the random process under study. This probability function is generally designated as $P(X \leq x)$ in the event of $X \leq x$ and is called the *probability distribution function* (PDF) or simply the *distribution function* of the random variable X. It is further expressed as $F(x)$, namely,

$$F(x) = P(X \leq x) \quad (-\infty < x < \infty) \tag{4.1}$$

Note that uppercase letters are used to express random variables, whereas lowercase letters are used to express the values of a random variable. Making this distinction can help you understand the associated abstract mathematical equations better.

Some random variables can only take nonnegative integer numbers as their value set, for example, counting the number of customers arriving at a banking center. And some random variables can take any values including fractions such as the interarrival time between the two customers who come one after another. Thus we have discrete random variables and continuous random variables.

4.2.2 Discrete Distribution and Probability Distribution Series

Mathematically, if a random variable X can only take a limited or infinite number of discrete values of $x_1, x_2, \ldots, x_k, \ldots$, we then call X a *discrete random variable*. If we express $P(X = x_k)$ as p_k or $P(X = x_k) = p_k$ ($k = 1, 2, \ldots$), then the probability distribution of the values that X can take is completely determined by the series $\{p_k\}$. We call $\{p_k\}$ the probability distribution series of X. The distribution function of X is the sum of all values of $\{p_k\}$ for $X \leq x$ such that

$$P(X \leq x) = F(x) = \sum_{x_k \leq x} p_k \tag{4.2}$$

where p_k is the probability corresponding to the kth value x_k of the discrete random variable X. p_k is also called the *distribution mass function* (DMF). Because of the summation over all discrete probabilities within the range of $X \leq x$, $F(x)$ is also called the *cumulative distribution function* (CDF).

To help understand Equation (4.2) better, let's take tossing a coin as an example. In this case, the outcome can only take one of the two values, $x_1 =$ "Heads" and $x_2 =$ "Tails." The chances for either side are $50/50$, so $p_1 = p_2 = \frac{1}{2}$.

Note that when the values of x are nonnegative integers, one can simply degenerate x_k into k for convenience.

Next, let's take a look at continuous distributions.

4.2.3 Continuous Distribution and Distribution Density Function

If the probability distribution function $F(x)$ of a random variable X can be mathematically expressed as

$$P(X \leq x) = F(x) = \int_{-\infty}^{x} p(t)\, dt \tag{4.3}$$

where $p(t)$ is nonnegative, then we call X a *continuous random variable* and $p(t)$ the *distribution density function* (DDF) (or simply distribution density). Again, $F(x)$ is called the cumulative distribution function (CDF) for the same reason as for the discrete distributions we discussed in the preceding section.

Equations (4.2) and (4.3) look simple. However, they represent the transition from a known and deterministic world to a partially known (probabilistic) and nondeterministic world through either summation for discrete or integration for continuous probabilities. This demonstrates the power of mathematics for describing and interpreting natural phenomena.

So far, we have introduced some basic concepts of probability theory such as random variable (discrete and continuous), probability distribution function, probability distribution series, distribution mass function, cumulative distribution function, and distribution density function. You'll understand better about these abstract concepts after we correlate them with queuing theory in the next section.

Appendices A through C provide a concise yet comprehensive coverage about random processes for those who wish to learn more, especially about some advanced concepts such as stochastic equilibrium and ergodicity, etc. However, this digression is not required for those who wish to get some immediate exposure to queuing theory as introduced in the remainder of this chapter.

4.3 APPLYING PROBABILITY THEORY TO QUEUING SYSTEMS

A queuing system has two mutually coupled processes: the arrival process and the service process: streams of customers or requests arrive, which are then serviced by the server. These two processes are stochastic or random to some extent. This can be further elaborated as follows:

- An arrival process is characterized by the number of arrivals during a given period of time and the interarrival time between two adjacent arrivals. Both the number of arrivals and the arrival interval are random, which makes an arrival process stochastic in nature. For example, a website receives requests from an ensemble of independent users spread all over the world. When, how often, and how many users would visit a website is undeterministic. We have to embrace this fact no matter how imperfect it is.

- As the arrival process is stochastic, any subsequent process driven by the arrival process is stochastic as well. This justifies why the service process is stochastic as well. Coupled with a random arrival process, different types of requests with different characteristics may take different amounts of time for the server to process. Therefore service times are random and follow certain probability laws.

- As the service time is random, response time and throughput of a queuing system that depend on service time are random as well.

So at this point it's clear that both the number of arrivals and the time intervals such as the arrival interval and service time cannot be predicted deterministically. Fortunately, probability theory and the laws of statistics give us the power to predict probabilistically the future. The gist of it is that when the event observation time is sufficiently long, random microscopic fluctuations tend to be smoothed out and small fluctuations in the end results are quite acceptable to us.

When we talk about statistics regardless of the context, certain probabilistic processes are implied. Probabilistic processes are described by their corresponding models. The following are some of the typical process models relevant to queuing theory:

1. *Markov (M) Process.* The Markov process is characterized by its memorylessness: the future states of the process are independent of its past history and depend solely on the present state. This type of process is named after A. A. Markov, who defined it a century ago.

2. *General (G) Process.* The process is not characterized by any single probability distribution because it's completely arbitrary.

3. *Deterministic (D) Process.* The process is predictable and characterized by various constants, for example, when the interarrival times are constant from one arrival to the next.

Relative to a general process, a Markov process is much easier to handle mathematically. Markov processes are representative of many random processes in reality, especially those random processes that can be found in queuing systems. For this reason, we'll concentrate on Markov processes in the remainder of this chapter.

4.3.1 Markov Process

When a Markov process is applied to the simplest queuing systems characterized by certain simple arrival and service time patterns, it implies that:

1. The number of arrivals follows the Poisson distribution.
2. The interarrival times follow the exponential distribution.
3. The service times follow the exponential distribution as well.

What does a Poisson distribution or exponential distribution mean exactly? Let's try to answer that question now.

Random processes are driven by random variables. As we discussed in Section 4.2, there are two types of random variables: *discrete random variables* and *continuous random variables*. A discrete random variable, such as the number of customers arriving at a banking center, can only take discrete values, whereas a continuous random variable, such as interarrival times and service times, can take any real values including fractions.

According to probability theory, discrete random events are characterized by *distribution mass functions*, whereas continuous random variables are characterized by *distribution density functions*. The Poisson distribution function is based on a distribution mass function that can be expressed mathematically as follows:

$$P(X = k) = p(k) = \frac{(\lambda t)^k e^{-\lambda t}}{k!} \tag{4.4}$$

where λ is the average arrival rate representing the number of events occurring per unit time *on average*, t is the observation period of $[0, t]$, which means from 0 through t, e represents the exponential function, k is the exact number of events expected to occur over the observation period, and $k!$ is the factorial of k. $P(X = k)$ should be read as "the probability that a random variable X takes a value of k."

Note that λt in Equation (4.4) is also the average number of occurrences $<k>$, where $< \cdots >$ represents averaging mathematically. Sometimes the Poisson distribution is expressed as

$$p(k) = \frac{(\lambda)^k e^{-\lambda}}{k!}$$

in place of Equation (4.4), but using λt instead of λ alone is more intuitive, because you can see both the average arrival rate λ and observation period t and know what they mean exactly. Another benefit of using λt instead of λ is that it will preserve the meaning of λ as the average occurrence rate for both the Poisson distribution and the exponential distribution, which helps minimize confusion.

The exponential distribution function is based on a distribution density function expressed mathematically as follows:

$$f(t) = \lambda e^{-\lambda t} \tag{4.5}$$

where λ is the average arrival rate representing the number of events that may occur per unit time *on average*, t is the observation period, and e represents the exponential function.

Now let's explain what Poisson distributions and exponential distributions mean exactly when they are associated with a Markov process in the context of software performance:

- The Poisson distribution shown in Equation (4.4) is a discrete probability distribution that represents a random arrival process with the probability of having exactly *k* events occurring in a fixed period of time with a known average rate of λ for those occurring events. These events are also called *arrivals, customers, requests, users,* and so on. In the context of software performance, such arrival events could be user's requests to a Web server, or the arrivals of service requests from one resource to another, from CPU to memory bus or to disk controllers for fetching or storing data.

- The exponential distribution shown in Equation (4.5) is used to model the time between independent events such as the interarrival time, service time, and response time. The reciprocal of λ, $\mu = 1/\lambda$, is called the *scale parameter* or *survival parameter*, as when $\lambda t = 1$ or $t = \mu$, $e^{-1} = (1/2.71828) = 37\%$, which means that the average survival probability for a biological system or a mechanical system has degraded from the initial 100% to 37%.

We are now clear that the Poisson distribution is about counting random events and the exponential function is about measuring time intervals such as service time and response time.

It can be proven mathematically that:

- If the random variable representing the number of event occurrences in some time interval follows the Poisson distribution, then the random variable representing the time between successive occurrences follows the exponential distribution.
- The exponential distribution function is the only continuous function that possesses the memoryless property. See Appendix B for a rigorous proof.

Next let's explore the Poisson distribution and exponential distribution numerically with concrete average arrival rates of λ in the context of queuing theory.

4.3.2 Poisson Distribution

Let's first plot the Poisson distribution and observe the probabilities as a function of both the mean number of occurrences λt or *n* and the arbitrary number of occurrences *k*. For convenience, from now on we use *n* in place of λt. Computation of the Poisson distribution can easily be done using Excel®. In Excel, this function is coded as POISSON (*k*, *n*, cumulative), where *k* and *n* are arbitrary and mean numbers of occurrences, respectively; *cumulative = false* implies distribution mass function and *cumulative = true* implies cumulative distribution function.

Figure 4.2 shows the Poisson mass function with three different values of $n = 1, 5$, and 10 for the mean number of occurrences of any events. Let's say the average interarrival time is 2 seconds, and the observation period of time is 10 seconds. This means that $\lambda = \frac{1}{2}$, $t = 10$, or $n = 5$, according to their respective definitions. In other words, it means that there are 5 occurrences every 10 seconds *on average*. Since this arrival rate of 5 requests per 10 seconds is an average value out of a random process, the probability for its exact occurrence is not 100%. Instead, the probability of seeing exactly 5 arrivals over a 10-second period is 17.5%, as calculated

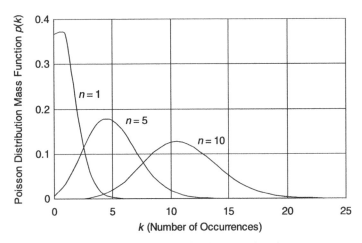

Figure 4.2 *Poisson distribution mass function.*

according to Equation (4.4) with $n = 5$. The probability of seeing exactly 4 arrivals over a 10-second period is 17.5% as well, and seeing exactly 6 arrivals over a 10-second period is 14.6%, and so on.

A cumulative distribution doesn't count exactly. Instead, it counts *up to* a certain point. For the *Poisson* distribution, its cumulative distribution function is

$$P(X \leq k) = F(k) = p(0) + p(1) + \cdots + p(k) \tag{4.6}$$

where $p(k)$ is given by Equation (4.4). Figure 4.3 shows the cumulative distribution function for the Poisson distribution. For example, for $n = 5$, the probability of finding *up to 5* arrivals is 62%, which includes the probabilities for finding exactly 0, 1, 2, 3, 4, and 5 arrivals.

Next, let's take a look at the exponential distribution function.

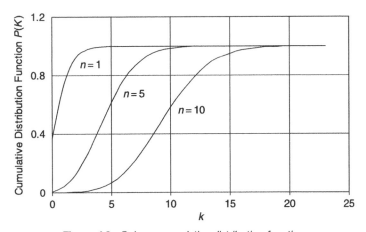

Figure 4.3 *Poisson cumulative distribution function.*

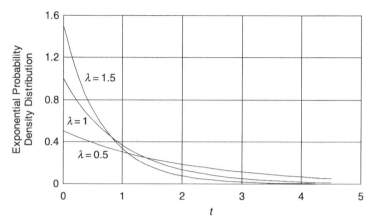

Figure 4.4 Exponential density distribution function.

4.3.3 Exponential Distribution Function

In Excel, the exponential function is coded as EXPONDIST (t, *lambda*, *cumulative*), where t represents the time interval of an arrival process or service time of a service process, *lambda* is the average arrival rate or service rate, *cumulative* = *false* implies density function, and *cumulative* = *true* implies cumulative function. For three different values of λ, Figure 4.4 shows the exponential density distribution function, whereas Figure 4.5 shows its cumulative distribution, which can be expressed as

$$P(T \leq t) = F(t) = 1 - e^{-\lambda t} \tag{4.7}$$

where λ is an arrival rate if it is associated with an arrival process or service rate if it's associated with a service process.

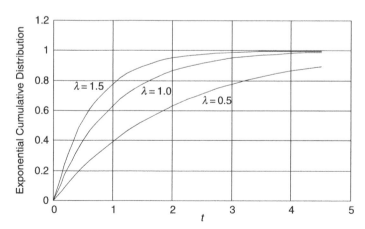

Figure 4.5 Exponential cumulative distribution function.

It's interesting to note from Equation (4.7) that when $P = 0.90$, which corresponds to the 90th percentile, $\lambda t = 2.3$ or $t = 2.3 / \lambda$, which is a characteristic interval for 90% of the events. This 90% is a more realistic measurement for the interarrival time or service time or response time than their corresponding mean values. Keep this in mind when you assess your response time measurement with your OLTP workload tests.

Note that both the Poisson distribution and exponential distribution have the same memorylessness property. The difference is that the Poisson distribution describes discrete events such as the number of occurrences, whereas the exponential distribution describes continuous entities such as interarrival times, service times, and response times.

A useful queuing model should represent a real-life system with sufficient accuracy and is analytically tractable. A queuing model based on the *Poisson* process and its companion exponential probability distribution meets these two requirements. A Poisson process models random events emanating from a memoryless process, such as a customer arrival process, a user request arrival process, or the completion of a request made to a Web server. That is, the length of the time interval from the current time to the occurrence of the next event does not depend on the time of occurrence of the last event. In the Poisson probability distribution, the observer records the number of events that occur in a time interval of fixed length. In the exponential probability distribution, the observer records the length of the time interval between consecutive events. In both, the underlying physical process is memoryless.

Queuing systems are frequently modeled as Poisson processes through the use of the exponential distribution. Together with the Poisson and exponential distributions, Table 4.2 lists some other distributions that are useful for characterizing queuing systems as well. Table 4.3 lists the typical usages of the distribution functions

TABLE 4.2   Common Probability Mass and Density Functions

Distribution	Expression
Poisson	$p(k) = ((\lambda t)^k / k!) \exp(-\lambda t)$, $k = 0, 1, 2, \ldots$; $\lambda > 0$
Exponential	$f(t, \lambda) = \lambda \exp(-\lambda t)$
Gamma	$f(t, \alpha, \beta) = [\beta^{-\alpha} / \Gamma(\alpha)]\, t^{\alpha-1} \exp(-t/\beta)$
Normal	$p_N(x) = [1/(2\pi)^{1/2}\sigma] \exp[-(x - \mu)^2 / 2\sigma^2]$
Uniform	$f(t) = 1/(b - a)$, $a < t < b$

TABLE 4.3   Mean (μ), Standard Deviation (σ), and Typical Usages of Common Probability Mass and Density Functions

Distribution	μ	σ	Usage
Poisson	λt	λt	Number of arrivals or occurrences
Exponential	λ^{-1}	λ^{-1}	Time interval
Gamma	$\alpha\beta$	$\alpha^{1/2}\beta$	Time interval
Normal	μ	σ	Mean error
Uniform	$\dfrac{(b - a)}{2}$	$\dfrac{(b - a)}{2\sqrt{3}}$	Network latency

listed in Table 4.2. Note that the exponential function is a particular case of gamma function with $\alpha = 1$ and $\lambda = 1/\beta$.

With a good basic understanding of what problems queuing theory solves based on probability theory, it's time to learn about the Kendall notation, which characterizes the queuing models based on the various aspects of a queuing system such as the arrival process, the service process, the capability of the server, and so on. This is our topic for the next section.

4.3.4 Kendall Notation

Based on the type of arrival process, the service time, and other characteristics of a queuing system, Kendall devised a set of notations for defining different types of queues symbolically [Kendall, 1981]. Because of its convenience for describing and characterizing a queuing system, Kendall notation has become the language of queuing theory. Fortunately, Kendall notation is very simple and intuitive, as described in Table 4.4.

In Kendall notation, a generic queue is represented as $\alpha/\sigma/m/\beta/N/Q$ symbolically with six symbols. Hence the Kendall descriptor $M/M/m/\infty/\infty/\text{FIFO}$ represents a queuing center with Markov arrival process, exponential service time distribution, m servers, infinite queuing capacity, infinite population, and first-in first-out (FIFO) service policy. Such a queuing center is denoted as $M/M/m$ queue conventionally, with the rest of it implied implicitly.

Kendall notation is both generic and specific. It can be applied to characterizing either a single queuing node or a queuing system that consists of multiple queuing nodes. The behavior of a single queuing node may predominantly determine the behavior of the entire system, or only contribute partially. The same performance metrics used for quantifying a queuing node are used for quantifying a queuing system as well. However, there are some notational differences in denoting a queuing node versus a queuing system, which will be clarified in the next section. This will help avoid confusion when we describe various queuing models in a later section.

4.3.5 Queuing Node versus Queuing System

A single queuing node is simply a single type of resource, such as computer CPUs, disks, or networks in the context of computer systems. Multiple queuing nodes or

TABLE 4.4 Kendall Notation

Symbol	Semantics
α	The type of probability distribution for an arrival process (e.g., Markov, general, etc.)
σ	The type of probability distribution for service time
m	The number of servers at a queuing center
β	The buffer size or storage capacity at a queuing center
N	The allowed population size, which may be finite or infinite
Q	The type of service policy (e.g., FIFO—first-in first-out)

TABLE 4.5 Notational Differences between a Queuing Node and a Queuing System

Metric	Node	System
Service time	S_i	S_0
Response time	R_i	R_0
Throughput	X_i	X_0

multiple subsystems may constitute a queuing system. A system is a top-level container, whereas nodes or subsystems are components. It's this *container–component* relationship that determines the overall performance of a queuing system.

Throughout this book, we adopt the following conventions in denoting a queuing node versus a queuing system:

- A queuing node is denoted with a subscript lowercase letter *i*.
- A queuing system is denoted with a subscript sign of zero.

In order to help reinforce the distinction between a *node* and a *system*, Table 4.5 summarizes some of the major metrics that have counterparts with each other. It is important not to confuse *node* with *system*. Of course, if it's only a single node, it's both a *node* and a *system*.

With this notational difference between a queuing node and a queuing system in mind, we can now move on to introducing various queuing models in the next section.

4.4 QUEUING MODELS FOR NETWORKED QUEUING SYSTEMS

Queues can be chained to form networked queuing systems where the departures from one queue enter the next queue. Queuing systems can be classified into two categories: open queuing systems and closed queuing systems. Open queuing systems have an external input and an external final destination. Closed queuing systems are completely contained and the customers circulate continually, never leaving the system. Of course, there could also be a situation in-between, for example, an open queuing system that contains internal feedback loops.

A queuing model is a procedure about how to calculate some of the performance metrics of a queuing system. For software, we are most concerned with *response time* and *throughput*. Response time pertains to user-activity driven OLTP workloads, whereas throughput pertains to batch jobs. OLTP scenarios resemble open queuing systems, whereas batch jobs resemble closed queuing systems, although a closed model applies to OLTP workloads as well.

In this section, I'll focus on the following three major entry points to queuing theory:

- *Little's law* which shows how the three major queuing metrics—throughput, response time, and queuing length—correlate with each other. This is a generic law that has no assumptions attached to it other than the equilibrium condition, which means that no customers are created or lost in the system. Little's law has been widely applied to solving software performance and scalability problems.

- *The M/M/1 open model* which assumes that customers enter and exit the system. This is an analytically tractable model and thus is very popular. The various analytical formulas of this model are commonly used to guide software performance analysis, optimization, and tuning efforts. It's the minimum that one should understand about queuing theory.

- *The M/M/m/N/N closed model* which assumes that there are a limited number of customers in the system. This model is defined by a set of recursive equations that can be solved easily to get more accurate results.

Throughput, response time, and queue length are the three metrics that can completely quantify the performance of a queuing system. That's how Little's law comes into play. Let's explore it in the next section.

4.4.1 Queuing Theory Triad I: Response Time, Throughput, and Queue Length (Little's Law)

An overview of queuing theory is incomplete without mentioning Little's law [Little, 1961]. Little's law simply states that the number of customers, both waiting for and receiving service, is equal to the product of throughput and response time:

$$N_i = X_i \times R_i \tag{4.8}$$

where X_i is the throughput at queuing node i.

Since response time can be expressed as $R = W + S$ in general, where W represents wait time and S service time, we can further decompose Equation (4.8) into

$$N_{i\_\text{wait}} = X_i \times W_i \tag{4.9a}$$

$$N_{i\_\text{busy}} = X_i \times S_i \tag{4.9b}$$

where N_{i_wait} and N_{i_busy} represent the number of customers waiting and the number of customers being serviced, respectively.

Little's law is intuitive. It can be proved as follows:

- Let R represent the average response time for a customer.
- Let T represent the total observation time.
- Let C be the number of customers departing the system over the time period T.
- Let N be the average number of customers in the system.

Then the probability that a customer is in the system is equal to R/T. According to this probability, on average, the number of customers who are in the system can be calculated as $N = C \times (R/T) = (C/T) \times R$, where by definition, $X = C/T$, and thus $N = XR$, which is equivalent to Equation (4.8). Note that Little's Law is valid for any $G/G/m$ queuing system.

To help understand Little's law, let's use an example.

■ **Case Study 4.1: Application of Little's Law**

A company is considering purchasing an IT help desk management system to help improve the productivity and efficiency of its employees. It is estimated that about 200 employees including IT support staff will use the help desk management system. It is further estimated that the application will be stressed by about 3% of the 200 users *concurrently*, namely, not all 200 employees will use the application at the same time. There will be four major user types, and the total average transaction arrival rate will be 9944 transactions per hour. Typical actions include signing-in, creating tickets, searching and modifying tickets, and signing-out. Each type of transaction is a specific combination of those typical actions. What would be the expected average response time for all user types when the system is operating under equilibrium conditions?

This question can be answered as follows:

- The transaction arrival rate or throughput would be $9944/3600 = 2.76$ transactions/second.
- The average number of concurrent users would be $200 \times 3\% = 6$.
- According to Little's Law, the average response time would be $R = N/X = 2.17$ seconds.

This example shows partially what software performance questions that Little's law can help answer. Note that when applying Little's law, the active response time includes the system busy time and system resource waiting time, but not the system idle time. The corresponding number of users is the count of the concurrent users whose requests are being executed concurrently in the system. One would arrive at wrong conclusions if the true meaning of *concurrency* pertaining to the state of a group of users is not understood correctly.

Next, let's elaborate on the two simplest queuing models, the $M/M/1$ open model and the $M/M/m/N/N$ closed model. These two models are the foundation for more complicated queuing models.

4.4.2 $M/M/1$ Model (Open)

Let's start with the simplest queue, the $M/M/1$ open model. The $M/M/1$ open model is most popular because of the following characteristics:

- It is analytically tractable so that one can use the fairly simple formulas derived from it to calculate *by hand* the important performance metrics, such as the response times and resource utilizations of a queuing system.
- It is fairly accurate for predicting the performance of a system operating under an equilibrium condition. An equilibrium condition is an ideal state for a system under which transactions flow smoothly.
- Very often it's good enough for back-of-the-envelope calculations, which can help show quickly what works and what doesn't. Back-of-the-envelope calculations are far more than a guess, although far less than a proof. The results

from back-of-the-envelope calculations are helpful in supporting some early decisions before major investments are made. It could be equally helpful in signaling troubling issues beforehand so that proactive measures can be taken to prevent disasters from happening.

Specifically to our interests, the $M/M/1$ open model illustrates all the basic concepts and elements of queuing theory, although it's simple. It's always good to start with something simple when you're learning something new.

To be generic, let's consider an $M/M/1$ queuing node with feedback, as shown in Figure 4.6. Here *feedback* means that some customers may come back and visit the queuing node more than once. In the context of software, *feedback* means multiple visits to a resource as required for completing a transaction at the system level.

The feedback in Figure 4.6 is denoted with three parameters: external arrival rate λ, internal arrival rate λ_1, and the probability p that customers return to the same queue.

Queuing with feedback is associated with a famous theorem, which is often called Jackson's theorem [Jackson, 1963]. It is about one of the assumptions made in studying queuing theory, which is the Poisson process as we stated earlier.

When there is no feedback, an arrival process is a Poisson process. When multiple arrival streams join the queue with feedback, the arrival process is no longer a Poisson process. However, Jackson's theorem states that although the arrivals into the queue are not Poisson, the queuing node's behavior statistically still follows the laws governed by a Poisson process.

Although extremely abstract, Jackson's work helped shed light on the fact that it's really the *service demand*, not the *service time*, that is most fundamental in determining the performance of a queuing system. This observation becomes obvious after we show how the response time of a queuing system can be calculated using the $M/M/1$ open model.

The $M/M/1$ open model begins with the following three assumptions:

1. An average arrival rate λ is known. This is usually not a problem, as arrivals are the workload driver to a system anyway.

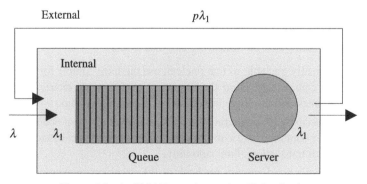

Figure 4.6 An M/M/1 queuing node with feedback.

2. The system is running under an equilibrium condition, which means that the average throughput X_0 is equal to the average arrival rate λ:

$$X_0 = \lambda \qquad (4.10)$$

This is another way of stating that there are no transactions lost in the system and they all run to completion in a steady state. We don't have a problem with this assumption either, as we can't afford to have a system that keeps losing transactions anyway.

3. The system's service demand for the resource in question is known, which is defined as

$$D_i = V_i \times S_i \qquad (4.11)$$

where the subscript i represents the ith queuing node, and V_i and S_i are the number of visits to the queuing node and average service time required per visit, respectively. This assumption is a little bit tougher in software, as it's necessary to have reliable tools to monitor the number of times a resource is accessed and the time duration taken for each visit to complete the task. However, it's not surprising at all, as theory is about calculating *unknowns* based on what we know partially.

A few comments about service time are in order.

- Measuring S_i may not be an easy task. It requires a well-controlled experiment with well-defined workload and very low system load. Service time is often approximated with the response time, which is what we can measure from end to end externally. Response time is defined as follows

$$R_i = W_i + S_i = S_i/(1 - U_i) \qquad (4.12)$$

where W_i is wait time, S_i is service time, and U_i is resource utilization. So when the system load is very low with utilization U_i not exceeding a few percent, we have

$$R_i \cong S_i \qquad (4.13)$$

Equation (4.13) shows how we can measure service time by measuring response time. In principle, we can never get the real service time, as from Equation (4.12) it requires measuring response time R_i with the condition of utilization $U_i = 0$, which means that the system is idle. But how do we measure it without even having the system running?

- With a queuing node with no feedback, service demand and service time are the same, namely:

$$D_i = S_i \qquad (4.14)$$

Now we are ready to proceed with the $M/M/1$ open model. Using this model, you can calculate the resource utilization U_i and the system response time R_0 of a queuing system as follows:

- Knowing the system throughput X_0 and the ith node's service demand D_i allows us to calculate the resource utilization U_i immediately according to

$$U_i = X_0 \times D_i \qquad (4.15)$$

- With the service demand D_i and utilization U_i known, we can then calculate the average residence time R_i' of a request at queue node i as follows:

$$R_i' = V_i \times R_i = D_i/(1 - U_i) \qquad (4.16)$$

- The total average system response time R_0 is the sum of residence times over all queue nodes from $i = 1$ through $i = K$, where K is the total number of nodes constituting the entire system; namely,

$$R_0 = \sum_{i=1}^{K} R_i' \qquad (4.17)$$

With Equations (4.8), (4.12), and (4.15), we can further obtain the average number of customers at queuing node i with given utilization:

$$N_i = U_i/(1 - U_i) \qquad (4.18)$$

or vice versa,

$$U_i = N_i/(N_i + 1) \qquad (4.19)$$

Note that the total number of customers in the queuing system is given by $N=\sum_i N_i$.

In summary, the $M/M/1$ model allows us to calculate the response time R_0 of an OLTP software system with given transaction arrival rate λ and premeasured service demand D_i or service time S_i without feedback. Service demand is one of the most basic elements for applying the $M/M/1$ queuing model to computing the performance of software systems.

Keep in mind that system throughput is a performance metric to be calculated for batch jobs, not for OLTP systems. With OLTP systems, throughput is the same as the arrival rate under the equilibrium condition. Throughput for batch jobs is computed using the $M/M/m/N/N$ closed model, which is a topic for a later section.

Feedback is an important factor in determining how to apply the analytical formulas derived from the $M/M/1$ model. In order to clarify, in the next section, we'll try to sort out all formulas presented so far so that the chances of using the wrong formulas in the wrong context will be minimized.

4.4.3 Queuing System: With Feedback versus Without Feedback

Perhaps the most confusing thing with queuing theory is that sometimes people use the terms of service demand, service time, response time, and residence time freely without regard to whether there is feedback involved or not. If there is feedback involved in a queuing system, then service demand and residence time are more appropriate to use than service time and response time, because it's incomplete to mention service time and response time without mentioning the number of visits to the queue. Of course, at the system level, we always use response time other than residence time to represent the performance of an OLTP software system.

To help avoid confusions, we sorted out all the formulas derived from the $M/M/1$ open model in Table 4.6. By setting $V_i = 1$ in all the formulas derived with feedback, you immediately get all the formulas for the case without feedback. Note that the symbols with subscript i denote the corresponding metrics for queue node i, whereas the symbols with subscript 0 denote the corresponding metrics at the system level.

Out of the formulas presented in Table 4.6, you may already notice that there is a prominent scaling factor between the residence time and the service demand or between the response time and the service time. This is a very important scaling relationship showing how the response time of a system can go up quickly with increasing resource utilization for a given service time value. This is one of those triads in queuing theory that you may find to be very useful very often. Let's see how this triad plays out in queuing theory in the next section.

4.4.4 Queuing Theory Triad II: Utilization, Service Time, and Response Time

The relationship among utilization, service time, and response time is as simple as Equation (4.12), which is rewritten below without regard to whether it's for a queuing node or a queuing system by omitting the subscript i for all symbols:

$$R = \frac{S}{(1 - U)} \qquad (4.20)$$

Figure 4.7 shows how quickly the response time can grow with increasing utilization. Assuming that the service time $S = 1$ second, the response time R would grow up to 2, 2.5, 3.3, 5, 10, and 20 seconds if the utilization U increases to 50%, 60%, 70%, 80%,

TABLE 4.6 Formulas Derived from the $M/M/1$ Model With and Without Feedback

Formula	With Feedback	Without Feedback
System throughput	$X_0 = \lambda$	$X_0 = \lambda$
Local throughput	$X_i = V_i \times X_0$	$X_i = X_0$
Service demand	$D_i = V_i \times S_i$	$D_i = S_i$
Utilization	$U_i = X_0 \times D_i$	$U_i = X_0 \times S_i$
Residence time	$R_i' = V_i \times R_i = D_i/(1 - U_i)$	$R_i' = R_i = S_i/(1 - U_i)$
System response time	$R_0 = \Sigma_{i=1}^{K} R_i'$	$R_0 = \Sigma_{i=1}^{K} R_i'$

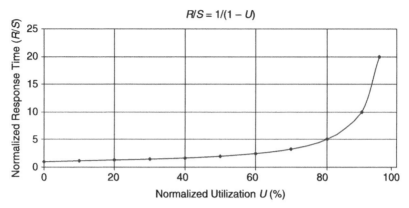

Figure 4.7 *Normalized response time versus system resource utilization.*

90%, and 95%, respectively. This is why you may hear the statement that the CPU utilizations of an OLTP software transaction system should be kept below about 70% so that the response time of the system would not exceed more than three times the service time.

It is interesting to note that the performance and scalability of a software system can be enhanced with the following two options:

- Multiple separate parallel queuing lines. In the context of computers, this scenario corresponds to scaling out to multiple computer servers.
- Single-queue multiserver queues. In the context of computers, this scenario corresponds to scaling up with multiple processors within a single computer server.

Let's examine quantitatively the response time scalability associated with these two types of more complex queuing systems in the next section.

4.4.5 Multiple Parallel Queues versus Single-Queue Multiple Servers

With m multiple parallel queue lines as shown in Figure 4.8, the treatment is simple: simply normalize the system utilization from U to $\rho = U/m$ with $0 \leq \rho \leq 1$ and

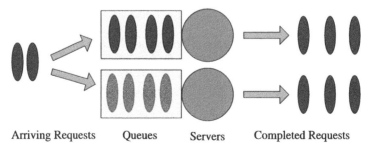

Arriving Requests   Queues   Servers   Completed Requests

Figure 4.8 *Multiple parallel queuing lines.*

Equation (4.20) still applies. This would lead to

$$R = \frac{S}{1 - \rho} \tag{4.21}$$

Figure 4.9 shows a single-queue multiserver scenario. Normalization of the system utilization from U to $\rho = U/m$ with $0 \leq \rho \leq 1$ still applies. However, the response time is now calculated with the so-called Erlang's C function $C(m, \rho)$, as shown below. Erlang was a Danish engineer who worked for the Copenhagen Telephone Exchange. He published the first paper on queuing theory in 1909.

$$R = S\left[1 + \frac{C(m, \rho)}{m(1 - \rho)}\right] \tag{4.22a}$$

$$C(m, \rho) = \frac{(m\rho)^m}{m!} \bigg/ \left[(1 - \rho)\sum_{k=0}^{m-1}\frac{(m\rho)^k}{k!} + \frac{(m\rho)^m}{m!}\right] \tag{4.22b}$$

Equation (4.22b) gives the probability that an arriving customer is delayed in the queue as a function of the number of servers (m) and load intensity (ρ). It can be approximated to give the following formulas for both response time and queue length:

$$R \approx \frac{S}{1 - \rho^m} \tag{4.23a}$$

$$N \approx \frac{m\rho}{1 - \rho^m} \tag{4.23b}$$

Let's compare Equation (4.21) with Equation (4.23a). Apparently, ρ^m is a lot smaller than ρ for large values of m, so we expect that a single-queue multiserver performs a lot better than multiple parallel queues. This seems to favor mainframe computers over modern, much less powerful but massively available computer systems. Let's use a chart to show this observation quantitatively.

With $m = 4$ for both scenarios, the normalized response time R/S is shown in Figure 4.10. Note that for the same utilization of $\rho = 50\%$, the response time degrades by 100% with the multiqueue scenario, but only 14% with the multiserver scenario. For $\rho = 70\%$, the response time degrades by 233% with the multiqueue scenario, but only 50% with the multiserver scenario. This analysis supports a well-known

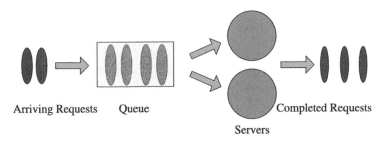

Arriving Requests   Queue   Completed Requests

Servers

Figure 4.9 *Single-queue multiserver queuing system.*

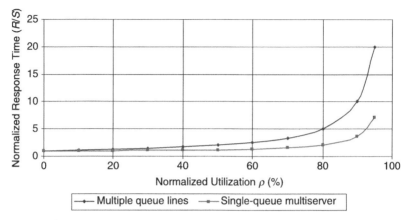

Figure 4.10 *Comparison of response time between multiple parallel queuing line scenario and single-queue multiserver scenario.*

best practice in the community regarding software performance and scalability that scaling up within the same system either by adding more processors or by using more powerful processors is more favorable than scaling out by adding more separate servers.

Next, let's explore the $M/M/m/N/N$ closed model, which applies to both the OLTP systems and batch jobs.

4.4.6 $M/M/m/N/N$ Model (Closed)

A closed queuing system, denoted as $M/M/m/N/N$ using Kendall notation, is described by the following set of recursive equations for each node:

$$R_i'[n] = D_i(1 + Q_i[n-1]) \tag{4.24a}$$

$$X[n] = \frac{n}{Z + \sum_{i=1}^{m} R_i'[n]} \tag{4.24b}$$

$$Q_i[n] = X[n]R_i'[n] \tag{4.24c}$$

where n is the queue length at the system level or the number of customers in the system, $R_i'[n]$ the residence time at queuing node i, $X[n]$ the system throughput, $Q_i[n-1]$ the queue length at queuing node i, and Z the think time. Equation (4.24a) is also called the arrival theorem in queuing theory.

The iteration starts with the initial conditions of $n = 1$ and $Q_i[0] = 0$, which leads to

$$R_i'[1] = D_i \tag{4.25}$$

Again, the service demand D_i is the entry point for solving the above set of recursive equations. This once more demonstrates the fundamental role of service demand in queuing theory.

The above set of equations can be solved using a program easily, for example, using a Java program as listed below:

```java
// a java program for solving M/M/1/N/N
// closed queuing model recursively

   public class closedModel {
    public static void main (String[] args) {
    double[] Qi = new double [100];
    double[] Rprime = new double [100];
    double[] X = new double [100];

    int m = 1;                  // # of queuing node
    int N = 50;                 // # of customers

    double Di = 0.25;          // service demand
    double Z = 2.0;                 // think time
    if (args.length == 2) {
       Di = Double.valueOf(args[0]).doubleValue();
       Z = Double.valueOf(args[1]).doubleValue();
    }

    Qi[0]=0.0;

    // iterate over the # of customers
    for (int n = 1; n < N; n++) {
       Rprime [n] = Di*(1.0 + Qi[n - 1]);
       X[n] = n/(Z + Rprime[n]);
       Qi[n] = X[n]*Rprime[n];

       // open model
       double Ui = X[n]* Di *100;
       double Ri = Di/(1.0 - Ui*0.01);

       System.out.println(``n = '' + n + ``Ui=''
              + Ui+``Rprime[n]=''+
              Rprime[n]+`''' + Ri+``X[n]=''
              + X[n]+``Q[n]=''+Qi[n]);
    }
    }
}
```

To run this program, open up a command prompt and then type

```
prompt> java closedModel <Di> <Z> >result_Di_Z.txt
```

where $<Di>$ and $<Z>$ represent the values for service demand and think time. The results will be directed into a text file that can be imported into an Excel spreadsheet for charting. Note that in the program, m is set to 1 and N is set to 50, so it's for a $M/M/1/$ 50/50 closed model. In the program, the service demand and think time are initialized to 250 milliseconds and 2 seconds, respectively, but different values can be input from the command line to overwrite the default values.

The above code includes the response time data based on the $M/M/1$ open model as well. Figure 4.11 shows the response time comparison between the closed and open models with the different think time values of $Z = 2, 5$, and 10 seconds, respectively. The service demand was fixed at 0.25 second for all runs. It is seen that for utilizations below 70%, the open model approximates the closed model well. This gives us confidence that the open model is sufficiently accurate with *utilizations* below 70% or so. A more detailed comparison between the real measurements and the open model predictions concluded similarly [Liu and Crain, 2004].

It's interesting to note that the open model response times for the three different values of think time Z overlap. This is expected since the open model is independent of think time, whereas the closed model isn't.

Figure 4.12 shows how the throughput varies with the number of users in a closed system, with the three different values of think time $Z = 2, 5$, and 10 seconds, respectively. It is seen that the knee of the curve moves toward more users with increasing think time. This is equal to saying that for a fixed number of users, the throughput of a system would be higher when the average user think time is smaller. In other

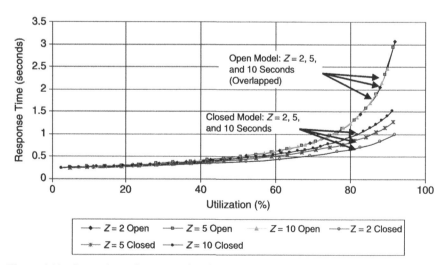

Figure 4.11 Comparison of response time between open model and closed model with different values of think time $Z = 2, 5$, and 10 seconds, respectively.

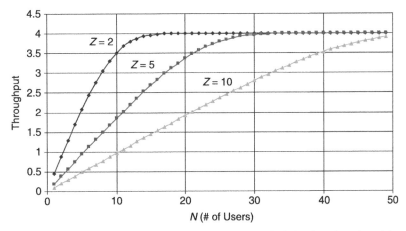

Figure 4.12 *Throughput versus think time Z in the* M/M/1/50/50 *closed model.*

words, for a fixed throughput, more and more users can be supported by the system with increasing average user think time. This is because longer think time means more users can use the system while some users are thinking without actually stressing the system.

Next, let's look at the response time versus the number of users. Figure 4.13 shows that for a given number of users, the response time varies drastically with think time Z. With a fixed number of users, longer average think time implies that the system would respond faster. In other words, for a fixed response time, longer user average think time implies that more users can be supported.

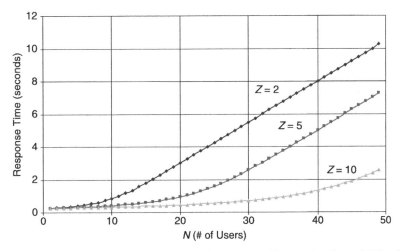

Figure 4.13 *Response times of a closed queuing system with a service time of 250 milliseconds and think times of 2, 5, and 10 seconds, respectively.*

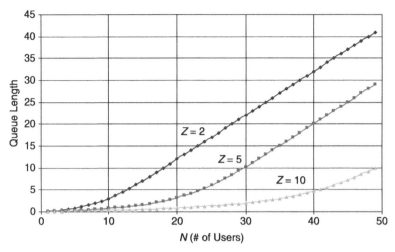

Figure 4.14 *Average number of users waiting to be serviced in a closed queuing system with think time Z = 2, 5, and 10 seconds, respectively.*

Figures 4.14 and 4.15 show the queue length and the number of active users with the three different values of think time $Z = 2$, 5, and 10 seconds, respectively.

Note that in Figure 4.14 the queue length represents the average number of users waiting to be serviced, in contrast with the number of users being serviced shown in Figure 4.15. Once again, for a fixed number of users, longer average think time implies that the system would become less jammed, as shown in Figure 4.14. It's also interesting to note from Figure 4.15 that with increasing average think time, more and more users can be serviced until the system becomes saturated and then only a fixed number of users can be serviced. Specifically, with those three different values of think time $Z = 2$, 5, and 10 seconds, the maximum number of users who can be serviced in this system are 8, 20, and 40, respectively.

Figure 4.13 demonstrates that the response time goes up linearly beyond some number of users in a closed queuing system. This behavior is very different from what we see in Figure 4.7, which shows that the response time in an open system rapidly approaches infinity when the system utilization approaches 100%. This discrepancy is purely due to the assumption with the open model that there are an infinite number of users in an open system, which is unrealistic. Let's clarify this discrepancy quantitatively in the next section.

4.4.7 Finite Response Time in Reality

With the open model, the response time goes up to infinity with the utilization approaching 100% according to $R = S/(1 - U)$, as shown in Figure 4.7. This is

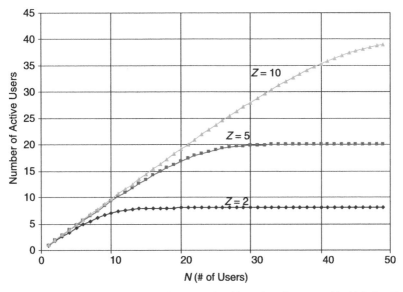

Figure 4.15   *Average number of users being serviced in a closed system with think time $Z = 2$, 5, and 10 seconds, respectively.*

purely an artificial effect, as can be demonstrated with the closed model in which the number of customers is finite.

To prove that there is no infinite response time in reality, let's begin with the definition of throughput for a closed model, similar to Equation (4.24b):

$$X[N] = \frac{N}{Z + R[N]} \qquad (4.26)$$

where X is the throughput, N the number of users in the closed system, Z the think time, and R the response time. To facilitate the discussion, we have omitted the subscript in Equation (4.26) to imply that we are considering a single queuing node.

Since our goal is to work out the maximum response time for a closed system, Equation (4.26) needs to be rearranged into the following form:

$$R[N] = \frac{N}{X[N]} - Z \qquad (4.27)$$

This equation shows the response time as a function of N. To normalize the response time using the service demand D, divide it by service demand D. Then we have

$$\frac{R[N]}{D} = \frac{N}{X[N]D} - \frac{Z}{D} \qquad (4.28)$$

Using the utilization law of $U = X[N]D = m\rho$ for a system that has m servers for a single queue and applying $\rho = 1$, we have

$$\left(\frac{R[N]}{D}\right)_{max} = \frac{N}{m} - \frac{Z}{D} \tag{4.29}$$

The condition of $\rho = 1$ corresponds to the extreme case of 100% resource utilization. This equation defines the maximum response time that an N-user closed system can have.

To help confirm that Equation (4.29) indeed represents the maximum response time for an N-user closed system when N is sufficiently large, three sets of data were obtained and displayed on the same chart shown in Figure 4.16:

- Response time versus the number of users for a closed system by solving Equation (4.24a) through (4.24c) with a service demand of 0.25 second and a think time of 2 seconds
- Response time of the corresponding open model using the intermediate results of the numerical solutions of the closed model
- Maximum response time calculated using Equation (4.29) with the same parameters used for solving the closed model

These sets of data describe the same queuing system either approximately or exactly. The closed model results are exact, whereas the open model results and the maximum response time calculations are approximate.

Figure 4.16 shows the comparison of response time among the three models, obtained when the above model was solved numerically. The upper curve corresponds to the open model, the lower curve corresponds to the maximum response time calculated according to Equation (4.29), and the curve in-between corresponds to the closed model. It is interesting that the two approximate approaches agree well with the closed model under their respective assumptions: namely, open model for light to normal

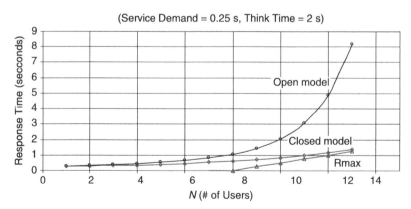

Figure 4.16 Comparison of response time among the open model, closed model, and maximum response time limit.

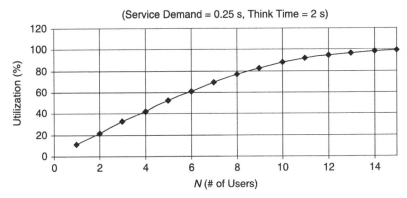

Figure 4.17   *Utilizations from solving the closed model associated with Figure 4.16.*

loads with $N < 7$ and Equation (4.29) for heavy loads with $N > 12$. The gap ($7 < N < 12$) between the two extreme conditions is filled in by the numerical solutions of the closed model.

Figure 4.17 shows the utilizations corresponding to different numbers of users, recorded when the above closed model was solved numerically. It confirms that for $N = 7$ the utilization is about 70%, and for $N = 12$, the utilization is about 95%. This once more demonstrates that one can use utilization to determine the validity of both the open model and the maximum response time for a large number of users. Again, it's a lot easier to use the system utilization rather than the number of users in a system to quantify the validity of the open model and the maximum response time limit model, because the former can be measured more conveniently than the latter. This validity issue for open models will be elaborated further in the next section.

4.4.8   Validity of Open Models

One must keep in mind that whenever an analytical formula is used for predicting or verifying the behavior of a system, it's necessary to make sure that the formula is used both in the right context and within the range of its validity.

The above statement applies to open queuing models as well. As we know, closed models are solved numerically, and the resultant numerical results can be taken as accurate solutions to real systems. Open models provide ready-to-use analytical formulas without requiring a program to solve a set of equations. This obvious analytical scaling relationship is a huge advantage of open models relative to closed models.

The question is: Under what conditions are the analytical formulas derived from the open models valid? As a matter of fact, this question has been answered with the concrete comparison data provided in the preceding section; but to underscore its importance, it's summarized again in this section.

There are quite a few different definitions of the validity of open models. But I have found that it's most convenient and practical to define it using the entities of resource utilization and queue length for the system in question. Essentially, the analytical formulas derived from open models are valid under either of the following conditions:

- The system is not near saturation or the utilization is below 70%. This statement is supported by both the quantitative numerical examples presented in the preceding section and some quantitative research [Liu and Crain, 2004].

- The system queue is empty or low, meaning that the system is not running near saturation and can take more loads without seeing significant impact on its performance.

There is a misconception that the analytical formulas derived with open models are valid if there are an infinite number of customers in the system. The assumption of infinite population size as implied by the Kendall notation $M/M/m/\infty/\infty/\text{FIFO}$ should be understood as the total number of customers processed by the system, not the number of customers in the system at any given instant. It's impossible to have an infinite number of customers in an open system at any given instant, because one of the driving input parameters to an open system is the average arrival rate, which is always finite.

The word *infinite* associated with the assumption for an open model should be understood as the ratio of the number of customers being serviced to the number of customers waiting in the queue. That ratio approaches infinity when the number of customers waiting approaches zero. That means that if there are more customers waiting than being serviced, then such systems cannot be accurately described with open models. The further away the system is from being defined by the above two statements, the less accurately such a system can be described with open queuing models. One can study this subject further with the help of the text by Gunther [1998] listed at the end of this chapter.

Approximate analytical formulas are useful not only for predicting the performance and scalability of a software system, but also for analyzing the performance and scalability bottlenecks based on real measurements. The concept of bottleneck is actually rooted in queuing theory, as we'll see in the next section.

4.4.9 Performance and Scalability Bottlenecks in a Software System

For batch jobs, the maximum throughput is achieved when the system is fully utilized. This can be confirmed with the utilization law of $U = XD$ that

$$X_{\max} = 1/D_{\max} \tag{4.30}$$

when $U = 1$. Equation (4.30) can be confirmed with Figure 4.12 that all curves with different think time values eventually got saturated with a maximum throughput of 4, which is due to the fact that a service demand of 0.25 second was used for all calculations.

Typically, for a system that uses multiple resources, total service demand is the sum of all service demands at different queuing nodes. The resource that contributes most to the total service demand is defined as the bottleneck. However, it might be difficult to compare the service demand among all queuing nodes, as service demand is hard to measure. One equally valid alternative is to use utilization instead of service demand to define bottlenecks, as is proved next.

For all resources, the following relationship holds true according to Equation (4.15):

$$\frac{U_i}{D_i} = \frac{U_j}{D_j} = \cdots = \frac{U_k}{D_k} \qquad (4.31)$$

which implies that large service demand corresponds to large utilization as well. Typically, resource utilizations are monitored with sufficient precision and therefore are an ideal metric for defining bottlenecks. This is especially true with the resource type of computer CPUs.

As far as the system bottleneck around the response time is concerned, the same guideline applies as well, as the response time is proportional to service demand or inversely proportional to the system idle time. Identifying system bottlenecks is the first step for optimizing and tuning software performance and scalability, whereas reducing service demands or system utilizations is the key to actually realizing tangible improvements on the performance and scalability of your software. We'll see such examples with the case studies provided later.

Before concluding queuing theory, I have to mention that I only covered some very basic aspects of queuing theory that are very likely to be used in your software performance work. This book is not about queuing theory; it's about practical software performance testing, analysis, optimization, and tuning, for which a basic knowledge about queuing theory is very helpful.

Instead of dragging you into more complicated queuing models, I'd like to direct you to the genealogy of the various major queuing models in the next section to help explain what we have covered and what we haven't. You can spend more time studying those models that have not been covered here with the appropriate texts that I'll recommend at the end of this chapter.

4.4.10 Genealogy of Queuing Models

Apparently it's impossible for this book to cover all queuing models. In order to have a good understanding of what we have learned about queuing theory after all, Figure 4.18 shows the genealogy of all queuing models described using the Kendall descriptors.

You can read this chart by following the leads below:

- The queuing policy of FIFO (first-in first-out) is implied for all models labeled on the chart.
- The genealogy first branched between Markov and non-Markov processes. You can ignore non-Markov processes as they are too complicated for real-life software applications.

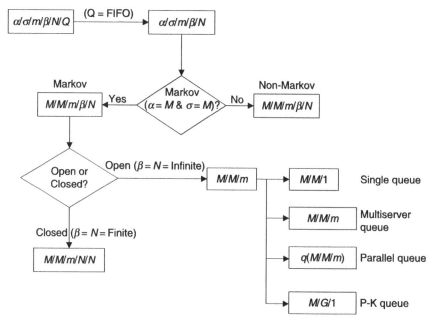

Figure 4.18 Genealogy of queuing models in Kendall notation.

- It then branched between the open and closed models. The closed models can only be solved numerically, whereas the open models are analytically tractable.
- For open models, we covered the simplest $M/M/1$ open model, parallel queues or multiple queue lines, and single-queue multiserver. There is a more generic model $M/G/1$, which takes the general distribution for the service time distribution. In this area, some pioneering work was done by Pollaczek and Khinchine, and you can delve deeper by reading other texts recommended at the end of this chapter.

This concludes our introduction to queuing theory. In the next two chapters, I'll concentrate on how queuing theory can be applied effectively to solving real performance problems for your software products.

4.5 SUMMARY

In this chapter, we explored queuing theory in the context of software performance and scalability. We introduced all basic concepts of queuing theory centered on response time for OLTP workloads and throughput for batch jobs. We provided a brief review of probability theory, which was necessary for understanding the Markov process and Poisson and exponential distributions upon which the subsequent queuing models were built. We covered in adequate depth both open models and closed models. We clarified infinite response time that is inherent with open models. We also explained how to identify bottlenecks using service demands and resource utilizations. This material is essential for applying queuing theory to solving real-world software performance and scalability problems.

Some of the highlights from this chapter include the following:

- Queuing theory is rooted in probability theory and statistics, and the performance behaviors of a software system can be described using queuing models. Because of the intrinsic stochastic nature of the performance of software, your measurements of response time and throughput contain inevitable errors. It is recommended not to interpret fluctuations in your test results of a few percent as performance gains or losses.

- The Markov random process is the foundation for establishing queuing models such as the $M/M/m$ open models, which are analytically tractable, as well as the $M/M/m/N/N$ closed models, which can be solved numerically to provide insight into queuing systems with a finite number of customers.

- The Markov process is characterized by the Poisson distribution and exponential distribution in the simplest case. The Poisson distribution describes the number of arrivals, whereas the exponential distribution describes time intervals such as interarrival time, service time, and response time.

- Open models deal with queuing systems with constant incoming and departing customers, whereas closed models deal with queuing systems with a fixed number of customers in the system. Open models are more applicable to OLTP workloads, whereas closed models are applicable to both batch jobs and OLTP workloads. Open models become less and less accurate when more and more customers are queued up in the system or when the system approaches saturation.

- Keep in mind that service demand is one of the most fundamental elements for calculating other queuing metrics, such as the utilization and response time. Service demand is also the indicator of performance bottlenecks. As service demand generally is hard to measure, one can use utilization instead to identify system bottlenecks.

- Software performance work is about applying queuing theory to analyzing performance bottlenecks and then removing bottlenecks to help build high-performance software products. By practicing, you'll become proficient in applying queuing theory to solving software performance problems.

I hope you will now consider applying queuing theory to solving your software performance and scalability challenges. It will be both fun and rewarding. Based on my own experience, I am confident that queuing theory can help you become more productive and efficient with your assignments to test, analyze, optimize, and tune the performance and scalability of your software. Chapters 5 and 6 will help you solidify what you have learned in this chapter by showing you how you can apply queuing theory to solving real-world software performance and scalability problems.

RECOMMENDED READING

For a brief review of probability, random variables, and random processes:

H. P. Hsu, "Theory and Problems of Probability, Random Variables, and Random Process," McGraw-Hill, 1997.

For a more rigorous mathematical treatment of queuing theory:

D. Gross, J. F. Shortle, J. M. Thompson, C. M. Harris, *Fundamentals of Queuing Theory*, 4th edition, Wiley Series in Probability and Statistics, 2008.

C. G. Cassandra and S. Lafortune, *Introduction to Discrete Event Systems*, 2nd edition, Springer Science Media, LLC, 2008.

G. Bolch, S. Greiner, H. de Meer, and K. Shridharbai, *Queuing Networks and Markov Chains: Modeling and Performance Evaluation with Computer Science Applications*, 2nd edition, John Wiley & Sons, 2006.

For some classical texts on queuing theory:

N. Gunther, *The Practical Performance Analyst*, McGraw-Hill, 1998.

R. Jain, *The Art of Computer Systems Performance Analysis*, John Wiley & Sons, 1991.

E. D. Lazowska, J. Zahorjan, G. S. Graham, and K. C. Sevcik, *Quantitative System Performance: Computer System Analysis Using Queuing Network Models*, Prentice Hall, 1984.

D. A. Menasce and V. A. F. Almeida, *Scaling for E-Business*, Prentice Hall PTR, 2000.

D. A. Menasce, V. A. F. Almeida, and L. W. Dowdy, *Performance by Design*, Prentice Hall, 2004.

The following three publications are seminal works about queuing theory quoted in the text of this chapter:

J. R. Jackson, Jobshop-like queuing systems, *Management Science*, Vol. 10, No. 1, 131–142, 1963.

D. G. Kendall, Some problems in the theory of queues, *Journal of the Royal Statistical Society Series B*, Vol. 13, 151–185, 1981.

J. D. C. Little, A proof for the queuing formula: $L = \lambda W$, *Operations Research*, Vol. 9, No. 3, 1961.

The following publications might be helpful if you are interested in how queuing theory can be applied to optimizing and tuning the performance and scalability of modern enterprise software applications:

H. H. Liu and P. V. Crain, An analytic model for predicting the performance of SOA-based enterprise software applications, in *CMG 2004 Proceedings*, Las Vegas.

H. H. Liu, Service demand models for enterprise software applications, in *CMG 2005 Proceedings*, Orlando, Florida.

H. H. Liu, Applying queuing theory to optimizing enterprise software applications, in *CMG 2006 Proceedings*, Reno.

EXERCISES

4.1. Explain conceptually the differences among *wait time*, *service time*, *response time*, *residence time*, and *think time*.

4.2. Explain conceptually the difference between *arrival rate* and *throughput*.

4.3. What are the characteristics of a Markov process?

4.4. What are the common usages of the Poisson and exponential distribution functions?

4.5. What is the Kendall descriptor used for?

4.6. Table 4.7 shows the load test results of an OLTP application with the given user types, the number of users and arrival rate for each user type. In the table, the arrival rate is measured in transactions per hour, and R represents the response time. Calculate the number of concurrent users for each user type. Compare with Exercise 3.6.

TABLE 4.7   An OLTP Load Test Profile

User Type	# of Users	Arrival Rate	R (s)	# of Concurrent Users
UT01	60	2749	2.53	( )
UT02	40	1572	1.87	( )
UT03	40	1400	2.08	( )
UT04	60	4223	0.89	( )

4.7. Why is Jackson's theorem an epoch-making advance in queuing theory?

4.8. Describe quantitatively the relationship among the *resource utilization*, *service time*, and *response time* for a single queuing node.

4.9. An OLTP workload consists of a single type of user activity of a Web application deployed on a single Web server, which serves static HTML contents. Statistically, the application requires an average service time of 200 ms on the Web server to process a user transaction. The Web server is shared with multiple applications. Calculate the average response time for the above user scenario when the Web server is already driven to 50% busy by some other applications.

4.10. What's the difference between computer server *scaling up* and *scaling out*? Which one is more effective and why?

4.11. Let's say the Web server is close to 100% busy for Exercise 4.9 and you are given the option of adding one more identical system or doubling the CPU capacity of the same server either by adding twice the number of identical processors or by replacing the existing processors with ones that are $2\times$ faster. Choose your option and justify it to your manager quantitatively.

4.12. Solve a closed model with the program provided in Section 4.4.6. Explain your observations.

4.13. How would you quantify that a resource is a bottleneck for a system?

4.14. Prove mathematically that for a batch job that consists of two consecutive activities that process the same number of objects, the combined throughput, X_0, can be calculated as follows:

$$X_0 = \frac{X_1 \times X_2}{X_1 + X_2}$$

where X_1 and X_2 represent the throughput values of the two consecutive activities, respectively.

4.15. An enterprise batch job is scheduled to run every night to reconcile the objects collected during the day. The batch job consists of two consecutive activities: validateObjects and checkInObjects. In order to isolate the performance issues, these two activities were run separately, and the throughput for each activity was measured separately as well. The measurements show that for reconciling 50,000 objects, the validateObjects activity took 9 minutes and 41 seconds, and the checkInObjects activity took 23 minutes and 9 seconds. Calculate the throughput for each activity first. Then calculate the combined throughput using the formula described in Exercise 4.14.

4.16. A software development team identified a 5–10% performance degradation with the product under development. After spending some time finding the root cause for that 5–10% degradation in vain, it was decided that they would move on since a 5–10% degradation would not be a show stopper. What can you make of this?

5

Case Study I: Queuing Theory Applied to SOA

"Think simple" as my old master used to say—meaning reduce the whole of its parts into the simplest terms, getting back to first principles.
—Frank Lloyd Wright

Queuing theory was developed for solving real problems. Specifically, in the field of software, queuing theory can be used not only for analyzing the performance and scalability bottlenecks of existing software applications based on traditional software architectures, but also for predicting the performance of software applications based on emerging software technologies such as the service-oriented architecture (SOA).

As a case study, this chapter will demonstrate how queuing theory can be applied to predicting the performance of SOA-based software applications. A well-developed sample medical record application built on BEA's XML Web services framework was used for this exercise.

Along with presenting this example, I'll show you how to carry out software performance tests with an end-to-end, well-thought-out procedure that consists of setting up a test bed, deploying the application, designing and implementing test scenarios, running the tests, collecting performance counters, and analyzing the test results. This procedure can be used as a reference for you to design and execute your performance and scalability tests as well.

Another purpose of this chapter is to help reconcile people's doubts about queuing theory such as "Is queuing theory accurate?" and "Does it really work?" The answers to such questions are both *yes* and *no*. Basically, a theory is accurate and works if all its assumptions are satisfied. As such, queuing theory is accurate when all its assumptions are satisfied, and it is not accurate when any of its assumptions are not satisfied.

Software Performance and Scalability. By Henry H. Liu
Copyright © 2009 IEEE Computer Society

To prove the above rationale, a fine experiment using an XML Web services application was designed and carried out. The measurements were then compared with the predictions based on queuing theory introduced in the preceding chapter. This chapter presents a summary of that experiment.

This will be a good opportunity for you to learn how to apply mature queuing theory to XML Web services as an emerging technology, so that you can design and develop better XML Web services applications. The performance and scalability characteristics of XML Web services are still an undefined territory. Along with this experiment, I believe some low-hanging fruits regarding some of the performance and scalability characteristics of XML Web services have been identified, which might be interesting to you as well.

Let's start with a brief introduction to the SOA, which has been the hottest topic in today's IT world. It's important to learn what the SOA is about because sufficient knowledge about the subject matter can help you design and carry out the performance and scalability tests more efficiently.

5.1   INTRODUCTION TO SOA

In this section, I'll introduce the background of the SOA to give you a clear perspective for the context of our discussions in this chapter.

Researchers and software engineers have been striving to simplify the software development process since the advent of computers decades ago. This movement has been driven by demands such as time-to-market and cost control associated with the development and maintenance of software applications. In this regard, shifts in the software architectural paradigm have been revolutionizing the way in which large-scale, mission-critical enterprise applications are built.

Interestingly, software architecture and state-of-the-art hardware technologies reinforce each other, giving software architects and developers greater flexibility for building simple yet functionally rich applications to meet the stringent business requirements of today's competitive markets. Along this path, the SOA has stimulated much interest by industry in this latest generation of software architecture for building flexible, low-cost enterprise software in place of tightly coupled legacy applications.

SOA emphasizes the functionality of software as either a reusable atomic service or a composite service that is built with a collection of atomic services. Each service is capable of completing a specific task for the client either independently or by collaborating with other services in a federated fashion to complete more complex tasks.

SOA is not a new thing. The earliest generation of service-oriented architectures includes DCOM [Eddon and Eddon, 1998], EJB/RMI [Anderson and Anderson, 2002], and CORBA/IIOP [Slama et al., 1999]. These SOA frameworks use different proprietary object communication protocols from different vendors. As the Internet becomes ubiquitous, the Hypertext Transfer Protocol (HTTP) has arisen as the dominating carrier communication protocol for delivering eXtensible Markup Language (XML) messages. This communication protocol innovation has led to XML Web services as a new generation of the SOA using open object communication protocols. The SOA based on XML Web services is a promising approach to building enterprise class software applications [Banerjee et al., 2001; Cauldwell et al., 2001; Glass, 2002; Microsoft, 2003].

Apparently, it's necessary to have a good understanding about what XML Web services are about before presenting the analytical performance model for XML Web services based enterprise applications. This will be the subject of the next section.

5.2 XML WEB SERVICES

Built on the introduction to XML Web services provided in Chapter 2, we now directly dive into the messaging mechanism of XML Web services. In order to build the queuing model for the XML Web services based enterprise applications, we have to understand how an XML Web service client consumes an XML Web service via message exchange.

As shown in Figure 5.1, a complete cycle of the XML Web service consuming process has to undergo the following steps:

1. The client program creates an XML Web service proxy object as a handle.
2. The client calls a method of the XML Web service on the proxy object.
3. The XML Web service infrastructure on the consumer side serializes the method call and arguments into a SOAP message and sends it to the XML Web service provider over the network.
4. The XML Web service infrastructure on the provider side deserializes the SOAP message and creates an instance of the XML Web service. The infrastructure then calls the method with the arguments on the XML Web service.
5. The XML Web service executes the method and returns the results to the infrastructure.
6. The infrastructure serializes the results into a SOAP message and sends them to the client over the network.
7. The infrastructure on the consumer side deserializes the SOAP message containing the method call results and sends them to the proxy object.
8. The proxy object sends the results to the client program.

Understanding how a software product works internally is very necessary for being able to carry out the performance and scalability tests successfully. Such detailed inner working information on a software application is also very necessary to determine what performance model to use to fully characterize its performance and scalability. Specifically, for XML Web services, Figure 5.1 is a good representation of its detailed inner working information. It shows how the XML Web service consumer and provider interact with each other to fulfill a service in the format of *request* and *response*. With the help of this flow chart, we can easily identify the following factors that can

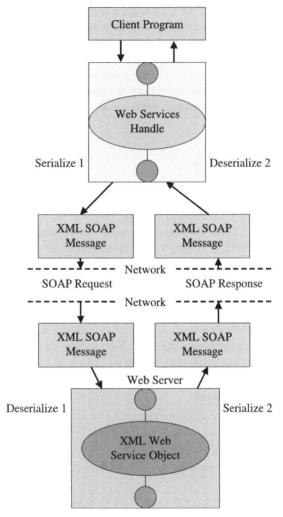

Figure 5.1   *Cycle of message exchange with XML Web services.*

affect the performance and scalability of XML Web services based enterprise applications:

- The client program as the service consumer sending the service request
- The XML Web service infrastructure on each side that supports the messaging mechanism by serializing objects into SOAP messages and deserializing SOAP messages back into objects
- XML SOAP message transfer over the network
- The XML Web service object as the service provider that works behind the scenes to fulfill the service request

In the next section, I'll show you how to construct an analytical model for predicting the performance of the SOA (XML Web services) based enterprise software applications based on the performance and scalability factors identified above.

5.3 THE ANALYTICAL MODEL

XML Web service is an exciting new software architecture that has emerged in recent years. However, the analytical models for software performance are quite mature relative to the evolution of new hardware and software technologies that have thrilled software practitioners during the past several decades. A few very excellent texts about how to establish queuing models for solving software performance problems are readily available [Gunther, 1998; Jain, 1991; Lazowska et al., 1984; Menasce and Almeida, 2000]. According to these texts, the acceptance criteria regarding the errors of those analytical models are: predicting system resource utilization—within 10%; system throughput—within 10%; and response time—within 30%; Of course, these numbers are approximate guidelines.

The software performance models can be further categorized into *system-level models* and *component-level models* [Menasce and Almeida, 2000]. The system-level models treat the actual system as a black box, in which only the external entities such as arrival rate and throughput are considered. The component-level models examine the system performance by decomposing the system into finer granularities of multiple hardware and software components, where each component is treated as a queue. This is the concept of queuing network models (QNMs), which can be further divided into *open models* and *closed models*, as we discussed in Chapter 4.

Depending on the number of classes of requests, models can be single-class or multiclass. Closed models have a fixed number of requests per class, whereas open models allow the number of requests per class to be variable in the system.

Based on how queuing theory works and how an XML Web services based application works, we can construct a QNM as shown in Figure 5.2 to represent all major performance factors in an XML Web services application system. This QNM is a collection of single queues, each of which mimics a single node or link in a real system. The model reflects the application system architecture composed of the flows of requests and responses from layer to layer.

An analytical model is attractive because of its simplicity and the power to predict the performance of a system that has not yet been built. A model is less useful if it's too complicated and provides no simple-to-use formulas. In this sense, the $M/M/1$ open model introduced in Chapter 4 is the most appropriate one to serve as the basis of the analytical model for predicting the performance of an SOA-based application. Without repeating the detailed description about how the model works, all of the performance metrics and laws for this model are recaptured in Table 5.1. For convenience, the formulas are renumbered.

As a brief review, let's explain what each symbol represents.

- λ—arrival rate
- X_0—system throughput

- V_i—number of visits to queuing node i
- S_i—average service time at queuing node i
- D_i—service demand at queuing node i
- U_i—resource utilization at queuing node i
- R_i'—residence time at queuing node i
- R_0—System response time

If you need a more detailed review about these formulas, revisit Chapter 4.

Remember that the software performance models are based on the two input parameters: The arrival rate λ and service demand D_i. Arrival rates are typically

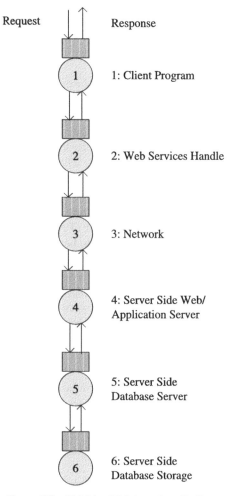

Figure 5.2 *QNM for SOA-based applications.*

TABLE 5.1   Performance Laws and Metrics for the $M/M/1$ Open Model

Law and Metric	Formula	
Equilibrium condition	$X_0 = \lambda$	(5.1)
Service demand law	$D_i = V_i \times S_i$	(5.2)
Utilization law	$U_i = X_0 \times D_i$	(5.3)
Residence time	$R_i' = V_i \times R_i = D_i/(1 - U_i)$	(5.4)
System response time	$R_0 = \sum_{i=1}^{K} R_i'$	(5.5)

given, whereas service demands must be measured. Once again, the service demand associated with each component is the core of a queuing model, as we'll see in the next section.

5.4 SERVICE DEMAND

The performance goal of a software system simply is to minimize the overall response time while maximizing the system throughput. According to Equation (5.4), the residence time at a queue can be minimized by reducing the service demand at the resource as well as the resource utilization. From a system's perspective, the slowest resource or most highly utilized resource should be optimized or tuned first in order to see the largest effect on the performance of the overall system. This simple principle is the entrie foundation for all software performance optimization and tuning activities.

Equation (5.2) further illustrates that reducing service demand D_i requires:

- Reducing the number of times a resource is accessed (V_i). This is a very applicable best practice in optimizing database-intensive software applications, as V_i corresponds to the number of round trips between a database server and its client. It is equally effective in optimizing network-intensive applications and can be implemented by minimizing the number of network round trips between two subsystems or processes. This is a well-known performance pattern and should be applied whenever possible.
- Reducing the absolute service time (S_i). This typically has a lot to do with adopting the most efficient algorithms for carrying out various performance-critical computing tasks. You can also minimize the service time by eliminating those computations that are actually not needed. Such extraneous computations that don't have to be performed in an application are termed "wastes" [Millsap, 2003]. Don't include *wastes* in your application and burn your valuable hardware resources for nothing. This sounds like a no-brainer, but it occurs quite often: for various reasons, such wastes have been built into or even shipped to customers together with the other useful functionalities of a product without realizing their unnecessary, negative impacts on the performance and scalability of the product.

The service demand at each queue depends largely on how a software system is designed. More efficient algorithms, better data access methods, and simplified business logic at the application implementation level are very effective common practices for improving the service time of a software system, as elaborated earlier.

On the other hand, the underlying hardware that provides the platform for the system software and application software to run on is also critical in determining the service time. Very often, faster hardware is the easiest solution if the problem is well understood and adding new hardware is affordable.

Besides, various tunings at the system level such as virtual machine heap allocation, garbage collection, processor affinity, and system and application configurations can often drastically improve the residence time at a specific resource by reducing the service demand and hence the system resource utilization.

In the next few sections, we'll explore the various components of this sample XML Web services application from the service time perspective.

5.4.1 Web Services Handle Creation

Object creation is an expensive operation. It may take hundreds of milliseconds to create an object. When an object is being created, its own constructor method and the constructors of all its parent classes have to be called. Those constructor calls not only consume local resources but also require the participation of distributed resources under certain circumstances.

With XML Web services, services are defined in text files according to the Web Services Description Language (WSDL) standards. Services are published dynamically by the service provider. The cost for creating a client proxy object or Web services handle is high, since the corresponding service definition file has to be fetched over the network. Additionally, the WSDL file has to be parsed as part of the object creation, which incurs additional cost relative to conventional object creation. Therefore, from the performance perspective, the client proxy object has to be cached.

5.4.2 XML SOAP Serialization/Deserialization

XML SOAP serialization and deserialization operations are responsible for converting back and forth between SOAP request/response messages and Java objects. Such operations need to be carried out on both the client and server sides. It might be time consuming to perform such operations, which is a concern from the performance and scalability perspectives.

XML SOAP serialization and deserialization operations are sometimes hidden from the user program, since they are performed by the supporting XML Web services infrastructure development kits and run-time libraries. In this case, the user does not have much flexibility to optimize serialization and deserialization processes. However, for large-scale enterprise applications, a specialized serializer has to be developed, which provides developers with another opportunity for optimizing the performance and scalability of the XML Web services based applications.

5.4.3 Network Latency

Since XML Web services are designed to integrate multiple services using SOAP over HTTP, network latency is one of the biggest concerns from the performance and scalability perspectives. Nowadays it's possible to have almost zero latency networks with the state-of-the-art network and cabling equipment in a typical LAN environment. However, network communications across WAN or even across continents are much slower. Networks such as home networks and 10-Mbps corporate networks are common as well. Network latency is one of the largest performance factors for XML Web services.

XML Web services SOAP messages can range from a few kilobytes to tens of kilobytes or even megabytes in large-scale enterprise applications. Depending on the bandwidth of the network and the size of SOAP messages, network latencies can be very significant. Table 5.2 shows typical network latencies with various commonly used networks.

Table 5.3 shows the network configurations labeled A through F in Table 5.2. As expected, network latencies are low when both the client and server sit on the same

TABLE 5.2 Network Latencies (Milliseconds) with Various Networks

Bytes	A	B	C	D	E	F
32	4	2	<1	<1	43	<3
64	4	2	<1	<1	44	<3
128	5	3	<1	<1	45	<3
256	6	3	<1	<1	44	<3
512	7	4	<1	1	45	<3
1024	10	7	<1	2	48	<3
2048	17	10	<1	3	51	<3
4096	33	–	1	7	55	<3
8192	50	30	2	14	64	<3
16384	96	32	3	27	80	3
32768	218	104	6	55	110	3
65400	372	204	12	110	172	3

TABLE 5.3 Networks Associated with Table 5.2

Network	Configuration
A	Wireless at home with DSL, 11 Mbps, Windows XP (Pentium IV, 2.66 GHz) to Windows XP (AMD Athlon XP, 2 GHz)
B	Direct hub connection with DSL, 100 Mbps, Windows XP (Pentium IV, 2.66 GHz) to Windows 2000 (Pentium III, 700 MHz)
C	Direct hub connection with DSL, 100 Mbps, Windows XP (Pentium IV, 2.66 GHz) to Windows XP (AMD Athlon XP, 2 GHz)
D	100-Mbps LAN, Windows XP to Windows XP
E	Corporate network from California to Kansas City, Windows XP to HP-UX 11
F	Same 100-Mbps LAN, Windows XP to HP-UX 11

high-speed LAN or when the message size is below 1 kilo-byte on a typical home network. Column E indicates that communication over long-distance networks is slow. Interestingly, this has in fact helped create a whole new segment of business in the software industry for those companies that provide content caching services distributed globally.

5.4.4 XML Web Service Provider

The XML Web service provider is the component that actually provides the client with the services the client requests. XML Web services are typically implemented as a stateless session façade object that delegates much of its work to other traditional session and entity objects that implement the business logic. However, this extra layer of overhead associated with the XML Web services façade could be high relative to the raw performance that the underlying business components have to offer. We will see some typical performance data in this regard in the section on test results later.

5.4.5 Database Server

The database is an important part of every enterprise application. Although it is not unique to XML Web services, its importance in the performance spectrum of XML Web services cannot be underestimated.

Although techniques for database optimization and tuning are often vendor specific, there are some aspects that are common for all types of database systems. To achieve the best possible database service times, one needs to make sure of the following:

- Adequate hardware capacity is assigned to the database server. This typically means using the latest computer servers with multicore processors and the fastest CPU clock rate.
- For a given type of database system, whether it's IBM DB2, Microsoft SQL Server, Oracle, or any other type of database systems, set all performance-sensitive parameters to their proper values. These parameters are typically related to memory, optimal query execution plans, and fast data retrieve and store from/ to the underlying physical disks.
- Adequate indexes are in place for all time-consuming SQL queries.
- Optimizer statistics are up to date. Without proper statistics gathered on the relevant tables and indexes, the SQL query optimizer is essentially blind in choosing most optimal execution plans, which often leads to slow queries and poor database performance.
- SQL queries are designed to be high performance. This is a whole separate area of database performance optimization and tuning on its own.
- Excessive logical reads are contained with a proper indexing scheme such as covering indexing scheme. Excessive logical reads are both a performance killer and a scalability killer. It is often masked with excessive database server

CPU utilizations. The larger the data volume for your test, the worse it is for your application. We'll see a concrete example about this issue in the next chapter.

To learn more about database optimization and tuning, one can consult the relevant texts that are readily available. For example, one can refer to Millsap [2003] for common performance tuning strategies on Oracle, which is one of the most widely used enterprise database products.

5.4.6 Data Storage

For database-intensive applications, adequate storage is very crucial for the overall performance and scalability of an application [Simitci, 2003]. Ideally, one should use enterprise class external storage for internal performance and scalability tests, but it might be difficult to have access to such high-end storage due to the budget constraint on the development systems in an organization. If you have to use local internal disks for your performance and scalability tests, here are some recommendations to keep in mind:

- Use the latest SCSI drives, which can provide much higher data transfer throughput than the outdated ones. Avoid putting all data for your database onto one single local disk: it is just as important to avoid putting the entire software stack onto one single low-end computer. Don't make the mistake of conducting the performance and scalability tests for your enterprise software applications using a low-end development computer system for all your software components and a low-end single disk for your database.

- Use multiple drives with data spread across at least three physical disks. With the latest computer systems, this can easily be achieved with an internal RAID configuration, such as RAID 0.

- Use one dedicated drive for transactional log files. Transactional logs are used to recover transactions in case of failures such as power outages. In Oracle, these logs are referred to as redo logs. Transactional logs are accessed sequentially, so it won't help to spread transactional logs across multiple disks.

- Take advantage of caching at the various levels such as at the disk level and disk controller level. However, be aware of the huge performance impact of caching at the file system level. All database systems cache data at the database system level. Caching data at the file system level causes data to be cached twice, which is known as double buffering. I'll give you a specific example of Oracle on the Veritas file system in the next chapter: once the double buffering was suppressed with the proper settings at both the database system level and file system level, the average read time was reduced from hundreds of milliseconds to submilliseconds, and the throughput was improved by as much as 13 times.

More details about storage are beyond the scope of this book. Let's move on to the inner workings of the sample application that will be tested against the performance model we established in Section 5.3.

5.5   MedRec APPLICATION

In order to make it possible to compare the analytical model and the actual measurements, we need to come up with a realistic application so that the model can be fed with the arrival rates and the measured service demands. A sample application from one of the leading application server vendors, BEA Systems, is well suited for this need [BEA, 2003]. This application is called Avitek Medical Records (MedRec). It is well documented and publicly available. The application allows patients, doctors, and administrators to manage patient data using a variety of clients. It was built with the best J2EE and XML Web services practices known today.

In order to help understand the performance model presented in Section 5.3, we explain in the next two sections how an XML Web service can be built by exposing a stateless session EJB as an XML Web service and how this XML Web service is consumed using SOAP in the MedRec application.

5.5.1   Exposing a Stateless Session EJB as an XML Web Service

BEA provides tools based on the open source Java compiling and packaging tool *Ant* for developing and deploying J2EE and XML Web services applications. These tools can be used for exposing stateless session Enterprise Java Beans (EJBs) as XML Web services. One of the tools, *autotype*, generates the following artifacts:

- Serialization and deserialization classes
- XML schema representation and type mapping information for the non-built-in Java data types that are used as parameters and return values of the EJB methods

The other tool, *source2wsdd*, generates the *web-services.xml* deployment descriptor file that describes the XML Web service.

In summary, the XML Web service architecture has introduced two extra layers to the application:

- The exposed XML Web service session EJB façade that takes incoming requests to the application and dispatches them to the underlying session and entity EJBs that implement the actual business logic.
- Object serialization. For the sake of interoperability with different types of clients, the methods of the Web service EJB use complex non-built-in data types as parameters and return values. The serialization classes convert those data types to their equivalent XML schema types, whereas the Web service EJB converts the data between the Web service data type and its equivalent value object used by other session and entity EJBs.

The next section examines how the client application uses a port object to invoke an XML Web service operation.

5.5.2 Consuming an XML Web Service Using SOAP

BEA provides a tool named *clientgen* for generating the Java API for XML-based RPC (JAX-RPC) stubs for the Web services deployed on both WebLogic Server and other application servers. JAX-RPC is a standard programming model for developing Web service clients and endpoints based on SOAP and WSDL. Clients can make calls to Web services through JAX-RPC. The call detail is transparent to the client with the underlying JAX-RPC run-time mechanisms, for example, SOAP protocol level mechanisms, marshalling, and unmarshalling. An overview of a JAX-RPC programming model can be found at http://java.sun.com/xml/xml_jaxrpc.xml.

In the MedRec application, the *PhysicianSessionEJB* is a Web service consumer that uses JAX-RPC to invoke the Web services object *MedRecWebServices*. The calls to each Web service method consist of the following two steps:

Step 1. Creating a *port* object with the JAX-RPC stub of the Web service. The following segment of the code shows how a port object is created:

```
wsdl_url = System.getProperty (''phys.app.wsdl.url'');
MedRecWebServices service=new MedRecWebServices_Impl
  (wsdl_url);
port = service.getMedRecWebServicesPort ();
```

where *phys.app.wsdl.url* is the URL of the WSDL of the deployed MedRecWebServices, passed in as a System Property.

Step 2. Invoking the Web service operation using the JAX-RPC stub:

```
RecordWS recordWS = PhysicianClientUtils.toRecordWS
  (pRecord);
port.addRecord (recordWS);
```

where the *PhysicianClientUtils.toRecordWS*( ) method is a utility that converts the standard *Record Value Object* to a Web service-specific data type.

As is seen, SOAP serialization/deserialization and HTTP send/receive are all encapsulated in the JAX-RPC stub implementation. The costs associated with those operations cannot be measured separately. They can only be inferred indirectly from the timing probes streamed to an output text file.

5.6 MedRec DEPLOYMENT AND TEST SCENARIO

We have secured enough knowledge about how this sample XML Web services application works. This is necessary for us to understand not only the performance model established for the SOA-based applications but also how to design and actually carry out the tests. Next, we need to deploy this application, develop and implement test scenarios, and actually execute the tests.

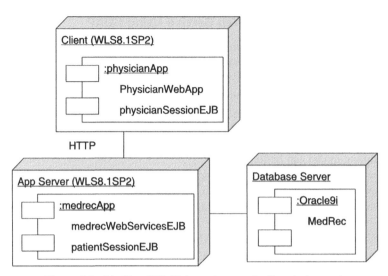

Figure 5.3   *MedRec XML Web services application deployment.*

Figure 5.3 shows the UML (Universal Mark-up Language) deployment diagram for the MedRec application from BEA Systems. The MedRec database was deployed on a stand-alone system. The components *physicianApp* and *medrecApp* can be deployed on one system or two separate systems.

The MedRec test scenario is depicted in the sequence diagram shown in Figure 5.4. The intention of the tests was to obtain measured data to help validate the performance model for SOA-based software applications. The tests were not designed for showing any software or hardware vendor-specific performance advantages over other similar products.

The performance test scenario shown in Figure 5.4 consists of a single query, findPatientByLastNameWild. This conforms to our single-class model. During each test run, streams of *findPatientByLastNameWild* queries were issued through the UI layer, which was built with the BEA version of *Struts* [Husted, 2003]. The *PhysicianSessionEJB* is the XML Web services client, which calls the XML Web services provider implemented as *MedRecWebServicesEJB* using SOAP over HTTP. *MedRecWebServicesEJB* was implemented as a session façade, which in turn calls *PatientSessionEJB* for carrying out the queries. *PatientSessionEJB* calls *PatientEJB* through the Value Object *Patient*. *PatientEJB* is the entity EJB that is an in-memory representation of the patient entity persisting in the database. For simplicity, the business session beans and entity beans are not shown in Figure 5.4.

A performance test script corresponding to the test scenario shown in Figure 5.4 was recorded and modified using the load test tool Microsoft Application Center Test (ACT), which is one of the most popular load test tools for testing Web applications on Windows/Intel platforms.

Figure 5.5 shows the test environment. The database was deployed on a stand-alone system. The application was installed on another separate system, which hosted both

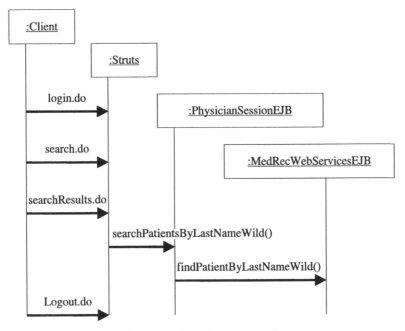

Figure 5.4 MedRec test scenario.

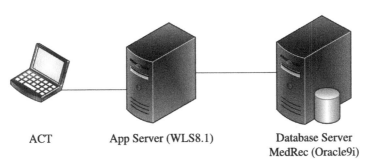

ACT   App Server (WLS8.1)   Database Server
                                          MedRec (Oracle9i)

Figure 5.5 XML Web services performance and scalability test environment.

the XML Web services provider and the client. The load test tool ACT was installed on a stand-alone system.

Let's examine the test results in the next section.

5.7 TEST RESULTS

Before presenting the test results, I need to make it clear that caching at the database level and application server level has huge effects on the performance numbers

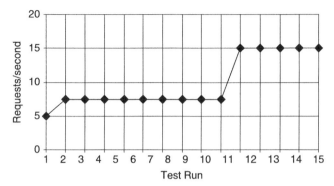

Figure 5.6   *Effects of caching on throughput.*

obtained with each run. After starting up the database server and application server, which were deployed on two separate Windows XP PCs, the first run was made with a single user, a single iteration, and zero *think time*, based on the test scenario shown in Figure 5.4. This run is shown in Figure 5.6 as Run 1. During this run, 15 requests were completed within 3 seconds.

Then the application server was restarted without restarting the database server, which effectively emptied the cached session objects on the application server. The same test as the first run was then repeated nine times, through Runs 2 to 10. A consistent throughput of 7.5 requests/second was achieved with each run. With these test runs, the database buffer cache helped reduce the total completion time from 3 seconds to 2 seconds for the same number of 15 requests total.

In order to see the effects of application server level caching on throughput, the same test was repeated five times more without restarting the application server prior to each run. Those five runs correspond to Runs 11–15 in Figure 5.6. The completion time further decreased from 2 seconds to 1 second. This has effectively tripled the throughput compared with Run 1. As is seen, caching is a very delicate issue to deal with in the actual performance and scalability tests.

In the following sections, we will look into the overhead of the XML Web services handle and the effects of caching the XML Web services handle on response times. I will show the throughput dynamics accompanied with bottleneck analysis.

5.7.1   Overhead of the XML Web Services Handle

The total time spent on the workload described in the previous section can be decomposed based on the QNM shown in Figure 5.2. The timing probes added to the XML Web services client and provider of this application allowed us to conduct this type of decomposition. The resultant resource profile including the overhead of the XML Web services handle is shown in Figure 5.7.

The pie chart shown in Figure 5.7 was based on the nine runs that had only a single user, single iteration, and zero think time with both the database server and application server restarted prior to each run. For this XML Web services query, the request and

Elapsed Time Apportionment in Milliseconds

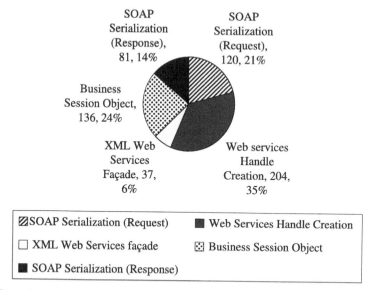

Figure 5.7 *Response time apportionment based on the QNM shown in Figure 5.2.*

response SOAP messages were 1 kB and 2 kB only, respectively. The application server and database server were connected to a 100-Mbps LAN corresponding to the Column C network configuration shown in Table 5.2. The network latency is negligible in this case.

It's interesting to see that XML Web services handle creation in this application took as much as 204 milliseconds out of a total response time of 583 milliseconds. In the next section, I will show how the handle can be cached in order to improve the overall response time.

5.7.2 Effects of Caching Web Services Handle

Figure 5.8 shows the test results obtained using the same test conditions as for Figure 5.7 except that the Web service handle was cached. Caching implementation for the Web service handle was easy as J2EE provides a simple solution to caching the properties of an EJB object through the *SessionContext* interface. The *SessionContext* interface provides access to the run-time session context that is maintained by the container. The container calls the *setSessionContext* method to pass the SessionContext object to an instance after the instance has been created. The session context remains associated with the instance for the lifetime of the instance [Shannon et al., 2000]. With the MedRec application, the handle was created as a *port* object, as shown in the code snippet in Section 5.5.2. The handle was then stored in the *PhysicianSessionEJB's SessionContext* object.

Elapsed Time Apportionment in Milliseconds

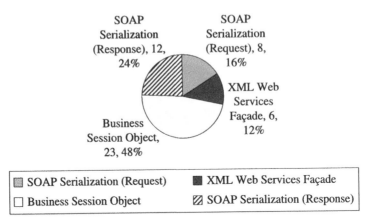

Figure 5.8   *Response time apportionment with cached XML Web services handle.*

It is seen that after the Web services handle was cached in the *SessionContext* object when the instance of *PhysicianSessionEJB* was created, the overhead associated with XML Web services has been reduced from 76% to about 50%, although it is still high and further optimizations in SOAP serialization are still needed.

In the next section, I will show the throughput dynamics for each performance test run. We will see that the request flow equilibrium was reached within the warm-up period and held steady afterwards.

5.7.3   Throughput Dynamics

In order to do a comparison with the analytical performance model described in Section 5.3, we conducted six *findPatientByLastNameWild* runs with 1, 3, 5, 7, 10, and 15 virtual users respectively, using ACT. A 20-second warm-up, 10-minute duration, and 250-ms total think time were specified for each run. There were five requests in the scenario:

- loginPage
- loginAction
- searchPage
- searchAction
- logout

A 50-ms think time was added after each request in order to have better control on the arrival rate. A text file that contains 10,006 patient last names was used in the test script to feed the patient search query.

Figure 5.9 shows the throughput dynamics in terms of requests/second versus time for the first five runs. As was described in Section 5.3, the analytical model was built on the assumption of operational equilibrium. Therefore, for each test run, we need to

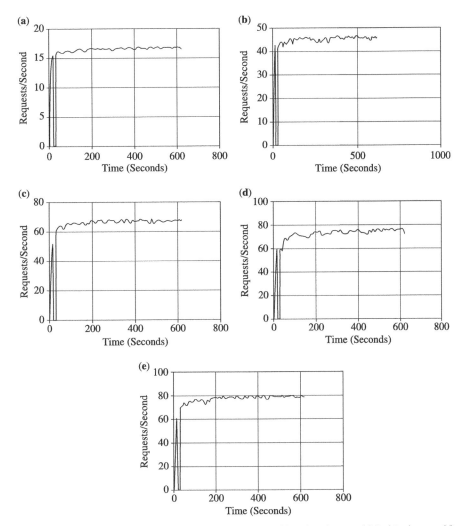

Figure 5.9 *Throughput dynamics with (a) 1 virtual user, (b) 3 virtual users, (c) 5 virtual users, (d) 7 virtual users, and (e) 10 virtual users.*

make sure that this assumption is met and the comparison between the model and the measurement is performed on a valid assumption.

As is shown, the throughput was saturated around 7 virtual users with a transaction rate of about 73 requests/second. A more detailed bottleneck analysis will be given next.

5.7.4 Bottleneck Analysis

We have collected detailed ACT test results and Windows® *perfmon* performance counter logs for diagnosing the bottlenecks attributable to the saturated throughput. Figure 5.10 shows the throughput in terms of requests per second (RPS) versus the

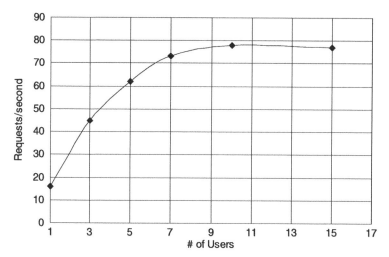

Figure 5.10   *Throughput versus the number of virtual users.*

number of virtual users. It is seen that the knee of the curve occurred around 7 virtual users. The knee of the curve is an indicator that the application has reached its capacity with the load around it.

Figure 5.11 shows the corresponding average response time of the *findPatientByLastNameWild* query. It is seen that beyond 7 virtual users, response time went up faster than a linear scaling trend, which also confirmed that the system had reached its scalability limit around 7 users.

Next, let's find out which resource was the bottleneck. The charts showing the various resource consumptions such as CPU, disk, network, and memory can reveal the resource that is the bottleneck preventing the application from being scalable beyond the knee of the curve.

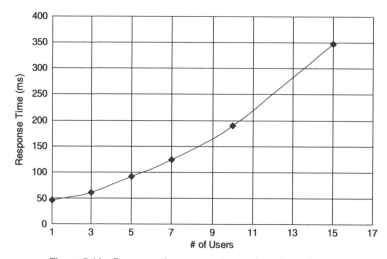

Figure 5.11   *Response time versus the number of virtual users.*

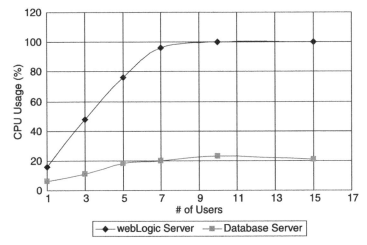

Figure 5.12 *CPU utilizations on the WLS and database server.*

Based on the *perfmon* performance counters, we can eliminate memory as a bottle-neck, as the largest working set from the WebLogic Server (WLS) process out of those six runs was about 110 MB, which means that less than half of the 256 MB heap memory was touched. Additionally, the throughput dynamics shown in Figure 5.9 indicate that no "thrashing" in throughput occurred due to insufficient JVM heap capacity.

We can also eliminate network as a bottleneck, since the maximum *Bytes Total/ second* was only 0.328 Mbps both on the database server and on the application server. That's a small fraction of the 100 Mbps total bandwidth. The disk did not seem to be the bottleneck either, as the disk busy time was less than 1%.

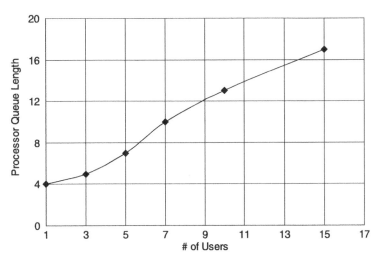

Figure 5.13 *Processor queue length on the WLS.*

Now let's concentrate on analyzing the CPU utilizations. Figure 5.12 shows the CPU utilizations on the WLS and database server. It is clear that the CPU utilization on the application server maxed out around 7 virtual users and beyond.

Figure 5.13 shows the processor queue lengths on the application server for those six runs. The processor queue length reached as high as 10 for the test case with 7 virtual users, which is far above the bottleneck threshold of 2 queued items per processor on the Windows/Intel platforms.

Based on the bottleneck analysis above, it is clear that using a more powerful server for the WebLogic application server would improve the scalability of this application beyond 7 users.

5.8 COMPARING THE MODEL WITH THE MEASUREMENTS

The analytical model described in Section 5.3 depends on the two input workload parameters: arrival rate and service demand. Here we assume a service demand of 50 ms for the application server, derived from the test results shown in Figure 5.7. From those six test runs discussed in the previous section, we obtained the arrival rate for each run by dividing the number of queries completed within the test duration of 10 minutes. Table 5.4 shows the derived arrival rates.

We then calculated the CPU utilizations using Equation (5.3). The results are shown in Table 5.5 along with the measured utilizations. The overall agreement between the model and measurement seems to be within the acceptance criteria we mentioned in Section 5.3.

Table 5.6 shows the response times calculated using Equation (5.4) along with the measured response times. As is often the case, measured response times have large

TABLE 5.4 Arrival Rate for Each Test Run

Number of Virtual Users	Number of Queries	Arrival Rate
1	1995	3.3
3	5438	9.0
5	7652	12.8
7	8744	14.6
10	9369	15.6
15	9211	15.4

TABLE 5.5 Calculated and Measured Utilizations (%)

	Utilization (%)	
Number of Virtual Users	Model	Measurement
1	17	16
3	46	40
5	64	73
7	72	95.6
10	88	99.9
15	86	99.9

TABLE 5.6 **Calculated and Measured Response Times**

		Response Times (ms)	
		Measurement	
Number of Virtual Users	Model	Average	Standard Deviation
1	50	46	9
3	70	60	17
5	117	92	24
7	150	124	42
10	350	190	67
15	300	348	126

variations around the average; therefore the standard deviation for each run is shown as well. Once again, the agreement between the model and measurement conforms to the acceptance criteria.

Figure 5.14 shows graphically the comparison between the measured and calculated application server CPU utilizations for different numbers of virtual users. The left bars show the CPU utilizations predicted using the analytical performance model, whereas the right bars show the measured CPU utilizations. The model prediction errors are 3.8%, 15%, −12%, −25%, −12% and −14% for those six test runs with 1, 3, 5, 7, 10, and 15 virtual users, respectively. The agreement between the model and the measurement is quite good given the fact that both theoretical models and experimental measurements contain certain levels of errors.

Figure 5.15 shows the comparison of the response times between the measurement and the model. With the measured data, both the average and error bars are shown. We used ±1 standard deviation to plot the error bars. It is seen that the calculated data are quite close to the measured average + standard deviation for the region prior to the knee of the curve, which is 7 virtual users.

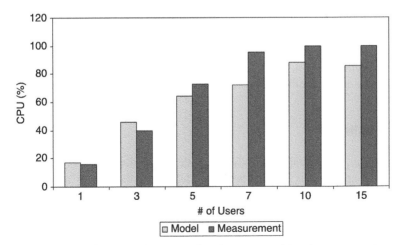

Figure 5.14 *CPU utilization comparison between model and measurement.*

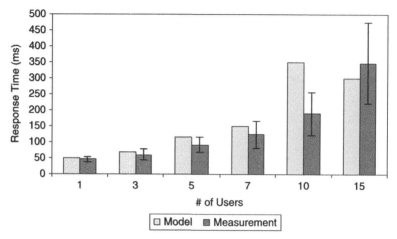

Figure 5.15   *Response time comparison between model and measurement.*

It is seen from Figure 5.15 that the model over-estimated the response time some-what compared with the measurements. This might have something to do with the fact that the queuing models described in Chapter 4 are based on the exponential distri-bution that has least information or highest entropy [Gross, 2008], which is equivalent to saying that the models estimate the response times conservatively.

In the next section I'll discuss the validity of the SOA performance model.

5.9   VALIDITY OF THE SOA PERFORMANCE MODEL

The validity of the SOA performance model studied in this chapter can best be con-firmed with the same preconditions described in Chapter 4 about the validity of the open models in general. Essentially, one can confirm with the comparison data pre-sented in the preceding section that the SOA performance model was more accurate with the smaller utilizations or lighter loads prior to the knee of the curve.

This concludes our first case study on applying queuing theory to predicting the performance and scalability of the SOA-based enterprise software applications.

5.10   SUMMARY

In this chapter, we presented an analytical model for predicting the performance of the SOA-based applications. Using the BEA MedRec application as an example, we demonstrated the applicability of the well-known queuing models to emerging technol-ogies such as XML Web services. Based on this exercise, we observed the following:

- The generic open QNM seems to apply well to the SOA-based applications in predicting both the system CPU utilizations and response times.

- Creating service handles is an expensive operation. Service handles must be cached at the component or application level to minimize their impact on the performance and scalability of the application.
- SOAP serialization and deserialization can be costly as well. An efficiently implemented serializer is necessary to minimize its impact on the performance and scalability of the XML Web services based applications.
- An interesting observation out of this exercise is that almost half of the total service response times are attributable to the XML Web services SOAP serialization and services façade, and the other half to the underlying business objects that fulfill the services. This 1 : 1 ratio between the XML Web services infrastructure overhead and the underlying business objects that carry out the core business logic may vary from application to application.

Since the service handle can be cached at the component or application level, the model can be applied to XML API driven, component-based enterprise applications as well. The observations out of this exercise are helpful for designing the performance-oriented, XML Web services based applications. They may have merits for exploring the Open Grid Services Architecture (OGSA) [Foster and Kesselman, 2004] as well in which XML Web services are potential basic building blocks and mechanisms.

RECOMMENDED READING

Some general texts on the SOA and XML Web services:

G. Anderson and P. Anderson, *Enterprise JavaBeans Component Architecture*, Prentice Hall, 2002.

A. Krowczyk, Z. Greenvos, C. Nagel, and A. Banerjee, *C# Web Services*, Wrox Press Ltd., 2001.

P. Cauldwell, R. Chawla, V. Chopra, G. Damschen, C. Dix, T. Hong, F. Norton, U. Ogbuji, G. Olander, M. A. Richman, K. Saunders, and Z. Zaev, *Professional XML Web Services*, WroxPress Ltd., 2001.

G. Eddon and H. Eddon, *Inside Distributed COM*, Microsoft Press, 1998.

G. Glass, *Web Services—Building Blocks for Distributed Systems*, Prentice Hall PTR, 2002.

Microsoft, *Developing XML Web Services and Server Components with Microsoft Visual Basic . Net and Visual C# .Net*, Microsoft Press, 2003.

D. Slama, J. Garbis, and P. Russell, *Enterprise CORBA*, Prentice Hall PTR, 1999.

Some texts on queuing theory and software performance tuning:

N. Gunther, *The Practical Performance Analyst*, McGraw-Hill, 1998.

M. Gurry and P. Corrigan, *Oracle Performance Tuning*, O'Reily & Associates, 1996.

R. Jain, *The Art of Computer Systems Performance Analysis*, John Wiley & Sons, 1991.

D. Gross, J. F. Shortle, J. M. Thompson, and C. M. Harris, *Fundamentals of Queuing Theory*, 4th edition, Wiley Series in Probability and Statistics, 2008.

E. D. Lazowska, J. Zahorjan, G. S. Graham, and K. C. Sevcik, *Quantitative System Performance: Computer System Analysis Using Queuing Network Models*, Prentice Hall, 1984.

D. A. Menasce and V. A. F. Almeida, *Scaling for E-Business*, Prentice Hall PTR, 2000.

C. Millsap, *Optimizing Oracle Performance*, O'Reilly & Associates, 2003.

H. Simitci, *Storage Network Performance Analysis*, John Wiley & Sons, 2003.

Some texts on developing SOA-based software applications:

BEA Systems, *BEA WebLogic Server MedRec Development Tutorial*, available at http://www.bea.com, 2003.

I. Foster and C. Kesselman, *The Grid 2: Blueprints for a New Computing Infrastructure*, Morgan Kaufmann, 2004.

T. Husted, *Struts in Action*, Manning, 2003.

B. Shannon, M. Hapner, V. Matena, and J. Davidson, *Java 2 Platform Enterprise Edition—Platform and Component Specifications*, Addison-Wesley, 2000.

Some publications on applying queuing theory to solving software performance problems:

H. H. Liu and P. V. Crain, An analytic model for predicting the performance of SOA-based enterprise software applications, in *CMG 2004 Proceedings*, Las Vegas.

H. H. Liu, Service demand models for enterprise software applications, in *CMG 2005 Proceedings*, Orlando Florida.

H. H. Liu, Applying queuing theory to optimizing enterprise software applications, in *CMG 2006 Proceedings*, Reno.

EXERCISES

5.1. Find a sample SOA application from one of the major SOA development infrastructure vendors such as BEA System, IBM, and Microsoft. Deploy the application on one or multiple physical systems by following the setup procedure downloaded with the application. Check out all the major functions of the application and make sure everything works as described in the document provided by the vendor. [*Note*: This is a good exercise for acquiring the skill set of performing routine tasks such as preparing a performance and scalability test environment and deploying a relatively complex application. This will also give you an opportunity to familiarize yourself with one of the leading SOA development platforms, which may help you land your first job in software if you are a college student or your next job for advancing your career either internally or externally.]

5.2. Find a free load test tool such as ACT from Microsoft or a commercial one if you have access to it. Design your use scenarios and develop the corresponding load test scripts. Include think times in your scripts. Test out your scripts thoroughly to make sure your scripts work properly. [*Note*: Developing load test scripts is another important skill set to have for coping with software performance and scalability challenges either with your current job or future job.]

5.3. Collect the throughput dynamics by varying the number of virtual users. Find the knee of the curve with your specific deployment. Analyze the system resource utilizations quantitatively and arrive at your conclusion about which resource is the bottleneck. [*Note*: This exercise will help you acquire the skill set for analyzing software performance and scalability bottlenecks.]

5.4. Develop a queuing model for the application under test. Compare your measurements with the predictions according to the queuing model. [*Note*: This is a very advanced exercise.]

5.5. Discover the ways in which you can optimize and tune the performance and scalability of your application even further. [*Note*: This is a good exercise whether you are a software developer or performance engineer.]

6

Case Study II: Queuing Theory Applied to Optimizing and Tuning Software Performance and Scalability

Mathematical reasoning may be regarded rather schematically as the exercise of a combination of two facilities, which we may call intuition and ingenuity.
—Alan Turing

A software system is unlikely to perform and scale without going through a rigorous performance and scalability engineering process. Such an engineering process typically includes two major activities: *optimization* and *tuning*. In the context of the software performance and scalability, *optimization* refers to the efforts of identifying and eliminating internal inefficient designs and implementations, whereas *tuning* refers to the efforts of establishing the optimal setting for every possible external configuration parameter. Both optimization and tuning must be incorporated into the development cycles of a software product to help achieve the best possible and predictable performance and scalability.

Software performance and scalability issues must be dealt with both rationally and quantitatively. One must understand that it's not a guessing game. All judgments and decisions must be based on quantitative performance and scalability test data. That's because system bottlenecks and implementation inefficiencies can only be revealed through analyzing quantitative performance and scalability test data, while prescriptions for removing bottlenecks and improving inefficient designs and implementations can only be carried out by following the performance and scalability laws defined in the framework of queuing theory.

Software performance and scalability test data in general refers to the data in the following three categories:

- Performance metrics data such as response time and throughput that quantify the performance of the software under test.
- System resource utilization data collected during a test with the various system resources such as CPU, disk, network, and memory.
- Profile data such as API profiling data and database statistical reports. API profiling data reveals the execution paths of the various software components, while a database statistical report summarizes by category the various activities that occurred inside a database execution engine for the duration of a test.

It's critical that test data meets the software performance data principles depicted in Chapter 3. After making sure that you have obtained reliable and quality performance and scalability test data, you should follow a rigorous methodology to analyze your data. Some people, especially those who tend to think more rationally and quantitatively, can drill down to the root cause of a software performance issue much faster than others. Trying to help you cultivate the habit of thinking more rationally and quantitatively on software performance and scalability issues is one of the main objectives of this book, in addition to helping you acquire the necessary technical skills.

Note that software performance and scalability analysis is only the first step toward solving a software performance or scalability issue. After identifying a bottleneck, you need to come up with some solutions for removing the bottleneck. If it requires recoding and recompiling some part of your software program, it's an optimization issue. If it requires you to adjust some of the settings external to your program without having to touch and recompile the source code, then it's a tuning issue. *Tuning* doesn't require recompiling your software, whereas *optimization* does.

You can tune your software all by yourself, by adjusting some of the external configuration parameters, and reconduct the same test to see how much improvement you can achieve. However, optimization may require you to work with your developers for a new version of your software that has the intended changes incorporated. Of course, if you are doing both coding and performance testing, everything is in your hands and it could be much faster for you to try out various implementations to see which changes are effective. Once again, you need very solid test cases as the basis for your optimization and tuning tests. The outcome of your optimization and tuning efforts strongly depends on what you are testing and how it is tested.

In this chapter, I'll first show you in Section 6.1 how to analyze software performance and scalability in general. In Section 6.2, I'll show you how to apply queuing theory to optimizing and tuning software performance and scalability. Plenty of case studies are presented—the result of measurements with real products—so you can be assured that the presented case studies are beyond academic exercises and can be applied to your product with the possibility that you will see similar positive results.

A software system can achieve its maximum sustainable performance and scalability only if a balance is reached among all mutually coupled resources. That's the subject of Section 6.3.

Let's start with analyzing software performance and scalability.

6.1 ANALYZING SOFTWARE PERFORMANCE AND SCALABILITY

Software performance and scalability analysis is basically a mission of finding the bottlenecks that are responsible for the poor performance and scalability of a software system deployed on a specific setup. Although there are many factors that may cause poor performance and scalability for a software system, typically there are only a few factors that are more responsible than others. This is especially true when the performance or scalability of the software in question is far below expectations.

Software performance and scalability analysis should start with an accurate characterization of the issue in question. As a software performance analyst, your characterization needs to be as quantitative as possible. If it's an OLTP system, you need to quantify what response times you are getting that are deemed as slow. If it's a batch job, you need to quantify what throughput numbers you are getting. So quantitatively characterizing a software performance or scalability issue is always the first step to take.

6.1.1 Characterizing Performance and Scalability Problems

The first step of software performance and scalability analysis is always to try to characterize the problem quantitatively. Remember that if the problem cannot be clearly characterized, then it's hard to solve it.

Let's use a real-life software scalability issue I experienced to illustrate how a full cycle of software performance and scalability analysis should be conducted. I'll start with the problem characterization first.

With this specific example, the application was deployed on two separate physical computer systems—one for the application server and the other for the database server. The application data were stored on an external SAN with a RAID 0 configuration. All systems were high end, running on a specific flavor of UNIX. A Java-based program was run to simulate creating objects by calling application server APIs with 15 threads. The performance of this object-creation test was measured in terms of objects created per second.

As you can see from Figure 6.1, the throughput of this creating object batch job deteriorated rapidly from 45 objects/second to 9 objects/second within about 50 minutes, with only 45 k objects created at the end of the test. The two charts represent the same test using time stamp and number of objects created as the x-axis, respectively.

As is seen, throughput was deteriorating rapidly with time or with more and more objects created. This is apparently a scalability alarm. What would happen if millions of objects are to be created in a real production environment with this issue not resolved prior to releasing to customers? The throughput may go down to zero with time, which is apparently unacceptable. The question now is what is causing this rapid throughput deterioration or poor scalability? To answer this question, we need

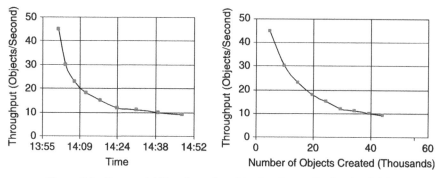

Figure 6.1   *Poor scalability of a real-world enterprise application batch job.*

to look at the system performance counters collected during the test. That's the topic of the next section.

6.1.2   Isolating Performance and Scalability Factors

Software performance and scalability analysis to some extent is similar to forensic medicine. You start with collecting the evidence before reaching conclusions. For diagnosing software performance and scalability problems, the evidence lies in the system performance counters collected during a test. Each system performance counter corresponds to a performance and/or scalability factor. By looking at the values of those performance counters, you determine whether the corresponding factors are important or not to your performance or scalability issue.

Performance counters are abundant, probably hundreds of them. Typically there is no need to record all performance counters. Refer to Chapter 3 for a review of what typical performance counters should be collected.

Table 6.1 is a summary of the recorded values of the relevant counters during the test associated with the poor scalability shown in Figure 6.1. It covers the four standard categories of resources: CPU, disk, network, and memory. One should take a layered approach by starting with one of the top categories and then diving in as needed.

A quick glance indicates that CPU utilizations on both the application server and database server were quite normal and the disk access time was normal as well.

TABLE 6.1   Summary of the Performance Counters Associated with the Scalability Problem Shown in Figure 6.1

Counter	Value
Average CPU utilization on the application server	10%
Average CPU utilization on the database server	36%
Average disk access time	7 milliseconds
Network	Not an issue
Memory	Not an issue

Network and memory weren't the problem either, as both the application server and the database server were located on a gigabits/second LAN and each server had 12-GB RAM, which was more than enough. If we saw hundreds of millisecond disk access times, we would have suspected that disk I/O was the problem, but that's not the case.

Since this was a database-intensive application, we actually should look at the database first before we suspect anything on the application server. For this specific test case, the database was running on Oracle 10g. Oracle 10g provides an excellent performance gathering and reporting tool for troubleshooting database performance issues. This tool was named AWR (Automatic Workload Repository), which evolved from *statspack* of the previous versions of Oracle.

This AWR tool is so useful that I rely on it to troubleshoot Oracle 10g performance issues both with my own performance and scalability tests and with customer's performance and scalability escalations. In fact, I have been using this tool exclusively for all my Oracle 10g related database performance analysis since it was released several years ago. I'll share with you here how I use this tool for my work as a software performance professional.

With an Oracle 10g AWR report, I always jump to the *Top 5 Timed Events* immediately after I open it in HTML format. From the top 5 timed events, you can get a good estimate of which resource is the potential bottleneck. If you don't see anything abnormal from the top 5 timed events, usually, that's an indication that database is not the problem.

Figure 6.2 shows the top 5 timed events associated with the poor scalability as characterized quantitatively in Figure 6.1. You can see immediately that 96.4% of the total database call time was attributed to the database CPU time. The percentages for all other wait events were insignificant.

After examining the top 5 timed events, I then always jump to the *I/O stats* section by following the link shown under Main Report in an AWR report. Since an AWR report is created in HTML, it's very easy to navigate around. Figure 6.3 shows what sections you can jump to by category from the Main Report.

Top 5 Timed Events

Event	Waits	Time (s)	Avg Wait (ms)	% Total Call Time	Wait Class
CPU time		35,539		96.4	
log file parallel write	87,410	1,004	11	2.7	System I/O
db file parallel write	7,551	89	12	.2	System I/O
Streams AQ: enqueue blocked on low memory	1	80	80,354	.2	Configuration
SQL*Net more data to client	303,635	35	0	.1	Network

Figure 6.2 Top 5 timed events from the Oracle 10g AWR report.

Main Report

- Report Summary
- Wait Events Statistics
- SQL Statistics
- Instance Activity Statistics
- IO Stats
- Buffer Pool Statistics
- Advisory Statistics
- Wait Statistics
- Undo Statistics
- Latch Statistics
- Segment Statistics
- Dictionary Cache Statistics
- Library Cache Statistics
- Memory Statistics
- Streams Statistics
- Resource Limit Statistics
- init.ora Parameters

Figure 6.3 *Main report of an AWR report.*

An AWR report is very lengthy. You may not need to go through the entire report every time you examine an AWR report. However, at a minimum you should check the following:

- *I/O Stats* section, which would take you to the I/O performance section. It's always helpful to verify whether I/O is a problem for your tests by looking at the average read time and average write buffer wait time from the I/O Stats section.
- *SQL Statistics* section that tells you whether there are hot SQLs or not.
- *init.ora Parameters* section, which is very useful for checking various Oracle configuration parameters, especially when the AWR report is from others instead of from your own test.

The I/O performance associated with this test is shown in Figure 6.4. The first row was for the user data table space, the second row for the Oracle UNDO table space, and

Tablespace IO Stats
- ordered by IOs (Reads + Writes) desc

Reads	Av Reads/s	Av Rd (ms)	Av Blks/Rd	Writes	Av Writes/s	Buffer Waits	Av Buf Wt (ms)
205	0	7.07	1.01	44,056	12	14,913	1.16
4	0	7.50	1.00	2,380	1	1,660	0.11
27	0	6.30	1.07	217	0	0	0.00
16	0	8.75	1.00	179	0	0	0.00

Figure 6.4 *I/O performance associated with the poor scalability shown in Figure 6.1.*

the remaining two for the SYSTEM table space. It's the user data table space that we are most concerned with.

From Figure 6.4, we see the following:

- During this test, a total number of 205 physical disk reads were performed. The read rate was less than 1 per second, which was rounded to zero. The average time per read operation was 7.07 milliseconds, which was at the low end of the normal range of 5–20 milliseconds. It is also seen that on average 1 data block was read.
- The second part of the I/O stats shows disk write performance. It indicates that a total number of 44,056 writes were performed during the test, with an average rate of 12 writes per second. This is not surprising at all, as this batch job was about creating objects after all, which incurs a lot more writes than reads.
- Oracle typically does not write data directly into physical disks. Instead, it writes data to the data buffer cache in memory first, and then flushes data from the data buffer cache to physical disks in bulk. This is why it lists the number of buffer waits and average buffer wait time for write activities. As is seen, the average buffer wait time was 1.16 milliseconds only, which was quite good.

So the question is: Where does Oracle spend so much CPU time as reported from the top 5 timed events? You can check out the *Time Model Statistics* section of the AWR report associated with the test. Figure 6.5 shows the time apportionment by Oracle on various database SQL execution activities. As is seen, the time spent on parsing and other activities is insignificant. However, the DB CPU time and SQL execution elapsed time were high. This indicates that we should look at the SQL Statistics section of the AWR report to find clues on why the DB CPU time and SQL execution elapsed time were so high for this test.

Again, you should get familiar with each statistic category of the Time Model Statistics report, because that's where you can get some hints about which parts of your Oracle database you should tune.

Oracle lists the top SQLs based on the following categories, as shown in Figure 6.6:

- *Elapsed Time*, which is the sum of wait time and service time in the context of queuing theory.
- *CPU Time*, which is the service demand in the context of queuing theory.
- *Buffer Gets*, which represents the number of logical reads. Logical reads read data from the data buffer cache in memory, whereas physical reads read data directly from the physical disks.
- *Reads*, which represents the number of reads by an SQL statement performed during the test.
- *Executions*, which represents the number of times an SQL statement was executed during the test.
- *Parse Calls*, which represents the number of times an SQL statement was parsed during the test.

Figure 6.6 shows all top SQLs ordered by *Elapsed Time*, *CPU Time*, and *Buffer Gets*, respectively. Note that the *Elapsed Time* and *CPU Time* show the fact that a

Time Model Statistics

- Total time in database user-calls (DB Time): 36878.7s
- Statistics including the word "background" measure background process time, and so do not contribute to the DB time statistic
- Ordered by % or DB time desc, Statistic name

Statistic Name	Time (s)	% of DB Time
DB CPU	35,538.91	96.37
sql execute elapsed time	34,509.38	93.58
parse time elapsed	439.28	1.19
hard parse elapsed time	10.06	0.03
hard parse (sharing criteria) elapsed time	0.19	0.00
PL/SQL compilation elapsed time	0.19	0.00
hard parse (bind mismatch) elapsed time	0.18	0.00
connection management call elapsed time	0.12	0.00
sequence load elapsed time	0.08	0.00
repeated bind elapsed time	0.01	0.00
PL/SQL execution elapsed time	0.00	0.00
DB time	36,878.65	
background elapsed time	1,475.24	
background cpu time	88.65	

Figure 6.5 Time model statistics associated with the poor scalability shown in Figure 6.1.

lot of time was taken for executing the first five SQLs, but these two metrics do not show the cause, namely, why so much time was spent on these hot SQLs. The *Buffer Gets* metric shows why, as I'll explain later.

Note from Figure 6.6c that the first five SQLs were responsible for the poor scalability shown in Figure 6.1, as they were accountable for 92% of the total elapsed time. Before explaining why these SQLs were costly, let's reveal the SQL text for each of the top 5 SQLs.

```
Query 1: SELECT documentId, classId, dataGroupId, consistencyId
            FROM objectTable WHERE objectId = <value>;
Query 2: SELECT documentId
            FROM objectTable WHERE objectId = <value>:
Query 3: SELECT documented, objectId
            FROM objectAssociationTable WHERE objectId = <value>;
Query 4: SELECT documentId, objectId
            FROM objectTable WHERE objectId = <value>;
Query 5: SELECT documentId, sourceObjectId, destObjectId, objectId,
            consistencyId FROM objectAssociationTable WHERE
            destObjectId = <value> and classId = <value>;
```

(a) **SQL ordered by Elapsed Time**

- Resources reported for PL/SQL code includes the resources used by all SQL statements called by the code.

- % Total DB Time is the Elapsed Time of the SQL statement divided into the Total Database Time multiplied by 100

Elapsed Time (s)	CPU Time (s)	Executions	Elap per Exec (s)	% Total DB Time	SQL Id
11,818	11,763	40,514	0.29	32.04	gsmv6cvsysnys
5,890	5,862	20,265	0.29	15.97	624kyhpq82nvm
5,768	5,763	19,986	0.29	15.64	1wfvddxcf841m
5,386	5,380	20,266	0.27	14.60	gfjauwnsqxzfx
4,915	4,911	19,680	0.25	13.33	6h79rp4gyts91
56	56	19,989	0.00	0.15	c070097bggvup
55	55	18,778	0.00	0.15	4pb2scqxpjgcn
49	49	20,279	0.00	0.13	7s4p3jnkpc5sy
28	28	9,273	0.00	0.08	1gbu3raazg6dy
28	28	9,236	0.00	0.08	ch8pbbp3r7xv0

(b) **SQL ordered by CPU Time**

- Resources reported for PL/SQL code includes the resources used by all SQL statements called by the code.

- % Total DB Time is the Elapsed Time of the SQL statement divided into the Total Database Time multiplied by 100

CPU Time (s)	Elapsed Time (s)	Executions	CPU per Exec (s)	% Total DB Time	SQL Id
11,763	11,818	40,514	0.29	32.04	gsmv6cvsysnys
5,862	5,890	20,265	0.29	15.97	624kyhpq82nvm
5,763	5,768	19,986	0.29	15.64	1wfvddxcf841m
5,380	5,386	20,266	0.27	14.60	gfjauwnsqxzfx
4,911	4,915	19,680	0.25	13.33	6h79rp4gyts91
56	56	19,989	0.00	0.15	c070097bggvup
55	55	18,778	0.00	0.15	4pb2scqxpjgcn
49	49	20,279	0.00	0.13	7s4p3jnkpc5sy
28	28	9,273	0.00	0.08	1gbu3raazg6dy
28	28	9,236	0.00	0.08	ch8pbbp3r7xv0

Figure 6.6 Top SQLs ordered by (a) Elapsed Time and (b) CPU Time.

(c) **SQL ordered by Gets**

- Resources reported for PL/SQL code includes the resources used by all SQL statements called by the code.
- Total Buffer Gets: 1,405,702,082
- Captured SQL account for 99.6% of Total

Buffer Gets	Executions	Gets per Exec	%Total	CPU Time (s)	Elapsed Time (s)	SQL Id
487,795,411	40,514	12,040.17	34.70	11762.78	11817.71	gsmv6cvsysnys
243,887,965	20,265	12,034.94	17.35	5861.58	5889.68	624kyhpq82nvm
222,103,691	20,266	10,959.42	15.80	5380.30	5385.82	gfjauwnsqxzfx
220,993,259	19,680	11,229.33	15.72	4910.95	4914.69	6h79rp4gyts91
219,156,990	19,986	10,965.53	15.59	5762.77	5767.73	1wfvddxcf841m
668,571	20,279	32.97	0.05	48.56	49.03	7s4p3jnkpc5sy
272,137	19,651	13.85	0.02	18.99	19.03	d0cp76dp8mfhq
271,772	19,675	13.81	0.02	18.03	23.92	ffbpj4hpp19ty
262,946	37,551	7.00	0.02	23.27	23.30	079k3hnw05pq4
227,517	19,626	11.59	0.02	14.10	14.13	1tdwt74ht67q6

Figure 6.6 (Continued) Top SQLs ordered by (c) Buffer Gets.

Note that the entity <value> in each WHERE clause represents the actual value for a specific column. The actual values taken are not important for our analysis here and are therefore masked out with the entity <value>.

To help understand better about the scalability issue caused by these five SQLs in question, Table 6.2 summarizes the percentage of elapsed time, number of executions, and number of logical reads (or Buffer Gets in Oracle's term) for each top query. In this context, logical reads and Buffer Gets are interchangeable.

Excessive number of logical reads is one of the most common factors affecting database performance and scalability. It gets worse and worse with increasing volume of data stored in a database. It's a very prominent show-stopper for the scalability of database-intensive software. To put it in perspective, this test incurred 205 physical reads and 44,056 physical writes, respectively, as shown in Figure 6.4, which pale in comparison with the hundreds of millions of Buffer Gets, as shown in Table 6.2.

TABLE 6.2 Statistic Data on the Top 5 SQLs in Question

Query Number (SQL Id)	Elapsed Time (%)	Number of Executions	Number of Logical Reads/ Buffer Gets (millions)
1 (gsmv6cvsysnys)	32.04	40,514	488
2 (624kyhpq82nvm)	15.97	20,265	244
3 (1wfvddxcf841 m)	15.64	20,266	222
4 (gfjauwnsqxzfx)	14.60	19,680	220
5 (6h79rp4gyts91)	13.33	19,988	210

One physical read certainly is a lot more expensive than one logical read. However, hundreds of millions of logical reads are a lot more expensive than hundreds of physical reads. Quantity *does* change the scale.

Previous research shows that a logical read in general takes about one-tenth of a physical read [Liu, 2005]. For example, a logical read typically is in the range of a fraction of a millisecond, whereas a physical read may take anywhere from a few milliseconds to tens or even hundreds of milliseconds.

What was causing so many logical reads then? Well, all explanations are arguable and subject to proof. For a software performance issue, if you ask ten different people, you will get ten different answers and every one has a different view from his/her perspective. But I know how it can be cured based on my experience.

The issue of excessive logical reads is not incurable. As a matter of fact, *covering indexes* are a very effective approach to coping with excessive logical reads [Liu, 2006]. I'll explain what a covering index is in the next section.

Prior to explaining the covering index, I'd like to mention that you are done as soon as you identify the bottleneck as a software performance analyst. You are now transitioning from the role of a performance analyst to that of a performance consultant. A performance analyst analyzes the problem, whereas a performance consultant gives prescriptions for fixing the problem, and immediate performance improvements should ensue.

6.1.3 Applying Optimization and Tuning

A covering index includes not only the columns from the *where clause* part but also the columns on the *select list* part of a *SELECT* SQL statement. The idea behind covering index is that the columns on the *select list* can be fetched together with columns from the *where clause*, thus saving additional I/Os.

Without further hesitation, I created the following three covering indexes:

- Index 1 on the columns of *objectId, documentId, classId, dataGroupId*, and *consistencyId* of the *objectTable*.
- Index 2 on the columns of *objectId* and *documentId* of the *objectAssociationTable*.
- Index 3 on the columns of *destObjectId, classId, documentId, sourceObjectId, objectId*, and *consistencyId* of the *objectAssociationTable*.

The test was repeated after adding these three covering indexes. See Figure 6.7 for the results. The lower curve represents the poor scalability before adding the covering indexes, whereas the upper curve represents the throughput after adding the covering indexes. The throughput is essentially flat now, which indicates good scalability.

It is seen that the covering indexes made a huge difference in improving the performance and scalability of this specific application. The efficacy of those covering indexes is shown clearly in Figure 6.7. The average throughput was improved from 15 objects/second to 71 objects/second. This is about 4.7 times better than before the covering indexes were added. More importantly, the high throughput after adding the covering indexes became sustainable.

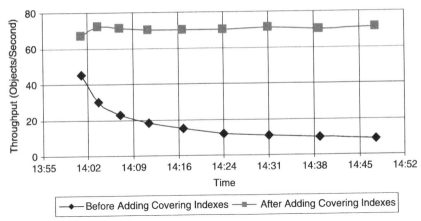

Figure 6.7   *Covering index as a prescription for curing excessive logical reads.*

TABLE 6.3   Number of Logical Reads Before and After Adding the Covering Indexes

Query Number	Before Adding Covering Indexes (millions)	After Adding Covering Indexes (thousands)
1	488	142
2	244	<102[a]
3	222	<102[a]
4	220	<102[a]
5	210	<102[a]

[a]The last four queries disappeared as hot SQLs in the AWR report after adding the covering indexes, and the 102,000 logical reads was from the 20th hottest SQL actually.

Table 6.3 shows quantitatively what a huge difference those covering indexes had made in effectively combating excessive logical reads for those top 5 SQL queries in question. The number of logical reads for those top SQLs were three orders of magnitude lower after adding the covering indexes.

Tablespace IO Stats
- ordered by IOs (Reads + Writes) desc

Reads	Av Reads/s	Av Rd(ms)	Av Blks/Rd	Writes	Av Writes/s	Buffer Waits	Av Buf Wt(ms)
204	0	4.95	1.00	46,323	61	39,101	0.75
43	0	0.47	1.00	1,767	2	3,821	0.12
52	0	6.35	1.00	401	1	0	0.00
40	0	7.00	1.00	275	0	0	0.00
0	0	0.00		9	0	0	0.00

Figure 6.8   *Disk read and write statistics after adding the covering indexes.*

Top 5 Timed Events

Event	Waits	Time(s)	Avg Wait(ms)	% Total Call Time	Wait Class
CPU time		1,713		50.8	
log file parallel write	36,463	566	16	16.8	System I/O
Streams AQ: enqueue blocked on low memory	2	523	261,699	15.5	Configuration
db file parallel write	4,709	69	15	2.0	System I/O
library cache pin	946	40	43	1.2	Concurrency

Figure 6.9 *Top 5 timed events after adding the covering indexes.*

After adding the covering indexes, the number of physical reads and writes for the user table space were 204 and 46,323, respectively, which were essentially the same as 205 and 44,046 before adding the covering indexes. And the average disk access time was reduced from 7 milliseconds to 5 milliseconds, which is inconsequential. See Figure 6.8 for the details about I/O statistics after adding the covering indexes.

It's necessary to mention that before creating these three covering indexes, those tables already had indexes on the *objectId*, *documentId*, and other *Id's*, but not as covering indexes. I point this out in case you are wondering about it at this point. There was a theory that if there were indexes on those columns in the *where clause*

Time Model Statistics

- Total time in database usercalls (DB Time): 3373.4s
- Statistics including the word "background" measure background process time, and so do not contribute to the DB time statistic
- Ordered by % or DB time desc, Statistic name

Statistic Name	Time (s)	% of DB Time
DB CPU	1,712.89	50.78
sql execute elapsed time	685.75	20.33
parse time elapsed	453.24	13.44
hard parse elapsed time	17.70	0.52
hard parse (sharing criteria) elapsed time	1.36	0.04
hard parse (bind mismatch) elapsed time	0.45	0.01
PL/SQL execution elapsed time	0.40	0.01
PL/SQL compilation elapsed time	0.20	0.01
sequence load elapsed time	0.12	0.00
repeated bind elapsed time	0.04	0.00
DB time	3,373.36	
background elapsed time	1,249.91	
background cpu time	33.43	

Figure 6.10 *Time model statistics after adding the covering indexes.*

of an SQL query, then Oracle would retrieve less data into the buffer cache and thus reduce excessive logical reads. I tried it and unfortunately that theory didn't work.

You might wonder what the *Top 5 Timed Events* look like after adding those covering indexes. Figure 6.9 shows the top 5 timed events after adding the covering indexes. In comparison with the top 5 timed events before adding the covering indexes as shown in Figure 6.2, we see that CPU time was reduced from 96.4% to 50.8%. Log file parallel write time has been reduced from 1004 seconds to 566 seconds, although percentage-wise it has gone up from 2.7% to 16.8%. The wait time with the Streams AQ: Enqueue blocked on low memory wait event has gone up. However, this didn't seem to be a problem for the system throughput as shown in Figure 6.7.

Figure 6.10 shows the time model statistics after adding the covering indexes. You can compare the time model statistics after adding the covering indexes with those before adding the covering indexes shown in Figure 6.5. It is seen that DB CPU and sql execute elapsed time were reduced significantly both percentage-wise and in terms of the total absolute time.

SQL ordered by Gets

- Resources reported for PL/SQL code includes the resources used by all SQL statements called by the code.
- Total Buffer Gets: 9,979,944
- Captured SQL account for 77.5% of Total

Buffer Gets	Executions	Gets per Exec	%Total	CPU Time (s)	Elapsed Time (s)	SQL Id
895,663	22,004	40.70	8.97	50.68	53.44	7s4p3jnkpc5sy
434,670	22,087	19.68	4.36	25.84	25.87	d0cp76dp8mfhq
433,035	22,135	19.56	4.34	23.07	27.98	ffbpj4hpp19ty
361,704	22,057	16.40	3.62	19.56	19.56	1tdwt74ht67q6
354,846	22,131	16.03	3.56	17.58	21.74	4su3ayym7r0hu
246,835	41,026	6.02	2.47	15.23	15.35	079k3hnw05pq4
240,067	10,665	22.51	2.41	30.01	30.57	1mca8yahft04j
230,826	21,600	10.69	2.31	22.66	25.63	5k3hvuaqvkbmr
223,167	9,855	22.65	2.24	28.04	28.40	4natsk0zggjbb
219,984	20,520	10.72	2.20	19.62	19.93	64n9254p0hpwk
188,114	21,600	8.71	1.88	19.71	20.24	cpmh76axk9xdz
187,413	20,777	9.02	1.88	9.57	9.68	b74wzp42akp78
180,826	11,070	16.33	1.81	15.00	15.00	gxfthzd310ahj
177,732	19,699	9.02	1.78	8.89	9.13	7jps580zc6vzb
171,753	10,665	16.10	1.72	14.07	14.12	8ssgkzkat29fs
146,401	22,139	6.61	1.47	13.69	14.62	76dbmn6tr9rx7
141,836	43,995	3.22	1.42	15.75	15.75	gsmv6cvsysnys

Figure 6.11 Buffer Gets statistics after adding the covering indexes.

Figure 6.11 shows the *Buffer Gets* statistics after adding those covering indexes:

- None of the SQLs had more than 1 million Buffer Gets.
- None of the SQLs had more than 10% of the total number of Buffer Gets. This means that the Buffer Gets issue has been conquered.
- Out of those top 5 SQLs that had hundreds of millions of Buffer Gets before adding the covering indexes, only one of them was captured after adding the covering indexes. This SQL had the SQL Id of gsmv6cvsysnys as you can see from Figure 6.11. Once again, this verifies the effectiveness of using the covering index to combat excessive Buffer Gets.

Figures 6.12 and 6.13 show the SQLs ordered by elapsed time and CPU time after adding the covering indexes, respectively. Both confirm that after adding the covering indexes, there were no more SQLs that were obviously a lot more expensive than others. In comparison with Figures 6.6a and 6.6b, none of the SQLs have *% Total DB Time* exceeding 2%. This indicates that SQL optimization and tuning are done with this specific test scenario and the database is no longer a bottleneck. It also indicates that an operational equilibrium has been reached, which is a prerequisite for sustainable performance and scalability.

I hope you have been convinced that software performance and scalability work isn't guess work. It requires a disciplined approach based on quantitative test data to resolve a software performance or scalability problem effectively.

SQL ordered by Elapsed Time

- Resources reported for PL/SQL code includes the resources used by all SQL statements called by the code.
- % Total DB Time is the Elapsed Time of the SQL statement divided into the Total Database Time multiplied by 100

Elapsed Time (s)	CPU Time (s)	Executions	Elap per Exec (s)	% Total DB Time	SQL Id
53	51	22,004	0.00	1.58	7s4p3jnkpc5sy
50	50	21,726	0.00	1.49	c070097bggvup
49	49	20,505	0.00	1.45	4pb2scqxpjgcn
31	30	10,665	0.00	0.91	1mca8yahft04j
28	28	9,855	0.00	0.84	4natsk0zggjbb
28	23	22,135	0.00	0.83	ffbpj4hpp19ty
26	26	10,389	0.00	0.78	ch8pbbp3r7xv0
26	26	22,087	0.00	0.77	d0cp76dp8mfhq
26	23	21,600	0.00	0.76	5k3hvuaqvkbmr
25	25	9,851	0.00	0.75	1gbu3raazg6dy

Figure 6.12 SQLs ordered by elapsed time after adding the covering indexes.

SQL ordered by CPU Time

- Resources reported for PL/SQL code includes the resources used by all SQL statements called by the code.
- % Total DB Time is the Elapsed Time of the SQL statement divided into the Total Database Time multiplied by 100

CPU Time (s)	Elapsed Time (s)	Executions	CPU per Exec (s)	% Total DB Time	SQL Id
51	53	22,004	0.00	1.58	7s4p3jnkpc5sy
50	50	21,726	0.00	1.49	c070097bggvup
49	49	20,505	0.00	1.45	4pb2scqxpjgcn
30	31	10,665	0.00	0.91	1mca8yahft04j
28	28	9,855	0.00	0.84	4natsk0zggjbb
26	26	10,389	0.00	0.78	ch8pbbp3r7xv0
26	26	22,087	0.00	0.77	d0cp76dp8mfhq
25	25	9,851	0.00	0.75	1gbu3raazg6dy
23	28	22,135	0.00	0.83	ffbpj4hpp19ty
23	26	21,600	0.00	0.76	5k3hvuaqvkbmr

Figure 6.13 SQLs ordered by CPU time after adding the covering indexes.

In the next section, I'll show you some very effective software performance optimization and tuning techniques based on queuing theory.

6.2 EFFECTIVE OPTIMIZATION AND TUNING TECHNIQUES

Optimization and tuning of the performance and scalability of a software system should focus on reducing the wait times and service demands, as we have learned from the queuing theory introduced in Chapter 4. Information about the wait times and service demands with a specific software product should come from rigorous performance and scalability testing and quantitative analysis of the test results.

There are some well-known performance and scalability patterns that are widely applicable, some of which are no-brainers. All software practitioners should become proficient in applying these performance and scalability patterns to designing, implementing, and deploying their products to achieve the best possible performance and scalability for their customers.

As a matter of fact, these performance and scalability patterns are deeply rooted in queuing theory. This explains why they are always effective. In this section, I'll introduce these performance and scalability patterns by associating them with the two key concepts of queuing theory—*wait time* and *service demand*. To reinforce the idea of associating the well-known performance and scalability patterns with queuing theory, I'll reformulate wait events and service demands in the next section in the context of enterprise software applications for which the most efficient computing resource utilizations are always aggressively sought.

6.2.1 Wait Events and Service Demands

Enterprise software applications typically adopt a multitier architecture consisting of a backend tier, a middle tier, and a front tier. The backend tier hosts data, the middle tier provides enterprise services that retrieve data from or add/update data at the backend, and the front tier sends user requests to the middle tier and renders results to the user.

Typically, the application server and database server constitute the major part of an enterprise software application deployment, as shown in Figure 6.14. For this reason, we omit the front tier for now.

In general, a database server and an application server communicate with each other using TCP/IP or some proprietary protocols. Enterprise data is stored on external storage configured at a proper RAID level. A database server accesses enterprise application data through gigabit storage area network (SAN) fabrics in order to minimize the data access latency.

A complete transaction in an enterprise software application consists of a "wait chain" as is shown in Figure 6.15. In this wait chain, a database server waits for the application data to come back from the disk arrays, and an application server waits for the application data to come back from the database server. Therefore the execution of a service call in an enterprise application can be considered as a series of cycles of service–wait–service–wait, as was illustrated in a research paper by Liu [2005].

If we treat each layer of an enterprise software application system as a queuing node, we can then immediately apply queuing theory introduced in Chapter 4 and shed some light on how the performance and scalability of an enterprise application can be optimized and tuned.

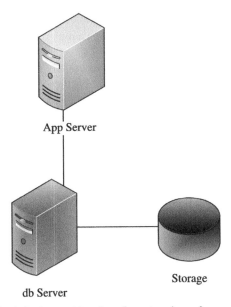

Figure 6.14 *A deployment topology for enterprise software applications.*

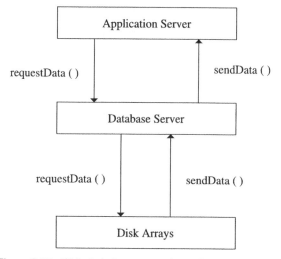

Figure 6.15 *Wait chain in an enterprise software application.*

Assuming that the service demands and wait times are represented as D_{app}, D_{db}, D_{disk}, W_{app}, W_{db}, and W_{disk} for the application server, database server, and disks in Figure 6.15, respectively, then, according to Equation (4.17), the total response time R_0 for an OLTP system at the system level can be decomposed into two parts as follows:

$$R_0 = \sum_i V_i \times W_i + \sum_i D_i \qquad (6.1)$$

where i iterates over the set of {app, db, disk}. Note that in this equation, the first term represents the wait times associated with the various resource wait events and the second term represents the service demands of the queuing nodes in a system. In an uncontended environment, all wait times are essentially negligible.

Similarly, applying Equations (4.8) and (6.1) at the system level, we can calculate the system throughput X_0 for the batch jobs as follows:

$$X_0 = \frac{N}{\sum_i V_i \times W_i + \sum_i D_i} \qquad (6.2)$$

where N is the total number of objects processed in a batch job.

It's clear from both Equations (6.1) and (6.2) that the efforts of optimizing and tuning the performance and scalability of an enterprise software application essentially fall into two categories:

• Minimizing the wait times at each layer as much as possible
• Reducing the service demands at each layer as much as possible

Note that from Equations (6.1) and (6.2), in an uncontended environment, both response time and throughput are determined by the sum of the service demands from all queuing nodes.

TABLE 6.4 Application Resource Bottlenecks

Application Type	Potential Bottleneck
Graphics, encryption	CPU, memory
Web application	Network
Enterprise application	I/O or CPU

As was stated in previous chapters, actual performance and scalability optimization and tuning efforts start with identifying bottlenecks. A resource is a bottleneck if it has the largest sum of wait time and service demand, as implied in Equations (6.1) and (6.2). When the bottleneck with a resource is removed, then the next bottleneck is identified and removed until a balance is reached among all resources. Removing bottlenecks one after another will lead to a balanced queuing system that will yield the best possible performance and scalability.

Characteristically, bottlenecks are implied when the type of application is known. As shown in Table 6.4, graphics and encryption applications consume more CPU power and memory. Web applications are dominated by network traffic, so the network is the most likely bottleneck. As enterprise applications incur intensive I/O activities and heavy validation logic, either I/O or CPU could be the bottleneck.

It's necessary to point out that the performance and scalability of an enterprise software application can be improved from multiple perspectives:

- Using faster hardware from the hardware perspective
- Adopting more efficient designs and implementations from the software perspective
- Using the optimal setting for every external configuration parameter from the system perspective

During the design and development stages, optimizations are applied from the software perspective, whereas after the product is released, the performance and scalability of an enterprise software application can be further improved by using the fastest possible hardware and applying system level tunings. Let's look at some examples.

6.2.2 Array Processing—Reducing V_i

Large-scale enterprise software applications require careful use of various performance and scalability patterns for the highest possible performance and scalability. One of the performance and scalability patterns is that round-trip communications between various tiers, especially between the application tier and database tier, should be minimized as much as possible. This way, the service demand, defined as the product of the number of round trips (V_i) and service time (S_i),

$$D_i = V_i \times S_i$$

can be decreased accordingly, resulting in better response time and throughput.

Array processing helps improve the performance and scalability of an enterprise software application by reducing the number of round trips V_i between an application server and a database server with batch operations on common data operations such as *insert* and *update*. Instead of issuing insert and update SQLs one by one, a bunch of inserts and updates, say, with a batch size of 10 or 100, can be issued to the database server as one call from the application server. This seems like common sense but is often ignored by developers until being caught during the performance assurance and acceptance test cycle.

Array processing is not a new performance optimization technique. It has been documented as a generic, programming language agnostic performance pattern [Smith and Williams, 2002]. It is supported explicitly in JDBC 2/Oracle JDBC driver [Bonazzi and Stokol, 2001; Harrison, 2001] with an *executeBatch* API from the *Statement* object.

Now let's see some real examples of array processing. Figure 6.16 is the first example of array processing. It shows the improvement in performance of the two APIs of a batch job from a real-world enterprise application, before and after implementing array processing with JDBC 2 and Oracle JDBC driver for the two APIs: saveRequest and saveRequestItems.

Without going into the details about how array processing was actually implemented in the application tested, it is seen that the first API (*saveRequest*) was made eight times faster and the second API (*saveRequestItems*) four times faster after the original implementation was replaced with array processing. A batch size of 10 was used for both API tests to achieve such a large amount of improvement. The optimal batch size may depend on the application design, implementation, and hardware. For your specific application and test environment, you should vary the batch size and find out the optimal batch size suitable for your application.

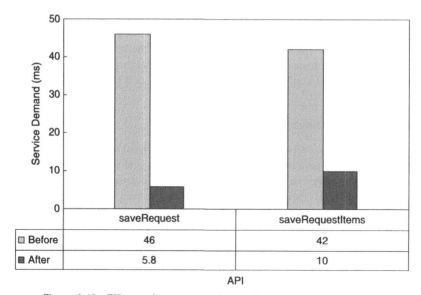

	saveRequest	saveRequestItems
☐ Before	46	42
▓ After	5.8	10

API

Figure 6.16 Efficacy of array processing on the two APIs of a batch job.

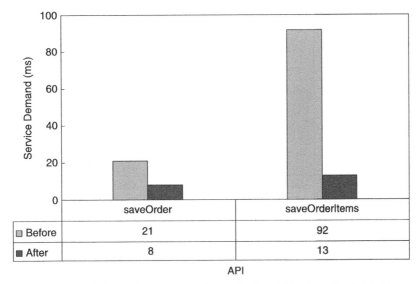

Figure 6.17 Efficacy of array processing on the two APIs of another batch job.

Figure 6.17 is the second example of array processing. It shows the improvement in performance of the two APIs of another batch job of the same enterprise application before and after implementing array processing. It is seen that the first API (*saveOrder*) was about three times faster and the second API (*saveOrderItems*) was about seven times faster after the original implementation was replaced with array processing. Again, for both APIs, a batch size of 10 was used.

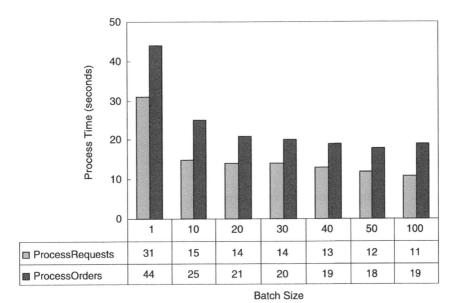

Figure 6.18 Effects of batch size on the processing time of two batch jobs.

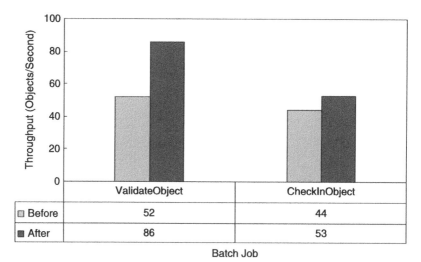

Figure 6.19   *Effects of array processing on an application built in Java/C/C++.*

	ValidateObject	CheckInObject
☐ Before	52	44
■ After	86	53

Batch Job

Figure 6.18 is the third example of array processing. It shows the effects of varying the array size in array processing implementation on the throughput of the two batch jobs of an enterprise application, *processRequests* and *processOrders*. The first batch job processed 497 requests, while the second batch job processed 571 orders. As is seen, a batch size of 10 gives a sharp improvement by as much as 100% on the throughput of the two batch jobs compared with the case of no array processing or a batch size of 1. Because of its significant effects on performance, array processing should be adopted and implemented with every enterprise software application during the early stages of the product development life cycle before performance assurance and acceptance tests begin.

As the last example of array processing, Figure 6.19 shows the performance improvements of an enterprise application built in Java/C/C++, after implementing array processing. In this case, the batch job *ValidateObject* was run first and then the batch job *CheckInObject* was run. The throughput of each batch job improved significantly: 65% for the first batch job and 20% for the second batch job. After it was verified to be optimal, a batch size of 100 was hard-coded into the application. Such improvements are significant as these batch jobs may run for days, depending on the volume of data to be processed.

6.2.3   Caching—Reducing Wait Time (W_i)

Caching helps reduce the wait time or data latency for objects that are fairly static and reused frequently. It is the most common performance optimization technique and certainly is implemented with every enterprise software application. It's safe to say that without caching, none of the enterprise applications would perform.

Caching can be implemented at various levels, for example, at the application server level, at the database level, and at the storage level. Developers are usually very good at implementing caching at the application level. However, human beings make mistakes, especially under tight schedules. Here are two examples of sudden performance degradation:

- In order to add a functionality requested by the customer, a small change was made to a production enterprise application that had been in use by millions of users for online shopping for years. Suddenly, the system was so slow that the users were not able to place purchase orders online anymore. The customer was losing revenue as every minute went by. What's the performance defect that had caused this incident?

- A large-scale enterprise application had undergone a thorough overhaul by retro-fitting and combining all major parts to make it perform better. Then, the routine performance regression test showed that it was 10–30 times slower than before. What could cause such enormous performance degradation?

In both cases, the performance degradations were caused by some objects that slipped away from caching in coding when changes were made. And in both cases, the defects were fixed in time. The moral of the story is that caching objects that are static at the application level plays a vital role in delivering decent performance for every large-scale enterprise software application. It's a smart guess that, in a situation where the performance of an application suddenly dropped drastically due to some changes in the code of an application, it might be because accidentally some objects slipped away from caching in coding.

Another interesting example of caching is at the storage level. I had been working on optimizing and tuning a real-life, large-scale enterprise application for more than a year using in-house hardware with local disks for the database server. Eventually, I got a chance to run the same tests on the production class hardware with advanced SAN storage for the database server. What kind of data latency disparity would you anticipate between local disks and SAN? Table 6.5 shows the difference between local disks (320 MB/s SCSI) and SAN for about 200,000 physical reads and writes.

It is seen that read/buffer wait latency was in the range of 10 ms with local disks, versus the submillisecond range with SAN. The difference comes from the fact that the SAN under test had a huge cache of 2 GB with cache-write enabled. With such a huge disparity in I/O latency between local disks and SAN, the throughput differed by as much as 2–3 times with the same workload.

TABLE 6.5 Comparison of Data Latency between Local Disks and SAN

I/O	Local Disk	SAN
Reads	201,400	201,800
Average reads/second	160	400
Average read time (ms)	9	0.21
Writes	238,300	124,700
Average writes/second	190	250
Buffer waits	5,300	12,000
Average buffer wait (ms)	11	0.12

6.2.4 Covering Index—Reducing Service Demand (D_i)

Database SQL tuning is a much broader category than can be covered in this book. Many excellent texts on SQL tuning are readily available [Harrison, 2001; Tow, 2004].

Most developers know how to index simple queries. In this section, we present an example beyond simple SQL indexing that can help combat excessive logical I/Os or Buffer Gets in Oracle terms. Excessive logical I/Os consume significant amounts of database CPUs and affect the throughput of batch jobs severely, as elaborated in Section 6.1.

This is another real-world example of software performance tuning out of my experience as a performance engineer. The performance issue centered on the following two SQLs, which are similar to each other:

```
Select C3 from T1 where C1=<value> and C2=<value> order by 1 ASC;
Select C3 from T2 where C1=<value> and C2=<value> order by 1 ASC;
```

The T1 and T2 tables from the above two SQLs store objects and relations, respectively. They are large tables that can contain millions of rows for objects and relations. The performance tests showed that the throughput was low even with both queries indexed on the C1 and C2 columns. The AWR report generated with the Oracle 10g performance diagnostics tool indicated that excessive Buffer Gets associated with these two SQLs were attributable to the large amounts of CPU time consumed on the database server.

Since the two SQLs were returning one column only from the data tables, it is a perfect situation where *covering index* (or data in index) can help. By appending

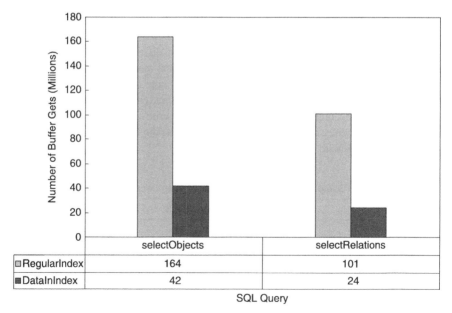

Figure 6.20 Combating excessive Buffer Gets with covering index or data-in-index (DII) optimization technique.

the C3 column to the indexes on the C1 and C2 columns of both tables, there would be no need for the two queries to touch the data tables, which not only helps save physical I/Os to the data tables but also helps avoid bringing too much data into the database buffer cache.

Figure 6.20 shows the significant reduction of Buffer Gets on both queries after this data-in-index optimization was applied. As is seen, the number of Buffer Gets had been reduced from 164 million to 42 million for the first query and from 101 million to 24 million for the second query. This optimization has not only improved the throughput of the batch job by as much as 55% but also helped improve the scalability of the batch job. Without this fix, more and more data would be brought into the database buffer cache when the volume of data to be processed becomes larger and larger, as was the case with the example elaborated in Section 6.1.

Indexing is not the only approach that can help enhance the performance and scalability of database-intensive enterprise applications. Properly configuring some of the database parameters can be equally effective, as is demonstrated next.

6.2.5 Cursor-Sharing—Reducing Service Demand (D_i)

This section presents another example about how the performance and scalability of an enterprise application can be improved by tuning the external configuration parameters, which helps reduce service demands. This example is Oracle 10g specific but might be applicable to other database products as well.

When a query is received by a database server, it must be parsed first. Parsing could be either a hard parse or a soft parse. A hard parse is very expensive since the database server treats each query as a new SQL and all data structure setup as well as all validation logic has to be repeated. Soft parse is less expensive as the database server may reuse the data structures already set up when the SQL was executed the first time.

With Oracle 10g, an initialization parameter named CURSOR_SHARING determines how an SQL is parsed. This parameter has three settings, EXACT (default), SIMILAR, and FORCE. Setting CURSOR_SHARING to EXACT incurs excessive hard parses and may hurt the performance and scalability of an application severely.

SQL statements that are identical, except for the values of some literals in the *where clause*, are called similar statements. Setting CURSOR_SHARING to either SIMILAR or FORCE allows similar statements to share SQL. The difference between SIMILAR and FORCE is that SIMILAR forces similar statements to share the SQL area without deteriorating execution plans, whereas setting CURSOR_SHARING to FORCE forces similar statements to share the executable SQL area, potentially deteriorating execution plans. Hence FORCE should be used as a last resort, when the risk of suboptimal plans is outweighed by the improvements in cursor sharing.

Setting CURSOR_SHARING to SIMILAR or FORCE can significantly improve the performance and scalability of the applications that have many similar statements but do not use bind variables. Figure 6.21 is an example showing the benefit (in terms of performance) of setting CURSOR_SHARING to SIMILAR or FORCE relative to the default setting of EXACT. Using the normalized throughput against the default setting of EXACT, it is demonstrated that the setting SIMILAR resulted in

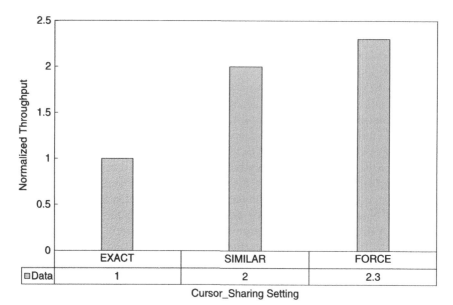

Figure 6.21 *Effects of the* CURSOR_SHARING *settings on the throughput of an enterprise application batch job.*

a 100% improvement over the setting of EXACT, and the setting FORCE resulted in a 15% improvement over the setting of SIMILAR.

Table 6.6 shows how the resource consumptions on the database server varied among the different CURSOR_SHARING settings, measured with the following counters:

(A) latch: library cache %Total Call Time

(B) % of DB Time of Parse Time Elapsed

(C) % of DB Time of Hard Parse Elapsed Time

Note that using the CURSOR_SHARING settings of SIMILAR and FORCE resulted in reduced memory usage, faster parses, and reduced latch contention. The end result was the improved performance and scalability for the application due to significant reduction in service demand on the database server.

In general, using SIMILAR or FORCE is faster than using EXACT. This is true even with the applications using bind variables. However, there is no guarantee that

TABLE 6.6   Resource Consumptions with Various CURSOR_SHARING Settings

Resource	EXACT	SIMILAR	FORCE
A	55	3.6	0.5
B	61	25.6	9.8
C	35	12.9	0.3

FORCE will always be faster than SIMILAR or vice versa. The performance and scalability test with a realistic workload is the only way to find out which setting is more suitable for your application.

6.2.6 Eliminating Extraneous Logic—Reducing Service Demand (D_i)

Enterprise applications are heavy on validating the business rules that must be enforced. Business rule validation may consume a significant amount of CPU resources both on the application server and database server. Without being assured by performance and scalability tests, it's easy for developers to code more validation logic than actually necessary.

For example, when new objects are inserted into a database, the application may fire database triggers to validate various attributes of each object before the object is allowed to be inserted into the database. To make it worse, triggers may trigger subtriggers. In one real-world experience, before tuning, as many as 130 triggers were fired every time a new object was inserted into the database. After examining the validation logic carefully, it was found that as many as half of the triggers actually never needed to be fired. By removing those extraneous triggers, the throughput of the application was increased by 35%. Eliminating extraneous triggers effectively reduced the service demands on the database server, which resulted in better throughput.

Here is another real-world example about how extraneous logic can impact the performance and scalability of a software product.

Prior to the scheduled RTM (release to market) for the new version of an enterprise application, the performance and scalability tests I conducted showed that the application throughput was degraded almost 6 times from 90 objects/second to 16 objects/second after another application component was installed on top of the existing application stack. The author identified the expensive SQLs caused by the new application component, using the performance troubleshooting methodologies introduced in this book. After working with the developer, who was familiar with the validation logic of the new application component, it was found that the expensive SQLs were issued from a legacy trigger that didn't have to be fired at all!

Since this issue was disrupting the RTM schedule for the product, the same performance and scalability test was conducted immediately with that legacy trigger disabled. Surprisingly, the throughput increased from 16 objects/second to 85 objects/second, which was only 6% below what was achieved without the new application component installed. This test cleared the hurdle for the successful RTM of the product within about 48 hours.

To reenforce the importance of having extraneous logic eliminated as much as possible, Figure 6.22 shows the throughput numbers associated with this real-world performance optimization experience. In Figure 6.22, the letter A represents the test case without new application component installed, the letter B the case with the new application component installed and the legacy trigger enabled, and the letter C the case with the new application component installed and the unnecessary legacy trigger disabled.

Without assurance and acceptance testing on the performance and scalability of a software system, it's hard to identify the unnecessary code logic that would waste CPU

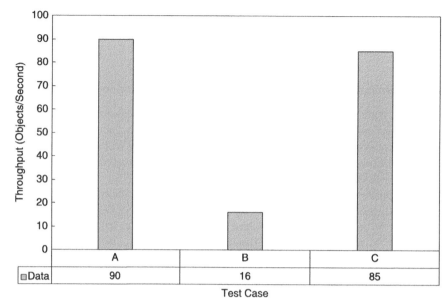

Figure 6.22   *A 6× performance degradation was effectively reduced to 6% after identifying and disabling an extraneous legacy trigger.*

resources and degrade the performance and scalability of an application. For large-scale enterprise software applications, rigorous performance and scalability testing will always be helpful in preventing your software with severe unnoticed performance and scalability defects from being shipped to customers.

6.2.7   Faster Storage—Reducing Data Latency (W_i)

I/O is an essential part of every enterprise application. It should be treated as the first potential bottleneck if it's known that the application incurs heavy I/O activities. In the context of queuing theory, faster I/O reduces data latency and therefore delivers higher throughput for the application that is I/O intensive.

Table 6.7 shows the vastly different I/O capabilities of the disk devices with different file systems and disk configurations. Both local disk configurations (I and II) were SCSI 320 but on different platforms. The tests for all configurations used the same workload of the same application, and the throughput was measured in terms of the objects that were inserted into a database over a period of time.

TABLE 6.7   Application Throughput (Objects/Second) versus I/O Rates from Different Disk Devices with Different File Systems and Disk Configurations

Configuration	Reads/Second	Writes/Second	Throughput
Local disk (I) (NTFS)	160	190	42
Local disk (II) (UFS)	54	52	27
SAN (RAID 0) (UFS)	400	250	90

In the next section, an example of using MPLS (Multi-Protocol Label Switching) to reduce the network latency will be presented to demonstrate how the response time of an enterprise application accessed by employees globally can be improved drastically.

6.2.8 MPLS—Reducing Network Latency (W_i)

MPLS stands for Multi-Protocol Label Switching. It is a concept and technology about network packet routing relative to the vanilla connectivity of VPNs (Virtual Private Networks). Its original goal was to bring the speed of Layer 2 switching to Layer 3. It allows routers to make forwarding decisions based on the contents of a simple label, rather than by performing a complex route lookup based on destination IP addresses. To make it simpler to understand, delivering a network packet using the vanilla connectivity of VPNs without MPLS is like sending a letter using regular mail, while delivering a network packet using MPLS is like sending a letter using express mail that allows a designated priority with guaranteed service, with the urgency of the content explicitly labelled on the envelope.

As enterprises have become more and more globally-based, MPLS has been massively adopted since 2001 as a more efficient approach to managing enterprise applications and moving information between different geographical locations. MPLS provides a high-degree of optimization and utilization of the available network bandwidth, and therefore, it's important to the organizations that need to ensure the low network latency for their business-critical applications.

In this section, we provide an example showing how MPLS had helped reduce network latency drastically for an enterprise application that manages help desk tickets for all the employees of a company located globally. The application was deployed in the United States, while users were spread across multiple countries in Asia. The application was accessed by employees using Web-based browsers. A typical use scenario for this application consisted of four actions: login, open console, search user and save ticket. Figure 6.23 shows three sets of response time data, demonstrating the obvious effects of MPLS on an application deployed globally:

- Users located in China accessing the application deployed in the United States using the direct IP-based routing without MPLS.
- Same users as the above case except that the network was MPLS enabled.
- Users located in India accessing the application deployed in the United States using a corporate MPLS network.

It is necessary to point out that the access path from Beijing, China, to Virginia, U.S. was with the application deployed in U.S. and users located in China, respectively, whereas the access path from India to U.S. was with the application deployed in California, U.S. and users located in India, respectively. The two different access paths were tested by two different (external and internal) teams independently. In each case, the response time of each action was measured manually, which represented the total end-to-end user time.

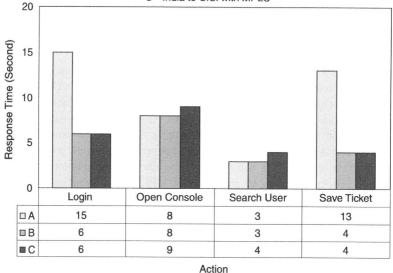

Figure 6.23 *Effects of MPLS on the performance of an enterprise application with two different access paths (China to U.S. and India to U.S.).*

It is seen that MPLS had resulted in drastic improvements on the response times of the login and save-ticket actions, as a result of network latency reduction expected from MPLS networks.

As a convenient tip, one can use the command *traceroute destination* to find out quickly if MPLS is enabled with the network connecting two different end points across the WAN. If the word *mpls* is explicitly embedded in the network router names out of some of the network hops from the output of the above command, then it's an MPLS enabled network. This was the case with the access path from U.S. to India shown in Figure 6.23, as is seen from the output of the *traceroute* command executed on a system in California against a server in India:

```
# traceroute serverInIndia
traceroute to serverInIndia (IP), 40 byte packets
 1 local-gw (IP) 0.693 ms
 2 sw-lan-core-usa-california (IP) 0.401 ms
 3 rtr-wan-core-usa-california (IP) 0.551 ms
 4 rtr-...-mpls-usa-california (IP) 0.951 ms
 5 IP (IP) 9.880 ms 73.410 ms 141.749 ms
 6 rtr-wan-...-mpls-india (IP) 298.106 ms
```

```
 7 rtr-wan-...-mpls-india (IP) 298.440 ms
 8 IP (IP) 298.362 ms
 9 IP (IP) 298.401 ms
10 serverInIndiaIP (IP) 299.171 ms
#
```

Note that the actual hostnames and IP addresses have been masked out, with some of the indicative words such as *gw (gateway), lan, wan, mpls, usa, india,* etc., preserved for identifying each hop.

There are not only performance and scalability patterns but also corresponding antipatterns. The next section shows an anti performance and scalability pattern that is commonly encountered with the database-centric enterprise applications.

6.2.9 Database Double Buffering—An Anti Performance and Scalability Pattern

Caching and faster storage are effective measures for boosting the performance and scalability of database-intensive enterprise applications. However, caching at multiple levels can hinder application performance sometimes. A well-known example is *double buffering* with some database systems, for example, with Oracle 10g on UNIX platforms.

Database systems store data on storage devices. In general, there is a file system between a database system and the data storage. Whenever a database system retrieves data from or stores data to the physical disks, the application data could be cached at both the file system level and the database system level. It is well known that, with newer versions of Oracle databases, bypassing caching at the file system level may improve application throughput tremendously. In this section, I'll share with you two examples out of my own experience.

The first example was with a real external customer. The customer had the following setup for a two-tier enterprise application:

- Application server: Intel dual dual-core at 3.0 GHz (4 CPUs), Windows 2003
- Database server: AMD quad dual-core at 2.8 GHz (8 CPUs), Oracle 10g on Solaris 10
- File system: Veritas
- Data storage: RAID 5 (7 disks) on EMC CLARiiON Cx700

The customer was experiencing very poor performance of 2.8 objects/second with the above setup and an enterprise application whose major functionality was to validate and insert objects into a database.

I repeated the same test as the customer did with a different set of hardware internally as follows:

- Application server: Windows 2003, 4 Intel Xeon® processors at 3.67 GHz
- Database server: identical system with Oracle 10g on Windows 2003 EE

- File system: NTFS
- Data storage: internal RAID 0 (3 disks)

Using the customer's data to drive my test, I got a good throughput of 25 objects/second. This is a factor of 9 difference in throughput between the two environments with the same workload. I needed to help the customer find out what was causing this huge difference.

After working closely with the customer, I found from the Oracle AWR reports from both environments that the average read time from my test was about 8 ms, versus as high as 145 ms from the customer's test. This discrepancy was quickly resolved with the help of a Veritas consultant on the customer's side. It turned out that the issue was related to one Oracle database parameter *filesystemio_options*. Because this parameter was set to *asynch* by default, Oracle wasn't bypassing caching at the Veritas file system level. The parameter *filesystemio_options* has four settings: {none | setall | directIO | asynch}. The implication of each setting is too complicated to be elaborated here. It depends both on the versions of Oracle and the OS. Check with your OS-specific Oracle documentation to be sure or test it yourself to find out which setting is more suitable for your application.

Since the Veritas consultant was very familiar with this issue, it was quickly resolved with the following two recommendations:

1. Set *filesystemio_options* to *directio* on Oracle's side.
2. Mount the file system with the following command:

```
mount -F vxfs -o
remount,cluster,mincache=direct,convosync=direct,
rw,nosuid,log,largefiles,noatime,ioerror=disable,
crw,dev=34432c9/dev/vx/dsk/oradirb_dg/data003_vol/
oradir/data003,.
```

where/data003 was the partition where the database data files were placed.

After the database server was rebooted with the above two changes in place with the customer's setup, the customer repeated the same test. The results were remarkable: average disk read time decreased from 145 milliseconds to 0.98 milliseconds and the throughput was improved from 2.8 objects/second to 23 objects/second.

It's necessary to point out that this *filesystemio_options/directio* setting of the Oracle database is not an issue on the Windows platform, as NTFS does not cache data. That's why with the default setting of *filesystemio_options* set to *asynch* on the Windows/NTFS configuration, a good throughput of 25 objects/second was achieved in my test environment. See Figure 6.24 for a summary of this interesting experience.

Another experience in double buffering was with Solaris, but it was an internal performance and scalability test experience I had, with the following setup:

- Application server: 8 CPUs at 1 GHz SPARC, Solaris 10
- Database server: 8 CPUs at 1 GHz SPARC, Solaris 10

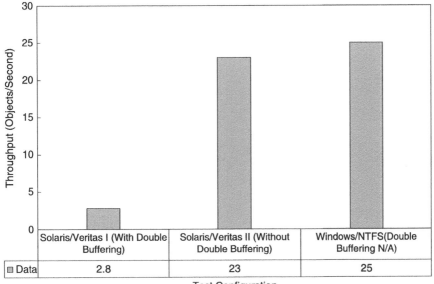

Figure 6.24 *Effects of double buffering on the performance of an enterprise application with Oracle 10g running on Solaris.*

- File system: UFS
- Data storage: internal RAID 0 (3 disks)

With the default setting of *filesystemio_options=asynch*, the AWR report showed that the average disk read time was 446 milliseconds. This is too far off the normal range of 5–20 milliseconds. My experience with that customer reminded me of the issue with caching at the file system level. I was motivated to disable caching at the file system level with Oracle 10g on Solaris.

After remounting the file system with the *directio* option and rebooting the database server, I repeated the same test. Once again, this tuning was very effective. This single change immediately brought the average disk read time from 447 milliseconds down to 10 milliseconds. And the throughput was improved from 49 objects/second to 145 objects/second. This is a factor of 3 improvement on throughput. See Figure 6.25 for a summary of this experience.

It's necessary to point out that with this experience:

- The parameter *filesystemio_options* was still set to the default value of *asynch*.
- The file system was UFS on Solaris, so a different command was used to remount the file system that hosted Oracle data files. To verify whether you have *forcedirectio* enabled on the partition that hosts your database data files, log into your

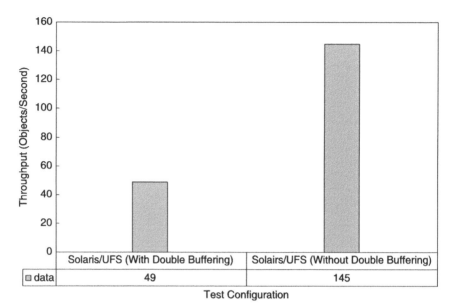

Figure 6.25 *Effects of double buffering on the performance of an enterprise application running on Solaris/UFS.*

Solaris system and issue the command of *mount*. Then you should see something similar to the following if you have *forcedirectio* enabled:

```
/data3 on/dev/dsk/c4t7d0s6
read/write/setuid/devices/intr/forcedirectio/
largefiles/logging/xattr/onerror=panic/dev=1d8000e
on Mon Jul 30 16:30:49 2007
```

However, check with your system administrator before applying this change.

To help summarize the above two examples of database double buffering that can significantly impact the performance and scalability of the enterprise software applications with lots of data inserts and updates, the test configurations and resultant average read times are recaptured and listed in Tables 6.8 and 6.9. For comparison purposes, the database write statistics corresponding to each test configuration are listed in Table 6.10 as well.

Note that from Table 6.10, the buffer wait time increased from 22 ms to 131 ms from the configuration of Solaris/Veritas I (with database buffering) to Solaris/Veritas II (without database buffering), whereas from the configuration of Solaris/UFS I (with database buffering) to Solaris/UFS II (without database buffering), the buffer wait time decreased from 187 ms to 1 ms. This discrepancy might have something to do with the two different settings of *directio* and *asynch* for the Oracle 10g parameter *filesystemio_options*.

TABLE 6.8 Configurations for Testing Double Buffering with Oracle 10g

Configuration	Server Hardware/OS/File System/Data Storage
Windows/NTFS	Application server: Windows 2003, 4 Xeon processors at 3.67 GHz, and 12 GB RAM. Database server: identical system, Oracle 10g Data storage: internal RAID 0 (3 disks)
Solaris/Veritas	Application server: Intel dual dual-core at 3.0 GHz (4 CPUs), Windows 2003 Database server: AMD quad dual-core at 2.8 GHz (8 CPUs), Oracle 10g on Solaris 10 File system: Veritas Data storage: RAID 5 (7 disks) on EMC CLARiiON Cx700
Solaris/UFS	Application server: 8 × 1 GHz SPARC, Solaris 10 Database server: 8 × 1 GHz SPARC, Solaris 10 File system: UFS Data storage: internal RAID 0 (3 disks)

TABLE 6.9 Average Read Time With and Without Double Buffering with Oracle 10g

Configuration	Reads	Average Reads/Second	Average Reads (ms)	With Double Buffering
Windows/NTFS	266,611	44	7.86	No
Solaris/Veritas I	422,733	13	145	Yes
Solaris/Veritas II	184,211	17	0.98	No
Solaris/UFS I	30,784	2	446.81	Yes
Solaris/UFS II	763,910	105	10.22	No

Based on these two examples with a real product and real customer, we see that the UNIX file system can significantly impact the performance and scalability of the enterprise applications, which incur a lot of insert and update disk activities. With UNIX file systems, data must be brought into the file system page cache from disks before being transferred to a database management system. When high volumes of data are being constantly modified, the file system page cache might be filled with data that becomes stale immediately. When all clean pages in file system page caches are used out, dirty pages have to be flushed out to disks. The operating system on the database server might then end up by repeatedly dirtying pages itself. By disabling caching at the file system level, caching can be managed more effectively by the database management system.

TABLE 6.10 Database Write Statistics Associated with Each Test Configuration

Configuration	Writes	Average Writes/Second	Buffer Waits	Buffer Waits (ms)
Windows/NTFS	775,054	127	25,713	4.10
Solaris/Veritas I	1,784,965	55	91,058	21.55
Solaris/Veritas II	964,148	89	45,338	130.72
Solaris/UFS I	368,246	21	290,224	186.95
Solaris/UFS II	580,105	80	429,432	1.04

Under certain circumstances, data access through a UNIX file system might incur double reading for a single write operation. Application data has to be read into the file system page caches first and then into database buffer caches. If the data in a database buffer cache is modified, it might need to be flushed out to the disks. Flushing data to disks takes time. It is possible that the file system may have reassigned the memory for the data flushed out to disks. In that case, the original data must be reread from the disk into the file system page cache. The end result is that one write has incurred two reads.

In this section, a number of examples out of my real-world software performance optimization and tuning practices have been presented to show how one can improve the response time and throughput by reducing the wait times and improving the service demands. Apparently, reducing the wait time and service demand can't be an endless loop. When should one stop? The answer lies in a very important empirical law, which implies that one should stop tuning further when a system is driven into a balanced queuing system. This is our subject for the next section.

6.3 BALANCED QUEUING SYSTEM

An important question in optimizing and tuning software performance and scalability is the following: How do we know that we have done enough and cannot do anything more to improve performance without going through some major changes either in software architecture or hardware architecture? The answer is that the system should be operating in an equilibrium state in terms of the resource utilizations of the various processes or subsystems. This leads to the concept of a *balanced queuing system*.

Traditionally, in a balanced queuing system, all queuing nodes have the same equal service demand. This poses a great challenge for evaluating whether a queuing system is balanced or not, as it's not easy to quantify service demands exactly [Liu, 2005].

Fortunately, there are always alternative approaches to achieving the same goal. A closer look at Equation (4.15),

$$U_i = X_0 \times D_i$$

reveals that for a stable system with constant throughput (X_0), the service demand (D_i) and utilization (U_i) are proportional to each other. This leads to a new definition for a balanced queuing system using the resource consumption metric of utilization:

A queuing system is balanced if all nodes have the same equal utilization.

A guideline for optimizing and tuning the performance and scalability of a software application can be derived based on the utilization-based definition of a balanced system:

A software system can achieve its best possible, scalable performance if it's a balanced system.

To demonstrate the utility of this empirical law, let's look at the experimental results from a setup that had both application server and database server (Oracle 10g) installed on a single four-CPU computer system. The system was driven with a batch workload that ran continuously to populate objects into the database. The system CPU utilizations were logged with Windows *perfmon* utility.

With this specific experiment, Figure 6.26 shows that although the total system CPU utilization was fairly constant, the CPU utilization ratio between the application server and the database server was not constant. Initially the application server CPU utilization and database server CPU utilization were about the same, and then with time, they bifurcated: the database server CPU utilization kept growing and the application server CPU utilization kept decreasing.

You may have noticed that the total CPU utilization of the system was pretty flat. That's because there were only two major processes running on the system: the application server process and database server process. Although the CPU utilizations with the two server processes were developing toward two different directions, the sum of the application server CPU utilization and database server CPU utilization was approximately equal to the total system CPU utilization, which was fairly constant.

Such abnormal database server and application server CPU utilization patterns indicate that the system was not balanced. It was quickly found out that the database server was executing an SQL query with a nonoptimal execution plan because of the lack of optimizer statistics or because the last gathered statistics became stale.

After updating the Oracle Schema statistics, the system was driven into a completely different state, as shown in Figure 6.27. As is seen, the CPU utilization ratio between the application server and the database server was fairly constant now, with exactly the same workload as for the system state shown in Figure 6.26. According to our definition of a balanced queuing system, Figure 6.27 corresponds to a balanced system, whereas Figure 6.26 doesn't. The throughput for the same batch job was improved by as much as 73% from a nonbalanced queuing system to

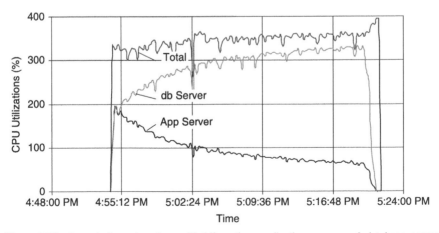

Figure 6.26 *An unbalanced system with bifurcating application server and database server CPU utilizations.*

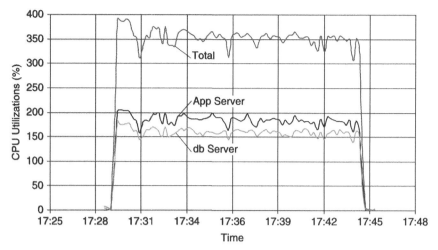

Figure 6.27 *A balanced system with constant CPU utilization ratio between the application server and the database server.*

a balanced queuing system. It's interesting that one can flip the state of the system by enabling/disabling the optimal execution plan for that SQL query with this specific example, as shown in Figure 6.28.

This guideline, based on the concept of balanced queuing systems, can be used as a generic guide to optimizing and tuning the performance and scalability of an enterprise software application. For example, let's say we have an enterprise application installed on one single system: namely, both the application server and database server are installed on the same single physical system. Then, we can monitor the

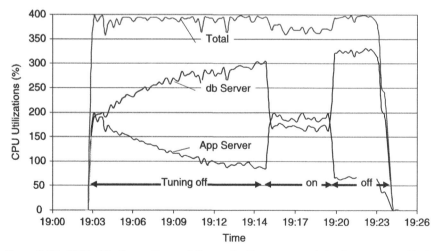

Figure 6.28 *CPU utilization patterns of the application server and database server with the tuning turned on and off.*

CPU utilizations of both the application server process and the database server process simultaneously when the performance and scalability tests are running. If the CPU utilizations of the application server and the database server are significantly disparate, then the optimization and tuning efforts should be focused on reducing the CPU utilizations of the server with the higher CPU utilization. Iteratively, we can help squeeze out every bit of performance and scalability for the application under development by driving it into a balanced state.

To help drive a system to a balanced state faster, it's desirable to use an application API profiler that generates API execution profiles such as shown in Figure 6.29.

The profile shown in Figure 6.29 would reveal immediately the following useful information on the execution of each API of the application:

- The percentage of the elapsed time or CPU time
- The absolute elapsed or CPU time
- The number of times an API was called

A profile can help nail down hot APIs immediately and drive the system to reach a balanced state quickly. Without such information, one has to infer based on the hot SQLs captured on the database side.

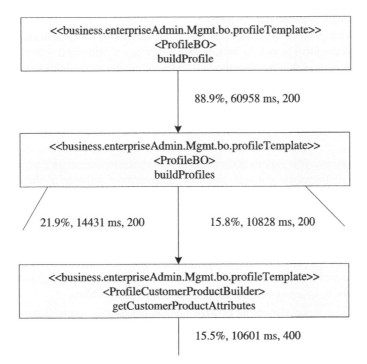

Figure 6.29 *An example profile for a J2EE enterprise application (note that each node is a J2EE method).*

Because of the prominent importance of API profiling to help optimize and tune the performance and scalability of a software system, the third part of this book is dedicated to API profiling. Hopefully, you'll enjoy reading that part as well.

6.4 SUMMARY

In this chapter, we started with showing how to conduct software performance and scalability analysis. A real example was used, detailing what steps to follow and what data to use for analyzing the performance and scalability of a software system. We illustrated how important rigorous, quantitative performance and scalability analysis is to optimizing and tuning the performance and scalability of a software system with a step-by-step procedure. We used results from a real product to convince you what a huge difference effective optimization and tuning practices can make to the performance and scalability of a software product.

We then demonstrated the applicability of queuing theory to optimizing and tuning the performance and scalability of a software system. We presented a number of optimization and tuning techniques that can result in immediate performance and scalability improvements when applied. These optimization and tuning techniques were presented in the framework of queuing theory by centering on the two key metrics of wait time and service demand, which essentially determine the response time and throughput of a software system.

We also proposed a new definition for balanced systems using utilizations instead of service demands. The two definitions using service demand and resource utilization are equivalent to each other, but the new definition using resource utilization makes more sense, as utilizations of a resource can be measured and monitored a lot more easily than service demands.

Based on the new definition for balanced systems, we derived a guideline for optimizing and tuning the performance and scalability of a software system, which states that *a software system can achieve its best possible, scalable performance if it's a balanced system*. This has turned out to be a very useful guide for optimizing and tuning the performance and scalability of the enterprise software applications both under development and after deployment.

Some of the major takeaways from this chapter include:

- Software performance and scalability analysis should consist of:
  - Accurate performance problem characterization. Try to be as quantitative as possible. Use response time for OLTP workloads and throughput for batch jobs to quantify the performance or scalability problem.
  - An accurate accounting of what hardware is used in terms of the number of CPUs, CPU clock rate, memory, data storage, and RAID configurations.
  - An accurate accounting of what software components are installed.
  - Detailed logging of the performance counters such as CPU utilization, disk utilization, memory utilization, and network bandwidth utilization.

- ○ Performance and scalability factor analysis to isolate the dominating factors that are potential bottlenecks.
- ○ Performance and scalability optimization and tuning prescriptions based on accurate performance and scalability factor analysis. Try to avoid guessing as much as you can, especially when you work with a customer.
- Think about optimizing and tuning the performance and scalability of a software system in the framework of queuing theory. Understand that the rationales for all software performance and scalability optimizations and tunings are rooted in queuing theory. You will be dealing with either excessive wait time or excessive service demand whenever you have a performance problem. Apply appropriate prescriptions accordingly.
- Understand all basic performance patterns and tuning techniques introduced in this chapter. It's very likely that by applying one or a few of them to your products, you'll see immediate impressive results.
- Whenever possible, check out whether your software is operating in a balanced condition. This is the only way to sustain the performance and scalability of your software.
- Appropriate database performance analysis skills are necessary to effectively troubleshoot database performance issues, which are always an important part of any enterprise software applications.
- The last point I'd like to make is that you really need a very effective API profiling tool to help you optimize and tune your software. Because having a profiler for optimizing and tuning your software is so important, I'll dedicate the remainder of this book to this subject. Hopefully, you'll continue reading through this book and become fully competent in conducting software performance and scalability work at a professional level.

Once again, I hope you will start applying what you have learned from reading this book.

RECOMMENDED READING

For software performance patterns, consult the following text:

C. Smith and L. Williams, *Performance Solutions—A Practical Guide to Creating Responsive, Scalable Software*, Addison-Wesley, 2002.

For applying queuing theory to optimizing and tuning the performance of software applications in general, see the following texts:

N. Gunther, *The Practical Performance Analyst*, McGraw-Hill, 1998.

D. A. Menasce and V. A. F. Almeida, *Scaling for E-Business*, Prentice Hall PTR, 2000.

D. A. Menasce, V. A. F. Almeida, and L. W. Dowdy, *Performance by Design*, Prentice Hall, 2004.

For SQL tunings, consult the following texts:

E. Bonazzi and G. Stokol, *Oracle 8i & Java, From Client/Server to E-Commerce*, Prentice Hall PTR, 2001.

Guy Harrison, *Oracle SQL High-Performance Tuning*, Prentice Hall PTR, 2001.

D. Tow, *SQL Tuning*, O'Reily & Associates, 2003.

For specific examples of applying queuing theory to optimizing and tuning the performance of enterprise software applications, see the following publications:

H. H. Liu and P. V. Crain, An analytic model for predicting the performance of SOA-based enterprise software applications, in *CMG 2004 Proceedings*, Las Vegas.

H. H. Liu, Service demand models for enterprise software applications, in *CMG 2005 Proceedings*, Orlando Florida.

H. H. Liu, Applying queuing theory to optimizing enterprise software applications, in *CMG 2006 Proceedings*, Reno.

EXERCISES

6.1. If you have access to an application that was built on Oracle 10g, create a relatively heavy workload, run the workload (which should last at least 20 minutes), and then generate an AWR report. Become familiar with how to read an AWR report by following the guidelines provided in this chapter.

6.2. What is a covering index? When would you consider using covering indexes? Analyze the expensive queries from your application and see if there is an opportunity for applying covering indexes to some of your database queries. If you do have a situation where covering indexes are applicable, you should expect huge performance and scalability improvements after you add proper covering indexes.

6.3. What is array processing? Analyze your application logic and find opportunities for applying array processing to your software product. Measure quantitatively how much improvement you can get if it's applicable and implemented properly. You should expect significant performance and scalability improvements after you implement array processing.

6.4. What is the Oracle CURSOR_SHARING parameter about? If you have access to an Oracle 10g based enterprise application, design a workload and measure quantitatively the impacts of the CURSOR_SHARING parameter with the three settings of EXACT, SIMILAR, and FORCE.

6.5. What is database double buffering? Is it potentially more of a problem on Windows or UNIX? How do you diagnose whether your application is being impacted by the anti performance and scalability pattern of database double buffering?

6.6. What is a balanced queuing system? Why is it useful for guiding the optimization and tuning efforts on the performance and scalability of a software system?

6.7. What does CPU utilization *bifurcation* refer to with a typical enterprise application deployment configuration consisting of one application server and one database server? How can you cure it and bring the performance and scalability of your software back to normal? If you have access to an application based on an application server and a database server, design a workload, run your test, and measure the CPU utilizations on both the application server and database server. Evaluate the CPU utilization trend for both the application server and the database server. Do you see bifurcating CPU utilizations between the application server and the database server? If you do, find the root cause and fix it.

Part 3

Applying API Profiling

Man is a tool-using animal. Without tools, he is nothing, with tools he is all.
—Thomas Carlyle, 1795–1881

One of the most effective approaches to identifying *quantitatively* the most expensive software program execution paths is through API profiling. API profiling generates detailed and quantitative execution profiles for a software program under test.

With the API profiling framework introduced in this part, one can easily turn the API profiling data into *performance maps* with which one can easily spot the most expensive execution paths. Developers can then figure out how to reduce the costs of the identified expensive execution paths by adopting more efficient designs and implementations, and thus improve the performance and scalability of the software system under development.

This last part of the book consists of the following four chapters:

- Chapter 7—Defining API Profiling Framework
- Chapter 8—Enabling API Profiling Framework
- Chapter 9—Implementing API Profiling Framework
- Chapter 10—Case Study: Applying API Profiling to Solving Software Performance and Scalability Challenges

The material selected for this part is self-complete from defining through enabling and implementing a simple API profiling framework, the *perfBasic* API profiling framework. The last chapter illustrates how you can apply API profiling to solving real-world software performance and scalability problems more efficiently, which is the ultimate goal of introducing API profiling framework in this book.

7

Defining API Profiling
Framework

Basic research is what I'm doing when I don't know what I'm doing.
—Jon von Neumann about Computer, Technology, and Science

As stated earlier in Chapter 3, the performance and scalability of a software system are determined by many factors. For complicated software systems, diagnosing the dominating performance and scalability factors is not an easy task. It requires software developers and performance professionals to possess both deep and broad knowledge and experience in all areas from hardware, to software, to performance and scalability problem diagnosis using adequate tools.

Diagnosing software performance and scalability defects with a software product could be a lot easier if an API profiling tool is available. API profiling can tell which APIs are slow, and based on that, one can drill down to the root causes. With an API profiling tool, one can save a lot of guess work in figuring out where things are slow.

From this chapter on, I'll focus on API profiling, as I have found out with my own software performance experience that an API profiling tool is necessary for carrying out software performance and scalability analysis at the source code level both effectively and efficiently.

API profiling is about getting a profile of how a software program spends its execution time with each of its APIs during a particular execution path. Based on the profile obtained, one can then track down the APIs that are implemented less efficiently. An API profiling tool is as important to a software developer or performance engineer as a stethoscope to a medical doctor. Medical doctors don't make stethoscopes themselves. However, we software engineers may have to make API profiling tools ourselves. Actually, it's not that hard to implement an API profiling framework.

Software Performance and Scalability. By Henry H. Liu
Copyright © 2009 IEEE Computer Society

I'll show you in the remainder of this book how you can make your own profiling tool if a commercial one is not readily available to you.

Let's begin with defining an API profiling framework in this chapter. In order to place it into appropriate context, it's interesting to see how software performance and scalability defects can propagate through various internal defense lines and be eventually caught by customers. This will be the topic for the next section.

7.1 DEFENSE LINES AGAINST SOFTWARE PERFORMANCE AND SCALABILITY DEFECTS

Two internal defense lines exist against software performance and scalability defects. As shown in Figure 7.1, the first defense line is before the performance and scalability defects slip out of the hands of the developers into the *builds* that are handed over to QA and performance test teams; the second defense line is a performance test team that captures the performance and scalability defects before they slip into production at a customer's site.

When severe performance and scalability defects slip into production at a customer's site, they will be caught eventually and the customer will have to file escalations back to the software provider. It would be ideal if all performance and scalability defects can be captured before a product gets out of the door, but in reality, that's hard to achieve, because it's almost impossible to test all use cases without knowing exactly how customers are going to use the product.

How effectively could each defense line work to capture most of the performance and scalability defects before a product is released? We don't have general statistics about this interesting subject. However, from a practical point of view, it would be desirable if the first defense line can capture 80% of all defects and the second defense line 15%, with only 5% of defects discovered in production at customers' sites. This ideal allocation on capturing performance defects is reenforced in Figure 7.2. Unfortunately, with those organizations who don't take software performance and scalability issues seriously, the reality might be just the opposite.

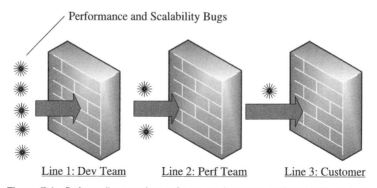

Performance and Scalability Bugs

Line 1: Dev Team   Line 2: Perf Team   Line 3: Customer

Figure 7.1 *Defense lines against software performance and scalability defects.*

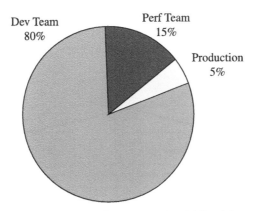

Figure 7.2 Goals for software performance and scalability defect capture ratios.

If we could achieve the goals of the performance and scalability capture ratios shown in Figure 7.2, obviously, software development costs would be significantly lower and customers would be a lot happier. How can we achieve these goals? That's the subject of this chapter. We need to provide an effective API profiling framework that all defense lines can rely on for capturing software performance and scalability defects. This framework has to be simple so that it can easily be implemented and used for solving real software performance and scalability problems.

Before outlining a generic API profiling framework step by step in this chapter, let's take some time to understand what constitutes a software program execution stack. Any API profiling framework has to fit into a generic software program execution stack in order to be useful.

7.2 SOFTWARE PROGRAM EXECUTION STACK

Software applications are written in popular high-level programming languages such as C/C++ and Java. Software programs are then compiled into machine language programs in native code format for the host platform before they can be run on a computer. As shown in Figure 7.3, the programs written in C/C++ are compiled first and then assembled to target a specific platform such as the various flavors of UNIX and Microsoft Windows, whereas the programs written in Java are first compiled into byte-code, which is platform independent. Java byte-code is then run in a Java Virtual Machine (JVM), which is a run-time environment for an underlying host platform.

Compilers and JVMs govern how a software program will eventually be executed on a host computer at the machine language level. All industry-strength compilers and JVMs have been carefully crafted, offering various compile and run-time optimization options for the user to try out for potential performance improvement. Details of the optimizations that can be achieved by choosing the proper compiler compile options and JVM run-time options are beyond the scope of this book. The reader should refer

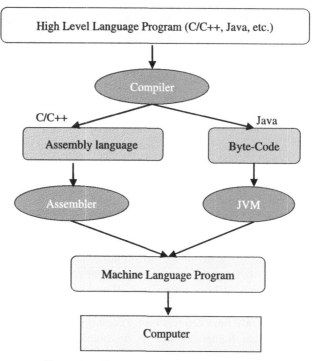

Figure 7.3 Software program execution stack.

to the platform-specific users' manuals for how to use these options for potential performance enhancements.

This book is focused on how an application can be profiled at the high-level language API level using a simple API profiling framework. This framework can be used by both performance engineers and developers. It should be used by developers to fence off the majority of the performance and scalability defects prior to a formal build release to the QA test team.

In the next section, I'll introduce the API profiling framework, which is the foundation for the remaining chapters in this book.

7.3   THE *PerfBasic* API PROFILING FRAMEWORK

It is necessary to point out that there are many commercially available API profiling tools on the market. These tools are very powerful and effective, yet hard to use and very costly. Even worse, some organizations paid a high price, but the profiler purchased was not used very often by their developers. Having observed such inefficiencies, the author is inspired with an idea of an open API profiling framework such as the *perfBasic* API profiling framework introduced in this book. Anybody can easily adapt and implement this API profiling framework. I am confident that once you try it out, you will discover that it's so useful that you will keep using it throughout your career.

The *perfBasic* API profiling framework is simple. It consists of the following steps:

- Insert statements into the source code of your application to generate perform-ance log data using a specific format. Typically, this would generate one or more text files that contain all information about how each API was executed within a specific time period driven by a specific workload.
- Parse the performance log data through a parser on a thread-by-thread basis. The parsed performance log data is written into one or more text files that can be understood by some graphics tools, which can be used to generate the so-called performance maps.

Performance maps are essentially the call-tree graphs that show all call stack hierarchies with all API profile information clearly labeled along each edge from a caller to a callee. The profile data includes the total elapsed time in both absolute units and percentages as well as the number of times each API was called. These types of intuitive performance maps are the key for developers to identify and fix performance and scalability defects quickly.

Since a chart can contain only a very limited amount of information, there are additional text files generated by the parser that summarize all performance pertinent details, especially the details about all SQL statements including their long texts for database-intensive applications.

Let's first begin with the performance logging format on which the *perfBasic* API profiling framework is based.

7.3.1 API Profile Logging Format

The granularity of application profiling is a very important issue. If it's too fine-grained, such as down to the assembly language level, then it would be beyond the comprehension of most developers and performance engineers and therefore would be unlikely to be utilized. If it's too coarse-grained, such as up to class and package level, it would not provide much useful information, and therefore it would be equally useless. The right granularity of application profiling is just down to the API level, which is at the *class method* level in Java and other object-oriented languages or *procedure* level in procedural languages. Developers just need to know which APIs are slow and then they can figure out why they are slow and how to fix them.

Let's begin with getting familiar with the logging format of the *perfBasic* API profiling framework.

The profile logging format for this API profiling framework is really simple. It follows a specific sequence as follows:

- <**firstEntry**>. This entry indicates the type of row, such as <API | SQL>.
- <**ThreadID**>. This entry is the ID number of an execution thread.
- <**TimeStamp**>. This entry indicates when an API call was logged.

- <**APISignature**>. This entry identifies the beginning or ending of an API call, signature of the API, and optionally API caller info such as caller's IP address. API signature should be preceded by a plus sign ($+$) to indicate the beginning or a minus sign ($-$) to indicate the ending of an API call. This will help the parser to determine when an API call began or ended.
- <ThreadGroupID>. This entry identifies the thread group to which the current thread belongs.
- <ServerID>. This entry identifies where this API was being executed.
- <ClientID>. This entry identifies where this API originated.
- <User>. This entry identifies who was making the API call.

The first four entries in the above list are mandatory; all others are optional. This list of entries provides just enough information for fully profiling an application at the right granularity.

If your application has already been implemented with similar logging capabilities, then just write an adapter to convert your original logging format into the format described above, and the rest of the framework will be the same. Or, you can define your own logging format and write your own parser as long as your implementation conforms to this framework, which was outlined prior to this section.

Next, we describe a log parser that takes the textual log files in the above format as input and generates output data files that are suitable for generating performance maps along with performance summarization files.

7.3.2 Performance Log Parser

The parser only understands what it is designed to understand. That is why it's important to stick to an all-agreed-upon logging format. Using the logging format introduced in the previous section for the *perfBasic* API profiling framework, the performance log parser works based on the following concepts:

- Namespace. The purpose of introducing the concept of namespace is simply to help identify and trace each unique execution path. For example, if API *createAccount* calls another API *getCustomerInfo* which in turn calls another API *getCustomerAddress*, then the namespace for this execution path simply is *createAcount.getCustomerInfo.getCustomerAddress*.
- Node. An API call is identified as a node on a performance map, which represents the various execution paths in a call-tree format. Nodes are classified into root node, intermediate nodes, and leaf nodes. A root node is the top node from which all thread executions originate; leaf nodes are those at the bottom of the application level; and intermediate nodes are those between a root node and leaf nodes.
- Link. Each execution path displayed on a performance map consists of nodes and links or edges in a top–down fashion, with each link representing an immediate caller-to-callee execution path. Each link has a label beside it to

indicate performance information such as the number of invocations and elapsed times in both absolute units and percentages. This information is key for developers to identify the performance and scalability defects and optimization opportunities at the application level.

These concepts will become clearer later in the context of performance maps with graphic illustrations. Let's concentrate on what a performance log parser does in this section.

A performance log parser in the context of the *perfBasic* API profiling framework is responsible for the following:

- Sorting log data by thread. After this step, the original log data will be split into multiple text files with one separate data file per thread. The performance log data will be analyzed on a thread-by-thread basis, because all threads were executed in parallel originally when the program was run, and all API calls must be re-played on a thread-by-thread basis in order for the call beginning and ending times to make sense.

- Processing log data by thread. After all performance log data has been sorted out onto the separate files identified by thread IDs, one can decide to process the performance log data of all threads or just certain threads. The parsing logic doesn't change from thread to thread.

- Looping through each thread file. Each line in a thread data file represents either the beginning or ending of an API call with the corresponding time stamp. Processing each line corresponds to associating it with a node if it's the beginning of an API call or with a link if it's the ending of an API call. If the current data line represents a self-node that has no ending call, then a method or procedure like *processCallEnd* must be called before moving to the next data line.

- Correlating call end time to its corresponding call start time. An execution path is essentially a call-chain with each intermediate node being both a callee and a caller. Besides, an API might be called multiple times. For each API call, its call end time must be correctly correlated to its call start time, with the number of invocations updated correctly as well. In order to handle correlation, one can use two dictionary data structures to store node information and link information, respectively, while using a stack data structure to facilitate walking-through the entire thread data file. All in all, it's very necessary to make sure that the parser generates accurate API call information for generating accurate performance maps.

- Emitting log data in proper format for generating graphic performance maps. The main goal of this API profiling framework is to convert hundreds of megabytes of textual performance log files into a single map so that hot APIs can be identified instantly by visual inspection. Therefore, at proper parsing stages and points, relevant data must be output to text files in graphics tool specific format. This typically happens immediately after processing a call start line or call end line. Then, a chosen graphics tool can be used to generate performance maps.

In the next section, we will introduce the concept of performance maps, which illustrate graphically hot APIs and hot execution paths in terms of response times. An API profiling tool and the performance maps it generates are very useful for developers to identify and fix performance and scalability defects before releasing to QA and performance test teams. I'd like to emphasize that an API profiling tool is as necessary to software developers as X-rays to medical doctors and dentists.

7.3.3 Performance Maps

The old saying of "a picture is worth a thousand words" is still true today. Instead of facing the challenge of reading and stepping through a 800-MB text log file for identifying performance and scalability problems, you can now achieve the same objective within minutes by reading a performance map that clearly shows hot APIs and hot execution paths.

Let's concentrate on how to decipher a performance map. A performance map is a graphic representation of all execution paths of all threads logged within a time duration using a specific workload driver. Each node on a performance map represents an API in the program as either a caller or a callee or both if it's an intermediate node. The connection between the two nodes from the source node to the target node constitutes a link, which represents a caller–callee relationship. The important execution history from API to API is represented by the label beside each link between each pair of caller–callee nodes. These labels indicate explicitly:

- The percentage of an API call relative to the total elapsed time
- The accumulated elapsed time of an API call in absolute time units, for example, in milliseconds
- The number of invocations of an API call

This doesn't seem to be a lot of information. However, this information is sufficient for identifying hot APIs and execution paths. The execution paths with the largest percentages of accumulated elapsed times are the hot execution paths, and the APIs along those hot execution paths are hot APIs. One should also watch out for the number of invocations of those APIs, which could indicate inefficient designs or implementations.

Figure 7.4 is an example performance map from a commercial application. This performance map contains the execution paths out of three threads, with each thread representing an independent call-tree trunk. Each trunk contains branches of its own, representing different execution paths of that thread. The thread ID, relative elapsed time percentage, the accumulated elapsed time in milliseconds, and the number of invocations are labeled beside each link. The hot execution paths are displayed in red to help enhance the readability for visual inspection.

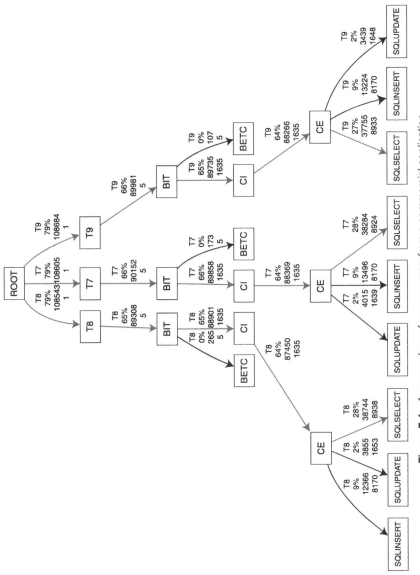

Figure 7.4 An example performance map from a commercial application.

In generating performance maps, one can use filters to filter out the low-impact execution paths. In general, one may need to try a few times in order to determine the most appropriate filtering threshold values.

Figure 7.4 was generated with a freely available graphics tool, *Graphviz dot* program. We will introduce this freely available graphics tool in detail in Chapter 9.

Although a performance map is a powerful vehicle for identifying performance and scalability defects, it's unrealistic to put all details such as the long SQL texts on a performance map. Performance maps can be augmented by additional summarization files that contain further details about each API call and execution path. The next section describes the contents of such additional summarization files.

7.3.4 Performance Summarization File

A performance map conveys information about the hierarchy of executions and hot execution paths in an easy-to-visualize format. A performance summarization file contains the whole history of all API executions in a more readable format than the original performance log data files. It should contain the following list of information for each API call:

- Elapsed time
- Thread ID
- Call count
- Full API signature

Filtering, sorting, and classifying can be applied to a summarization file to make more detailed, drill-down performance data analysis easier. For example, you may not want to include those API calls whose elapsed times are below a certain threshold to help reduce the volume of the data to be viewed; you may want to sort all API calls based on the API type and elapsed time; you may want to view the accumulated elapsed time for an API rather than each individual call elapsed time; or you may want to separate APIs from SQL statements.

In the next chapter, I'll introduce how one can easily enable the *perfBasic* API profiling framework by inserting profiling enabling statements in the source code of a software product.

7.4 SUMMARY

In this chapter, we defined three software performance and scalability defect defense lines and proposed a practical defect capturing ratio for each defense line. The majority of software performance and scalability defects should be contained at the development stage. In order for this to happen, developers need an effective API profiling tool, which can help them identify software performance and scalability defects within minutes.

We then justified that software performance profiling at the API level is the right granularity. Profiling at lower levels would mostly be interesting to vendors who manufacture hardware or system software such as virtual machines, compilers, and operating systems.

We then defined an API profiling framework (*perfBasic*) that is simple to implement and easy to use for developers and performance engineers to identify application, system, and database bottlenecks. The framework consists of a standard logging format, the basic functions of a commensurate parser, and the notions of performance maps and summarization files. We expect that performance maps will be the most frequently used vehicle for solving most of the performance and scalability defects before a drop of a software product under development is made available for quality and performance assurance tests.

We will devote the next three chapters to enabling, implementing, and applying the *perfBasic* API profiling framework to solving real-world performance and scalability problems.

EXERCISES

7.1. Describe the three defense lines against software performance and scalability defects for a software product. What will be the consequences if a software product is released to customers with significant performance and scalability problems?

7.2. Describe the concept of a software execution stack using a layered approach. Why is it important to understand the software execution stack associated with a specific software product for helping solve performance and scalability problems?

7.3. What is a *framework* in general? What's the difference between a framework and an implementation? Give some examples of frameworks and implementations in the software industry.

7.4. What is the *perfBasic* API profiling framework? What logging format does it use? Devise a software program and describe how the *perfBasic* API profiling framework can help you diagnose performance and scalability problems.

7.5. What are software performance maps? What information does a software performance map convey in general? Why is it useful for helping identify the most expensive calling paths with a software program?

7.6. If you have experience in using a commercial API profiling tool or an internal one, how convenient is it? Can it actually generate performance maps?

8

Enabling API Profiling Framework

Genius is 1 percent inspiration and 99 percent perspiration.
—*Thomas Alva Edison*

Enabling the *perfBasic* API profiling framework is easy if your existing applications already have the capability of writing API calls to external log files in the text format. If such log files already contain the API profiling data specified by the *perfBasic* API profiling framework, then you only need to rewrite your logged data according to the logging format required by the *perfBasic* API profiling framework. This can easily be done using an adapter program, as will be elaborated in the next chapter.

For an application that has no built-in capability of logging API calls, API profiling statements can be inserted into its source code using an external program such as *perfLog.java* written by the author for illustration purposes. In this chapter, I will briefly walk through the source code of this program with you. This will expose some issues with enabling API profiling to profile existing software. The task is as easy as inserting profiling statements into the source code of a program as the beginning or ending statement in a method or procedure. However, there are many delicate issues to deal with.

Although *perfLog.java* is implemented in Java for enabling Java applications, it can be used as a useful reference for implementing an enabling program for applications written in any other high-level programming languages.

Let's first begin with the overall structure of *perfLog.java*.

8.1 OVERALL STRUCTURE

The program *perfLog.java* is implemented in Java using *eclipse*, which is one of the most popular open source IDEs (integrated development environments) in the software development community. Figure 8.1 shows the structure of this program

Figure 8.1 perfLog.java in eclipse.

in *eclipse* with all global parameters and methods included. Those items preceded with ▲^{S} symbols are variables, while those preceded with ●^{S} symbols are methods. In the subsequent sections, I will give a brief overview of how this program works, followed by a code listing showing some implementation details.

8.2 GLOBAL PARAMETERS

This program has the following five global parameters:

- *createApfWriterMethodName*, which represents the method to be added to the original source code for creating a file writer object that will be used to write actual API profiling log data.
- *debug*, which specifies whether debugging information will be written when *perfLog* program is being executed.
- *fileWriter* of type *PrintWriter*, which is used for rewriting the original source code and inserting profiling statements immediately following the *method* signature and immediately prior to the *return* statement or ending of a method.
- *logPerfDataMethodName*, which represents the name of the method that must be added to the original source code for writing the API calls to the external text files. This parameter is used to avoid adding profiling statements to the logging method, which may otherwise cause endless recursive calls to the logging method itself.
- *mainAddProfilingBeginAfter*, which specifies the first executable statement in the main program after which the profiling begin statement will be inserted.
- *mainAddProfilingEndAfter*, which specifies the statement in the main program before which the profiling end statement will be inserted.

These parameters are initialized with the help of an external *properties* file named *apf.properties*. Figure 8.2 shows a sample *apf.properties* file.

In the next section, we'll introduce the main processing logic coded in the main method of *perfLog.java*. From the code listing for the main method, you will also see how the above global parameters are initialized.

```
// file apf.properties
sourceDir=../bstPerfTest/src/com/bst/cdmi/perf/
targetDir=../bstPerfTestStaging/src/com/bst/cdmi/perf/
createApfWriterMethodName=cdmiPerfTest.createApfWriter
mainAddProfilingBeginAfter=createApfWriter("perfLogData.apf");
mainAddProfilingEndAfter=apfWriter.close();
logPerfDataMethodName=cdmiPerfUtil.printLogData
debug=on
```

Figure 8.2 A sample apf.properties *file.*

8.3 MAIN LOGIC

As shown in Code Listing 8.1, the *main* method calls the method *getPropertiesHandle* ( ), which returns a *Properties* object pointing to *apf.properties* file. This object is then used to initialize all the global parameters prior to main logic execution.

The main method then calls the method *getFiles* ( ) with a given *soureDirectory* to get a list of Java source files contained in this file directory. The next method call to *processFiles (files, targetDir)* processes each source file by parsing it and adding profiling statements within its methods, which is the main purpose of this program.

Code Listing 8.1: main Method of *perfLog.java*

```
public static void main(String[] args) {
  Properties apfProps=getPropertiesHandle();
  mainAddProfilingBeginAfter=apfProps
       .getProperty(''mainAddProfilingBeginAfter'');
  mainAddProfilingEndAfter=apfProps
       .getProperty(''mainAddProfilingEndAfter'');
  System.out.println(mainAddProfilingBeginAfter);
  System.out.println(mainAddProfilingEndAfter);
  String sourceDir=apfProps.getProperty(''sourceDir'');
  String targetDir=apfProps.getProperty(''targetDir'');
  debug=apfProps.getProperty(''debug'', ''off'');
  System.out.println(''debug'' + debug);
  logPerfDataMethodName=apfProps
       .getProperty(''logPerfDataMethodName'');
  createApfWriterMethodName=apfProps
       .getProperty(''createApfWriterMethodName'');
  ArrayList files=getFiles(new File(sourceDir));
  processFiles(files, targetDir);
}
```

In the next section, we'll introduce the *processFiles* ( ) method, which initiates enabling API profiling on each method of each source file in the specified source directory.

8.4 PROCESSING FILES

The logic of the *processFiles* ( ) method is simple. It loops through each file with the same logic of creating a file writer object using the target file name, adding profiling statements within each method of that class, and then closing the file writer. Code Listing 8.2 shows how this method is implemented.

Code Listing 8.2: processFiles Method of *perfLog.java*

```
public static void processFiles(ArrayList fileNames,
         String targetDir) {
```

```
for (int i = 0; i<fileNames.size(); i++) {
    String fileName = fileNames.get(i).toString();
    String targetFile = targetDir
     + fileName.substring(fileName.lastIndexOf(''\\'')+1);
    fileWriter = createWriter(targetFile);
    addProfiling(fileName);
    fileWriter.close();
}
}
```

In the next section, we'll present the core logic of this program, the *addProfiling* ( ) method, which implements how enabling statements are inserted into each method of the class to be profiled.

8.5 ENABLING PROFILING

Enabling profiling is as simple as adding profiling statements at the beginning and ending places within each method of the class to be profiled. This is achieved through the *addProfiling* ( ) method of the *perfLog.java* program.

As shown in Code Listing 8.3, this method loops through each line in the source code with the following core logic:

- It first checks and processes comment blocks. How comment blocks are processed is deferred to the next section.
- It then updates the *scopeLevel* variable and *classLevel* variable. The *scopeLevel* variable is used to help identify whether the current line is a method signature line, a normal code line within the method, or the end of a method definition, whereas the *classLevel* variable is used to track inner classes. The *scopeLevel* variable is updated with the utility method *countLeftBrackets* ( ), while the *classLevel* variable is updated with the utility method *isClassBeginLine* ( ).
- It then checks whether the current line is a method begin line. If it is, it calls *processMethodBeginLine* ( ) to process the method begin line, in which an API profiling statement indicating beginning of an API call is added to the original source code; it also updates three variables: *numOfStart*, *scopeLevel*, and *methodName*. The variable *numOfStart* is used to check the balance of method begin and end lines, as each method has only one begin line and one end line. The other two variables of *scopeLevel* and *methodName* are used later to identify whether a method end line has been reached.
- For those typed methods that return values, for example, a string, a number, or an object instance, their *return* statements must be properly identified and dealt with, as one cannot add a profiling statement after a *return* statement and prior to the enclosing bracket of the method. Whether it's a typed method that contains *return* statement(s) is indicated by the value of the Boolean variable *isTypedMethod*.

- The return statements are checked with the method of *isReturnStatement* ( ), and processed with the method of *processReturnLine* ( ).
- It then checks whether the current line represents the end of the method being processed by calling *isMethodEndLine* ( ) with the parameters passed in. If it does, the method of *processMethodEndLine* ( ) is called to process the end line of a method, in which an API profiling statement indicating the end of an API call is added prior to the method ending bracket. This is where the variable *isTypedMethod* is useful, as there is no need to add a profiling statement at this point if the method is a typed one with a return statement, since an API profiling statement has already been added prior to a return statement. The two variables of *numOfEnd* and *methodName* are updated then.
- Beyond the cases described above, the current line is just a normal source statement within a method, and it is just rewritten to the target source file. However, it doesn't just end here. It calls the *processMainMethodProfiling* ( ) method as shown in Code Listing 8.4 to check whether the current line needs to be followed by a profiling statement indicating the start of the call to the *main* method. This mechanism is implemented with the parameter *mainAddProfilingBeginAfter*, which is set in the *apf.properties* file and initialized as one of the global parameters for the program.

Code Listing 8.3: addProfiling ( ) Method of *perfLog.java*

```
public static void addProfiling(String fileName) {
    BufferedReader reader = createReader(fileName);

    String line = '''';
    int numOfStart = 0;
    int numOfEnd = 0;
    int numOfReturn = 0;
    int classLevel = 0;
    int scopeLevel = 0;
    String methodName = '''';
    String debugInfo = '''';
    boolean isTypedMethod = false;
    boolean isReturnProcessed = false;
    String className = getClassName(fileName);
    Stack scopeStack = new Stack();
    scopeStack.push(''root'');
    String scope = ''root'';
    while ((line = readNextLine(reader)) != null) {
      line = processComment(reader, line);
      int scopeLevelChange = countLeftBrackets(line);
      scopeLevel = scopeLevel + scopeLevelChange;
      scope = '''';
      if (scopeLevelChange > 0) {
        scope = getScope(reader, line);
```

```
  if (scope ! =  '''') {
    scopeStack.push(scope);
  }
  } else if (scopeLevelChange < 0) {
    scopeStack.pop();
  }
  if (scope.equals(''array initializer'')) {
    scopeStack.pop();
    scopeLevel--;
  } else if (isClassBeginLine(line)) {
    scopeStack.push(''class'');
    classLevel++;
    debugInfo = getDebugInfo(scopeStack, classLevel,
    scopeLevel);
  printSourceLine(line, debugInfo);
} else if (isStartsWithIf(line)) {
  if (processStartsWithIf(reader, line, methodName) > 0) {
    scopeStack.push(''if'');
    scopeLevel++;
  }
} else if (isMethodBeginLine(line)) {
  scopeStack.push(''method'');
  isReturnProcessed = false;
  numOfReturn = 0;
  String methodLine = processMethodBeginLine(reader,
    className, line);
  isTypedMethod = getMethodType(methodLine);
  numOfStart++;
  if (!line.trim().equalsIgnoreCase(methodLine.trim())) {
    scopeLevel++;
  }
  methodName = className+''_''
    + getMethodName(methodLine);
  } else if (isReturnStatement(line, methodName)) {
    isReturnProcessed = processReturnLine(reader, line,
      methodName);
    numOfReturn++;
  } else if (isMethodEndLine(line, methodName, scopeLevel,
    classLevel)) {
    processMethodEndLine(line, isReturnProcessed,
      methodName);
    numOfEnd++;
    checkWellFormed(isTypedMethod, methodName,
      numOfReturn);
    methodName = '''';
  } else {
```

```
    debugInfo = getDebugInfo(scopeStack, classLevel,
      scopeLevel);
    printSourceLine(line, debugInfo);
    processMainMethodProfiling(line, methodName);
  }
}
try {
  reader.close();
} catch (IOException ioe) {
}
System.out.println(fileName +'': numOfStart = ''+numOfStart
  + ''numOfEnd = ''+numOfEnd + ''\n'');
}
```

Code Listing 8.4: processMainMethodProfiling ( ) of *perfLog.java*

```
public static void processMainMethodProfiling(String line,
        String methodName) {
  if (line.contains(perfLog.mainAddProfilingBeginAfter)) {
      fileWriter.println(line);
      fileWriter.println(''\t\t'' + logPerfDataMethodName
        + ''(\''''+getLogFormat(methodName, true)+''\ '');'');
  }
}
```

The implementation for enabling the *perfBasic* API profiling framework should be as generic as possible. One example out of many potential coding practices is inner classes. In the next section, we describe how inner classes are dealt with in this enabling program of *perfLog.java*.

8.6 PROCESSING INNER CLASSES

Inner classes are tracked using the variable *classLevel* in the *addProfiling* ( ) method with the statement

```
classLevel=classLevel+isClassBeginLine(line);
```

in conjunction with the method *isClassBeginLine* ( ) as shown in Code Listing 8.5.

Code Listing 8.5: isClassBeginMethod ( ) of *perfLog.java*

```
public static boolean isClassBeginLine(String line) {
  boolean IsClassBeginLine = false;
```

```
if (hasAccessSpecifier(line) && line.contains(``class'')) {
   IsClassBeginLine = true;
}
return IsClassBeginLine;
}
```

As is seen, this method depends on the access specifiers and the keyword *class* to determine whether the current line is a class begin line. The specifiers are Java specific and defined in the *hasAccessSpecifier* ( ) method, as shown in Code Listing 8.6.

Code Listing 8.6: hasAccessSpecifier ( ) of *perfLog.java*

```
public static boolean hasAccessSpecifier(String line) {
   String[] tokens = { ``public'', ``private'', ``protected'',
            ``final'', ``native'', ``synchronized''};
   boolean hasIt = false;
   for (int i = 0; i < tokens.length; i++) {
     if (line.contains(tokens[i])) {
        hasIt = true;
     }
   }
   return hasIt;
}
```

In the next section, we'll discuss how *comments* are dealt with in this API profiling enabling implementation.

8.7 PROCESSING COMMENTS

Java uses either "//" or "/* comments */" to indicate comment lines or comment blocks in the source code of a Java program. The following code listing shows how the comment statements are processed in the *processComment* ( ) method of *perfLog.java*. As is seen, both types of comments are processed in the same *while* loop. The comments are written back to the target source file.

Code Listing 8.7: processComment ( ) of *perfLog.java*

```
public static String processComment(BufferedReader reader,
            String line) {

   while (line.trim().startsWith(``//'')
      || line.trim().startsWith(``/*'')) {
      if (line.trim().startsWith(``//'')
         || (line.trim().startsWith(``/*'') && line.trim()
                  .endsWith(``*/''))) {
```

```
        printSourceLine(line);
        line = readNextLine(reader);
      } else if (line.trim().startsWith(''/*'')) {
        while (!line.trim().endsWith(''*/'')) {
          printSourceLine(line);
          line = readNextLine(reader);
        }
        if (line.trim().endsWith(''*/'')) {
          printSourceLine(line);
          line = readNextLine(reader);
        }
      }
    }
    return line;
}
```

In the next section, we'll discuss how the method begin lines are processed.

8.8   PROCESSING METHOD BEGIN

Enabling API profiling consists of adding profiling statements following the begin line and prior to the end line of a method of the class to be profiled. Whether the current line is a method begin line is determined by calling the method *isMethodBeginLine* ( ), as shown in Code Listing 8.8.

Code Listing 8.8: isMethodBeginLine ( ) of *perfLog.java*

```
public static boolean isMethodBeginLine(String line) {
    boolean isMethodBeginLine = true;
    if (!hasAccessSpecifier(line) || !line.contains(''('')
        || line.endsWith('';'') || line.startsWith(''//'')
        || line.contains(''class'') || line.length() < 3) {
        isMethodBeginLine = false;
    }

    return isMethodBeginLine;

}
```

As seen from the above code listing, a line is a method begin line if all of the following conditions are satisfied:

- It has an access specifier similar to those defined in Code Listing 8.6 for defining a class begin line.
- It contains the left round bracket "(" indicating the beginning of the argument list.

- It does not end with ";".
- It does not start with "//".
- It does not contain the key word *class.*
- And its length is longer than 3.

This lengthy list of conditions helps guarantee in most cases that a method begin line can be identified correctly.

Code Listing 8.9 shows how a profiling statement is added after the begin line of a method to indicate the start of an API call:

- It first keeps reading until reaching the left curly bracket of "{" just in case the method signature expands into multiple lines.
- Then the name of the method is extracted using the entire line that defines the method.
- Then it checks whether this method is excluded from being profiled. For various reasons, some methods may not be profiled. Also, the *main* method requires a different treatment, which is excluded from being processed at this point as well.
- If the method is to be profiled, a profiling enabling statement is written after the method signature line with the help of one parameter and one method. The parameter *logPerfDataMethodName* specifies which profiling statement to use, which must be preexisting in the original source code. The method *getLogFormat* ( ) determines what logging format to use to indicate whether the API profiling log data represents the *begin* or *end* of an API call. As shown in Code Listing 8.10, the begin of an API call is indicated by the method name preceded by " + ", whereas the end of an API call is indicated by the method name surrounded by the signs of "−" and "OK".

Code Listing 8.9: processMethodBeginLine ( ) of *perfLog.java*

```
public static String processMethodBeginLine(
          BufferedReader reader, String className,
          String line) {
    String methodLine = '''';
    String methodName='''';
    while (!line.contains(''{'')) {
      printSourceLine(line);
      methodLine = methodLine + line.trim();
      line = readNextLine(reader);
    }
    printSourceLine(line);
    methodLine = methodLine + line.trim();
    methodName = className +''_'' + getMethodName(methodLine);
    if (isProfiledMethod(methodName)
        && !methodName.endsWith(''main'')) {
```

```
      fileWriter.println(``\t\t'' + logPerfDataMethodName
        + ``(\''\'' + getLogFormat(methodName, true) + ``\'');'');
  }
  return methodLine;
}
```

Code Listing 8.10: getLogFormat ( ) of *perfLog.java*

```
public static String getLogFormat(String methodName,
      boolean isStart) {
  String format=``'';
  if (isStart) {
    format = ``+'' + methodName;
  } else {
    format = ``-''+methodName+``OK'';
  }
  return format;
}
```

In the next section, we'll discuss how the *return* statements are dealt with.

8.9 PROCESSING RETURN STATEMENTS

For the typed methods that return values, the profiling statement indicating the end of an API call must be added immediately prior to the return statement. This doesn't sound too complicated, but actually it has a lot of variations in Java on how the keyword *return* could appear on a source line.

Processing return statements is preceded by determining whether a line containing the keyword return is a return statement by calling the *isReturnStatement ( )* method, as shown in Code Listing 8.11. When receiving a line, this method cuts off the *comment* part on the line and checks whether the *return* keyword is still on the line. If yes, it returns *true*; otherwise it returns *false*.

Code Listing 8.11: isReturnStatement ( ) of *perfLog.java*

```
public static boolean isReturnStatement(String line,
      String methodName) {
  boolean isReturnLine=false;
  String testLine=removeAppendedComment(line);
  if (testLine.trim().startsWith(``return'')
      && !isLiteral(testLine, ``return'')) {
    isReturnLine=true;
  }
  return isReturnLine;
}
```

When it is determined that the current line is a return statement, the method *processReturnLine* ( ) is called to process the return statement. As shown in Code Listing 8.12, the *processReturnLine* ( ) method first checks whether this method is to be profiled. If it is, the *processReturnLine* ( ) method simply calls the *printReturnLine* ( ) method to print the return line with the proper ending API call statement inserted. Otherwise, the line is printed as a normal source line.

Code Listing 8.12: processReturnLine ( ) of *perfLog.java*

```
public static boolean processReturnLine(BufferedReader reader,
        String line, String methodName) {
  boolean isReturnProcessed=false;
  if (isProfiledMethod(methodName)) {
     printReturnLine(reader, line, methodName);
     isReturnProcessed=true;

  } else {
    printSourceLine(line);
  }
   return isReturnProcessed;
}
```

In the next section, we'll discuss the *processMethodEndLine* ( ) method.

8.10 PROCESSING METHOD END

The method processMethodEndLine ( ) is simple, as shown in Code Listing 8.13. It first makes sure that the method is to be profiled and that the method is not a typed method. If these conditions are satisfied, the profiling enabling statement is written to the target source file similar to how the profiling statement is written in the method of *processMethodBeginLine* ( ) described previously. The only difference is that *false* is passed to the *getLogFormat* ( ) method as the second argument to indicate that this is the end of a method call.

Code Line 8.13: processMethodEndLine ( ) of *perfLog.java*

```
public static void processMethodEndLine(String line,
        boolean isReturnProcessed, String methodName) {
  if (isProfiledMethod(methodName) && !isReturnProcessed) {
    printSourceLine(''\t\t'' + logPerfDataMethodName + ''(\''''
        + getLogFormat(methodName, false)+''\'');'');
    if (methodName.endsWith(''main'')) {
      fileWriter.println(''\t\t''
          + perfLog.mainAddProfilingEndAfter);
    }
```

```
   }
   printSourceLine(line);
}
```

In the next section, we'll discuss how the main method is treated differently from the other methods.

8.11   PROCESSING MAIN METHOD

The *main* method should be treated differently when adding profiling enabling statements in it, because it provides the entry point to the entire program, and some operations must be conducted first before profiling can start. For example, the file writer object must be created at the beginning of the main method before the profiling log data indicating the start of the main method execution can be written using a file writer. For the same reason, this file writer object cannot be closed until the profiling statement indicating the end of the main program execution has been executed. This is why the main method has to be treated differently from the other methods.

Adding profiling statements in the main method depends on the following two parameters that need to be set up in the *apf.properties* file:

*   The first parameter *mainAddProfilingBeginAfter* represents the statement in the main method of the source program to be profiled after which the profiling statement indicating the begin of the call to the main method should be added. Usually, the parameter *mainAddProfilingBeginAfter* is set to something similar to *apfWriter = createWriter ("logPerfTest.apf")*; which should be the first executable statement in the main method of the source program to be profiled. This statement creates a file writer object that will be used later by the profiling statements inserted into each method to write the profiling log data or the API calls into the file specified as the argument of the *createWriter ( )* method.

*   The second parameter *mainAddProfilingEndAfter* takes care of adding the profiling statement to indicate the end of the main method execution in the main method of the source program to be profiled before the file writer object is closed. Similar to the first parameter described above, this parameter is set in the *apf.properties* file, similar to something like *apfWriter.close ( )*; prior to the enclosing curly bracket of "}" for indicating the end of the main method in the source program to be profiled.

Adding profiling statements in the main method of a source program to be profiled is spread over several other methods as well, which has already been discussed in the previous sections. Here is a recap of how it is handled in several other methods:

*   In Section 8.5 about the *addProfiling ( )* method, Code Listing 8.3 contains a statement that calls the method *processMainMethodProfiling ( )* to check

whether it's time to write the profiling statement indicating the *begin* of the call to the main method. Code Listing 8.4 shows how the profiling statement would be written if the condition is satisfied.

- In Section 8.8 about the *processMethodBeginLine* ( ) method, Code Listing 8.9 has a statement toward the end showing that writing profiling statement for the main method is excluded. This exclusion is necessary because of the call to the method *processMainMethodProfiling* ( ) in the *addProfiling* ( ) method as described above.
- In Section 8.10 about the *processMethodEndLine* ( ) method, Code Listing 8.13 indicates that a line containing the value of the parameter *mainAddProfiling EndAfter* is written when it encounters the end of the main method of the source program to be profiled.

This profiling enabling program, *perfLog.java*, has been tested with the *perfLog.java* program itself as well as the framework implementation program to be described in the next chapter. In addition, a specifically designed program, *perfLogTest.java* in the same package, has been used for testing the correctness of the *perfLog.java* program. Let's discuss this test program in the next section.

8.12   TEST PROGRAM

The test program, *perfLogTest.java*, is designed to test the correctness of the profiling enabling program, *perfLog.java*. The test scenarios include multiple return statements in various situations as well as an inner class and its methods.

If you are interested in the details of each test scenario, consult Code Listing 8.14.

Code Listing 8.14: perfLogTest.java

```
package logParser20;
/*
 * Test program designed to test the correctness of the profiling
 * enabling program perfTest.java @author henry h liu 2007
 */
public class perfLogTest {
    String desc = ''Java program for testing perfLog.java'';

    // This is a commment line
    /*
     * This is a comment block
     */
    // Constructor
    public perfLogTest(String desc) {
        this.desc = desc;
    }
```

```java
// getter - typed method
public String getDesc() {
    return desc;
}

// setter - non-typed method
public void setDesc(String s) {
    desc = s;
}

/*
 * keyword return contained in a String; muliple instances of the
 * keyword return in an if-return statement; last return statement
 * containing return keyword in a String
 */
public String returnTest0() {
    String x = ``split return''
    if (x.equals(``\\ \ ``return'' + ``\\ return''))
        return ``return''; // return return
    return x + ``return split in two lines'';
}

// return in two split lines
public String returnTest1() {
    String xxxxxxxxxxxxxxxxxxxxxxxxxxxxxxxxxxxxxx = ``split return'';
    return xxxxxxxxxxxxxxxxxxxxxxxxxxxxxxxxxxxxxx
        + ``return split in two lines'';
}

// return in string, followed by a real return statement
public String returnTest2() {
    String x = ``return in if line'';
    if (x.length() > 1)
        x = ``return test 2''; // return in string
    return x + ``return in if line'';
}

// return in a string in a separate line of an if statement; two
// return statements, one in an if statement and the other in a
// block
public String returnTest3() {
    String x = ``return in comment line'';
    if (x.length() > 1)
        x = ``return test 3''; // return in string
    if (x.equals(``y''))
```

```
            return (x + ``return and if on the same line'');
        {
            return x + ``return in two lines'';
        }
    }

    // inner class test
    public class inner {
        int x = 0;

        public inner(int x0) {
            x = x0;
        }

        public int getX() {
            return x;
        }

        public void setX(int i) {
            x = i;
        }
    }
}
```

8.13 SUMMARY

In this chapter, we demonstrated how the *perfBasic* API profiling framework can easily be enabled. A reference implementation of enabling this API profiling framework in Java has been discussed in detail by walking through all its major methods. Various design and implementation issues encountered in developing this program have been addressed. For the complete source code listing, download *perfLog.java* and all the relevant files from this book's website.

In the next chapter, we will concentrate on how a parser can be implemented to facilitate parsing the API profiling data logged using this API profiling framework. In the last chapter of this book, we'll demonstrate how to apply this API profiling framework to solving real-world software performance and scalability problems using a few concrete case studies.

RECOMMENDED READING

The following book is an excellent text about how to program in Java:

C. S. Horstmann and G. Cornell, *Core Java 2, Volume I—Fundamentals and Volume 2—Advanced Features*, Prentice Hall, 2003.

EXERCISES

8.1. List the basic steps for enabling the *perfBasic* API profiling framework.

8.2. If you are a software developer, consider enabling the *perfBasic* API profiling framework for probing performance and scalability problems with your product. The code snippets provided in this chapter may help you get started.

9

Implementing API Profiling Framework

If I had stayed for other people to make my tools and things for me, I had never made anything.
—*Sir Isaac Newton*

A framework is not an implementation. It simply is a specification on paper. A framework can be implemented in any high-level programming language, on any hardware platform, and by any organization or individual who has an interest in it. In this chapter, we describe in detail an example implementation of the *perfBasic* API profiling framework in Java. This is the implementation that has been used to generate all performance maps presented throughout this book.

One of the key points that this book intends to convey to software developers and performance engineers is that performance maps are the most efficient approach to identifying performance and scalability defects at the development stage of a software product. In order to generate performance maps using the API profiling data logged during a performance test run, we must use some sort of graphics tools.

In the next two sections, I will introduce two graphics tools for generating performance maps, one is the free *dot.exe* program from Graphviz (http://www.graphviz.org), and the other is a commercial tool from ILOG® (http://www.ilog.com). Let's first begin with the *dot.exe* program, which is a very powerful and easy to use graphics tool available for free.

9.1 GRAPHICS TOOL—*dot*

dot is one of the graphics programs made available by Graphviz (Graph Visualization Software). The best way to learn about *dot* is to download a copy of it and start to experiment with it yourself. Here is a list of the Web links that are helpful for you to get started:

- Download the software: http://www.graphviz.org/Download.php.
- Documentations: http://www.graphviz.org/Documentation.php. You can download the user's guide to *dot* and *neato* in PDF format from here.
- Frequently asked questions: http://www.graphviz.org/doc/FAQ.html.

The following graphics tools are available from Graphviz:

- *dot* making "hierarchical" or layered drawings of directed graphs
- *neato* and *fdp* making "spring model" layouts
- *twopi* making radial layout
- *circo* making circular layout

Most of the time, we use *dot* and *neato*. Both *dot* and *neato* share the same DOT language, which defines the format of the text input file for the *dot* and *neato* programs.

In order to understand how *dot* works, let's begin with an example. Assuming that you have installed the Graphviz package on your computer, now create a text file named *dotDemo.dot* that has the following lines:

```
digraph G {
    driver -> parser;
    driver -> params;
    driver -> utility;
    parser -> processLogByThread;
    processLogByThread -> processThreads;
    processLogByThread -> xmlProcessing;
}
```

Then, issue the following command at a DOS command line:

```
dot.exe -Tgif dotDemo.dot -o dotDemo.gif
```

In addition to the *gif* graphics file output format, you can also specify *ps*, *svg*, *jpg*, and so on. It seems that files generated with the *gif* format have better display quality than *jpg*, although both *gif* and *jpg* are bitmap type of graphics format. Files created with *ps* and *svg* format are better suited for embedding in a document to be published or importing into other graphics software such as Adobe® Illustrator®, which is a vector-based drawing program. Unlike bitmap graphics, vector graphics can scale without losing the details of a graphic when being enlarged. A vector graphic can be converted into a bitmap graphic through a process called *rasterizing*.

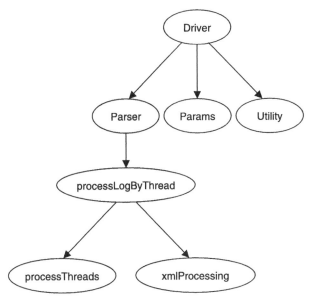

Figure 9.1 *An example* dot *demo.*

Now you have a file named *dotDemo.gif* created. Open this file and you should see a drawing similar to Figure 9.1.

This example shows how easy it is to use *dot*. Of course, you can make it a lot fancier by exploring many features of *dot* yourself, for example, adding colors. The user's guide to *dot* contains all the details about how you can specify the layout, node and edge attributes, and so on.

Sometimes, you may want to use a different Graphviz tool if you don't get what you want, especially the layout. For example, the diagram in Figure 9.2 was created with *dot*, with everything clotted into a line, which is hard to view.

Now, with the same *dot* file, using the program *neato*, it can be turned into a different layout, as shown in Figure 9.3, that can be zoomed and easily viewed.

This example shows that choosing an appropriate layout is an important issue, as the whole point of a performance map is about easier visual inspection.

In the next section, we'll discuss how performance maps can be generated with a commercial graphics tool such as ILOG.

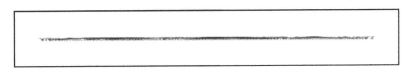

Figure 9.2 *A hard-to-view flat tree structure created with* dot.

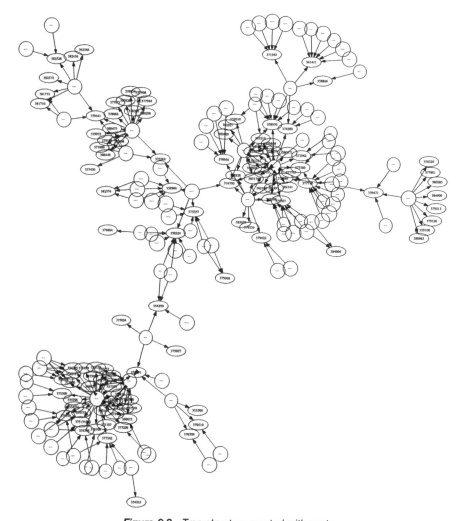

Figure 9.3 *Tree structure created with* neato.

9.2 GRAPHICS TOOL–ILOG

ILOG Visualization software is an advanced technology that translates raw data into useful information. It's another very powerful graphics tool for drawing performance maps with the XML data generated using the API profiling framework presented in this book.

In this section, we describe how one can use the ILOG JViews Diagrammer to draw structured data such as performance maps. To get a basic understanding of how the ILOG JViews Diagrammer works, let's begin with a simple example.

It's important to choose an appropriate layout when drawing performance maps in order to achieve the desired visual comfort level. In most cases, the tree layout results

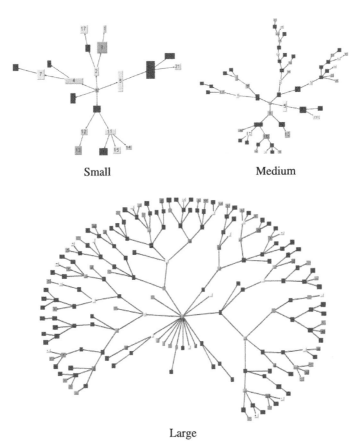

Small   Medium

Large

Figure 9.4 *Three tree structures generated using ILOG JViews Diagrammer.*

in the most balanced and aesthetic graphs. The graphs shown in Figure 9.4 illustrate three tree structures in small, medium, and large configurations that can be generated with the ILOG JViews Diagrammer.

Although these three tree structures differ in complexity, they were created with the same steps:

1. Structural data was written in an XML data file that conforms to a specific schema.
2. A cascading style sheet (CSS) file was used to specify *layout*, *node*, and *link* styles.
3. A Java applet was run to draw the graph based on the data input file and the CSS file described in Steps 1 and 2. The only difference among those three graphs is that a different XML data file was used for each of them.

Next, let's learn a little bit about graphics resolution, which should help you decide how you can generate crisp, clear performance maps.

9.3   GRAPHICS RESOLUTION

Sometimes you may want to generate a high-resolution performance map or a graphic in general to make it look crisp and clear. Instead of talking about color theories, I'll give you some tips about how you can manage the quality of your graphics.

Computer graphics fall into two main categories: bitmap images and vector graphics. Bitmap images are created using a square or rectangular grid of colored squares called pixels. Bitmaps are most suited for continuous tone images such as photographs. In order to create the illusion of continuous tone, pixels must be small enough. The resolution of a bitmap image is measured by the number of pixels in an inch. Thus bitmap images are termed resolution dependent.

Vector graphics are created with lines and curves, which are defined by mathematical objects called vectors. Vectors use geometric characteristics to define the object. Vector graphics consist of anchor points and line segments, which together are referred to as paths. Computer graphics rely on vectors to render bold graphics that must retain clean, crisp lines when scaled to various sizes.

Now from a practical point of view, the graphics created in the format of *gif* or *jpg* are bitmap images, while the graphics created in the format of *ps*, *eps*, or *svg* are vector graphics. To create the most desirable effects when a graphic is displayed or printed, fluency with resolution terminology is helpful, as summarized below:

- Pixels per inch (PPI) for bitmap images. The recommended PPI for a bitmap graphic is 72 to be used on a Web page, or 250–300 to be printed in a formal document.

- Dots per inch (DPI) for an output device such as a printer. The resolution of a desktop printer is between 600 and 1200 DPI, which is good enough for printing texts. For printing bitmap images, a minimum resolution of 2400 DPI is required to create the desired effects.

- Lines per inch (LPI) for a printed page. LPI or "line screen" measures the number of lines per inch printed for an image on a page. It is also called screen frequency. A standard LPI is around 150 LPI for color printing.

So, in summary, the visual quality of a displayed or printed graphic depends on the raw resolution of the displaying or printing device as well as the resolution of the graphic defined in PPI. The quality of printed output depends on the resolution of both the output device (dpi) and the screen frequency (lpi). For example, a production class image-setter with a resolution of 2400 dpi and a screen frequency of 177 lpi produces a higher quality image than a desktop printer with a resolution in the range of 300 to 600 dpi and a screen frequency of 85 lpi. However, a high screen frequency alone does not guarantee high-quality output. The screen frequency must be configured properly according to the class of the paper, the inks, and the printer to print high-quality, professional-looking graphic.

Next, let's move on to the implementation of the *perfBasic* API profiling framework in Java and see how performance maps can be generated with Graphviz graphics software and ILOG Visualization software.

9.4 IMPLEMENTATION

An implementation of the *perfBasic* API profiling framework can help turn the humongous performance log data text files into the succinct performance maps that software developers and performance engineers can use to identify application, database, and system bottlenecks quickly with minimum learning efforts.

In this section, we present a reference implementation of the *perfBasic* API profiling framework in Java. Java has evolved into a robust, mature, and easy to program language during the past ten years and has been embraced by a large community of programmers. So it's one of the ideal high-level programming languages for implementing this API profiling framework.

The implementation of the *perfBasic* API profiling framework consists of the following Java classes:

- *driver.java*. This class provides the main method as an entry point to the program.
- *params.java*. This class initializes all global parameters.
- *logReader.java*. This class reads an API profiling log data file and writes to multiple files sorted by threads.
- log*Writer.java*. This class writes API call data into text files in a specific format for the graphics tools to generate performance maps.
- *Node.java*. This class represents an API call in a call tree structure.
- *Link.java*. This class represents an immediate caller–callee relation in a call tree structure.
- *CallRecord.java*. This class represents each API call with detailed call information such as call start time and call end time.
- *utility.java*. This class provides various methods for manipulating date and time stamps and for creating Java I/O readers and writers.
- *parser.java*. This class parses an API profiling log data file.
- *xmlProcessor.java*. This class generates an XML file with complete information such as call count and aggregated elapsed time for XML-based graphics tools to generate performance maps.
- *analyzer.java*. This class generates detailed summarization text files for all API calls to help facilitate the drill-down type of performance and scalability analysis.
- *adapter.java*. This class converts custom API profiling log data files from non-standard format into standard format for the parser to process.

Let's discuss each Java class in detail in the following sections.

9.4.1 driver

The driver program is implemented in *driver.java*, as shown in Code Listing 9.1. It is coded following the logic as shown in the *main* ( ) method of Code Listing 8.1.

- It first calls *System.currentTimeMillis* ( ) to record the program start time.
- It then calls the static method *init* ( ) of *params.java*, which initializes all global parameters for all the remaining classes of this implementation. The parameter class is a convenient way for centralizing all parameters used by various classes in one place.
- The next call to *utility.display* ( ) outputs the string passed in as an argument to standard output. This method simply is a wrapper of the Java system method *System.out.println (String s)*.
- Note that the program assumes that the API profiling log data conforms to the standard log format. If not, then one should use an *adapter* program to convert the log data from nonconforming to conforming format. An adapter is another Java class that converts log data from its native to the standard format.
- Then it tests to see if the log file is already sorted by thread. If it is, then the thread information file is read through the static method of *getThreadInfo* ( ) of the *logReader* class. Otherwise, the static method *sortLogByThread* ( ) of the logReader class is called to read the original raw API profiling log data, which is sorted and then output to the multiple text files with each file containing the log data from one specific thread only.
- Then a parser object is created to start parsing the API profiling log data. The entry method of the parser object is *processLogByThread* ( ), which initiates processing each thread in a thread loop.
- The total processing time is reported after parsing is complete.

Code Listing 9.1: driver.java

```
package logParser20;

import java.io.FileWriter;
import java.io.PrintWriter;
import java.io.IOException;

import logParser20.logReader;
import logParser20.params;
import logParser20.parser;
import logParser20.utility;

public class driver {
   public static PrintWriter apfWriter;

   public static void main(String[] args) {
     String apfLogFile = System.getProperty(''apfLogFileName'');
     if (apfLogFile != null) {
         createApfWriter(apfLogFile);
     }
```

```
long startTime = System.currentTimeMillis();
params.init();
utility.display(``parsing log file: '' + params.logFileName);

if (params.logFileIsSortedByThread) {
   utility.display(``skip reading mixed data files ...'');
   logReader.getThreadInfo(params.threadInfoFileName);
} else {
   utility.display(``reading raw data files ...'');
   logReader.sortLogByThread();
}
parser Parser = new parser();
Parser.processLogByThread();
utility.display(``Total processing time =''
      + (System.currentTimeMillis() - startTime)+``ms'');
params.sumWriter.close();
if (apfWriter != null) {
   apfWriter.close();
}
}

public static void createApfWriter(String apfFileName) {
   try {
      apfWriter = new PrintWriter(new FileWriter(apfFileName),
               true);
   } catch (IOException ioe) {
      utility.display(``Error in creating writer with''
         + apfFileName);
   }
}
}
```

From Code Listing 9.1, note that this driver program is API profiling enabled as well with an *apfWriter* object created at the beginning of the program.

Following the sequence of the program execution logic, let's discuss the next Java class, params.java, in the next section.

9.4.2   Global Parameters

The *params.java* class is a container for all global parameters as listed below:

- *description*, which provides a textual description about the subject.
- *maxThreads*, which represents the maximum number of threads that will be processed.
- *threadSample*, which specifies the thread sampling interval to limit the number of program execution threads to be processed.

- *inputFileDir*, which specifies the directory containing the input files.
- *outputFileDir*, which specifies the directory that will hold the output files.
- *threadFileDir*, which specifies the directory that will hold all data files for all threads.
- *logFileName*, which specifies the name of the API profiling log data file.
- *logFileIsSortedByThread*. If this parameter is set to false, the original API profiling log data is read and then written to the multiple text files thread-by-thread. If set to true, then data will be read directly from the thread files.
- *threadInfoFileName*, which represents the name of the file containing the thread information for the parser to read all thread files.
- *callTreeDotFile*, which is related to *dot*-generated performance maps only. It represents the name of the *dot* file for the graphics tool *dot* to use to generate performance maps.
- *callTreeXMLFile0*, which is related to XML file based performance maps only. It represents the name of the initial XML file that serves as a holder of the data structure for all nodes and links with details left open to be filled in after the entire parsing is complete.
- *callTreeXMLFileFinal*, which is related to XML file based performance maps only. This is the final XML file with all missing information from callTreeXMLFile0 filled in eventually. This is the file that XML-based graphics tools will use to generate performance maps.
- *graphByThread*, which is related to *dot*-generated performance maps only. It controls whether each thread will be shown as a separate branch of the call tree.
- *subGraph*, which is related to *dot*-generated performance maps only. It controls whether the call tree will be drawn using the functionality of subGraph of *dot*.
- *traceTreeWalkThrough*, which controls whether debugging information will be displayed along with parsing.
- *dotLinkLabelHorizontal*, which controls whether the items in a label beside an edge of a *dot*-generated performance map will be written all horizontally.
- *threadPercentTimeFilter*, which represents an elapsed time threshold value below which a thread will be excluded from processing.
- *elapsedTimeThresholdInMS*, which represents an elapsed time threshold value in milliseconds, below which an execution path (edge or link) will be excluded in the generated performance maps.
- *elapsedTimePercentRed*, which represents an elapsed time threshold value in percentage, above which an execution path (edge or link) will be colored in red to indicate that it's a hot path.
- *deleteThreadFiles*, which controls whether the thread files will be deleted at the exit of the program execution.
- *relativeToLogOnTime*, which controls whether all time stamps will be absolute or relative to the time when logging started.
- *ignoreLinesIdentifiers*, which provides an option for ignoring the lines that match the identifiers defined in the *log.properties* file.

- *callEndIdentifiers*, which specifies the identifiers defined in the *log.properties* file to indicate what lines are call end lines.
- *selfNodeIdentifiers*, which specifies the identifiers defined in the *log.properties* file to indicate what lines are API calls that have no call end time.
- *sumWriter*, which is a Java writer object used for writing parsing summary files.
- *xmlProcessing*, which controls whether XML processing will be initiated after parsing is complete. Specify *false* if XML based graphics tool is not going to be used for generating performance maps.
- *profilingOn*, which is a parameter for controlling profiling this reference implementation itself.

The class *params.java* works as follows:

- It uses a Java properties object in its *init* ( ) method to initialize all parameters using a property file named *parser.properties*.
- Then all initial parameters are written into a summary file using the *writeParams* ( ) method.
- There is a method named *getIdentifiers* ( ) that is used to extract the identifiers specified in another properties file *log.properties*.

The *parser.properties* file and *log.properties* file need to be set up correctly before running this API profiling log data parser. We will leave the details about how to set up these files to the next chapter.

In the next section, I'll describe how the *logReader* class is implemented. This is the class that implements the logic for reading in API profiling log data.

9.4.3 logReader

The class *logReader* has the following two major functions:

- *sortLogByThread* ( ), which sorts an original API profiling log data file into multiple files with each file containing the data for a thread only. This is a preparation for the parser to parse the log data on a thread-by-thread basis in a thread loop.
- *getThreadInfo* ( ), which is used to skip re-sorting an original API profiling log data file. The parser will start parsing directly with the thread files created when the original log data were sorted by the *sortLogByThread* ( ) method. This is designed to avoid repeatedly calling the *sortLogByThread* ( ) method, which might be very time consuming for large log data files.

After the *sortLogByThread* ( ) method is executed, the following information about the execution of each thread will be available for the parser to use:

- *threadTimeMin*, which is the earliest start call time for a thread.
- *threadTimeMax*, which is the time stamp of the last call end time for the same thread.
- *threadTimeDelta*, which is the difference between threadTimeMax and threadTimeMin and represents the total elapsed time for a thread.

- *allThreadTimeMin*, which is the earliest call start time of all threads.
- *allThreadTimeMax*, which is the latest call end time of all threads.
- *allThreadTimeTotal*, which is the difference between allThreadTimeMax and allThreadTimeMin and represents the total logging period for the entire execution.
- *threadIndexMax*, which represents the actual number of threads read in the original log data files.

See the source code that can be downloaded from this book's website about how this *logReader* class is implemented, if you are interested in the details.

In the next section, I will introduce the counterpart of the *logReader* class—the *logWriter* class.

9.4.4   logWriter

The *logWriter* class is used by the parser class to write API call data in *dot* format or XML format when it needs to. The functions of each method are described below to show exactly what each method is designed for:

- *writeDotRelation* (*PrintWriter logWriter, String fromId, String fromName, String relationId, String toId, String toName, int threadId, int count, int elapsedTime*). This method writes a *dot* edge with the parameters given in the argument list.
- *logWriteNode* (*PrintWriter logWriter, Node node*). This method writes an API call as an XML node.
- *logWriteNodeProperty* (*PrintWriter logWriter, String userObject*). This method writes a property XML element with the parameters given in the argument list.
- *writeLink* (*PrintWriter logWriter, Link link*). This method writes an XML link element with the parameters given in the argument list.
- *writeEndNode* (*PrintWriter logWriter*). This method writes an end XML node with the parameter given in the argument list.
- *writeLinkProperty* (*PrintWriter logWriter, long callCount, long elapsedTime*). This method writes a link property XML element with the parameters given.

The data written by a logWriter object is used by the graphics tools to generate performance maps. So the output format must conform to the specifications associated with each graphics tool.

See the source code downloadable from this book's website about how this logWriter class is implemented.

In the next section, I will describe the *Node* class. This class describes the XML node that the parser composes as it parses along. The purpose of the Node class is for writing data in XML format so that XML-based graphics tools can use it to generate performance maps.

9.4.5 Node

Each API call is represented as a node on performance maps. The *Node* class has all the attributes that are required for completely characterizing an API call. A Node has the following attributes:

- *Id*, which uniquely identifies an XML node. It consists of two parts: Namespace and Name. Namespace is simply a concatenation of its ancestor callers, and Name is the current method name.
- *Namespace*, which is simply a concatenation of the ancestor callers of the current API.
- *Name*, which is the name of the current API.
- *callStartTime*, which is the call start time of the current API.
- *callEndTime*, which is the call end time of the current API.
- *elapsedTimeSum*, which is the aggregated elapsed call time of the current API.
- *callCountSum*, which is the aggregated call count of the current API.
- *type*, which is the type of the current API.
- *text*, which is the entire text of the current API call.

The values of some of the attributes may need to be aggregated progressively with parsing, for example, *elapsedTimeSum* and *callCountSum*. Also, not all the attributes have their values available when the call was encountered the first time. For example, *callEndTime* is not available until all of its callees have been processed. This is a delicate issue and has been carefully considered in the parser class.

The methods of the *Node* class are all getter and setter classes that are self-explicit. See the source code downloadable from this book's website about how this *Node* class is implemented.

In the next section, I will introduce the *Link* class, which describes the call path from Node A to Node B.

9.4.6 Link

The *Link* class describes a link between the two nodes that has a caller–callee relationship. It has the following attributes:

- *sourceNode*, which is the caller node of an immediate caller–callee relationship.
- *destNode*, which is the callee node of an immediate caller–callee relationship.
- *name*, which is the name of an immediate caller–callee relationship.
- *callCount*, which is the total number of executions for an immediate pair of caller and callee.
- *elapsedTime*, which is the elapsed time of the executions for an immediate pair of caller and callee.

- *isLink*, which is an attribute of the XML format defined for a Link element.
- *color*, which indicates what color to use for drawing an immediate caller–callee relationship.
- *namespace*, which is simply a concatenation of the names of all ancestor callers of the current caller in an immediate caller–callee relationship.
- *id*, which uniquely identifies an immediate caller–callee relationship.

The attributes *callCount* and *elapsedTime* are the two most important attributes for performance maps. Based on these two metrics explicitly displayed on performance maps, software developers and performance engineers can quickly identify the application, database, and system bottlenecks.

The methods of the *Link* class are all getter and setter classes that are self-explicit. See the source code downloadable from this book's website about how this *Link* class is implemented.

In the next section, I will introduce the *CallRecord* class. This class is used for writing performance summarization files that contain the details of each API call that are hard to include and display on performance maps. Performance summarization files are used for deeper, drill-down type of analysis of performance and scalability issues.

9.4.7 CallRecord

The *CallRecord* class has the following attributes:

- *threadId*, which indicates from which thread this call came.
- *hashCode*, which is the hash code for the API text of the call.
- *elapsedTime*, which is the elapsed time of the call.
- *callCount*, which is the number of times the call was made.
- *text*, which is the entire text of an API.

The methods of the *CallRecord* class are all getter and setter classes that are self-explicit. See the source code downloadable from this book's website about how this *CallRecord* class is implemented.

In the next section, I will introduce the utility class that is used by other classes for the utility type of operations.

9.4.8 utility

The *utility* class is designed for providing convenience in manipulating date and time stamps and in creating Java I/O reader and writer objects. Each method of the *utility* class is simple enough that the reader should be able to understand it just by reading the comments and its implementation. See the source code downloadable from this book's website if you are interested in knowing what utility functions are provided and how they are implemented.

In the next section, I will introduce the *parser* class. This is the most sophisticated class of the API profiling framework implementation. It's the class that parses the API profiling log data and generates the output data that can be used by the graphics tools to generate performance maps.

9.4.9 parser

Parsing API profiling log data starts with the *processLogByThread* ( ) method, as is shown in the driver class described in Section 9.3.1. It is important to note that the API calls out of all program execution threads are intermingled. After they are segregated into multiple thread files, they must be processed on a thread-by-thread basis, because threads run in parallel with overlapping timings.

There are two delicate issues that must be dealt with carefully when designing the parsing algorithm for implementing this API profiling framework:

- Whether the API profiling log data conforms to the standard format is unknown until exceptions are thrown during parsing. Whenever this happens, the parsing logic needs to be examined and the bugs identified must be fixed before it can move along. This may happen very often, as the API profiling log data files are usually humongous and may contain many unexpected variations.
- Even if the log data conforms to the standard log format, there are still chances that generated performance maps may not be displayed properly, for example, with orphan nodes. Also, all quantitative metrics such as the elapsed time and call count must be accurate. This calls for a robust implementation of the parsing logic.

After lengthy debugging and experimentation, I eventually came up with the implementation of a parser as shown in the source code downloadable from this book's website. In case you are motivated to look at the code of *parser.java*, here is a sample. The core logic is implemented in the *threadLoop* ( ) method. It will become clear what it does after going over the following pseudocode.

Pseudocode for the Parsing Logic of the *threadLoop* Method in *parser.java*

```
process the root node first;
for (each thread) {
    exclude this thread if it's insignificant;
    clear the callPath HashSet;    \\ keeps track of where an API call
                        \\ is in a call path that are multiple
                        \\ levels deep
    process the thread node;  \\ the level immediately below root node
    read each line from the data file for this thread {
        if ( isCallEnd ) {
                        processCallEnd;
                    } else { // nonCallEnd
```

```
                                    processCallStart;
                                    if ( isSelfNode ) {
                                    processCallEnd;
                                    } // end selfNodeCheck
                     } // end if ( isCallEnd )
                  } // end read each line from the thread file
   } // end for each thread
   post check call stack;
```

In this implementation, two data structures have been used, one of which is named *callPath* of the type HashSet, and the other named *callStack* of the type Stack. The data structure *callPath* keeps track of whether the current call has been encountered so far, and the HashSet data structure is an ideal choice relative to other data structures such as HashMap, List, and Stack. That's because we are not interested in the order in which the items are stored. Instead, we are interested only in quickly finding out whether an item already exists in that data structure.

The data structure *callStack* keeps a stack of API call nodes that are on the stack so far. Let's say we have a segment of API call log data that represents the call sequence as shown in Figure 9.5. Let's see how parsing should proceed.

In Figure 9.5, each letter represents the name of an API method call, with "+" sign denoting the call start and "−" sign the call end. Then, two issues must be taken into account:

- First, the call path of A → B → C must be remembered so that when the same call path is encountered again later, it will not be written to the external XML file again, which would be against the XML format rules adopted by XML-based graphics tools. Instead, only its call count and elapsed time will be updated.
- Second, when a new API call is encountered, it must be pushed into the stack, so prior to "C−" that represents the end of the C API call, the stack must already have "A+ B+ C+" so that when "C−" is encountered, "C+" would be popped off the stack to indicate that the C API call is complete in a full call start and end cycle. Similarly, by the time the B API call end "B−" is encountered, the parser would know that this end of call should be correlated to its

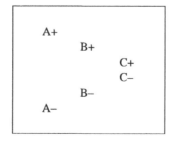

Figure 9.5   An illustrative API call stack.

start of call, which is "B+ ". The correlation of the start and end of a call is maintained by the *push* and *pop* operations of this stack data structure. Stack is an ideal data structure for this purpose, as it is most suitable for indicating the *start* and *end* of an API call.

The last statement of *postCheckCallStack* ( ) will make sure that those calls that remain on the stack with no call ends encountered at the completion of parsing will be processed as well so that the XML and *dot* files written for drawing performance maps will be well formatted.

In addition to the core parsing logic described above, the *threadLoop* ( ) method also takes care of initiating writing XML and *dot* data files that will be used by the graphics tools to generate performance maps. The XML file needs to have its beginning line written before the body lines can be written. The *dot* file can wait until the end of parsing in the *threadLoop* ( ) method.

Some other major parsing methods include the following:

- *isCallEnd* ( ). This method uses *callEndIdentifiers* to help determine whether the current data line represents the end of an API call. You may want to add additional identifiers if you are using an adapter to convert your native API profiling log data from nonconforming format into conforming format.
- *processCallEnd* ( ). This method depends on namespace to uniquely identify an immediate caller–callee relationship. It first pops the callee off the call stack and updates the attributes for the callee. It then peeks at the caller from the call stack and constructs a *Link* object. If the caller–callee relation instance associated with this *Link* object has not been encountered so far, the data structure *callPath* is updated with this *Link* instance, and a *Link* element is written to the XML file that keeps track of all API calls. The aggregated attribute values of this caller–callee relationship such as the call count and elapsed time are updated in the *HashMap* data structure *relations*. This data structure is used later during the XML processing stage to complete the call tree XML file with all missing information at this parsing stage.
- *processCallStart* ( ). This method processes a data line that represents a call start. It first gets the namespace from the content of the current call stack. It then constructs a *Node* object by calling the *makeNode* ( ) method. The *makeNode* ( ) method makes a node by extracting the node attribute values such as name, call start time, type, and text out of the current thread data line. This node is pushed onto the call stack as one more API call on top of the current call path maintained in the *callStack* data structure. If it represents a new call path, then it is entered into the *callPath HashSet* and an XML node representing this new API call is written to the XML file that keeps all unique API call paths. This is necessary so that when the same path is encountered again it will not be written to the XML file again.
- *isSelfNode* ( ). This method is designed to deal with special situations such as calls that have call start and call end time stamps all on one data line. Such lines typically represent status reports indicating that some events have occurred.

- *processRootNode* ( ). The root node is the node that spawns all threads. On performance maps, the root node is the origin of all execution threads, which in turn spawn more execution paths on its own. It follows a simple logic of making a new node, pushing it to the call stack, writing it to the XML file, and registering it in the *callPath* data structure.

- *processThreadNode* ( ). Thread nodes are those nodes that fall immediately below the root node. The logic of *processThreadNode* ( ) is similar to *processRootNode* ( ) except that a link needs to be constructed from the root node to the thread node and this link needs to be processed by calling the *processRelation* ( ) method.

Whether you want to use this implementation for your API profiling or you want to implement your own parser, it's worthwhile to study the source code *parser.java* downloadable from this book's website to get familiar with the details of the parsing logic adopted in this reference implementation. It's fun to implement a parser. If you make a mistake in your parser implementation, you will not see the desired output and the call tree graphs will end up with intermingled orphan nodes and links. The order and beauty of those call tree graphs only come with a correctly implemented parser.

In the next section, I'll describe the *xmlProcessor* class, which is meant for finalizing the XML data file used by XML-based graphics tools.

9.4.10 xmlProcessor

During the parsing stage, the raw API profiling log data is transformed into two data files, one of which is a *dot* file for the *dot* graphics tool, and the other is an XML file that can be used by the XML file based graphics tools such as ILOG to generate performance maps. The *dot* file is self-complete and ready for use. However, the XML file generated during the parsing stage is more or less a holder for the call tree structure only and more detailed information such as the call count and total elapsed time for each specific call path is unavailable until parsing is complete.

Taking the initial XML file generated during the parsing stage as input, the *xmlProcessor* class completes filling in each node and link in the call tree structure with correctly aggregated information such as the call count and elapsed time for each API call.

In addition to this initial XML file, *xmlProcessor* depends on another data structure of type *HashMap* to update all nodes and links. An instance of this *HashMap* object would contain the following information for each immediate caller–callee relationship:

- Call count, which is the total number of times that an API call was made
- Elapsed time, which is the total elapsed time aggregated over all the calls with an API
- Last call end time, which is the call end time of the last call made with an API

Based on the initial XML file and the relation data structure, the *xmlProcessor* class uses the following methods to generate the final XML file that can be used by XML-based graphics tools to generate performance maps:

- *updateAllLinks* (*HashMap relations*). This method updates each *treelink* element with the aggregated call count, elapsed time, and call end time for the caller. It also updates the text content of the property element that is used as a label for that link.
- *updateAllDestNodes* (*HashMap relations*). This method updates each treenode element with the aggregated call count, elapsed time, and call end time.
- *treeFilter* (*Document doc*). This method walks through the entire call tree and removes those nodes whose elapsed times are smaller than a certain specified threshold value, for example, 10 milliseconds. It might be necessary to apply filtering when a call tree structure becomes too crowded to be displayed. Filtering also helps identify hot program execution paths more quickly.
- *writeDocumentToFile* (*Document doc*). Using an XML serializer object, this method writes the modified, final XML document from memory to an external file, which is the XML file that XML-based graphics tools can use to generate performance maps.

XML processing is simple in logic. However, depending on the size of the XML document to be processed, it might be time consuming relative to the parsing time. It may also take a lot of memory. It can be skipped by specifying *xmlProcessing* = *false* in the *parser.properties* file if you do not plan to use XML-based graphics tools and the *dot* format output file is the only one desirable.

See the source code for *xmlProcessor.java* downloadable from this book's website for the implementation details about this class. In order to be able to understand the code, it might be necessary to acquire some knowledge about XML processing in Java in general.

In the next section, I will introduce the last Java class of this implementation, *analyzer*. This class writes detailed summarization files about every API call so that the details for each API call will be available for drill-down type of performance and scalability analysis.

9.4.11 analyzer

A performance map is a convenient means for facilitating communications on software performance and scalability issues. However, it's impractical to put everything on a performance map. The details about every API call have to go to the external text files.

During the parsing stage, every API call is written to an external data file that acts like a warehouse for all call records. This data can be processed only after parsing is complete. The *analyzer* class is designed just for this purpose.

```
adapter.java          adapter.properties  ✕

description=perfBasic test
adapter=bstAdapter
logFileName=test_5_5_021308_0.log
inputFileDir=input
```

Figure 9.6 *An example* adapter.properties *file.*

The *analyzer* class works as follows:

- The entry method *processData* ( ) is called to initiate processing. It creates an ArrayList object to contain all call records.
- Then the method *sortDataByThread* ( ) is called to sort out all the call records on a thread-by-thread basis.
- Then the method *outputCallRecord* ( ) is called to write the information such as the call count, elapsed time, and thread about each call to an external text data file.

See the source code for *analyzer.java* downloadable from this book's website for the implementation details about this class.

In the next section, I'll discuss the *adapter* class that is used to convert custom log files from nonstandard to standard format to suit the parser designed to conform to the *perfBasic* API profiling framework.

9.4.12 adapter

The *adapter* class is a separate program that is run first if the API profiling log data files were generated from custom logs. In order to run this program, the information as specified in the *adapter.properties* file as shown in Figure 9.6 needs to be provided. This file provides the information on which custom adapter class to use, which customer log file to work on, and where that file is located.

When a custom log file is to be converted, an option is provided through the use of a *log.properties* file for ignoring some of the lines in the log file that are used as annotations other than API call records. We'll see such an example later when we present a case study of generating performance maps based on custom logs.

The further details of the *adapter.java* class and *bstAdapter.java* class are omitted here, since they are application specific.

This class concludes our introduction on the reference implementation of this API profiling framework.

9.5 SUMMARY

In this chapter, we introduced a reference implementation of the *perfBasic* API profiling framework. It helped expose various issues in implementing such an API profiling

framework to turn humongous API profiling log data files into convenient performance maps. The implementation can be used for identifying various performance
and scalability defects with any software applications programmed in high-level
programming languages.

I would like to emphasize that this tool should be used in conjunction with other
performance and scalability analysis tools such as the system performance analysis
tools and database performance analysis tools if the database is part of the application
as well.

I will show in the next chapter how the *perfBasic* API profiling framework can be
used to help solve performance and scalability problems in the real-world situations.

EXERCISES

9.1. Download the free graphics tool *dot* and experiment on the examples provided
with it.

9.2. Study the reference implementation of the *perfBasic* API profiling framework
and explain how it is designed and implemented. Explain the concepts of
nodes and links.

9.3. Explain how the parser works. Experiment with it and you may find out that it's
simple conceptually but complex to implement.

9.4. What is an adapter from the software design pattern perspective? Write an adapter
to convert your custom API profiling log data in compliance with the *perfBasic*
API profiling framework if you already have an API profiling framework
implemented for your product.

Case Study: Applying API Profiling to Solving Software Performance and Scalability Challenges

Plato is my friend—Aristotle is my friend—but my greatest friend is truth.
—*Sir Isaac Newton*

API profiling is the most efficient approach to optimizing and tuning the performance and scalability of a software system. It provides such vital information for an API as how many times it was called, how long on average the calls took, and whether it's a hot API or not in terms of its elapsed time percentage relative to the total execution time of the program.

Without API profiling, it's hard for the software developers to gain inside knowledge about the performance of each individual API of a software program. Without being equipped with an API profiling tool, software developers would have to speculate, which can rarely lead to fruitful outcomes toward solving software performance and scalability issues. API profiling is as important for software developers to identify and fix software performance and scalability defects as the blood tests and X-ray examinations for medical doctors to diagnose and cure diseases of their patients.

In order to efficiently optimize and tune the performance and scalability of a software system, every software development team should have an API profiling tool in place. In general, there are three sources of API profiling tools:

- Commercial tools such as VTune™ from Intel™, Quantify™ from IBM, and Vantage Analyzer for J2EE™ from Compuware™, and so on.
- Most large-scale software applications have their own built-in implementations of logging for debugging functionality and performance problems. However, in most cases, such log files are written in text format and can be as large as hundreds of megabytes or even up to gigabytes. It's very hard to navigate such text files using a text editor such as Notepad™ or Word™ and try to find clues visually.
- If you have neither a commercial API profiling tool nor a built-in API logging mechanism with your product, you might choose to implement the *perfBasic* API profiling framework introduced in this book to help support the performance optimization and tuning work for your product.

Built on the previous few chapters, in this chapter, I will help you understand how API profiling can be applied to solving your performance and scalability problems. I'll show you:

- How to use the reference implementation of the *perfBasic* API profiling framework to enable API profiling.
- How to parse the API profiling log data using the log parser introduced in Chapter 9.
- How to generate and read performance maps to solve real-world software performance and scalability problems. When API profiling data is transformed into performance maps, software developers can easily identify the performance and scalability bottlenecks based on the elapsed time percentages. After the expensive execution paths are identified, various well-known or creative optimization and tuning techniques can be applied to fix the performance and scalability problems.

This chapter essentially completes what we started with defining, enabling, and implementing the *perfBasic* API profiling framework described in detail in Chapters 7 through 9.

Let's first start with how API profiling can be enabled with a software product based on the material we presented in the previous few chapters.

10.1 ENABLING API PROFILING

It's beyond the scope of this book to describe how API profiling can be enabled with a commercial profiling tool or an existing custom logging framework. Instead, I will describe how you can use a program similar to the *perfLog.java* program introduced in Chapter 8 of this book to enable logging, if you don't have a commercial tool or your own tool. For a small software development project, this program of *perfLog.java* can be easily rounded out by an experienced developer to suit your special needs and it might be just sufficient with some further enhancement if necessary.

In order to understand how API profiling can be enabled using the *perfLog.java* program, it is beneficial to review briefly the material presented in Chapters 7 through 9. Here is a recap:

- In Chapter 7, I defined an API profiling framework named *perfBasic*. I introduced a standard logging format, emphasized the need for a log parser, and emphasized the goal of transforming humongous text log files into convenient performance maps.
- In Chapter 8, I introduced an API profiling enabling program named *perfLog.java*. This program simply adds profiling statements to existing software source code to write API call data into external log files. I described how this program can be used to generate API call log files.
- In Chapter 9, I introduced the implementation of the *perfBasic* API profiling framework with a Java-based parser. This parser parses the original API profiling log data and generates the data suitable for generating performance maps.

Let's take a step-by-step approach and see how the program *perfLog.java* can be used to enable API profiling.

10.1.1 Mechanism of Populating Log Entry

First of all, a mechanism of populating each log entry must be implemented for each method to be profiled. This mechanism will be product specific, as there is no generic framework that will work for all products. However, it should not be that hard, as developers know how to retrieve the following log entries with the software product they are familiar with:

- *API type*, which could be API, SQL, or application specific types such as FILTER.
- *ThreadID*, which is available only with multithreaded programs. For single-threaded programs, use a dummy integer number for the threadID.
- *Call time stamp*, which can be implemented using language-specific utility APIs. In Java, *System.currentTimeMillis ( )* can be used.
- *ServerID*, which is product specific.
- *ThreadGroupID*, which is product specific.
- *ClientID*, which is product specific.
- *UserID*, which is product specific.
- *API signature*, which along with its call time stamp information indicates the start and end times of the API call.

Consult Chapter 7 for the concrete format of each log entry. Assuming that this mechanism has already been implemented, let's see what step-by-step procedure we should follow to enable API profiling using *perfLog.java*.

10.1.2 Source and Target Projects

It's obvious that the first step for enabling an API profiling framework is to identify the source code that will be API profiling-enabled. Also, it's better to put the API profiling-enabled code in a staging area that is separate from the original source code. This is because you may need several iterations to make sure that the original source code is transformed correctly into target API profiling-enabled code.

It's very important that you use a good IDE (integrated development environment) such as *eclipse* (http://www.eclipse.org). *eclipse* is the IDE that I have been using for all my development work, including all the API profiling related programs introduced throughout this book. With an IDE, you can catch displaced profiling statements visually immediately. And an IDE is convenient for debugging as well.

Here is a procedure for setting up the source and target projects:

- Create a project for the source code to be transformed with correct project, source directory, and package structure. Copy or check all source code into appropriate packages. Add appropriate jar files and verify that the source code has no compiling errors.
- Create a target project that will contain the modified code with profiling statements inserted. You can follow the same procedure as for the source code except that you don't copy all the code into the target package directories.
- Identify the packages and class files that will not be profiled. Copy these files into the appropriate package directories of the target project.
- Add proper jar and library files to the target project as you did with the original source project.

The *eclipse* screenshot shown in Figure 10.1 is an example illustrating both the source project of *bstPerfTest* and the target project of *bstPerfTestStaging*, where *bst* is an alias for a fictitious company named "Best Software Technologies."

In the source and target projects, the first package under the *src* directory, *com.bst.cdmi.cdm*, contains those Java classes that will not be profiled; the second package under the *src* directory, *com.bst.cdmi.perf*, contains those Java classes that will be profiled. The Java package *com.bst.cdmi.perf* contains the source files into which profiling statements will be inserted.

After setting up the source and target projects, the next step is to set up the *apf.properties* file, which is a configuration file for the enabling program *perfLog.java*. This file contains the information that is needed by the enabling program to insert enabling statements into the source files to be profiled.

10.1.3 Setting *apf.properties* File

An *apf.properties* file provides the *perfLog.java* program with some of the initial parameters. Figure 10.2 shows what entries are specified in an *apf.properties* file as input.

The *sourceDir* and *targetDir* entries describe where to pick up the source files to be transformed and where to put the target files that will have profiling

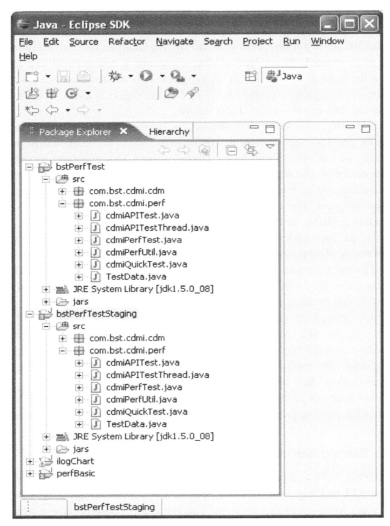

Figure 10.1 *An example showing the source and target projects (*bstPerfTest *and* bstPerfTestStaging*) in eclipse.*

```
sourceDir=../bstPerfTest/src/com/bst/cdmi/perf/
targetDir=../bstPerfTestStaging/src/com/bst/cdmi/perf/
createApfWriterMethodName=cdmiPerfTest.createApfWriter
mainAddProfilingBeginAfter=createApfWriter("perfLogData.apf");
mainAddProfilingEndAfter=apfWriter.close();
logPerfDataMethodName=cdmiPerfUtil.printLogData

debug=on
```

Figure 10.2 *Enabling program input parameters set in* apf.properties.

statements inserted, as was discussed in the previous section. The three entries following the sourceDir and targetDir entries, *createApfWriterMethodName*, *mainAddProfilingBeginAfter*, and *mainAddProfilingEndAfter*, need some explanation.

The entry *createApfWriterMethodName* represents a new method that must be added in the main method of the driver program. This method creates a Java writer object prior to program execution start. This writer object is used for writing API profiling log data into the external text log file.

The next entry, *mainAddProfilingBeginAfter*, instructs the *perfLog* program where to insert the profiling begin statement in the main method of the program to be profiled. Apparently, we can't write profiling log data before the I/O writer object is created and becomes available. The statement specified as the value of this entry, *createApfWriter ("perfLogData.apf");*, must be the first executable statement in the main method of the driver program. The file *perfLogData.apf* eventually will contain the profiling log data that conforms to the standard log format.

Similar to *mainAddProfilingBeginAfter*, the entry *mainAddProfilingEndAfter* instructs the *perfLog* program to insert API call end profiling data after the statement specified by this parameter. In this case, it's the *apfWriter.close();* statement as specified in the above file for this parameter. The writer object should not be closed before the last API call profiling data is written to the external log file.

The next entry, *logPerfDataMethodName*, defines the name of the method that is used to write the API call profiling data into the external log file. In Figure 10.2, this method is implemented in the Java class *cdmiPerfUtil* with the name of *printLogData*. This method must be excluded from being profiled; otherwise, it will initiate an endless chain of self-recursive calls.

The last entry of *debug* is used for tracking parsing workflow as well as for debugging the *perfLog* program. Parsing workflow is the subject for the next section.

10.1.4 Parsing Workflow

To profile the APIs of a program, that program must be API profiling-enabled first. Enabling API profiling for a program is the process of adding profiling statements in the proper locations of that program. This process is similar to how a program is parsed during the compile stage with a high-level programming language compiler.

Figure 10.3 is a sample excerpt of a program that has been API profiling-enabled using the *perfLog.java* program. Let's use this sample to show the parsing workflow for adding profiling statements into the source code of a program.

The sample output shown in Figure 10.3 was generated with debug turned on. The comment appended to the end of each statement in the target source file is the debugging information generated when the source code of the program was parsed for adding API enabling statements. The debugging information helps track the scope changes of a statement as the original source code is read and parsed for adding profiling statements in proper places of each method of the program to be profiled. It shows how the *perfLog.java* program determines the locations for inserting API call begin and end profiling statements by tracking the scope changes marked by the left and right curly brackets.

```
public class cdmiAPITestThread extends Thread {//class:2:1:1
//class:2:1:1
        public String[] getInstanceIds(String className, ArrayList list,
                        int maxInstances) {
                cdmiPerfUtil.printLogData ("+cdmiAPITestThread_getInstanceIds");
                String[] instanceIds = new String[maxInstances]; //method:3:1:2
//method:3:1:2
                int imax = list.size(); //method:3:1:2
                for (int i = 0; i < maxInstances; i++) {//for:4:1:3
                        int randomPick = (int) (Math.random() * (float) imax); //for:4:1:3
                        instanceIds[i] = list.get(randomPick).toString(); //for:4:1:3
                        // System.out.println(instanceIds[i] + " "
                        // +list.get(randomPick).toString() );
                }//method:3:1:2
                {
                cdmiPerfUtil.printLogData ("-cdmiAPITestThread_getInstanceIds OK");
                return instanceIds;
                }
        }
//class:2:1:1
```

Figure 10.3   *Sample output of a target file with profiling enabled.*

To be more specific, the debug information appended to each statement represents the name of the scope, for example, *class, method, for, if, while*, and *try*, the number of the scope names currently on the *scopeStack* data structure, the class level, and the scope level. Let's walk through the sample output shown in Figure 10.3 to understand what the debugging information means exactly:

- Initially, *root* was assigned to the scope name. Since there is only one item on the scope stack data structure, the size of the scope stack data structure was 1. Both class level and scope level were 0. This is why we see //*root:1:0:0* appended to the first *import* statement.
- After the class begin statement is read, the scope name is *class*, and the stack size, class level, and scope level were all increased by 1, which led to //class:2:1:1 appended to the class definition line of *public class cdmiAPITestThread extends Thread {*.
- After the string array definition line of *String[] instanceIds = new String [maxInstances];*, *method* became the scope name, stack size changed to 3, class level remained at 1, and the scope level changed to 2, which led to //method:3:1:2 appended to this method definition line.
- When the for loop was encountered, the scope name changed to *for*, stack size increased to 4, class level remained at 1, and the scope level increased to 3.
- After the for loop, the scope name changed back to *method*, and the stack size and scope level all decreased by 1 while the class level still stayed at 1.
- At the end of the method definition for the *getInstanceIds* ( ) method, the scope name, stack size, class level, and scope level all came back to what they were before the method definition line.

Figure 10.3 also shows how the beginning profiling statement and the ending profiling statement look in a profiled method. For the method shown there, the API call begin profiling statement is represented by *cdmiPerfUtil.printLogData ("+cdmiAPITestThread_getInstanceIds");*, whereas the API call end profiling statement is represented by *cdmiPerfUtil.printLogData ("−cdmiAPITestThread_ getInstanceIds OK");*. Note the use of the plus sign for signaling the API call begin, and the minus sign and the keyword *OK* for signaling the API call end. This is required according to the standard logging format we defined in Chapter 7 about the *perfBasic* API profiling framework.

After the original source code is rewritten with the API profiling statements inserted, it's necessary to verify that the profiling statements have been inserted at the correct locations in each method to be profiled. This is the topic of the next section.

10.1.5 Verifying the Profiling-Enabled Source Code

Verification of the profiling-enabled source code is very necessary to guarantee that the modified program will stay the same as it was except that it will emit API call data when the program is executed. The functions of the program should not change at all. Depending on the coding habits of the programmers and the complexity of the program, you may encounter some of the following problems:

- It's very possible that API profiling statements were displaced in some methods. For example, Java requires that some statements must be the first executable statements in a method, such as the *super* method call shown in Figure 10.4. Whenever something like this happens, the error must be corrected manually.
- Java has variations of complicated control statements such as *if, if − then, if { } else if, try { } catch ( ) { }, do { } while;, while ( ) { }, switch*, and so on. When these structures contain *return* statements, make sure that an API call end statement is eventually executed in this method regardless of which *if-condition* is met. Missing a matching API call begin or end statement may result in log parsing failing later when the log data is parsed for generating performance maps.

This *perfLog.java* program is meant to help developers catch performance defects during the early stage of a software development project. It's not meant for production use, and therefore the inserted profiling statements should not be compiled into the release version of the software. Of course, if it has been used extensively and has

```
//class:2:1:1
        public cdmiAPITestThread(ARServerUser con, String name) {
            cdmiPerfUtil.printLogData
                    ("+cdmiAPITestThread_cdmiAPITestThread");
            super(name);//method:3:1:2
            context = con;//method:3:1:2
//method:3:1:2
```

Figure 10.4 *A Java method that contains* super *method.*

proved to be robust enough, it can be used in production as well, which may help debug production execution errors and performance issues as well. All in all, use it with caution when deploying it in a production environment.

In order to help hedge against parsing errors and failures, it's necessary that programmers adhere to certain best programming practices, as recommended in the next section.

10.1.6 Recommended Best Coding Practices

A well-structured software program is always more desirable than a convoluted, spaghetti-like program. Well-formed coding styles will not only enhance the readability of a software program, but also make it easier for a compiler to come up with the most efficient and optimized execution paths, although it doesn't make a software program more correct.

In order to make it easier to write an API profiling-enabling program, the following best coding practices are recommended:

- Single entry–single exit. For typed and nontyped methods, it's acceptable to have multiple exits with various if–like statements from the language grammar point of view. However, multiple exits require inserting multiple API call end statements within a method, which adds complexity for an API profiling-enabling program to work correctly. Keep in mind that every API call begin log entry must have a corresponding API call end log entry; otherwise, the log data cannot be parsed correctly later for generating performance maps. Single entry–single exit will guarantee that every API call begin log entry will have a matching API call end log entry.

- Don't add ad hoc comments everywhere in a software program. Always put comments prior to a class definition, a method definition, a block definition, or a statement. Figure 10.5 shows the comments spread between the condition and the action statement of an *if* statement. The program *perfLog.java* can handle situations like this, but it has made its parsing logic a lot more complicated than it should be.

- A cleaner implementation is always better. Avoid deeply embedded *if* blocks as it will increase the complexity of the parsing logic. Also, as a side effect, deep and interwoven control structures make it difficult for the compiler to optimize the execution of a program as well.

```
cdmiAPITestThread.java  ✕

if (i % cdmiPerfTest.sampleInterval == 0) // control the
        // volume of data to
        // be written
    threadWriter.println("ith, " + i + ", " + getName() + ", "
        + (( TestData) vData[k].get(i)).toString());
```

Figure 10.5 *Poorly placed comment statements.*

```
cdmiAPITest_printARException not well-formed (void: 1 exits)
..\bstPerfTest\src\com\bst\cdmi\perf\cdmiAPITest.java: numOfStart = 26 numOfEnd = 26

..\bstPerfTest\src\com\bst\cdmi\perf\cdmiAPITestThread.java: numOfStart = 16 numOfEnd = 16

..\bstPerfTest\src\com\bst\cdmi\perf\cdmiPerfTest.java: numOfStart = 19 numOfEnd = 19

cdmiPerfUtil_printARException not well-formed (void: 1 exits)
cdmiPerfUtil_PrintBulkEntryReturnList not well-formed (void: 1 exits)
cdmiPerfUtil_createGuid not well-formed (typed: 2 exits)
cdmiPerfUtil_PrintStatusInfoList not well-formed (void: 1 exits)
..\bstPerfTest\src\com\bst\cdmi\perf\cdmiPerfUtil.java: numOfStart = 9 numOfEnd = 9

cdmiQuickTest_cleanUp not well-formed (void: 1 exits)
cdmiQuickTest_cleanUpSystem not well-formed (void: 2 exits)
cdmiQuickTest_GetListInstancesTest not well-formed (void: 2 exits)
cdmiQuickTest_printARException not well-formed (void: 1 exits)
..\bstPerfTest\src\com\bst\cdmi\perf\cdmiQuickTest.java: numOfStart = 30 numOfEnd = 30

..\bstPerfTest\src\com\bst\cdmi\perf\TestData.java: numOfStart = 5 numOfEnd = 5
```

Figure 10.6 An example report from perfLog.java showing the well-formed-ness and matching number of entries and exits for each class that was profiling enabled.

At the end of execution, *perfLog* outputs information about the well-formed-ness of each method to be profiled. Figure 10.6 shows an example output, which contains two pieces of information for each method:

- A typed method is not well formed if it has more than one exit (return) statement. A nontyped method is not well formed if it has exit (return) statements.
- The total number of entries and exits for each class is reported. Even if the number of exits matches the number of entries for a class, it doesn't guarantee the correctness of profiling statement insertion, but a nonmatching report definitely signals the errors of profiling statement insertion for that class.

Most professional programmers make a conscious effort to code in standard styles, which is the best assurance for a software program to be coded in a standard, professional-looking way. One can also use the built-in source code formatter of an IDE such as *eclipse* to help enforce adopting standard coding styles.

10.1.7 Enabling Non-Java Programs

The program *perfLog.java* works only with the software programs coded in Java. Different high-level programming languages have different grammar rules, and the profiling-enabling program such as *perfLog.java* can't be language agnostic. However, the parsing logic and the techniques we illustrated in *perfLog.java* are still applicable to the software programs written in non-Java programming languages. Using *perfLog.java* as a reference, an experienced programmer should have no difficulties writing a profiling-enabling program for targeting the non-Java-based software products within a matter of weeks.

In the remaining sections of this chapter, I will focus on how to apply API profiling to help solve performance and scalability problems during the early stage of a software development life cycle. Software developers should use API profiling techniques with the goal of releasing a product with no major performance and scalability defects.

10.2 API PROFILING WITH STANDARD LOGS

In this section, I use a real example and demonstrate how to run an API profiling-enabled program to generate API call log data that conforms to the standard logging format as specified in Chapter 7. I will also show how to use the reference implementation of the *perfBasic* API profiling framework introduced in Chapter 9 to parse the API call log data generated from running an API profiling-enabled program. I then complete this section by showing how to generate performance maps using the output of the parsing program.

Let's first begin with how to generate the API profiling log data with an API profiling-enabled software program.

10.2.1 Generating API Profiling Log Data

The example application chosen for demonstrating how to generate API profiling log data is a real application capable of populating enterprise asset data into a database for enterprise service management. The functions and other details of this application are not important here. We are not interested in showing what this program could do exactly from the application perspective. We are interested only in how this application can be profiled using the *perfBasic* API profiling framework introduced in this book.

The application to be profiled is a multithreaded program, which is more interesting than a single-threaded program, as it's more challenging in general to profile a multithreaded program than a single-threaded program. In reality, most enterprise software programs are multithreaded for better performance and scalability.

This program consists of two packages, one of which is named *com.bst.cdmi.cdm* and the other is named *com.bst.cdmi.perf*. The *cdm* package contains about 40 Java classes that represent various IT asset data models, whereas the *perf* package contains the following six Java classes:

- *cmdiPerfTest.java*. This class is the driver for launching the program.
- *cmdiAPITestThread.java*. This class implements the multithreading mechanism for using multiple threads to populate IT asset data.
- *cmdiAPITest.java*. This class provides the core function of inserting IT asset data objects into the database. It is executed by each thread.
- *cmdiPerfUtil.java*. This class is a utility class.
- *cdmiTestData.java*. This class is an abstraction of API performance test data.
- *cdmiQuickTest.java*. This class functions as a test harness for performing quick performance regression tests on certain core APIs.

In order to avoid generating too much log data, none of the classes in the *cdm* package were profiled. The methods of these classes are essentially getters and setters. Such classes are ideal candidates for being excluded from profiling as they perform neither complicated logic nor database calls. The classes contained in the second package of *com.bst.cdmi.perf* were profiling-enabled using the program *perfLog.java*.

After running this API profiling-enabled application using a typical workload with ten threads, the API call log data was dumped to an external text file named

```
description=perfBasic test
logFileName=perfLogData_demo1.apf
maxThreads=50
threadSample=1
logFileIsSortedByThread=false
threadInfoFileName=threadInfoFile.txt
outputFileDir=results
inputFileDir=input
threadFileDir=threads
callTreeDotFile=data/callTree.dot
callTreeXMLFile0=data/callTree0.xml
callTreeXMLFileFinal=data/callTreeFinal.xml
graphByThread=true
subGraph=false
traceTreeWalkThrough=false
dotLinkLabelHorizontal=false
threadPercentTimeFilter=1
elapsedTimeThresholdInMS=1000
elapsedTimePercentRed=10
deleteThreadFiles=false
relativeToLogOnTime=true
xmlProcessing=true
profilingOn=false
```

Figure 10.7   parser.properties *file for the parser to parse the log data.*

perfLogData.apf. In the next section, I will show how to parse this log file using the reference implementation of the *perfBasic* API profiling framework to generate the output that can be used for generating performance maps.

10.2.2   Parsing API Profiling Log Data

In order to parse the API profiling log data using the reference implementation of the parser for the *perfBasic* API profiling framework, we need to compose a *parser. properties* file to instruct the parser how to parse the log data file. Figure 10.7 shows the content of the *parser.properties* file constructed in the *eclipse* IDE.

Each entry in the file is explained as follows:

- *description* indicates what this test is about.
- *logFileName* indicates the name of the API profiling log data file to be parsed.
- *maxThreads* indicates how many threads will be processed at most.
- *threadSample* specifies sampling intervals for limiting the number of threads to be processed.
- *logFileIsSortedByThread* controls whether to read data from the original raw data file or from the sorted thread data files.

- *threadInfoFileName* represents the name of the thread information file generated when the raw log file was processed the first time.
- *outputFileDir* indicates where the output files should go.
- *inputFileDir* indicates where to pick up the input log file.
- *threadFileDir* indicates where the sorted thread files should go.
- *callTreeDotFile* indicates the name of the output file that will be used by the *dot* program to generate performance maps.
- *callTreeXMLFile0* indicates the initial, incomplete XML file for using XML-based graphics tools to generate performance maps.
- *callTreeXMLFileFinal* indicates the final, complete XML file for using XML-based graphics tools to generate performance maps.
- *graphByThread* indicates whether the performance maps will be drawn with each graph as a separate call tree branch.
- *subGraph* indicates whether all APIs having the same node name will be clustered together.
- *traceTreeWalkThrough* indicates whether call tree walk-through will be traced to help debug in case the parser is unable to parse successfully to the end.
- *dotLinkLabelHorizontal* indicates whether the entries of each dot link label such as elapsed time percentage, absolute elapsed time, and call count will be placed horizontally.
- *threadPercentTimeFilter* sets a filter for excluding those threads whose elapsed times in percentage are insignificant.
- *elapsedTimeThreasholdInMS* sets a threshold in milliseconds for excluding those APIs whose elapsed times are insignificant.
- *elapsedTimePercentRed* sets a threshold above which a call path will be labeled in *red* and *bold* font to help draw attention to it.
- *deleteThreadFiles* indicates whether the thread files will be deleted at the end of parsing.
- *relativeToLogOnTime* indicates whether the call time stamp is absolute or relative to the time when logging was turned on.
- *xmlProcessing* indicates whether XML output files will be generated for using XML-based graphics tools to generate performance maps.
- *profilingOn* indicates whether the parser program will be profiled as well if it's profiling-enabled.

This seems to be a long list of entries, but every one of them is necessary for the desired flexibility in parsing. Usually, most of the entries will stay fixed and only a few of them need be changed when parsing different log files.

At the end of parsing, the parser will generate the following output:

- A file named *callTree.dot* for using the *dot* program to generate performance maps

- A file named *callTreeXMLFinal.xml* for using XML-based graphics tools to generate performance maps
- A text file with the postfix of *_summary* in the file name that summarizes parsing
- A text file with the postfix of *_data* in the file name that contains all API call data
- A text file with the postfix of *_callCost* in the file name that contains all API calls in each thread sorted by call cost in terms of the total elapsed time
- A thread information file in the threads directory that contains enough information for the parser to read log data without going through the initial step of sorting data by thread again
- All thread files that contain log data sorted by thread

Next, let's see how performance maps can be generated based on the output from the parser. This would be the fun part of API profiling and parsing, as it's so easy to identify software performance and scalability problems with the help of performance maps.

10.2.3   Generating Performance Maps

Generating performance maps is easy, as long as the map input data files generated by the parser conform to the format required by each specific graphics tool.

In this section, we'll concentrate on how to generate performance maps using the graphics tool *dot* introduced in Chapter 9. *dot* is a powerful, yet easy to learn and easy to use graphics tool for displaying structural data such as software API call trees in the form of performance maps.

If you are new to *dot*, you are strongly encouraged to experiment with it, as it's not only very useful, but also a lot of fun.

The *dot* grammar is really simple. Figure 10.8 shows the *dot* file generated by the parser *logParser.java* with the API profiling log data collected with the application described in the preceding section.

This *dot* input file starts with

```
digraph G {
```

and ends with

```
}.
```

Then, at the beginning of the data section inside it, you can define how a *node* will be displayed with attributes such as *shape*, *style*, *color*, and so on, as shown in the following data line:

```
node[shape=``box'',style=``filled'',color=``lightgoldenrod''];
```

The rest of it is simple; it either defines a concrete node or a concrete edge or link that connects a node with its immediate descendant. A concrete node is defined with an ID followed by [. . .] with the node attributes such as *label* in it. A *label* represents the text

```
digraph G {
node[shape="box"];
ROOT_T0_cdmiAPITestThread_run[label="cdmiAPITestThread_run"];
ROOT_T0_cdmiAPITestThread_run_cdmiAPITestThread_createObjectT
ROOT_T0_cdmiAPITestThread_run->ROOT_T0_cdmiAPITestThread_run_
ROOT_T0_cdmiAPITestThread_run_cdmiAPITestThread_createObjectT
ROOT_T0_cdmiAPITestThread_run_cdmiAPITestThread_createObjectT
ROOT_T0_cdmiAPITestThread_run_cdmiAPITestThread_createObjectT
ROOT_T0[label="T0"];
ROOT_T0_cdmiAPITestThread_run[label="cdmiAPITestThread_run"];
ROOT_T0->ROOT_T0_cdmiAPITestThread_run[style="bold",color="re
ROOT_T0[label="T0"];
ROOT_T0_cdmiPerfTest_main[label="cdmiPerfTest_main"];
ROOT_T0->ROOT_T0_cdmiPerfTest_main[style="filled",color="blue"
ROOT_ROOT[label="ROOT"];
ROOT_T0[label="T0"];
ROOT_ROOT->ROOT_T0[style="bold",color="red",label="100%\n18971
ROOT_T0_cdmiAPITestThread_run_cdmiAPITestThread_createObjectTe
ROOT_T0_cdmiAPITestThread_run_cdmiAPITestThread_createObjectTe
ROOT_T0_cdmiAPITestThread_run_cdmiAPITestThread_createObjectTe
ROOT_T0_cdmiAPITestThread_run_cdmiAPITestThread_createObjectTe
ROOT_T0_cdmiAPITestThread_run_cdmiAPITestThread_createObjectTe
ROOT_T0_cdmiAPITestThread_run_cdmiAPITestThread_createObjectTe
ROOT_T0_cdmiAPITestThread_run_cdmiAPITestThread_createObjectTe
ROOT_T0_cdmiAPITestThread_run_cdmiAPITestThread_createObjectTe
}
```

Figure 10.8   A dot *input file for generating a performance map.*

that will be displayed on the map for that node. The third line in Figure 10.8 is an example of how a concrete node is defined.

A concrete edge is defined with the following format:

nodeA_id -> nodeB-id [attrib1=value1, attrib2=value2, ...];

where *nodeA_id* is the node id of the source node, and *nodeB_id* is the node id of the destination node. You can easily identify the edges in Figure 10.8 by following the above format.

This *dot* file shown in Figure 10.8 might look visually noisy, but it doesn't matter much, because most of the time we will not look at this file. We will look at the performance maps instead.

Assuming that the *callTree.dot* input file is well formed, namely, it conforms to the *dot* format specification, generating a performance map is as easy as executing a command on a Windows™ DOS™ command line similar to the following:

dot.exe -Tgif callTree.dot -o callTree.gif

In the above command, the first entry of *dot.exe* simply invokes the *dot* program, the second entry of *−Tgif* specifies the output graphics format, the third entry of *callTree.dot* specifies the *dot* input file, and the last entry of *−o callTree.gif* specifies the output graphics file, which is the actual performance map.

In general, it's more convenient to put the *dot* command in a *.bat* file so that you can just double click on that *.bat* file to generate the performance map when parsing is complete and the proper *.dot* file has been generated. You can also modify the generated *.dot* file and rerun the *dot* command without going through the parsing process again. To prevent the generated *callTree.dot* file from being overwritten, rename both the *.dot* file and the *.bat* file and move them to a different directory. You can also share the performance maps with other team members through an internal website.

Executing the above command with the *dot* file generated for this example resulted in the performance map shown in Figure 10.9. In the next section, I'll describe how to

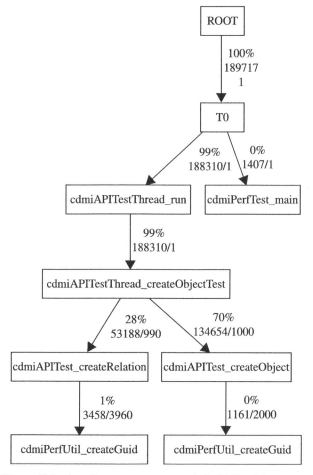

Figure 10.9   *A performance map generated with the* dot *program.*

make sense out of a performance map such as this one for solving real performance and scalability problems.

10.2.4 Making Sense Out of Performance Maps

In order to make sense out of the performance maps, we need to get familiar with the structure and labels shown on a performance map. Using Figure 10.9 as an example, let's walk through that map and illustrate all the useful information contained there as follows:

- The top edge from ROOT to T0 implies the main thread spawned when the program was invoked. The label near the edge shows that this path represents 100% of the total elapsed execution time, which was 189717 ms, and that it was invoked only once.

- Then the execution started to branch. The left branch represents the *main* method call of the *cdmiPerfTest.java* program. This branch rounded down to 0% of the total elapsed execution time, which was 1407 ms only, and of course, it was invoked only once. The parser doesn't show fractions of percentages, as we probably don't care about any execution paths that are at least 10% or below, in order to pinpoint the most expensive APIs.

- If you are familiar with Java, you would recognize that the API call of *cdmiAPITestThread* run on the left branch of this call tree represents the work that each thread would do to actually carry out the task of the API performance test, which is what that API performance test driver was designed for. Since this branch represents 99% of the total elapsed time of 188310 ms, let's concentrate on this branch only.

- We can immediately recognize that this thread spent its entire time executing a *cdmiAPITestThread.createObjectTest* call. Immediately beneath it, there are two expensive calls: *cdmiAPITest.createRelation*, which took 28% of the total elapsed time or 53188 ms out of 990 invocations, and *cdmiAPITest.createObject*, which took 70% of the total elapsed time or 134654 ms out of 1000 invocations. This clearly indicates the focus for the performance optimization, since the other API calls were just noise compared with the above two API calls in terms of the total elapsed time. In general, elapsed time is what we care about most with the performance of the APIs of a program.

- We can further identify that the *cdmiAPITest.createObject* API call is 2.5 times more expensive than the *cdmiAPITest.createRalation* API call. This indicates further which one should be the primary focus. This kind of information out of a performance map tells developers immediately where the performance optimization and tuning efforts should be focused.

It is necessary to point out that you can drill down further into the APIs of the underlying packages called by the above two methods if those packages were profiled as well. Typically, we don't want to drill down all the way into the JVM, the operating system level APIs, or even the assembly language levels, as there is not very much we can do at these levels.

Note that we have applied filtering to filter away those nodes whose elapsed times are less than 1000 milliseconds. If we did not apply this filter, the resultant performance map would be hard to read with a page size like this book.

In this section, I demonstrated how to apply API profiling and generate performance maps using the API profiling log data that conforms to the standard logging format. In the next section, I'll show how to adapt custom API call log data to generate performance maps.

10.3   API PROFILING WITH CUSTOM LOGS

Some software programs may already have their internal logging APIs in place for generating API profiling log data in a specific text format. Such logs can be used for troubleshooting functional and performance bugs. However, it might be hard to make sense out of a gigabyte text log file, for example, even for developers who are most familiar with the log content.

It's actually very easy to turn a large text file into a performance map in graphics format as shown in the previous sections. A gigabyte text log file is huge in size. However, it represents well-structured data that are repeated API calls. This well-structured data can be turned into graphic maps for easier visual inspection. A software program such as the log parser introduced in Chapter 9 can do this kind of work very easily. In the context of the *perfBasic* API profiling framework proposed in this book, all we need is an adapter software program that can transform the log data in its original log format into standard format, and then the rest of it is easy—essentially it's the same to parse transformed log data as if it were written in standard format in the first place.

In this section, I demonstrate how performance maps can be generated with custom logs from an existing software program. I'll start by using an adapter to transform custom API profiling log data into the standard format that conforms to the specification of the *perfBasic* API profiling framework.

10.3.1   Using Adapter to Transform Custom Logs

As one of the many software design patterns that are widely used in designing software programs, an adapter is responsible for transforming data from one format into another. This is exactly what we need for turning API profiling log data from its custom format into standard format.

Although developing an adapter software program should not be too difficult, the concrete implementation of an adapter may differ from one custom logging format to another. However, all implementations may have to deal with the following common issues:

- Custom logs may contain ad hoc data lines for debugging functionality bugs. These lines should be ignored during data format transformation for the purpose of generating performance maps. The pattern for ignoring such lines can be specified in an external file, and then applied as custom log data is read and rewritten into another text file in the standard format.

- Custom logs may contain API calls that have no time stamps. Such lines must be ignored as well.
- With custom logs, the first API call may only signify the start of logging when logging was enabled initially. There might be a delay from turning logging on to actually recording real API calls under a concrete test workload. When a test run is complete, logging should be turned off immediately to avoid capturing irrelevant log data. There are two gaps here, one from turning logging on to test start, and the other from test end to turning logging off. These factors should be taken into account when generating and interpreting performance maps. However, they can be ignored if the gaps are insignificant relative to the test duration.
- Another trivial issue is that one can choose to rewrite log data using timings relative to the time when logging was turned on. This provides convenience for measuring the time durations for API calls in a more sensible way, as the absolute time stamps in milliseconds might be astronomically large.

Other than these issues, developing an adapter to transform log data from its original format into standard format should be easy. As long as an adapter does its work correctly, we shouldn't see a huge difference in generating performance maps between using standard and custom logs. In the next section, I'll provide an example showing how custom API profiling logs can easily be turned into performance maps.

10.3.2 Generating Performance Maps with Custom Logs

Generating performance maps with custom logs starts with converting logs from custom format to standard format. After custom API profiling logs are transformed and rewritten into the log files that conform to the standard logging format of the *perfBasic* API profiling framework, the procedure for generating the performance maps with custom logs is the same as with standard logs. For this reason, we will not repeat the procedure for generating performance maps here.

Now let's use one of the custom logs to illustrate how to generate performance maps with custom logs. First, let's list some of the issues that need to be taken care of with custom logs:

- Custom logs are typically large in size, ranging from a few megabytes up to gigabytes. It saves time if the custom logs are converted into standard logs first, and then subsequent parsing always uses the same converted standard logs. This is feasible, as the adapter and parser are separate programs that can be run separately.
- If custom logs contain too many threads, you may want to limit the number of threads to be processed and displayed in the format of graphic performance maps. For well-written, multithreaded programs, executions within the same group of threads are well balanced among all the threads. Thus the call tree structure and the performance metrics such as the elapsed time and call count will be similar from one thread to another among the same group of threads. Including

too many threads may divert one's attention and adversely affect separating the wheat from the chaff. For this purpose, a parameter named *threadSample* can be used to help control the number of threads to be displayed on a performance map when dealing with multithreaded log data. For example, if you set *threadSample* to *n*, which is an integer number, that means only every *n*th thread will be processed and displayed on the performance map.

- When log files are too large, XML processing can be very time consuming. In this case, you can either turn off XML processing or apply filtering to limit the number of XML nodes in a call tree structure to be processed.
- You may need to experiment with the parameters of *threadSample* and *elapsedTimeThresholdInMS* in the *parser.properties* file a few times in order to arrive at satisfactory performance maps.

Figure 10.10 shows the performance map generated from a real custom log. This log contains a total number of 30 execution threads from an application programmed in C/C++. The application validated 25k objects against a database that was to contain all the objects accumulated over time.

When this performance map was generated, the following settings were adopted for some of the parameters specified in the *parser.properties* file:

- The elapsed time threshold was set to 70 seconds in order to limit the number of API nodes appearing on the map.
- *dotLinkLabelHorizontal* was set to true in order to have a more balanced aspect ratio.

Also, the following *log.properties* were used with this example:

```
includeLines={``[''}
ignoreLines={``Trace Log'', ``+SSI'', ``End of filter
processing'', ``Restart of filter processing'', ``Call
Guide'', ``Checking''}
callEnd={``OK''}
selfNode={``COMMIT WORK'', ``Set LOB'', ``Trace Log''
temp={``Start filter processing'', ``Stop filter
processing''}
```

Besides, a *rankdir = LR* statement was added at the beginning of the *callTree.dot* file for the desired orientation.

It is interesting to mention that after being converted to standard format, the original log file was reduced from 500 MB to a standard log file of 102 MB. It's apparently much easier to view a map than viewing a text file of hundreds of megabytes. However, due to the limited page size of the book, it's challenging to show clearly the entire structure of this performance map with so many threads, but this should not be a problem for two reasons. First, we are only interested in showing its overall structure here. Second, this will not be a problem in its real use, as you can either view it on a larger screen or print it out on poster-size paper.

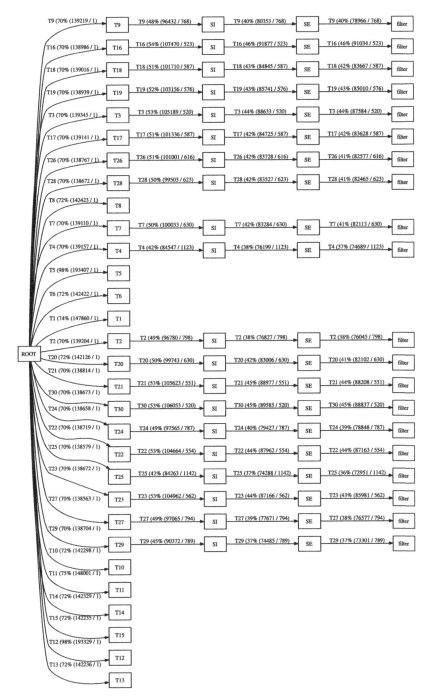

Figure 10.10 A performance map generated with a custom log file.

Printing a performance map out on poster-size paper is handy for communication among the team members who have common interests in it. Using a colored format will further enhance its appeal and visibility. From physiological point of view, a better structured performance map with some sort of aesthetics in it can draw more attention and get all stakeholders more focused on it. Keep in mind that software programs are a product of the mind, and the mind can be affected in many ways.

Based on the structure of this performance map, we can immediately recognize that there are two groups of threads here, one of which makes more and deeper API calls than the other. The actual content of this performance map is not important here, but it illustrates how much easier it is to get to the execution details of a large software program with a performance map than with a 500-MB text log file.

Since all threads within the same thread group bear similar API call tree structure and similar performance metrics, we applied a thread sampling filtering to choose one out of every five threads. The resultant performance map is shown in Figure 10.11. Also, only its core part is shown in order to make it more readable.

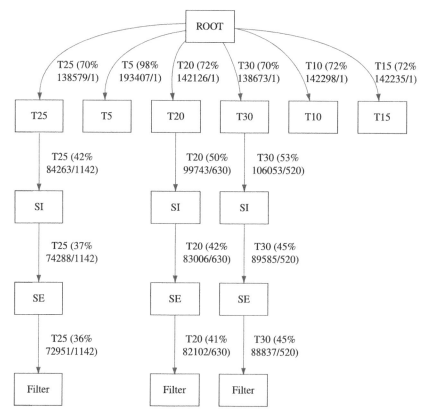

Figure 10.11   Core part of the same performance map as shown in Figure 10.10 with thread sampling set to choose one of every five threads out of a total of 30 threads.

As seen from Figure 10.11, a performance map is helpful not only for diagnosing software performance and scalability defects, but also for debugging multithreaded programming. Balance in terms of the execution time among all threads is a good measure of the effectiveness of the multithread implementation for a software program. Multithreading is one of the most effective programming techniques for enhancing software performance and scalability, especially with the latest computer processors that have been designed to support parallelism to the largest extent. Readers are strongly encouraged to implement multithreading for a software program whenever possible.

To increase the complexity, I'll demonstrate in the next section how to generate performance maps with combo logs, some of which are custom logs and some are standard logs. This is especially applicable when an application server has its APIs exposed to client programs, which deliver services to their users by calling the application server APIs. The application server generates its custom logs, whereas the ad hoc lightweight client programs generate standard logs.

10.4 API PROFILING WITH COMBO LOGS

In this section, let's use a real application to demonstrate how API profiling can be applied when we have a situation of a multithreaded client calling multithreaded server APIs. This is a very common scenario of a client/server programming model in practice. The client side typically is thin and simple, which is an ideal case for applying the simpler, easy-to-implement *perfBasic* API profiling framework.

This application was written in Java. Its major functionality was for populating IT asset data into a database by calling the server APIs directly. The server APIs were Java wrapper APIs of the corresponding underlying APIs implemented in C/C++. The number of threads on the client side can be configured based on the thread pools on the server side. In order to make it more manageable, we limited the number of threads to three on the client side and the number of threads to seven on the server side. A typical workload was executed and the API profiling logs were collected on both the server side and client side. The performance maps were generated for both the client and server. Let's first look at the client side performance map in the next section.

10.4.1 Client Side Performance Map

Without going into the subtleties of how API profiling was enabled, how log files were parsed, and how performance maps were generated, the client side performance map is shown directly in Figure 10.12. This performance map was obtained with an elapsed time filter of 1000 milliseconds. Again, the following abbreviations were used in order to make all information visible:

- A—*cdmiPerfTest*
- B—*cdmiAPITestThread*
- C—*cdmiAPITest*

- D—*cdmiPerfUtil*
- CO—*createObject*
- CR—*createRelation*

In Figure 10.12, we see four threads from T0 through T3. The first thread, T0, was the main thread launched when the client program *cdmiPerfTest* started execution. Its method *cdmiPerfTest.APITest* ( ) spawned three worker threads of T1 through T3, which all populate IT asset data concurrently.

Those three threads of T1, T2, and T3 were very well balanced, as the portion of elapsed time was quite uniform among them. All these threads called the method of *cdmiAPITestThread.createObjectTest* ( ), which in turn called the other two methods of *cdmiAPITest.createObject* ( ) and *cdmiAPITest.createRelation* ( ). The elapsed times in percentage for the two methods of *createObject* ( ) and *createRelation* ( ) were 77% and 21% for the T1 thread, 77% and 20% for the T2 thread, and 78% and 21% for the T3 thread, respectively. These percentage numbers differ by less than 1% from thread to thread. This implies that a remarkable multithreading model was working behind the scenes, which resulted from the robust implementations of not only the application server and client but also the underlying hardware, operation system, middleware, Java, and C++ execution environments.

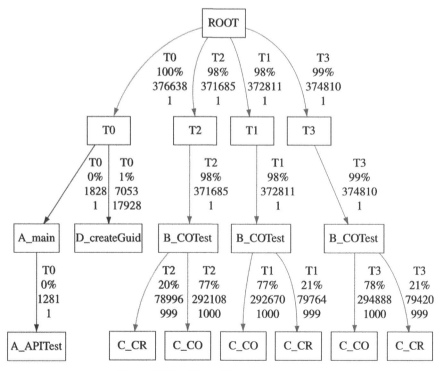

Figure 10.12 Client side performance map.

After reducing the elapsed time filtering value from 1000 milliseconds to 10 milliseconds, further API call details were revealed. As shown in Figure 10.13, the two most expensive methods, *cdmiAPITestThread.createObject* ( ) and *cdmiAPITestThread.createRelation* ( ), spent 99% of the time on the remote server side, which means that the time spent locally was negligible. This confirms the lean logic on the client side. Here only a portion of the performance map for the T3 thread is shown. The other two threads, T1 and T2, had exactly the same structure as T1, with the elapsed time differing by less than 1% from T3. Also, a uniform data population model was used and all three threads had the same amount of work to do.

In the next section, we will look at the corresponding server side performance map. The performance maps on both sides will be correlated to help get a consistent view about the overall performance of the application.

10.4.2 Server Side Performance Map

Figure 10.14 shows the server side performance map generated with the server side custom logs, collected under the same workload as for the client side performance map. It is seen that the server side performance map contains deeper API calls than the client side. This design principle of *thin* client favors better overall system performance.

When Figure 10.14 was generated, an elapsed time threshold value of 10 milliseconds was applied to filter out those API calls whose contributions to the total elapsed time were insignificant from the performance point of view. It is meant to show the overall structure of the server side performance map, not the details of every API call. Although the visual clarity is limited by the page size of the book, we can still see that:

- There are seven threads under the root node, one of which (T0) was the admin thread, three (T1, T2, T3) from the lightweight thread group, and three (T4, T5, T6) from the heavyweight thread group.
- The execution paths with more levels were from the lightweight threads, and the execution paths with fewer levels were from the heavyweight threads. The lightweight threads fetch less data from the database for minimizing the response time, whereas the heavyweight threads return more data from the database for maximizing the throughput.
- Once again, all threads within a particular thread group bear similar structures with comparable elapsed times, which imply a well-balanced multithreading execution model.
- Each lightweight thread started to fan out beneath the API node *CE*. This fan-out call tree structure originated from the filter operations with the mixed SQL operations. This design choice is beyond the scope of this book. We'd like to remind the reader that we are only interested in how to profile APIs. The design logic behind the software program being profiled is less interesting.

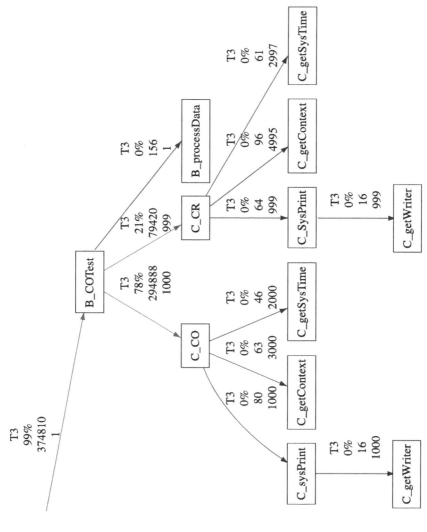

Figure 10.13 Portion of a performance map showing negligible local execution time on the client side.

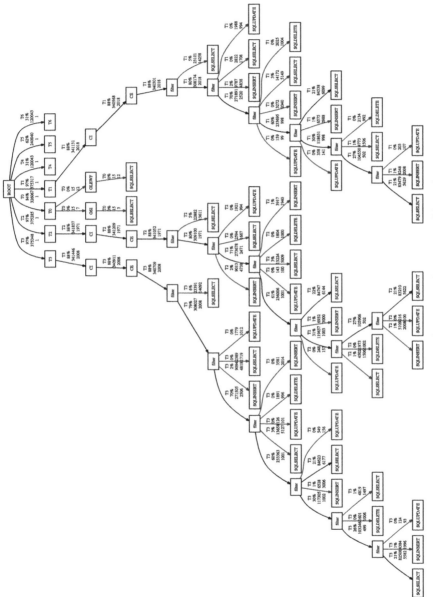

Figure 10.14 Illustrative overall structure of the server side performance map.

Viewing the overall structure of the server side performance map shown in Figure 10.14 is like viewing a forest from a height of 1000 feet, in the sense that we don't see details immediately from it. It gives us an immediate feel about how the software program is designed overall.

Now let's zoom in and see the trees, namely, examining the execution details of each expensive execution path. For this purpose, Figure 10.15 shows the top portion of the server side performance map shown in Figure 10.14. It clearly shows that for this workload, the lightweight threads were heavily utilized relative to the heavyweight threads, based on the relative elapsed time percentage of each thread. Although the elapsed time percentages of the heavyweight threads ranged from 31% to 62%, they were idle most of the time, which was why no API calls lasted longer than 10 milliseconds beneath them. Whether lightweight threads or heavyweight threads were used depends on the workload of the execution tasks, but we are less concerned with that here.

It is seen from Figure 10.15 that the percentage of the elapsed time for each light-weight thread from T1 to T3 under the root node was 97% uniformly across the board, which corresponds to 375 seconds in absolute time units. Once again, this indicates a good balance among all the threads.

All lightweight threads called the API *CI* as shown under each thread from T1 to T3. Since this is a server side API written in C++, its elapsed time of 341 seconds can be used to measure the overhead of its corresponding Java API wrapper. This is easy math, given its parent elapsed time shown above it, which is 375 seconds.

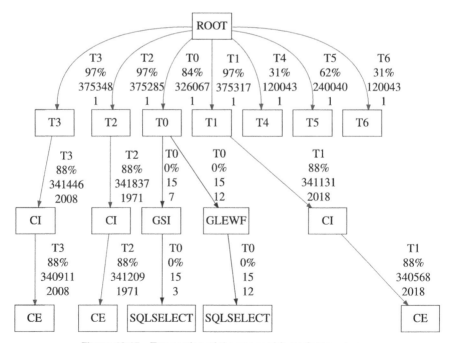

Figure 10.15 *Top portion of the server side performance map.*

Based on these two numbers of 341 and 375 seconds, it can easily be calculated that the Java wrapper overhead was only 9%. This clearly shows that this wrapper layer for the product was sufficiently lean and should not be the performance optimization focus.

Next, let's drill down to the bottom of the call tree. Figure 10.16 shows the sub call tree beneath the API *CE* shown in Figure 10.15. It was taken from the T1 thread but

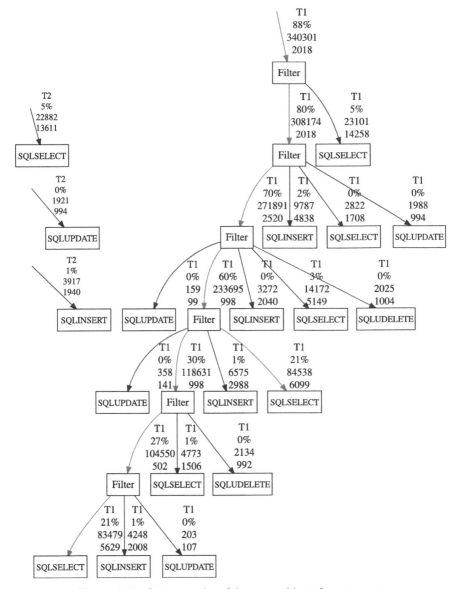

Figure 10.16 *Bottom portion of the server side performance map.*

applies to the T2 and T3 threads as well, due to the structural similarity that we mentioned previously. This sub call tree shows that each lightweight thread spent about half of its time executing two SQL statements, one of which was executed 6099 times, and the other was executed 5629 times. These are the potential areas where significant performance improvements could be realized.

This might be a good opportunity for discussing about how we drill down to the expensive API calls following the execution paths shown on a performance map in general. Let's use Figure 10.16 as an example with the following top–down procedure to show how to look for the expensive execution paths:

- First, we see from the top that this execution path represents 88% of the total execution time or 340301 milliseconds in absolute time units. This amount of execution time was accumulated over 2018 calls.

- Next, we see two branches: one was accountable for 80%, and the other for 5% of the total execution time. Note that these two execution paths don't add up to 88% of the total execution time of their parent API call. That's because that 88% includes local time spent within that method and time spent calling other APIs whose time portions were too small to be included with the filter specified when the original log data file was parsed. Remember that we are not interested in doing exact math here. Instead, we are trying to identify which execution paths are the most expensive ones that constitute the system bottlenecks and performance optimization opportunities.

- Following that 80% total execution time branch, we came down to the next API call that was accountable for 70% of the total execution time. With the same approach, we came down to the API call that was accountable for 60% of the total execution time.

- Next, we see another two branches: one was an SQL query that was accountable for 21%, and the other was a filter start operation that was accountable for 30% of the total execution time.

- That filter start operation initiated another two filter start operations in a self-recursive fashion. Eventually, it ended with an SQL query that was accountable for 21% of the total execution time. SQL queries are leaf nodes, which indicate performance optimization opportunities if their time apportionments are large.

- Since these two SQL queries constitute 42% of the total execution time, it's worthwhile to investigate how these two SQL queries could be executed more efficiently either by adding proper indexes or by rewriting them. SQL tuning itself is another interesting territory and the reader can find plenty of good textbooks about it.

- Apparently, SQL queries were accountable for only half of the total execution time. The other half was spent on the application logic. One common performance defect is that some waste logic is executed repeatedly which might not have to be executed at all. Domain expert developers can apply their product-specific knowledge and help shed the extraneous application logic that affects the performance and scalability of the software product under development.

In the next section, I'll use a real-world example to demonstrate how API profiling can be applied to solve real software performance and scalability problems.

10.5 APPLYING API PROFILING TO SOLVING PERFORMANCE AND SCALABILITY PROBLEMS

In this last section, a real software performance optimization experience is presented to show how performance maps can be used to guide performance optimization efforts. This optimization effort was initiated to improve the performance of an application server API named GR (Get Records). The GR API is used heavily by all custom applications and its performance is very critical.

The GR API is called by custom applications to retrieve a series of objects from the database based on certain selection criteria. It also calls other application server APIs to complete the query. In order to get focused on the main subject of applying API profiling and optimizing the performance of a software program guided by performance maps, I'd like to remind the reader that the domain context associated with this API is not very important here. The important thing here is to demonstrate how API profiling and performance maps can be utilized to guide performance efforts in a real software development process.

Let's start with the baseline performance of this API in the next subsection.

10.5.1 Baseline

Baseline performance refers to whatever performance you have observed which you would like to take as an initial start point. It's extremely important that the baseline performance is carefully established first. It must be established carefully because that's the yardstick you will use to measure and assess your ongoing performance optimization efforts. If the baseline is shaky, for example, the baseline numbers are not repeatable from run to run, then how would you accurately calculate how much performance improvement you have achieved with whatever optimizations you applied?

In addition to adhering to the performance data principles introduced in Chapter 3, here is a list of things that you need to pay attention to when establishing baseline performance:

- The test scenarios must be representative. Different scenarios may result in different performance numbers. For example, retrieving all objects with all attributes of each object retrieved will certainly run slower than retrieving all objects with one or a few attributes retrieved for each object. Typically, at least three scenarios should be considered: worst, normal, and best.

- The test environment must be stable. Ideally, a completely isolated test environment should be used. It's not unusual that the test environment may actually consist of servers that reside on a corporate network. If this is the case, you might see that the performance numbers you obtain depend on when you run the test; you may get better performance numbers at night when the network is nearly idle, and you may get worse performance numbers in the morning when the network is busy with everybody using it.

- The test duration must be sufficiently long. The longer the test duration, the more repeatable the test results will be. Empirically, the test duration should be at least 5 minutes.

- Keep all test conditions and settings that affect the performance test results the same from conducting baseline tests to optimization tests except those you intentionally take as variables. This usually is called apple-to-apple comparison except for the factors that are being tested. For example, when testing a different algorithm or a different system level setting or database level setting, make it the only variable for interpreting the test results. Another recommendation is that you may want to restart your application server and/or database server to make sure that you are not observing performance improvement that actually results from picking up data from caching that occurred when the baseline test was run.

The list of things that you need to pay attention to when establishing a good baseline performance can grow longer, but let's stop here and get back to the main objective of this section, namely, showing how API profiling and performance maps can help solve real performance problems.

Figure 10.17 shows the baseline performance map of the GR API we mentioned in the beginning of this section. We have applied a filter of 10 milliseconds, so those API calls with less than 10 ms elapsed times have been eliminated from showing up on this performance map.

First of all, note that this was a multithreaded scenario, as there are three threads, T0, T3, and T8. T0 is the admin thread, which doesn't do actual user work other than administration work. T8 had a small elapsed time of only 31 milliseconds, which is negligible. The T3 thread did most of the work based on its large total elapsed time of 53625 milliseconds, as shown on the map.

It's easy to recognize that the GND API underneath the GR API had made a total number of 4005 SQL SELECT calls. The avoidance of excessive SQL calls from an application server is one of the most effective software performance optimization techniques. SQL calls will incur not only large elapsed times on the database server, but also network latencies between the application server and the database server. This is why excessive SQL calls are expensive from the performance perspective.

One of the performance patterns associated with database-intensive applications is to minimize the number of SQL calls from an application server to the database server. This will reduce not only the number of network round trips but also various SQL execution overhead incurred on the database side.

With the above performance pattern in mind, we naturally infer that if we could reduce the number of SQL calls from the GND API, it might help improve the

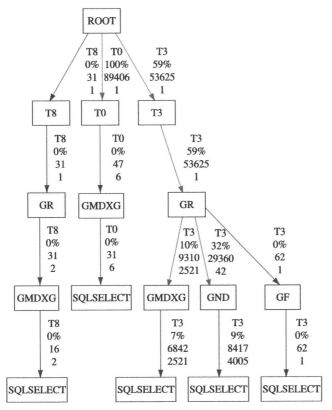

Figure 10.17 Performance map of the baseline test.

performance of its parent API GR. This inference resulted in an optimized implementation of this GR API, which will be discussed in the next subsection.

10.5.2 Optimization

Based on the above idea of reducing the SQL call count from the GND API, the query logic of GR API was redesigned and implemented. The resultant performance map of the optimized implementation is shown in Figure 10.18.

As we can see, the total elapsed time of the GR API has been improved from 54 seconds (baseline) to 44 seconds, which represents a 19% improvement. I'd like to mention that in order to make sure that we were measuring real performance improvement, we restarted both the database server and application server prior to starting the tests when taking both the baseline and optimized performance measurements. This way, we guaranteed that the optimization test was not taking advantage of the data cached from the baseline test.

In the next section, I'll offer a quick analysis of how this performance improvement was achieved in this specific performance optimization effort.

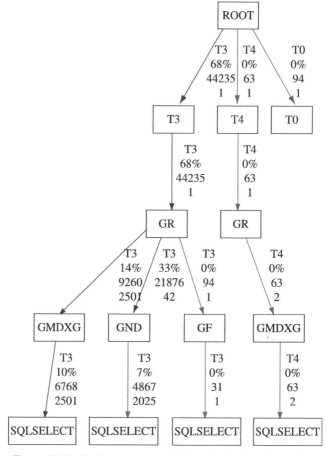

Figure 10.18   Performance map of the optimized implementation.

10.5.3   Analysis

Performance optimization analysis aided with performance maps is easy. You just need to compare the two performance maps from the baseline test and the optimization test.

Table 10.1 shows the comparison between the baseline and optimization tests from the elapsed-time-to-elapsed-time and call-count-to-call-count perspectives. Based on

**TABLE 10.1   Comparison of Elapsed Time (Milliseconds)/
Call Count of the API GND and Associated SQLs Based
on the Baseline and Optimization Performance Maps**

Test	GND	SQL SELECT
Baseline	29360/42	8417/4005
Optimization	21876/42	4867/2025

this table, it's obvious that the realized performance gain for the GR API is due to the reduction in the number of SQL calls from the GND API. Nothing is ambiguous here when the analysis is based on the quantitative information shown explicitly on performance maps.

10.6 SUMMARY

In this chapter, we focused on how to apply API profiling to develop high-performance, scalable software programs. A detailed procedure was developed on how to enable API profiling, how to parse API profiling log data, and how to generate performance maps. API profiling was demonstrated using the *perfBasic* API profiling framework with standard logs, custom logs, and combo logs. This chapter concluded with a real example showing the usefulness of API profiling and performance maps in guiding practical performance optimization efforts.

For your convenience, Table 10.2 shows what programs and property files are needed in order to fully utilize the *perfBasic* API profiling framework for solving your performance and scalability problems.

I hope you will apply what you have learned from this book to your software product and see immediate performance and scalability improvements. Specifically, I envision that you will:

- Design and conduct your performance and scalability tests carefully so that your test results will be reliable and valid.
- Interpret your test results based on queuing theory so that you can identify the performance and scalability bottlenecks faster.
- Use API profiling to aid your optimization and tuning efforts for improving the performance and scalability of your software product. This approach can help you gain a deeper understanding of which APIs are preventing your software from performing better and why.

I hope you have enjoyed reading this book. More importantly, you should keep practicing the knowledge and skills you have acquired from this book so that you can optimize and tune the performance and scalability of your software programs more effectively and efficiently.

Good luck!

TABLE 10.2 Programs for the *perfBasic* API Profiling Framework

Program	Required File	Purpose
perfLog.java	apf.properties	Enabling API profiling
adapter.java	adapter.properties	Converting custom log files into standard format
paser.java	parser.properties log.properties	Parsing log file for generating performance maps

EXERCISES

10.1. Apply the *perfBasic* API profiling framework to a sample application or a real application. Follow the steps listed below:

- Apply a workload to the application and collect the API profiling log data.
- Generate the performance maps based on the API profiling log data from the preceding step.
- Identify the most expensive calling paths.
- Improve the performance of the application by modifying the design and implementation to reduce the execution times of the most expensive calling paths identified from the preceding step.
- Compare the performance maps before and after the improvements.
- Quantify the improvements in a brief summary report.

10.2. Revisit the performance map shown in Figure 10.9. Identify the two most expensive APIs. Then apply Amdahl's law:

- Assuming that you could improve the performance of the most expensive API by 50%, how much overall improvement could you expect?
- Assuming that you could improve the performance of the second most expensive API by 50%, how much overall improvement could you expect?
- Assuming that you could improve the performance of both APIs by 50% each, how much overall improvement could you expect?

10.3. Based on the quantitative case study described in Section 10.4, how would you quantify the performance overhead of the wrapper APIs in general? Devise a program that uses wrapper APIs and prove your approach.

Stochastic Equilibrium and Ergodicity

> *So much of life, it seems to me, is determined by pure randomness.*
> —*Sidney Poitier*

In this appendix, a more thorough covering of random processes is provided to accommodate the needs of those who wish to dive deeper on the theories about random processes and those who wish to know more about how some of the important concepts derived thereof can be borrowed to help understand software performance and scalability challenges better. It is particularly important to understand the concepts of stochastic equilibrium and ergodicity, not only because they are the foundations on which most of the useful queuing models are built, but also because they represent the desirable conditions that many systems are designed to develop into.

A.1 BASIC CONCEPTS

We continue with where we left off in Section 4.2 by further elaborating on the concept of random variables.

A.1.1 Random Variables

In probability theory, a random variable is a variable whose values are random and to which a probability distribution is assigned. For example, when you access a Web

Software Performance and Scalability. By Henry H. Liu
Copyright © 2009 John Wiley & Sons, Inc.

application, there can only be one of the two outcomes: Available (A) or Unavailable (U). If you access the same Web application twice over a time period, based on the status of the Web application at the time it was accessed, then there could be two out of the four possible outcomes to describe your experience: (UU, UA, AU, AA). If we assign a random variable (X) to denote the number of times the Web application is available, corresponding to the above experience, there could be three possible cases: none of the two accesses available (0), one time out of the two accesses available (1), and both accesses available (2). Now we have a new space of {0, 1, 2} to describe the availability of the Web application, and we can assign $x_0 = 0$, $x_1 = 1$, $x_2 = 1$, $x_3 = 2$ as the values that the random variable X can take for those four possible accesses.

As we see from the above example, a random variable is really not a variable at all in the traditional sense as in the deterministic world. Instead, it is a mapping or function. If we use ζ to denote a single sample point, then the random variable $X(\zeta)$ is a single-valued real function that assigns a real number as the value of $X(\zeta)$ corresponding to each sample point. We call this value set the *state space* (or *range*) of the random variable $X(\zeta)$ in contrast with the *sample space* of ζ. Note that two or more different sample points might take the same value of $X(\zeta)$, for example, both $X(\zeta_1 = UA)$ and $X(\zeta_2 = AU)$ can take the same value of 1 with the above example, but two different numbers, for example, any of the two values in the state space {0, 1, 2}, cannot be assigned to the same sample point.

With the above example, the sample variable ζ belongs to the sample spaces of $S_0 = \{\Phi\}$ (empty space), $S_1 = \{U, A\}$, $S_2 = \{UU, UA, AU, AA\}$, ..., and $S_i = \{UU...U, ..., AA...A\}$, ..., etc. Apparently, for any dynamic processes, the random variable X is a function of time t as well, namely, $X = X(\zeta, t)$. If t is fixed, X can possibly take any values corresponding to various sample points of ζ in the sample spaces described above. If ζ is fixed, the values the random variable can take vary as well. Unless explicitly noted, $X(\zeta, t)$ is simply denoted as $X(t)$, in which case $X(t)$ is considered a *generic* random variable. The specific values the random variable $X(t)$ takes over time are called a *sample path* or a *realization* of the random process represented by the random variable $X(t)$.

Let's next introduce the concept of random variable vector.

A.1.2 Random Variable Vector

The values that a random variable X takes vary with time t. Therefore, we can view the random variable X at various time instants as representing the states of a random process. Thus, at various time points of $t_0 < t_1 < t_2 < \cdots < t_n$, the vector

$$\mathbf{X} = [X(t_0), X(t_1), \ldots, X(t_n)] \tag{A.1}$$

constitutes a random variable vector which can take values represented by the following state vector

$$\mathbf{x} = [x_0, x_1, \ldots, x_n] \tag{A.2}$$

In this case, we say the random variables $\{X(t_k)\}$ are indexed by *parameter t*. Based on t being discrete or continuous, we can have discrete-time processes and continuous-time processes. In combination with the possibility of the random variable X (or *state* of the process) being discrete or continuous, we can have discrete-time and discrete-state processes (*DTDS*), discrete-time and continuous-state processes (*DTCS*), continuous-time and discrete-state processes (*CTDS*), and continuous-time and continuous-state (*CTCS*) processes. Discrete-state processes are also known as *chains*, in which case, $X(t_k)$ is simplified to X_k.

Then, a random process is fully characterized by a joint CDF as follows:

$$F_X(x_0, \ldots, x_n; t_0, \ldots, t_n) = P[X(t_0) \leq x_0, \ldots, X(t_n) \leq x_n] \tag{A.3}$$

In summary, the mathematical symbols and expressions introduced above represent the following entities:

- $\{t_k\}$ (discrete) or $\{t, t \in R\}$ (continuous), where R is a set of all real numbers, represents the *index set* or *parameter space* of the random process.
- $\{X_k\}$ (discrete) or $\{X(t)\}$ (continuous) represents the *state space* of the random process.
- $\{x_k\}$ (discrete) or $\{x(t)\}$ (continuous) represents the *sample paths* or *realizations* of the random process.
- $\{X_k \leq x_k\}$ (discrete) or $\{X(t_k) \leq x_k\}$ (continuous) represents the *event space* of the random process.
- $P[E_k]$ represents the probability measure of the random process for a given event E_k.

It's helpful to be able to fully understand these concepts when studying random processes.

A.1.3 Independent and Identical Distributions (IID)

To simplify the mathematical treatment, one can assume that all the random variables in a random variable vector are mutually-independent and have the identical distribution (IID). Then, we can simplify (A.3) and immediately arrive at:

$$F_X(x_0, \ldots, x_n; t_0, \ldots, t_n) = F_X(x_0, t_0) \ldots F_X(x_n, t_n) \tag{A.4}$$

It is seen that under the premise of IID, the entire random behavior of a random process can be described by a single CDF, $F_X(x_k, t_k)$, for any $k = 0, 1, \ldots, n$. Fortunately, for many random processes in reality, the IID assumption is well-satisfied, which makes all the analyses based on the IID assumption valid and useful.

A.1.4   Stationary Processes

A stationary random process is defined by the following stationary property of its CDF:

$$F_X(x_0, \ldots, x_n; t_0 + \Delta t, \ldots, t_n + \Delta t) = F_X(x_0, \ldots, x_n; t_0, \ldots, t_n) \qquad (A.5)$$

The above equation implies that the probability distribution of a stationary random process is time-invariant. The stationarity guarantees that the measurement taken at time t is statistically distinguishable from the same measurement taken Δt time units earlier or later, where Δt is arbitrary. Any processes under regular conditions can be considered as stationary processes, for example, the traffic flow on a highway on regular workdays. Another example is a Web application accessed by the users during non-peak hours during which the access patterns are more likely to be evenly distributed.

In some cases, (A.5) might hold only for some number $n \leq k$. Then we say that the random process is stationary up to order k only. When $k = 2$, the process is said to be *wide-sense stationary* (*WSS*) or *weak stationary* in contrast to *strict-sense stationary* defined by (A.5).

A.1.5   Processes with Stationary Independent Increments

Random processes are often studied over a series of time intervals defined by

$$0 < t_1 < t_2 < \cdots < t_n$$

in order to observe the incremental changes in the states of the processes:

$$X(0), \; X(t_1) - X(t_0), \; X(t_2) - X(t_1), \ldots, X(t_n) - X(t_{n-1})$$

If such incremental state changes are independent and satisfy the stationary condition that $X(t) - X(s)$ has the same distribution as $X(t + h) - X(s + h)$ for all s, t, $h \geq 0$, $s < t$, then the process $X(t)$ is said to have *stationary independent increments* (SII). Note that processes with stationary independent increments are not the same as stationary processes. As a matter of fact, processes with stationary independent increments are non-stationary. For example, Poisson processes possess the SSI property, but their mean and variance are time-dependent and proportional to time t. In addition, SSI is not the same as IID, either. The concept of SII measures the stationarity of incremental changes in the states of the underlying random processes, while the concept of IID is used to characterize the probability distributions of the random variables associated with the underlying random processes.

The concepts of stationarity and IID help simplify the analysis of many random processes significantly. They are indispensable for arriving at the analytical solutions of the state probability equations describing the evolution of some particularized random processes. Apparently, designing systems that can reach stationary states is of great practical interest.

A.2 CLASSIFICATION OF RANDOM PROCESSES

It's helpful to put all typical random processes into perspective based on the defining characteristics assigned to them. In this section, we briefly review a few random processes that are representative and closely correlated with each other. These processes include:

- General Renewal Processes
- Markov Renewal Processes
- Markov Processes

A.2.1 General Renewal Processes

A *general renewal process* is a continuous-time and discrete-state chain that describes an *inter-arrival process*. It is characterized by the following parameter and state spaces:

- Parameter space: $0 \leq t_1 \leq t_2 \leq \ldots t_k \ldots \leq t_n$, where t_k represents the kth time point at which an event reoccurs or renews. The inter-arrival time $S_k = T_k - T_{k-1}$ is a random variable which is also referred to as the kth *state holding time*. The random variable T_k is called the kth *jump time*. An inter-arrival process is called a *renewal process* if the random variables $\{S_k, k = 1, 2, \ldots\}$ constitute a sequence of IID variables; otherwise, it is just a generic inter-arrival process.
- State space: $N(0) \leq N(t_1) \leq N(t_2) \leq \ldots \leq N(t_n)$, where $N(t_k)$ is a random variable counting the number of occurrences up to the kth time point. Note that a renewal process has no particular constraint on the random variables $\{N(t_k)\}$ at all. Therefore, it's more appropriate to classify a renewal process as an arrival process than a counting process, because its constraint is on the inter-arrival times, not on the number of events counted.

Conceptually, general renewal processes are important, as many random processes are particularized based on them, as is shown in the next section.

A.2.2 Markov Renewal Processes

A general renewal process becomes a Markov renewal process if the probability of a state transition depends on the current state only. A Markov renewal process is also known as a Semi-Markov process, as that constraint on state transitions is the first Markovian property for a Markov process, as is discussed next.

A.2.3 Markov Processes

Markov processes are particularized and from Markov renewal processes with an additional constraint imposed that the random time intervals between successive state transitions follow the exponential distribution that possesses the memoryless property. The two constraints on the two aspects of a Markov process (states and inter-event times) can be summarized as follows:

- Markovian Property 1 (MP1). The first Markovian property about state transitions is referred to as the memoryless property of state transitions: the next future state of the process depends *conditionally* and *only* on its current state. For continuous-state Markov processes, this implies that

$$P[X(t_{k+1}) \leq x_{k+1}|X(t_k) = x_k, X(t_{k-1}) = x_{k-1}, X(t_0) = x_0]$$
$$= P[X(t_{k+1}) \leq x_{k+1}|X(t_k) = x_k] \tag{A.6a}$$

And similarly, for discrete-state Markov chains, MP1 implies that

$$P[X(t_{k+1}) = x_{k+1}|X(t_k) = x_k, X(t_{k-1}) = x_{k-1}, X(t_0) = x_0]$$
$$= P[X(t_{k+1}) = x_{k+1}|X(t_k) = x_k] \tag{A.6b}$$

And for discrete-time Markov chains, MP1 implies that

$$P[X_{k+1} = x_{k+1}|X_k = x_k, X_{k-1} = x_{k-1}, X_0 = x_0]$$
$$= P[X_{k+1} = x_{k+1}|X_k = x_k] \tag{A.6c}$$

- Markovian Property 2 (MP2). The second Markovian property is about the memoryless property of the time intervals between adjacent state transitions: how long the process will remain in the current state is irrelevant of how long the process has been in the current state. This is equivalent to saying that the time intervals between the adjacent state transitions follow the exponential distribution for continuous-time Markov chains or geometric distribution for discrete-time Markov chains, since the exponential distribution and the geometric distribution are the only distributions that possess the memoryless property in the continuous and discrete parameter spaces, respectively. To help understand the memoryless property better, Appendix B is provided to show a rigorous mathematical proof of the memoryless property for the exponential distribution.

The analysis of Markov and Semi-Markov chains has provided a rich framework for studying many real life random processes, particularly in the areas of applying queuing theory to solving software performance and scalability problems.

So far, we have introduced many basic concepts of probability theory and random processes. Next, we'll concentrate on finding the state probabilities of a given random process at any time instant, which is the central objective of applying probability theory to studying random processes. Since the analysis of most queuing systems is based on Markov chains, we'll limit ourselves to Markov chains from this point on.

Let's start with the discrete-time Markov chains first. Although we are eventually more interested in continuous-time Markov chains which are more relevant to the queuing theory in the context of software performance and scalability, discrete-time

Markov chains provide an easier entry and are more straightforward to allow us to capture all the essence more conveniently. The analysis of continuous-time Markov chains parallels that of discrete-time Markov chains.

A.3 DISCRETE-TIME MARKOV CHAINS

The subject of finding the state probabilities of discrete-time Markov chains at any time instant can be formulated as follows:

For a given initial state distribution and given state-to-state transition probabilities, how can we find out the state probabilities of a system at any time instant?

Since the transition probabilities fill the bridge between the initial states to any subsequent states for a random process, let's start with understanding the transition probability matrix for a discrete-time Markov chains first.

A.3.1 Transition Probability Matrix and C-K Equations

For discrete-time Markov chains, we use symbols i and j to denote the current and next states respectively. Thus, the *transition probability* describing a system to transit from state i to state j at time instant k can be expressed as follows:

$$p_{ij}(k) = P[X_{k+1} = j | X_k = i] \tag{A.7}$$

This equation is equivalent to Equation (A.6c) by setting $x_k = i$ and $x_{k+1} = j$ in (A.6c). Note that the state transition probabilities described above must satisfy the normalization condition of

$$\sum_{all\ j} p_{ij}(k) = 1 \tag{A.8}$$

Equation (A.7) represents the *single-step state transition probability* of a system from state i to state j at the kth time point. It can be extended to study the *n-step state transition probabilities* with a single mathematical symbol $p_{ij}^{(n)}(k)$ as follows:

$$p_{ij}^{(n)}(k) = P[X_{k+n} = j | X_k = i] \tag{A.9}$$

Note the change from X_{k+1} in (A.7) to X_{k+n} in (A.9). Very often, we are interested in the transition process internal to the n-step transition expressed by (A.9). This can be easily achieved by assuming an intermediate state r with $i < r < j$ at time point m with $1 < m < n$. Then, by the rule of total probability, (A.9) can be rewritten as

$$p_{ij}^{(n)}(k) = \sum_{all\ r} P[X_{k+n} = j | X_{k+m} = r, X_k = i] \cdot P[X_{k+m} = r | X_k = i] \tag{A.10}$$

By applying the memoryless property of Markov chains to the first term of the right-hand-side of (A.10), we have

$$P[X_{k+n} = j | X_{k+m} = r, X_k = i] = P[X_{k+n} = j | X_{k+m} = r] = p_{rj}^{(n-m)}(k) \qquad (A.11)$$

Since the second term on the right-hand-side of (A.10) is $p_{ir}^{(m)}(k)$, (A.9) now becomes

$$p_{ij}^{(n)}(k) = \sum_{all\,r} p_{ir}^{(n-m)}(k) p_{rj}^{(m)}(k) \qquad (A.12)$$

The above equation is the *Chapman–Kolmogorov (C-K) equation* expressed with higher-order transition probabilities.

Apparently, a simpler case is that $p_{ij}(k)$ is independent of k, namely, the transition probability from state i to state j is a constant regardless of the time instant at which the transition occurs. This is the assumption of *homogeneity*. *Homogeneity* is a standard term in statistics, which implies that the statistical properties of any one part of an overall dataset are the same as any other part. Note that under the assumption of homogeneity, the states of a random system are still random.

Under the above premise that $p_{ij}(k)$ is independent of k, we obtain a *homogeneous* Markov chain, and Equation (A.7) can be simplified at follows with p_{ij} in place of $p_{ij}(k)$:

$$p_{ij} = P[X_{k+1} = j | X_k = i] \qquad (A.13)$$

By placing p_{ij} in the location of the *i*th *row* and *j*th column of a matrix, we can obtain the *state transition probability matrix* **P**:

$$\mathbf{P} = [p_{ij}] \qquad (A.14)$$

The above equation represents the single-step state transition probabilities in matrix format. Similar to (A.9), we can further define the homogeneous *n-step* state transition probability $p_{ij}^{(n)}$ as:

$$p_{ij}^{(n)} = P[X_{k+n} = j | X_k = i] \qquad (A.15)$$

In matrix format, Equation (A.15) is equivalent to:

$$\mathbf{P}^{(n)} = \mathbf{P} \cdot \mathbf{P} \cdots \mathbf{P} = \mathbf{P}^n \qquad (A.16)$$

An element of the transition probability matrix **P** can be expressed as:

$$p_{ij}^{(n)} = \sum_{all\,r} p_{ir}^{(m)} p_{rj}^{(n-m)} \quad (0 < m < n) \qquad (A.17)$$

which again implies that one can divide the total number of state transitions into a two-stage jump, first m steps and then $(n-m)$ steps, respectively. Equation (A.17) is the *homogeneous Chapman–Kolmogorov equation*. By setting $m = n - 1$ and $m = 1$, respectively, we can obtain the *forward* and *backward* C-K equations as follows:

$$\mathbf{P}^{(n)} = \mathbf{P}^{(n-1)} \cdot \mathbf{P} \qquad (forward) \qquad \text{(A.18a)}$$

$$\mathbf{P}^{(n)} = \mathbf{P} \cdot \mathbf{P}^{(n-1)} \qquad (backward) \qquad \text{(A.18b)}$$

In the next section, we define the state probabilities and correlate them with the transition probabilities.

A.3.2 State Probability Matrix

The state probability defines the unconditional probability of a system at state j at some time instant regardless of its initial state. For discrete-time Markov chains, the probability of a system at state j at time instant k can be expressed as follows:

$$\pi_j^{(k)} = P[X_k = j] \qquad \text{(A.19)}$$

We can then define the state probability vector for discrete-time Markov chains as follows:

$$\boldsymbol{\pi}^{(k)} = [\pi_0^{(k)}, \pi_1^{(k)}, \ldots] \qquad \text{(A.20)}$$

Then, the initial state probability vector of a Markov chain can be expressed as:

$$\boldsymbol{\pi}^{(0)} = [\pi_0^{(0)}, \pi_1^{(0)}, \ldots] \qquad \text{(A.21)}$$

Now, given the initial state probability vector of Equation (A.21) and the transition probability matrix of Equation (A.14) for discrete-time Markov chains, how can we find the state probabilities of the system at state j at time instant k as expressed in Equation (A.20)? The answer is the following:

$$\boldsymbol{\pi}^{(k)} = \boldsymbol{\pi}^{(0)} \mathbf{P}^k, \quad k = 1, 2, \ldots \qquad \text{(A.22)}$$

Note that in some other texts, the state probability vector $\boldsymbol{\pi}^{(k)}$ might be denoted as $\boldsymbol{\pi}(k)$ in place of $\boldsymbol{\pi}^{(k)}$.

Thus, given initial state probabilities and transition probabilities for a homogenous discrete-time Markov chain, one can solve Equation (A.22) to obtain the state probabilities of the system at various states at time instant k. This type of analysis of finding the state probabilities of a random process within a limited number of time units is known as *transient analysis*. It might be more interesting to find out the *limiting* state probabilities of a system when it operates for a long period of time and settles down to the *stationary* state (or *steady state*). This is equivalent to solving Equation (A.22) with sufficiently large values of k. However, this is not always an easy task. Under such circumstances, we compromise for knowing under what conditions such limiting state probabilities exist. In order to answer such questions, we need to characterize the states of the discrete-time Markov chains first.

A.3.3   Classification of States and Chains

In this section, we present a series of definitions to characterize miscellenaeous types of states of discrete-time Markov chains. These definitions include:

- *Absorbing states.* State j is said to be an absorbing state if $p_{jj} = 1$; that is, once trapped in an absorbing state, it can never leave.
- *Irreducible Chains.* A chain is said to be irreducible if there exists an n such that $p_{ij}^{(n)} > 0$ for all state pairs (i, j). Thus, the idea of *irreducibility* means that within a finite number of time steps, any state of the system can reach any of all other states, or in other words, all states are mutually reachable.
- *Aperiodic Chains.* A chain is said to be *aperiodic* if all of its states are *aperiodic*. A state is said to be *aperiodic* if it can not be revisited *periodically* with a *fixed* number of time units that is large than 1. Mathematically, the aperiodicity is defined by the greatest common divisor (GCD) of the set of integers $\{n\}$ for which $p_{ij}^{(n)} > 0$. The GCD n must be equal to 1 in order for a state to be qualified as being *aperiodic*. Those with GCD > 1 are *periodic* states.
- *Positive Recurrent Chain.* A chain is said to be *positive recurrent* if all its states are *positive recurrent*. A state is said to be positive recurrent if it can definitely come back to the same state within a finite number of time units. Mathematically, it is defined by the total recurrence probability f_{jj} which is defined as

$$f_{jj} = \sum_{n=1}^{\infty} f_{jj}^{(n)} \tag{A.23}$$

where $f_{jj}^{(n)} = \sum_{k \neq j} p_{jk} f_{kj}^{(n-1)}$ $(n = 2, 3, \dots)$ is the probability of a system at state j returning to the same state j for the first time in n time units. If $f_{jj} = 1$, then state j is said to be a *recurrent* state; if $f_{jj} < 1$, then state j is said to be a *transient* state. A state j with $f_{jj} = 1$ is a *positive recurrent* state if its mean recurrence time

$$m_{jj} = \sum_{n=1}^{\infty} n f_{jj}^{(n)} \tag{A.24}$$

is finite, namely, if $m_{jj} < \infty$; otherwise, if $m_{jj} = \infty$, state j is said to be a *null recurrent* state.

The above definitions provide foundation for discussing the limiting state probabilities of Markov chains. We defer the discussion about the limiting state probabilities of Markov chains in the context of statistical equilibrium and ergodicity until after we discuss the state probabilities of continuous-time Markov chains.

A.4 CONTINUOUS-TIME MARKOV CHAINS

The analysis of the state probabilities of continuous-time Markov chains parallels that of discrete-time Markov chains. However, since we are dealing with continuous time, the concept of *transition rate matrix* is introduced to describe the dynamic change of the state probabilities with time. This is reflected in the C–K equations for continuous-time Markov chains described below.

A.4.1 C–K Equations

Assuming that the system is in state i at time t and in state j at time $t + \tau$, then the transition probability of a system from state i at time t to state j at time $t + \tau$ can be described with the following transition function:

$$p_{ij}(t, t + \tau) = P[X(t + \tau) = j | X(t) = i] \tag{A.25}$$

Again, we assume that we are dealing with *homogenous* Markov chains. Then for any time instant t, p_{ij} depends on τ only, namely:

$$p_{ij}(\tau) = p_{ij}(t, t + \tau) = P[X(t + \tau) = j | X(t) = i] \tag{A.26}$$

Without going through the lengthy process of mathematical derivation, the forward C–K equation for the state probability vector $\boldsymbol{\pi}(t)$ of homogeneous continuous-time Markov chains is given as follows:

$$\frac{d\boldsymbol{\pi}(t)}{dt} = \boldsymbol{\pi}(t)\mathbf{Q} \tag{A.27}$$

where $\mathbf{Q}$ is the so-called *transition rate matrix* which is also known as the *intensity matrix* (or *infinitesimal generator*) of the continuous-time Markov chains. With (A.27), all state probabilities as the elements of the state probability vector $\boldsymbol{\pi}(t)$ must satisfy the normalization condition $\sum_j \pi_j = 1$.

In the next section, we explore the implications of the transition rate matrix for continuous-time Markov chains.

A.4.2 Transition Rate Matrix

Each element of the transition rate matrix, q_{ij}, is time-independent for homogenous continuous-time Markov chains. To gain insight into the implications behind those transition rate matrix elements, Equation (A.27) can be expanded with each transition rate element exposed explicitly in a set of scalar differential equations:

$$\frac{d\pi_j(t)}{dt} = q_{jj}\pi_j(t) + \sum_{i \neq j} q_{ij}\pi_i(t) \quad (j = 1, 2, \ldots) \tag{A.28a}$$

$$\frac{d\pi_0(t)}{dt} = q_{00}\pi_0(t) \quad (j = 0) \tag{A.28b}$$

Note that in (A.28a) the state probability for state j, $\pi_j(t)$, has been separated out from the sum over all i. Note also that the above equations resemble a generic form of equations that can be expressed as $df(t)/dt = \beta \cdot f(t)$ with β being the decaying rate (if $\beta < 0$) or growth rate (if $\beta > 0$) of the entity that $f(t)$ represents. The components of the transition rate matrix $\mathbf{Q}$ can thus be interpreted as follows:

- $j = i$. This case corresponds to the transition rate matrix element q_{jj}. Since q_{jj} is time-invariant under homogeneity assumption, we can apply the limiting condition of $t \to 0$, under which $q_{jj} = (d\pi_j(t)/dt)|_{t=0}$ or $-q_{jj} = [d(1 - \pi_j(t))/dt]|_{t=0}$. As $1 - \pi_j(t)$ is the departure probability of the system at state j, $-q_{jj}$ is the *departure rate* of the system at state j.
- $i \neq j$. In this case, $q_{ij}\pi_i$ can be taken as the amount of state probability carried by the process from state i to state j, or in other words, q_{ij} can be considered as the instantaneous event arrival rate of the system from state i to state j.

It can be proven that every row of the transition rate matrix satisfies the condition $\sum_{all\,j} q_{ij} = 0$, or,

$$q_{ii} = -\sum_{all\,j \neq i} q_{ij} \tag{A.29}$$

which is equivalent to saying that the departure rate at state i is equal to the sum of all arrival rates from all other states.

The above interpretations about the elements of the transition rate matrix will become clearer after we introduce the birth–death chains later.

Since the performance measures of continuous-time Markov chains can be observed at various time points, to some extent, equivalent discrete-time Markov models should exist to bridge the gap between continuous-time and discrete-time Markov chains. That's the concept of imbedded Markov chains as introduced in the next section.

A.4.3 Imbedded Markov Chains

We started discussing continuous-time Markov chains with the concept of transition rate matrix instead of transition probability matrix as in the case of discrete-time Markov chains. That's because as a matter of fact, the transition probabilities for continuous-time Markov chains are defined with the concept of transition rate matrix which applies to continuous-time Markov chains only. This is made possible with the concept of imbedded Markov chains for which the random state variables $\{X_1, X_2, \ldots, X_k, \ldots\}$ are defined at random time instants $\{T_1 < T_2 < \cdots < T_k < \cdots\}$ to model the continuous-time Markov chains. Then, the state transition probabilities for *discretized* continuous-time Markov chains can be expressed as

$$P_{ij} = P[X_{k+1} = j | X_k = i] \tag{A.30}$$

which is similar to (A.13) defined for discrete-time Markov chains.

It can be proved that the transition probabilities defined in (A.30) are correlated to the transition rate matrix for continuous-time Markov chains as follows:

$$P_{ij} = \frac{q_{ij}}{-q_{ii}}, \quad (j \neq i) \tag{A.31}$$

By use of (A.29), one can further prove that $\sum_{j \neq i} P_{ij} = 1$, which implies that all diagonal elements $P_{ii} = 0$. This remarkable result is consistent with the nature of continuous-time Markov chains that the state of the systems modeled with continuous-time Markov chains changes *continuously* with time, unlike the real discrete-time Markov chains that changes of states are always triggered passively.

Next, we discuss the concepts of stochastic equilibrium and ergodicity which are directly related to the queuing models presented in this book.

A.5 STOCHASTIC EQUILIBRIUM AND ERGODICITY

The concepts of *stochastic equilibrium* and *ergodicity* are essentially two different terms with the same meaning: a system that evolves for a long time tends to "forget" its initial states when it has run for sufficiently long. For random processes, they mean that the state probabilities will become time-independent eventually, although the states of the processes will still be random. It is emphasized again that stochastic equilibrium and ergodicity do not mean that a system driven by random processes will evolve into a deterministic system when the associated state probabilities reach their limiting distributions.

Let's first define what the concept of ergodicity means to stochastically dynamic systems in the next section.

A.5.1 Definition

The mathematical definition of ergodicity for random variables is that their time averages equal their corresponding ensemble averages for certain or all moments. First, let's define what it means by "ensemble."

An *ensemble* is essentially a collection of identical copies of a real system, with each of which representing a possible state that the real system might be in. In the context of random processes, an ensemble is the collection of all sample paths of the random variables representing the underlying random process. Although these random variables might be mutually independent and follow the same probability distribution, they in general start with different initial states and therefore exhibit different sample paths over time. See Figure A.1 for the illustration of a single sample path (upper graphic) versus multiple paths initiated from different initial states (lower graphic).

The kth-moment time average of a random variable vector along a particular sample path $\{x_0(t)\}$ from $t = 0$ to $t = T$ is calculated as follows:

$$<x_0^k> = \frac{1}{n}\sum_{i=1}^{n} x_0^k(i) \qquad x: discrete$$

$$= \frac{1}{T}\int_0^T [x_0(t)]^k dt \quad x: continuous$$

(A.32)

where n represents the number of time points in the case of discrete distribution.

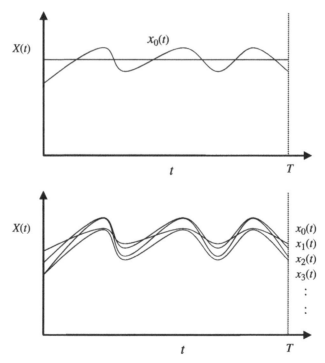

Figure A.1 *Ergodicity: time averaging vs. ensemble averaging.*

The kth-moment *ensemble average* (or *statistical average*) of a random variable vector at time $t = T$ can be expressed as:

$$m_k(T) = E[X_T^k]$$

$$= \lim_{N \to \infty} \sum_{i=1}^{N} x_i^k(T) p_i(T) \quad X : discrete$$ (A.33)

$$= \int_{-\infty}^{\infty} x^k f_X(x)\, dx \qquad X : continuous$$

where E represents *Expected* value or *ensemble average*. For discrete-time chains, N is the dimension of the random variable vector or the dimension of the ensemble, $x_i(T)$ is the state of the *i-th* random variable over the *i-th* sample path at time T, $p_i(T)$ is the state probability of the *i-th* random variable taking the value of $x_i(T)$ at time instant T. For continuous-time chains, f_X is the distribution density function of the generic random variable X. A system is said to be ergodic if the condition $< x_0^k > = m_k(T)$ is satisfied.

Note that a random process might be ergodic with respect to certain moments only. A random process is fully ergodic if it is ergodic with respect to all its moments.

The significance of the ergodic property for a random process is that one can determine the measures of a stochastic system by starting from a particular initial state and then follow along with time taking the average from a single sample path or realization, rather than from all possible paths originated from all possible initial states.

The ergodicity for a dynamic system implies that limiting state probabilities exist so that the system will eventually develop into a steady state. In the next section, we define the limiting state probabilities for discrete-time and continuous-time Markov chains.

A.5.2 Limiting State Probabilities

Determining the stochastic equilibrium or ergodicity of a stochastic system is not always an easy task. It turns out that it has a lot to do with the limiting state probabilities of a random system. Let's concentrate on the subject of the limiting state probabilities of a Markov chain next.

Depending on whether it's a discrete-time Markov chain or a continuous-time Markov chain, the long-run behavior of a Markov chain is defined by its limiting state probabilities as follows:

$$\pi_j = \begin{cases} \lim\limits_{n \to \infty} \pi_j^{(n)} & (for\ discrete-time\ Markov\ chains) \quad (A.34a) \\ \lim\limits_{t \to \infty} \pi_j(t) & (for\ continuous-time\ Markov\ chains) \quad (A.34b) \end{cases}$$

As stated in the next section, limiting state probabilities may be obtained from solving stationary equations for stochastically dynamic systems.

A.5.3 Stationary Equations

The limiting state probabilities defined in (A.34a) and (A.34b),

$$\boldsymbol{\pi} = [\pi_0, \ \pi_1, \dots]$$

should be a solution to the following *stationary* (or *steady-state*) equations for the discrete-time and continuous-time Markov chains, respectively, along with their respective normalization condition:

$$\boldsymbol{\pi} = \boldsymbol{\pi}\mathbf{P}, \quad \boldsymbol{\pi}\mathbf{e} = 1 \quad (\textit{for discrete}-\textit{time Markov chains}) \tag{A.35a}$$

$$\boldsymbol{\pi}\mathbf{Q} = 0, \quad \boldsymbol{\pi}\mathbf{e} = 1 \quad (\textit{for continuous}-\textit{time Markov chains}) \tag{A.35b}$$

The state probability vector must satisfy the normalization condition $\sum_j \pi_j = 1$ in order for $\{\pi_j\}$ to qualify as legitimate state probabilities.

It must be pointed out that the limiting state probabilities must satisfy (A.35a) or (A.35b), but the solutions from (A.35a) or (A.35b) may not be limiting state probabilities. So (A.35a) is the necessary but not sufficient condition for (A.34a), and the same deduction logic applies to (A.35b) and (A.34b) as well.

Note that there are several alternative terms interchangeable with the word "*limiting*," such as *steady-state*, *stationary*, and *equilibrium*, etc. They all mean being *time-invariant* or *time-independent* in the long run.

Now we are in a position to discuss the ergodic theorems for discrete-time and continuous-time Markov chains. Note that ergodicity is conceptually simple but very complex to quantify. Many theorems exist about ergodicity and covering all of them is far beyond the scope of this text. We'll introduce only a few of them here, and the reader is referred to the texts dedicated to the whole topic of ergodicity.

A.5.4 Ergodic Theorems for Discrete-Time Markov Chains

Theorem A.1. For a discrete-time Markov chain, *irreducibility* and *positive recurrence* are the two minimum requirements for the existence of a non-degenerate solution to the stationary equations

$$\boldsymbol{\pi} = \boldsymbol{\pi}\mathbf{P}, \quad \boldsymbol{\pi}\mathbf{e} = 1$$

such that the solution vector $\boldsymbol{\pi} = [\pi_0, \pi_1, \dots]$ where $\pi_j = 1/m_{jj}$ with m_{jj} given by (A.24). Note that the solution exists doesn't guarantee the stationarity of the solution and hence the ergodicity to the system.

Theorem A.2. If an *irreducible* and *positive recurrent* discrete-time Markov chain starts with its initial state probability vector equal to that obtained as the non-degenerate solution to the stationary equations shown in Theorem A.1, then the system will stay stationary and hence *ergodic*.

Theorem A.3. If a discrete-time Markov chain is not only *irreducible* and *positive recurrent* but also *aperiodic*, the process is *ergodic* with its *limiting state probability* *vector* equal to the non-degenerate solution obtained from the stationary equations shown in Theorem A.1, regardless of its *initial state probabilities*.

Theorem A.4. A discrete-time Markov chain is *positive recurrent* if it has a finite *irreducible* set of states.

Theorem A.5. If a discrete-time Markov chain is *irreducible* and *aperiodic* but consists of *transient* states or *null current* states, then the following result

$$\pi_j = \lim_{n \to \infty} \pi_j(n) = 0$$

holds true for all states j, and no *limiting* or *stationary* probability distribution exists. This theorem is complementary to the first theorem described above, stating under what conditions a non-degenerate solution to the stationary equations shown in Theorem A.1 does not exist. Of course, when a solution to the stationary equations shown in Theorem A.1 does not exist, the system is not ergodic.

EXAMPLE A.1

As an example, consider the following transition probability matrix for a two-state homogeneous Markov chain:

$$P = \begin{bmatrix} 1 - \alpha & \alpha \\ \beta & 1 - \beta \end{bmatrix} \quad 0 < \alpha < 1, \ 0 < \beta < 1$$

By use of the characteristic equation of P, it can be shown that the n-step transition probability of P is

$$P^n = \frac{1}{\alpha + \beta} \left\{ \begin{bmatrix} \beta & \alpha \\ \beta & \alpha \end{bmatrix} + (1 - \alpha - \beta)^n \begin{bmatrix} \alpha & -\alpha \\ -\beta & \beta \end{bmatrix} \right\} \quad 0 < \alpha < 1, \ 0 < \beta < 1$$

Apparently, with $0 < \alpha + \beta < 2$, the limiting n-step transition probability matrix is reduced to

$$\lim_{n \to \infty} P^n = \frac{1}{\alpha + \beta} \begin{bmatrix} \beta & \alpha \\ \beta & \alpha \end{bmatrix}$$

Note that the above limiting transition probability matrix has the same rows.

Now, let us examine the states of this two-state homogenous Markov chain:

- First of all, it is *irreducible*, as all the off-diagonal elements are larger than zero, therefore, the two states can reach each other mutually.
- Secondly, it is *aperiodic*, since all the diagonal elements are larger than zero.
- Thirdly, none of the states is *absorbing*, as neither of the diagonal elements equals one.
- Finally, it is *positive recurrent*. This seems to be less obvious, since it's not an easy task to show that $f_{jj} = 1$ and $m_{jj} < \infty$ as defined by (A.23) and (A.24) for

arbitrary values of α and β. However, according to Theorem A.4, it is positive recurrent.

- Because of the above properties, it has a *steady state*. It can be easily verified that the stationary state probability distribution $\pi = \frac{1}{\alpha+\beta}[\beta, \alpha]$ regardless of the initial states. Therefore, it is ergodic. Note that the stationary state probability distribution is the same as the row of the limiting transition probability matrix.

The reader is encouraged to continue exercising with the above example in two specific cases: $\alpha = \beta = 1$ and $\alpha = \beta = \frac{1}{2}$, respectively. Describe the states of the chains and determine whether they are ergodic in these two cases by use of the theorems given.

It is clear that when designing a discrete-time Markov chain system, it's desirable to make it eventually *irreducible*, *aperiodic* and *positive recurrent*, in order for it to be *ergodic* and reach *steady state* (or *equilibrium*) in the long run.

A.5.5 Ergodic Theorems for Continuous-Time Markov Chains

Ergodicity gets slightly simpler with continuous-time Markov chains, as is indicated by the theorem below:

Theorem A.6. For a *continuous-time* Markov chain, *irreducibility* and *positive recurrence* are the two *sufficient* conditions for the existence of the *stationary* state probabilities as a non-degenerate solution to the stationary equations

$$\pi Q = 0, \quad \pi e = 1$$

such that the solution vector $\pi = [\pi_0, \pi_1, \dots]$ where $\pi_j = 1/m_{jj}$ with m_{jj} given by (A.24). Note that in this case the solution is the limiting state probability vector regardless of the *initial state probabilities* and regardless of the *aperiodicity*.

Ergodicity is a classical and broad topic. It has many applications in many fields. Before concluding this section, we present another theorem published in 1969 by A. G. Pakes (A. G. Pakes, "Some Conditions for Ergodicity and Recurrence of Markov Chains," *Operations Research*, 17:1048–1061, 1969).

Theorem A.7. A *irreducible*, *aperiodic* discrete-time Markov chain is *positive recurrent* and hence *ergodic* if there exists a nonnegative solution of the inequalities

$$\sum_{j=0}^{j=\infty} p_{ij}x_j \leq x_i - 1 \quad (i = N, N+1, \dots) \tag{A.36a}$$

such that

$$\sum_{j=0}^{j=\infty} p_{ij}x_j < \infty \quad (i = 0, 1, \dots, N-1) \tag{A.36b}$$

where N is any fixed positive integer. This theorem was proved by showing that there exists a nonnegative integer j such that all state probabilities $\pi_j > 0$ for all j.

In the next section, we consider the birth–death chains, which will not only help us solidify what we have learnt so far about the concepts of stochastic equilibrium and ergodicity but also provide a foundation as the basis of all the queuing models covered in this book.

A.6   BIRTH–DEATH CHAINS

The concept of *birth–death* chains is illustrated in Figure A.2. Birth–death chains provide good examples of continuous-time Markov chains. Therefore, we can apply the procedure we presented in the previous section about continuous-time Markov chains to carry out the steady-state analysis of birth–death chains. We begin with the transition rate matrix for birth–death chains first in the next section.

A.6.1   Transition Rate Matrix

The transition rate matrix of a birth–death chain is expressed as follows:

$$
\begin{aligned}
q_{ij} &= 0 & &\text{for all } j > i+1 \ \text{and} \ j < i-1 \\
q_{j,j+1} &= \lambda_j > 0 & &j = 0, 1, \ldots \\
q_{j,j-1} &= \mu_j > 0 & &j = 1, 2, \ldots
\end{aligned}
\tag{A.37}
$$

With the diagonal elements calculated using (A.29), the transition rate matrix of birth–death chains can be fully expressed in matrix format as follows

$$
Q =
\begin{bmatrix}
-\lambda_0 & \lambda_0 & 0 & 0 & \cdots \\
\mu_1 & -(\lambda_1 + \mu_1) & \lambda_1 & 0 & \cdots \\
0 & \mu_2 & -(\lambda_2 + \mu_2) & \lambda_2 & \cdots \\
0 & 0 & \mu_3 & -(\lambda_3 + \mu_3) & \cdots \\
\vdots & \vdots & \vdots & \vdots & \vdots
\end{bmatrix}
\tag{A.38}
$$

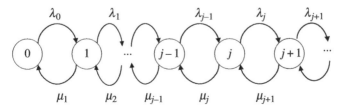

Figure A.2   Birth–death chains.

The reader is recommended to verify the elements of the above matrix against Figure   showing the state transitions from state to state for birth–death chains. As is seen:

- Each state of a birth–death chain can be considered as a counter representing the population size at that state. In the context of computers and software, typical examples of "population" include the number of messages with a messaging server, the number of HTTP requests with a Web server, or service requests with any software or system resources of a computing device in a broader sense, etc.
- The concept of birth–death corresponds to the arrival and departure occurrences in a queuing system. A transition from state j to state $j + 1$ is a *birth* (or arrival), and a transition from j to $j - 1$ is a *death* (or departure). The state transition probabilities beyond its neighboring states of a system are zero except at the initial state $j = 0$ at which only a birth is possible.

Given the transition rate matrix (A.38) for birth–death chains, the next step is to solve the C–K equations for birth–death chains, which is the topic of the next section.

A.6.2 C–K Equations

Substituting the transition rate elements of Equation (A.28) with those of (A.38), we have the equations for describing the evolution of states for a birth–death chain:

$$\frac{d\pi_j(t)}{dt} = -(\lambda_j + \mu_j)\pi_j(t) + \lambda_{j-1}\pi_{j-1}(t) + \mu_{j+1}(t)\pi_{j+1}(t) \quad j = 1, 2, \ldots \quad \text{(A.39a)}$$

$$\frac{d\pi_0(t)}{dt} = -\lambda_0\pi_0(t) + \mu_1\pi_1(t) \quad \text{(A.39b)}$$

Next, we explore the solutions of (A.39a) and (A.39b) in two special cases:

- The pure birth chain (all $\mu_j = 0$ for $j = 1, 2, \ldots$) with constant birth rates of $\lambda_j = \lambda$ for all $j = 0, 1, 2, \ldots$. This assumption results in the well-known Poisson processes with the state probabilities of

$$\pi_j(t) = \frac{(\lambda t)^j}{j!} e^{-\lambda t} \quad (t \geq 0, j = 0, 1, 2, \ldots)$$

The Poisson processes are discussed in more detail in Section 4.3.
- Limiting state probabilities of the birth–death chains under stochastic equilibrium (or steady-state) conditions.

Next, let's discuss the equilibrium states of birth-death chains.

By setting $d\pi_j(t)/dt = 0$ and $d\pi_0(t)/dt = 0$ in (A.39a) and (A.39b), we can obtain the equilibrium equations of the birth–death chains as follows:

$$-(\lambda_j + \mu_j)\pi_j(t) + \lambda_{j-1}\pi_{j-1}(t) + \mu_{j+1}(t)\pi_{j+1}(t) = 0 \quad (j = 1, 2, \ldots) \qquad \text{(A.40a)}$$

$$-\lambda_0\pi_0(t) + \mu_1\pi_1(t) = 0 \qquad \text{(A.40b)}$$

In the next section, we discuss how one can solve the above equations to obtain the limiting state probabilities for birth–death chains.

A.6.3 Limiting State Probabilities

Using a recursive approach starting with π_0 and π_1, we can obtain the equilibrium state probabilities of birth–death chains as follows:

$$\pi_j = \left(\frac{\lambda_0 \cdots \lambda_{j-1}}{\mu_1 \cdots \mu_j}\right) \pi_0 \qquad \text{(A.41)}$$

The above equilibrium state probabilities are incomplete without knowing the initial state probability π_0. By applying the normalization condition of $\sum_j \pi_j = 1$, we can find the initial state probability π_0 as follows:

$$\pi_0 = \frac{1}{1 + \sum_{j=1}^{\infty} (\pi_j/\pi_0)} = \frac{1}{1 + \sum_{j=1}^{\infty} \left(\frac{\lambda_0 \cdots \lambda_{j-1}}{\mu_1 \cdots \mu_j}\right)} \qquad \text{(A.42)}$$

The equilibrium state probabilities of the birth–death chains are fully described by Equations (A.41) and (A.42). They are the basis for exploring the ergodicity of birth–death chains, as will be demonstrated in the next section.

A.6.4 Ergodicity

Now let's see under what conditions a birth–death chain is ergodic. For this purpose, the big sum term in (A.42) gets our attention immediately. If that term does not converge, or if the birth rates are larger than the death rates, then the chain cannot be positive recurrent with $\pi_0 = 0$, and therefore, an equilibrium or ergodic state cannot be reached, which means that the system associated with this process will never become stable. On the other hand, if the death rates are larger than the birth rates, then eventually the initial state of the system will be re-visited with $\pi_0 \to 1$, and the system will reach the equilibrium or ergodic state.

In general, it's desirable to maintain the following condition

$$\frac{\lambda_j}{\mu_j} < 1 \tag{A.43}$$

so that the system can operate under equilibrium conditions. In the context of computers and software, this implies that the service completion rates should be faster than arrival rates, which calls for proper sizing of the hardware capacities required to support the projected workloads. This belongs to the category of *capacity planning* which has been a standard practice of the IT department of every organization.

To see how the analysis of birth–death chains is applied to queuing systems whose inter-arrival times and service times follow the exponential distribution which possesses the memoryless property as proven in Appendix B, refer to Appendix C: the $M/M/1$ queues derived from birth–death chains.

Memoryless Property of the Exponential Distribution

I have memories—but only a fool stores his past in the future.
—David Gerrold

We mentioned in Chapter 4 that a Markov process is characterized by its unique property of memoryless-ness: the future states of the process are independent of its past history and depends solely on its present state. We further learnt that Poisson processes constitute a special class of Markov processes for which the event occurring patterns follow the Poisson distribution while the inter-arrival times and service times follow the exponential distribution. We have also learnt that if the event occurring patterns follow the Poisson distribution, then the inter-arrival times and service times follow the exponential distribution, or vice versa. It is important to understand that all these statements are supported by the fact that the exponential distribution is the only continuous distribution that possesses the unique property of memoryless-ness.

Now let's mathematically prove the memoryless property of the exponential distribution. Surprisingly, the proof is very simple.

First, let's state the following conditional probability law that

$$P(A \mid B) = P(A \cap B)/P(B) \tag{B.1}$$

which can be read as "given the event B, the probability of the event A is equal to the joint probability of A and B divided by the probability of the event B."

Software Performance and Scalability. By Henry H. Liu
Copyright © 2009 IEEE Computer Society

Let T be the variable representing the random inter-arrival time between two successive arrivals at two time points, then according to Equation (4.7), we have the following probabilities for the two mutually-exclusive events:

- Having an arrival within a period of t seconds:

$$P(T \leq t) = 1 - e^{-\lambda t} \tag{B.2}$$

- No arrival yet for a period of t seconds:

$$P(T \geq t) = e^{-\lambda t} \tag{B.3}$$

Then we wish to prove that

$$P(T \leq t + \Delta t \mid T \geq t) = P(0 \leq T \leq \Delta t) \tag{B.4}$$

The left-hand-side of the above equation represents the probability of having an arrival by waiting Δt seconds longer under the condition that no arrival has occurred during the past waiting period of t seconds with $t \geq 0$; the right-hand-side represents the probability of having an arrival if waiting for another Δt seconds. The equation states that the probability of having an arrival during the next Δt seconds is independent of when the last arrival occurred.

With the help of Equations (B.1)–(B.3), we can prove that

$$P(T \leq t + \Delta t \mid T \geq t) = \frac{P[(T \leq t + \Delta t) \cap (T \geq t)]}{P(T \geq t)}$$

$$= \frac{e^{-\lambda t} - e^{-\lambda(t+\Delta t)}}{e^{-\lambda t}} = 1 - e^{-\lambda(\Delta t)}$$

$$= P(0 \leq T \leq \Delta t)$$

As an example, let's say that there has been no arrival during the last 10 seconds. Then the probability of having an arrival within the next 2 seconds is independent of how long there has been no arrival so far, namely, $P(T \leq 10 + 2 \mid T \geq 10) = P(T \leq 2)$. Do not mistakenly think that $P(T \leq 10 + 2 \mid T \geq 10) = P(T \leq 12)$.

This completes the proof of the memoryless property of the exponential distribution.

Appendix C

M/M/1 Queues at Steady State

The theory of probabilities is at bottom nothing but common sense reduced to calculus; it enables us to appreciate with exactness that which accurate minds feel with a sort of instinct for which often times they are unable to account.
—Pierre-Simon Laplace

In this appendix, we demonstrate how to analyze the behavior of a queuing model using the theoretical framework about random processes we formulated in Appendices A and B. The simplest queuing model, the M/M/1 queues, is chosen for this purpose. Although extremely simple, the M/M/1 model is sufficient for demonstrating the standard procedure of deriving various performance metrics of a queuing system based on the theoretical framework established for describing stochastic processes. In addition, the M/M/1 model reveals many basic facets of a wide range of more complex queuing models.

The analysis of M/M/1 queuing model can be carried out by applying the limiting state probability results of birth–death chains obtained previously. Let's start with reviewing the major results of birth–death chains presented in Appendix A. We assume that the reader is already familiar with some of the basic concepts and metrics about queuing systems introduced in Chapter 4 of this book.

C.1 REVIEW OF BIRTH–DEATH CHAINS

The key results of birth–death chains are the limiting state probabilities as repeated below for the initial state probability π_0 and limiting state probability π_n, together

Software Performance and Scalability. By Henry H. Liu
Copyright © 2009 John Wiley & Sons, Inc.

with the normalization condition for the state probabilities:

$$\pi_0 = \frac{1}{1 + \sum_{n=1}^{\infty} \left(\dfrac{\lambda_0 \cdots \lambda_{n-1}}{\mu_1 \cdots \mu_n} \right)} \tag{C.1a}$$

$$\pi_n = \left(\frac{\lambda_0 \cdots \lambda_{n-1}}{\mu_1 \cdots \mu_n} \right) \pi_0 \quad n = 1, 2, \ldots \tag{C.1b}$$

$$\sum_n \pi_n = 1 \tag{C.1c}$$

Another statement we need to make is that we'll use a generic random variable (X) instead of a random variable vector to represent the random states of the system. Similarly, a generic random variable (T) is used to denote the random inter-arrival times between successive arrivals. These choices are well justified under the assumption of IID we discussed previously.

The $M/M/1$ model represents a queuing system that is characterized as follows:

- Markov arrival process which implies the Poisson distribution for the number of customers in the system and exponential distribution for the inter-arrival times
- Markov service pattern which implies that service times obey the exponential distribution
- Single server for all customers
- Infinite system storage capacity
- First-come first-served policy

Then the generic birth–death model can be simplified for the $M/M/1$ model with the following arrival and departure rates:

$$\lambda_n = \lambda \quad \text{for all } n = 0, 1, \ldots$$
$$\mu_n = \mu \quad \text{for all } n = 1, 2, \ldots$$

Then (C.1a) and (C.1b) can be simplified as follows:

$$\pi_0 = 1 - \rho \tag{C.2a}$$
$$\pi_n = \rho^n (1 - \rho) \tag{C.2b}$$

where $\rho = \lambda/\mu < 1$ represents the load intensity.

Now we can proceed to derive all major performance metrics of $M/M/1$ queues based on Equations (C.2a) and (C.2b).

C.2 UTILIZATION AND THROUGHPUT

The utilization (U) of an $M/M/1$ queuing system can be obtained with the initial state probability π_0 which defines the relative portion of the time when the system is empty and the server is idle. It is simply

$$U = 1 - \pi_0 = \rho \tag{C.3}$$

The system throughput (X_0) is defined by the portion of the total service rate when the system is busy, which is

$$X_0 = \mu\rho = \lambda \tag{C.4}$$

This conclusion can also be obtained by the implicit premise that we are examining the behavior of a stable $M/M/1$ system under steady-state or equilibrium condition so that the system throughput equals the arrival rate.

Note that we use the symbol X_0 to denote the system throughput here in order to be consistent with what is used to denote the system throughput in Chapter 4 of the main text. Although it might be confused with the random variable X_0 in the context of discussing random processes, its meaning should be clear in its local context here.

Next, let's calculate the average queue length for an $M/M/1$ system.

C.3   AVERAGE QUEUE LENGTH IN THE SYSTEM

The average queue length is the average number of customers in the system, which can be calculated according to the state probabilities (C.2b) as follows:

$$E(N) = \sum_{n=0}^{\infty} n\pi_n = (1 - \rho) \sum_{n=0}^{\infty} n\rho^n = \frac{\rho}{1 - \rho} \tag{C.5}$$

To keep it simple, we have omitted the lengthy mathematical derivations for arriving at (C.5).

Next, let's calculate the average system time for an $M/M/1$ system.

C.4   AVERAGE SYSTEM TIME

The average system time $E(S)$ is the average residing time for customers in the system, which can be calculated according to Little's Law as follows:

$$E(S) = \frac{E(N)}{X_0} = \frac{1/\mu}{1 - \rho} \tag{C.6}$$

This result is straightforward with no complicated mathematical derivations involved. Note that $1/\mu$ is simply the average service time which measures the average time for customers from entering to departing the system when the system load is low. The average system time includes the system wait time when the system needs to wait for the availability of some system resources but excludes the user wait time before entering the system.

Next, let's calculate the average wait time for an $M/M/1$ system.

C.5 AVERAGE WAIT TIME

The average wait time $E(W)$ is the average time that customers wait for being serviced by the system. It is equal to the average system time subtracting the average service time which is $1/\mu$. It thus follows that:

$$E(W) = E(S) - \frac{1}{\mu} = \frac{(1/\mu)\rho}{1 - \rho} \qquad (C.7)$$

From (C.7), one can also get the average queue length in the queue alone $E_q(N)$, which by Little's Law, is equal to the throughput $(\mu\rho)$ multiplied by the average wait time in the queue expressed by (C.7), or:

$$E_q(N) = (\mu\rho)E(W) = \frac{\rho^2}{1 - \rho} \qquad (C.8)$$

Since the purpose of this appendix is to demonstrate how queuing systems are analytically treated with a generic theoretical framework describing random processes, more complex queuing systems are covered in Chapter 4 of the text. Also the reader is suggested to reconcile the inconsistencies of the terminologies and symbols used here and in the main text by following Table C.1. The two sets of terminologies for describing the same set of queuing system performance metrics stem from two different perspectives: one from the statistical perspective and the other from the application perspective.

TABLE C.1 Queuing System Performance Metrics

Statistical Perspective		Application Perspective
Average queue length:	$E(N)$	N_i in (4.18) (System size)
Average system time:	$E(S)$	R_i in (4.12) (Response time)
Average wait time:	$E(W)$	W_i in (4.12) (Wait time in the queue)
Service time:	$1/\mu$	S_i in (4.12) (Service time)

One can follow a similar procedure to analyzing the behavior of an $M/M/1$ queue to carry out the analysis of more complicated queues. To explore further, refer to the more in-depth texts on queuing theory recommended at the end of Chapter 4.

Index

Agile software, software development
    process, 83–84
Amdahl's law, performance, and scalability
    testing, 97–99
Application binary interface (ABI),
    application programming interfaces
    (APIs) contrasted, 45
Application programming interface (API),
    44–47
  generally, 44–45
  Google, 46–47
  Java, 45–46
  scalable performance, 2
  Windows, 45
Application programming interface (API)
    profiling, 249–338. *See also*
    Java application programming
    interfaces (APIs); Performance
    and scalability testing
  defense lines, 252–253
  defined, 251–252
  execution stack, 253–254
  overview, 249
  perfBasic, 254–260
    generally, 254–255

logging format, 255–256
log parser, 256–258
performance maps, 258–260
summarization file, 260
Application programming interface (API)
    profiling case study, 303–338
  combo logs, 325–333
    client side performance map, 325–327
    server side performance map,
        327–334
  custom logs, 320–325
    adapter, 320–321
    performance map generation,
        321–325
  enabling, 304–312
    apf.properties file settings, 306–308
    best coding practices, 311–312
    generally, 304–305
    mechanism of populating log
        entry, 305
    non-Java programs, 312
    parsing workflow, 308–310
    source and target projects, 306
    verification of profiling-enabled
        source code, 310–311

Software Performance and Scalability. By Henry H. Liu
Copyright © 2009 John Wiley & Sons, Inc.

Application programming interface (API)
    profiling case study (*Continued*)
    overview, 303–304
    performance and scalability problems,
        333–337
        analysis, 336–337
        baseline, 333–335
        optimization, 335–336
    standard logs, 313–320
        data generation, 313–314
        parsing, 314–316
        performance map analysis, 319–320
        performance map generation, 316–319
Application programming interface (API)
    profiling enablement, 263–280. *See
        also PerfBasic* (API profiling)
    begin line, 272–274
    comments processing, 271–272
    enabling profiling, 267–270
    end line, 275–276
    files processing, 266–267
    global parameters, 265
    inner classes processing, 270–271
    main logic, 266
    main method processing, 276–277
    overview, 263
    return statements processing, 274–275
    structure, 264–265
    test program, 277–279
Application programming interface (API)
    profiling implementation, 281–301
    adapter class, 300
    analyzer class, 299–300
    CallRecord class, 294
    driver program, 286–289
    global parameters, 289–291
    graphics tool:
        dot and *neato*, 281–284
        ILOG, 284–285
        resolution, 286
    Link class, 293–294
    logReader, 291–292
    logWriter, 292
    Node class, 292–293
    overview, 286–287
    parser class, 294–298
    utility class, 294
    xmlProcessor class, 298–299
Application software, categorization, 54–55

Aristotle, 503
Array processing, optimization, and tuning
        software application (queuing
        theory), 223–226

Babbage, Charles, 3, 6
Backus, John, 8
Balanced queuing system, optimization, and
        tuning software application (queuing
        theory), 240–244
Batch jobs:
    networked queuing systems, 170–171
    scalability testing, 75–82
    software performance testing, 86–95
BEA Systems, 188–191
Begin line, application programming
        interface (API) profiling
        enablement, 272–274
Benchmarking, performance benchmarking
        testing, 74
Bifurcating, 241
BIOS (Basic Input/Output System),
        systems software categorization, 53
Bottlenecks:
    central processing unit (CPU), *perfmon*,
        119–121
    disk I/O bottlenecks diagnosis, *perfmon*,
        121–124
    networked queuing systems, 170–171
    Perfmon, multithreading, 51–52
    service-oriented architecture (SOA)
        application (queuing theory), test
        results, 197–200
    Task Manager, 125–128
    Von Neuman, John, 8
Business software, application software
        categorization, 54

Cache memory:
    optimization and tuning software
        application (queuing theory),
        226–227
    storage and hierarchy, 22–23
Carlyle, Thomas, 249
Central processing unit (CPU):
    bottlenecks diagnosis, *perfmon*, system
        performance counters, 119–121
    hyperthreading, 11–13
    Perfmon, multithreading, 48–52

performance and scalability testing
factors, 100–103
von Neumann machine, 7–8, 18
Chip, defined, 20
Chipset, defined, 20
Chipsets, Intel Core microarchitecture,
20–21
C language, 42
C++ language, 42, 253–254
Client/server architecture, enterprise
software, 57–59
Closed model ($M/M/m/N/N$), networked
queuing systems, 162–166
COBOL, 42
Componentry, enterprise software, 61
Computer technology. *See also* Intel Core
microarchitecture; Intel machine
advances in, 5–6, 18
Intel Core microarchitecture, 13–17
Intel machine, 9–17
sizing hardware, 35–37
Sun machine, 17–18
Turing machine, 6–7
von Neumann machine, 7–8, 18
Zuse machine, 8
Continuous distribution and distribution
density function, 145
Continuous random variable, 145
Covering index, optimization, and tuning
software application (queuing
theory), 228–229
Cursor-sharing, service demand reduction,
optimization and tuning software
application (queuing theory),
229–231

Database-centric application software
categorization, 55
Database deadlocks, performance, and
scalability testing factors, 110
Database double buffering, optimization,
and tuning software application
(queuing theory), 235–240
Database statistics, performance, and
scalability testing factors, 107–108
Data latency reduction, optimization, and
tuning software application (queuing
theory), 232–233
Da Vinci, Leonardo, 135

Defense lines, application programming
interface (API) profiling, 252–253
Deterministic process, probability
theory, 146
Device drivers, systems software
categorization, 53–54
Discrete distribution and probability
distribution series, 144
Discrete random variable, probability
theory, 144
Disk I/O bottlenecks diagnosis, *perfmon*,
system performance counters,
121–124
Distributed mass function, probability
theory, 144–145
Distribution density function:
continuous distribution, 145
probability theory, 144–145
Distribution functions, probability theory,
143–145

Edison, Thomas Alva, 263
Electronic Discrete Variable Automatic
Computer (EDVAC, Von Neumann
machine), 7–8
End line, application programming interface
(API) profiling enablement,
275–276
Enterprise software, 55–63
client/server architecture, 58
componentry, 61
defined, 55–57
monolithic architecture, 57
multithreading, 47
N-tier architecture, 60
service-oriented architecture, 61
three-tier architecture, 59
Entertainment software, application
software categorization, 53
Exponential distribution function:
memoryless property of, 361–363
probability theory applications,
146–151
Extraneous logic elimination, service
demand reduction, optimization, and
tuning software application (queuing
theory), 231–232
Extreme programming, software
development process, 84–86

Feedback, networked queuing systems, 159
Finite response time, networked queuing
  systems, 166–168
FORTRAN, 42

Galileo Galilei, 135
Gates, Bill, 42
Genealogy, networked queuing systems,
  171–172
General process, probability theory, 146
Gerrold. David, 361
Google application programming interfaces
  (APIs), 46–47

Hard disks, memory and storage
  hierarchy, 23
Hardware, performance and scalability
  testing factors, 100–103
Hardware platform, 5–37. *See also* Intel
  Core microarchitecture; Intel
  machine
  Intel Core microarchitecture, 13–17
  Intel machine, 9–17
  scalable performance, 3
  sizing hardware, 35–36
  Sun machine, 17–18
  Turing machine, 6–7
  von Neumann machine, 7–8, 18
  Zuse machine, 8
Hardware principle, software performance
  data principles, 129–130
Hierarchy, memory, and storage, 22–23
Hyperthreading, Intel machine, 9–13

Institute for Advanced Studies (IAS,
  Princeton University), 18
Intel Core microarchitecture, 13–17
  chipsets, 20–21
  motherboards, 19–20
  networking, 27–28
  processors, 18–19
  RAIDs, 23–27
  storage, 21–23
  Turing model, 30–35
Intel machine, 9–17
  historical perspective, 9
  hyperthreading, 9–13
  multicore architecture, 13–16
  system monitoring tools, 17

Internal application software
  categorization, 55

Java application programming interfaces
  (APIs), 45–46, 253–254. *See also*
  Application programming interface
  (API) profiling
Java virtual machine (JVM), 43–44
Jackson's Theorem, 156

Kendall notation:
  networked queuing systems, 152

Languages, software stack, 42–44, 253
Leonardo da Vinci, 135
Licensing, performance, and scalability
  testing factors, 110
Linux platforms, system performance
  counters, 128–129
Little's law, networked queuing systems,
  154–155
Logging format, *perfBasic*, API profiling,
  255–256
Log parser, API profiling, 256–258

Main memory, memory, and storage
  hierarchy, 23
Markov process:
  memoryless property, 344
  probability theory applications, 144–146
Mathematical symbols, queuing theory, 142
Media software, application software
  categorization, 54
Medical records (MedRec) application:
  queuing theory, 188–191
  test results, 191–198
Memory, storage, and hierarchy, 22–23
Memory leaks:
  Turing model, 30–35
  perfmon, system performance counters,
    118–119
Memoryless property, of exponential
  distribution, 361
Method begin line, application
  programming interface (API)
  profiling enablement, 272–274
Method end line, application programming
  interface (API) profiling
  enablement, 275–276

Microsoft Windows. *See* Windows
Middleware software, categorization, 55
$M/M/m/N/N$ model (closed), networked
    queuing systems, 162–166
Monolithic architecture, enterprise
    software, 57
Moore, Gordon E., 5–6
Moore's law, 5–6
Motherboards, Intel Core microarchitecture,
    19–20
MPLS, 233
Multicore architecture, Intel machine,
    13–16
Multiple parallel queues, single-queue
    multiple servers versus, 160–162
Multithreading, software platform, 47–53

Networked queuing systems, 153–172
    feedback, 156
    finite response time, 166–169
    genealogy, 171–172
    generally, 153
    Little's law, 154
    $M/M/m/N/N$ model (closed), 162–166
    multiple parallel queues versus single-
        queue multiple servers, 160–162
    open model ($M/M/1$), 155–159
    open model validity, 169
    system bottlenecks, 170
    utilization, service time, and response
        time (Triad II), 159
Networking, Intel Core microarchitecture,
    27–28
Newton, Isaac, 303
Noninteractive batch jobs, performance
    metrics, 1
N-tier architecture, enterprise software,
    60–61

Online transaction processing (OLTP):
    hyperthreading, 9
    performance metrics, 87
    queuing systems, 153, 158–159
        (*See also* Queuing theory)
    scalability testing, 75–82
    software performance testing, 86–95
Open model ($M/M/1$):
    networked queuing systems, 155–159
    validity of, 169–170

Operating system (OS):
    performance and scalability testing
        factors, 103–107
    systems software categorization, 55
Optimization and tuning software appli-
        cation (queuing theory), 205–245
    balanced queuing system, 240–244
    overview, 205–207
    performance and scalability, 208–220
        application, 215–220
        factor isolation, 208–215
        problem characterization, 207–208
    techniques, 220–240
        array processing, 223–226
        caching, 226–228
        database double buffering, 235–240
        data latency reduction, 232–233
        generally, 220
        service demand reduction, 228–231
            covering index, 228
            cursor-sharing, 229–231
            extraneous logic elimination,
                231–232
        wait events and service demands,
            221–223
Optimization testing, performance
    optimization and tuning testing,
    70–74

PerfBasic (API profiling), 254–260.
    See also Application programming
    interface (API) profiling case study;
    Application programming interface
    (API) profiling enablement;
    Application programming interface
    (API) profiling implementation
    generally, 254–255
    logging format, 255
    log parser, 256–258
    performance maps, 258–260
    summarization file, 260
Perfmon:
    CPU bottlenecks diagnosis, system
        performance counters, 111–128
    disk I/O bottlenecks diagnosis, system
        performance counters, 121–125
    memory leak diagnosis, system
        performance counters, 118–119
    multithreading, 47–53

Performance:
  scalability contrasted, 1–2 (*See also*
      Scalable performance)
  software platform, 42
Performance and scalability testing,
      67–135. *See also* Application
      programming interface (API)
      profiling
  Amdahl's law, 97–99
  application programming interface (API)
      profiling case study, 333–337
  factors in, 99–111
    database deadlocks, 110
    database statistics, 107
    generally, 99
    hardware, 100
    licensing, 110
    operating system, 103
    SQL server parameterization, 108
  optimization and tuning software
      application (queuing theory),
      205–240
    factor isolation, 208
    problem characterization, 207
  overview, 65–68
  performance benchmarking testing, 75
  performance optimization and tuning
      testing, 70–75
  performance regression testing, 68
  performance testing merits, 82
  QA testing, performance testing
      compared, 82
  scalability testing, 75
  software development process, 83–86
    agile software, 83
    extreme programming, 84
  software performance, 86–95
    batch jobs, 92
    generally, 86–95
    online transaction processing (OLTP),
      87
  software performance data principles,
      129–131
  software performance measurements,
      stochastic nature of, 95
  system performance counters, 111–129
    generally, 111–112
    perfmon:
      CPU bottlenecks diagnosis, 119

      disk I/O bottlenecks diagnosis, 121
      memory leak diagnosis, 118
      Task Manager, system bottlenecks
        diagnosis, 125
      UNIX/Linux platforms, 128
      Windows performance console, 112
  test types, 68
Performance benchmarking testing, 75
Performance maps (API profiling), 258,
      316–327
  client side, 325
  server side, 327
Performance optimization and tuning
      testing, 70
Performance regression testing, 68
Performance testing:
  merits of, 82
  QA testing compared, 82
Platform principle, software performance
      data principles, 129
Plato, 137, 303
Poisson distribution:
  memoryless property, 361–363
  probability theory applications, 148
Probability distribution series and discrete
      distribution, 144
Probability theory, 142–145
  continuous distribution and
      distribution density
      function, 144–145
  discrete distribution and probability
      distribution series, 144
  generally, 142–143
  random variables and distribution
      functions, 143–144
Probability theory applications, 145–152
  exponential distribution function, 150
  generally, 145–146
  Kendall notation, 152
  Markov process, 146
  nodes versus systems, 152
  Poisson distribution, 148
Process, thread contrasted, 47
Processors, Intel Core microarchitecture,
      13–16
Product engineering software, application
      software categorization, 54
Programming languages, software stack,
      42, 253

QA testing, performance testing
    compared, 82
Quality principle, software performance
    data principles, 131
Quantitativeness, scalable performance, 6
Queue length, queuing systems, 154
Queuing nodes, queuing systems contrasted,
    probability theory applications, 152
Queuing systems, queuing nodes contrasted,
    probability theory applications, 152
Queuing theory, 135–177
  concepts in, 139–141
  mathematical symbols in, 142
  medical records (MedRec) application,
    188
  networked queuing systems, 153
    feedback, 159
    finite response time, 166
    genealogy, 171
    generally, 145
    Little's law, 154
    $M/M/m/N/N$ model (closed), 162
    multiple parallel queues versus single-
      queue multiple servers, 160
    open model $(M/M/1)$, 155
    open model validity, 169
    system bottlenecks, 170
    utilization, service time, and response
      time (Triad II), 159
  optimization and tuning software
    application, 205–249
    overview, 205–207
    performance and scalability, 207–220
      application, 215–220
      factor isolation, 208–215
      problem characterization, 207–208
  optimization and tuning software
    application techniques, 220–235
    array processing, 223
    balanced queuing system, 240
    caching, 226
    database double buffering, 235
    data latency reduction, 232
    generally, 220
    service demand reduction, 228–232
      covering index, 228
      cursor-sharing, 229
      extraneous logic elimination, 231
    wait events and service demands, 221

  overview, 139
  performance and scalability testing,
    137–138
  perspective on, 135
  probability theory, 143
    continuous distribution and
      distribution density function,
      145
    discrete distribution and probability
      distribution series, 144
    generally, 143
    random variables and distribution
      functions, 144
  probability theory applications,
    145–153
    exponential distribution function, 150
    generally, 145
    Kendall notation, 152
    Markov process, 146
    nodes versus systems, 152
    Poisson distribution, 148
  service-oriented architecture (SOA)
    application, 177–201
    analytical model, 181
    demand, 183
      database server, 186
      data storage, 187
      generally, 183
      network latency, 185
      object creation, 184
      XML SOAP serialization/
        deserialization, 184
      XML Web service provider, 186
    model/measurement comparisons,
      198
    overview, 177
    test results, 191
    validity, 200
    XML Web services, 179

RAIDS. *See* Redundant arrays of
    inexpensive disks (RAIDs)
Random variables, probability theory, 143
Reality principle, software performance
    data principles, 130
Redundant arrays of inexpensive disks
    (RAIDs):
  Intel Core microarchitecture, 13–17
  Perfmon, multithreading, 47

Registers, memory and storage
hierarchy, 22
Regression tests, performance regression
testing, 68
Reliability principle, software performance
data principles, 130
Response time:
online transaction processing (OLTP), 1
queuing systems, 154
utilization, service time, and networked
queuing systems, 155

Scalability. *See also* Scalable performance
performance contrasted, 1–2
software platform, 41
Scalability testing, 75
batch jobs, 76
generally, 75
online transaction processing (OLTP),
77–82
Scalable performance, 1
factors in, 3–4
Intel Core microarchitecture, 13–17
chipset, 20–21
motherboard, 19–20
networking, 27–28
processors, 18–19
RAIDs, 24
storage, 22
Turing model, 6, 30
sizing hardware, 35
software platform, 41
Service demand(s):
covering index, 228
cursor-sharing, 229
wait events, 221
Service level agreement (SLA), Intel Core
microarchitecture and Turing
model, 35
Service-oriented architecture (SOA),
177–201. *See also* XML Web
services
analytical model, 181
demand, 183
database server, 186
data storage, 186
generally, 183–184
network latency, 185
object creation, 184

XML SOAP serialization/
deserialization, 184
XML Web service provider, 186
enterprise software, 55–61
model/measurement comparisons, 198
overview, 177–179
test results, 191
validity, 200
XML Web services, 179
Service time, utilization, response time, and
networked queuing systems, 159
Single-queue multiple servers, multiple
parallel queues versus, 160
Single-user application software
categorization, 54
Sizing hardware, 35
SOA. *See* Service-oriented architecture
(SOA)
Software development kit (SDK),
application programming interfaces
(APIs), 44
Software development process, 83
agile software, 83
extreme programming, 84
Software performance data principles, 129
Software performance measurements,
stochastic nature of, 95
Software performance testing, 86
batch jobs, 86–95
generally, 86
online transaction processing (OLTP),
87–95
Software platform, 42–63
application programming interfaces
(APIs), 44–47
generally, 44
Google, 46
Java, 45
Windows, 46
categorization, 53
enterprise software, 55
client/server architecture, 58
componentry, 61
defined, 55
monolithic architecture, 57
N-tier architecture, 60
service-oriented architecture, 61
three-tier architecture, 59
multithreading, 47

overview, 42
scalable performance, 3
software stack, 42, 253
Software stack:
    application programming interface (API)
        profiling, 254
    languages, 42
SQL server parameterization, performance,
    and scalability testing factors, 108
SQL tuning, optimization, and tuning
    software application, 228
Storage:
    data latency reduction, optimization, and
        tuning software, 232
    Intel Core microarchitecture, 13–17
Summarization file, API profiling, 260
Sun machine, 17–18
System bottlenecks. *See also* Bottlenecks
    networked queuing systems, 170
    Task Manager, 125
System monitoring tools, Intel machine, 17
System performance counters, 111
    generally, 111
    perfmon:
        CPU bottlenecks diagnosis, 119
        disk I/O bottlenecks diagnosis, 121
        memory leak diagnosis, 118
        Task Manager, system bottlenecks
            diagnosis, 125
        UNIX/Linux platforms, 128
        Windows performance console, 112
Systems software, categorization, 53

Task Manager, system bottlenecks
    diagnosis, 125
Testing software, scalable performance, 3
Thread, process contrasted, 47
Three-tier architecture, enterprise
    software, 59
Throughput:
    noninteractive batch jobs, 1
    queuing systems, 152
Tuning testing and performance
    optimization testing, 70

Turing, Alan, 6–7, 205
Turing machine:
    computer technology, 6–7
    Intel Core microarchitecture, 13–17

UNIX/Linux platforms, system
    performance counters, 128
Utilization, service time, response
    time, and networked queuing
    systems, 159

VMWare^{TM}, 43
Volume principle, software performance
    data principles, 130
Von Neumann, John, 7–8
Von Neumann bottleneck, 8
Von Neumann machine, computer
    technology, 7–8, 18

Wait events:
    optimization and tuning software
        application, 205–244
    service demands, optimization, and
        tuning software, 221
Web application software categorization, 55
Windows, application programming
    interfaces (APIs), 45
Windows performance console, system
    performance counters, 111
Wright, Frank Lloyd, 177

XML Web services. *See also* Service-
    oriented architecture (SOA)
    API profiling implementation,
        287–300
    medical records (MedRec)
        application, 188
    service-oriented architecture (SOA)
        application (queuing theory),
        177–179
    test results, 191

Zuse, Konrad, 5, 8
Zuse machine, computer technology, 8

Printed and bound by CPI Group (UK) Ltd, Croydon, CR0 4YY

27/10/2024

14580252-0003